A Fragile Legacy of Well-Being

A Fragile Legacy of Well-Being

Three Families and the Trajectory of America: 1750–2019

DAVID E. STUART

CULTURAL IMPACTS PUBLISHING | SANTA FE, NM

© 2019 by David E. Stuart
All rights reserved. Published 2019
Printed in the United States of America

Maps are courtesy of Bird's Eye View Maps

Cover illustration courtesy of Vecteezy.com
Designed by Felicia Cedillos

CONTENTS

LIST OF TABLES   vii
PREFACE   xi
ACKNOWLEDGMENTS   xv
NAMED INDIVIDUALS   xvii

Part 1
Old Robert's America

Chapter 1. The American Advantage   3
Chapter 2. On Braddock's Road, 1800   8
Chapter 3. Family Origins and the Hunger for Self-Sufficiency   12
Chapter 4. Transportation, Infrastructure, and Frontier Efficiencies   25
Chapter 5. Regional Culture, History, and Changes   36
Chapter 6. 1812 and 1813: War and Its Consequences   50
Chapter 7. Family Networks, Work, and Population Growth   59
Chapter 8. The Twilight of Self-Sufficiency   74

Part 2
At the Forks of the Ohio: Vandergrift, Hart, and Densmore

Chapter 9. Vandergrift, Hart, and Densmore   93
Chapter 10. Angst, Iron, and the Drumbeats of War   105
Chapter 11. The 1860s—Whose War Was It?   113

Chapter 12. Cousins in the Nation's Industrial Bull's-Eye   124

Chapter 13. Iron, Industrial Efficiencies, and Consequences   150

Chapter 14. Postwar Culture: Class, Labels, and Consequences, 1861–1879   179

Chapter 15. Continuing Unrest: the 1870s   219

Chapter 16. Pittsburgh's Symphony of Iron: The Densmores   226

Chapter 17. The 1890s: Both the Gay and the Dour   260

Part 3
The 1900s

Chapter 18. Middle-Class Dreams   283

Chapter 19. Paths to Well-Being   311

Chapter 20. The Great Emptiness   320

Chapter 21. How Many Americas?   326

APPENDIX   341

NOTES   349

REFERENCES   379

INDEX   387

TABLES

1.	Average Male Heights in the United States	6
2.	Life Expectancy at Birth in the United States	6
3.	Round Trip from Southern Adams County, Pennsylvania, to Connellsville, Winter 1800	47
4.	US Population, Number of Households, and Family Members, 1790–1830	66
5.	Wagoner vs. Colyer: Comparison of Old Robert's Invested Work Calories	70
6.	Old Robert's Known Children with Hannah Glenn	77
7.	Individual Wagon Transport Efficiencies and Three Wagon Hauls from Hagerstown to Brownsville and Return, 1789–1845	96
8.	Vandergrift Boats Sold, Commandeered, Lost, or Leased in the Civil War	141
9A.	Ollie Densmore's Apprenticeship in Iron work at Oliphant's in Fairchance, 1853–1860	236
9B.	Ollie Densmore's Roller Years at Anchor Works in Birmingham, 1861–1896	237
9C.	Ollie Densmore's Iron Career, 1853–1896 (Summary of Tables 9A and 9B)	237
10.	F. H. O. Densmore's Identifiable Crew Members as Listed in Diffenbacher's 1883–1884 and 1884–1885 Directories	245
11.	H. O. Densmore's Crew: Tonnage of Rolled Specialty Iron per Pay Period, 1886–1887	253
12.	All American Male Heights Compared to All European Males, 2016–2017	335
A1.	Male Heights	341
A2.	Enlistment Heights of Densmore Men Before 1832	342
A3.	Enlistment Heights of Hart Men in the War of 1812	342

A4.	Enlistment Heights of Vandergrift Men Before 1820	343
A5.	Enlistment Heights of Hart Men in the Civil War	344
A6.	Enlistment Heights of Densmore Men in the Civil War	344
A7.	Enlistment Heights of Vandergrift Men in the Civil War	345
A8.	Enlistment Heights of Densmore Men in World War I	346
A9.	Enlistment Heights of Hart Men in World War I	346
A10.	Enlistment Heights of Vandergrift Men in World War I	347

For H. Thomas Densmore, Educator and Master Cabinetmaker

PREFACE

This book addresses the role of well-being in the United States across nearly three centuries. In fact, a striking Colonial American advantage in height, longevity, and lower infant mortality, when compared to the European world of the mid-1700s, may well have contributed to our founding.

Well-being is a complex concept that depends on many factors. These include nutrition, family income, early childhood diseases, home environment, physical environment, household crowding, work intensity, social identity, position, and genetics. Well-being *is* complex, a realm that involves medicine, nutrition, ecology, work culture, economic trends, statistics, and demography.

As a young, restless anthropologist, I observed eye-popping contrasts in well-being in Appalachia, the tobacco-growing South, Mexico, Ecuador, Peru, bush country Alaska, Guatemala, Honduras, and many places in between. I knew the contrasts when I saw them, as I did on one particular cool day while walking along a rough, narrow portion of the Pan-American Highway in the Andes. From out of nowhere an immaculate, black Mercedes sedan appeared and pulled up alongside of me. That got my attention—rural southern Ecuador was not typically Mercedes country. A window rolled down, and a gentleman in a beautifully tailored dark suit, his "brolly" between his legs, greeted me. Apparently I had caught his attention, and he had questions—rural southern Ecuador was not white American scholar country, either. I was out of place. I answered his questions as a small caravan of rural, Quechua-speaking farmers stopped their donkeys to watch.

In truth Mr. Mercedes and I were *both* out of place in those indigenous Quechua farmers' view of *their* world. But Mr. Mercedes likely owned a huge hacienda house and half the land in sight. I owned my gear, my Master's diploma, and the promise of five hundred dollars and airfare to the States at the end of my research gig. The indigenous Quechua men and boys watching from thirty feet away owned half their yearly harvest as sharecroppers, a sixteenth share in the three donkeys (I had asked), the clothes on their backs, and some portion of a mud-brick house and a few guinea pigs. Collectively, we offered a momentary tableaux that many might call the "Developing World."

A clearer analysis suggests that three strikingly different well-beings met on a highway at ten thousand feet in elevation. As an elite member of the hacendado class, Mr. Mercedes would likely live to about seventy-five years. The Quechua men could expect to survive into their late forties. As an American male in the 1960s, I could expect about seventy-one years, but family genetics cast a shadow over the outcome.

In truth, though many Americans detest facing it, one could have found a similar tableaux in the sharecroppers' rural tobacco belt around Durham, North Carolina, or on a gravel road in coal country above the Tug Fork River that separates West Virginia from Kentucky. Our coal barons and large-scale rural landlords are rather like Mr. Mercedes—their methods of extracting wealth play a role in the well-being of those entangled in their enterprises.

We often find the same thing in archeological work when ancient burials and skeletal remains are analyzed. There is a rhythm to the measurable trajectories of individual and family well-being that fluctuates over long spans of time due to a society's cycles of growth, stasis, retrenchment, or fragmentation.

Some years ago I wrote *Anasazi America*, which chronicled the impressive rise, spread, and tragic undoing of the ancient Southwest's fabulous Chaco Canyon society. Its technological, agricultural, and brilliant logistical efficiencies drove rapid growth in population, scale, and complexity. It was a sweet ride until erratic cycles of rainfall then true drought in the early 1100s punched holes in its logistical tires as crop yields dwindled. To the Chacoans, corn yields were as crucial as petroleum is to us. Famine, conflict, and fragmentation ended that integrated world in just forty years, after more than three centuries of triumph.

Chacoan burials of the late eleventh and early twelfth centuries yielded tantalizing clues to Chacoan on-the-ground dynamics and the trajectory of its citizens' well-being. By about 1100 AD in Chaco Canyon, the Great House– dwelling elite class measured about two inches taller than the adult farmers who died both younger and shorter in their modest houses within sight of those Great Houses. That two-inch difference in male heights at death nagged at me—I knew it was key to a dynamic I did not fully understand. What was clear was that the well-being of Chaco's elite was rather like that of Mr. Mercedes, while its farmers were like that of the Quechua sharecropping farmers in Ecuador.

Years later I came across Robert Fogel's book, *The Escape from Hunger and Early Death*.[1] That book and its data tables made it crystal clear that a population's most effective short-term biological response to protracted insufficient nutrition was not mass death but reduction in a generation's stature. Tables and statistical details were right there in front of me. Fogel, I discovered, was but one of a substantial group of scholars working on the frontiers of applied statistics, economics, demography, and historical data sets to define and clarify well-being.[2] These scholars' use of data was brilliant, but they referred to no real individuals. Hence this book.

It turns out that the Chacoan Great House elites had not been sharing wisely—their burials were replete with precious uneaten food, and their storerooms, when excavated, often provided surprisingly large caches of uneaten dried corn. Meanwhile, contemporaneous nearby farmer burials almost never included food offerings—food had become more precious among them than the shale or exotic seashell necklaces that signaled prosperity in Chacoan society. As Chacoan society came undone, its elites invested in more Great Houses rather than expanding irrigation systems to bolster outlying small farmers' crop outputs. Compromised well-being, it seems, was a major key to the Chacoan story of decline.[3]

Since no data sets parallel to the extensive European military records analyzed by Fogel and his colleagues were likely ever to be found in the Chacoan archaeological record, I wondered if well-being was also a key to our American story. But even our own massive historical records since European settlement proved problematic. We know how tall Benjamin Franklin was (5'9"), but for his father, Josiah, there is no data. Nor is there any for his fifteen siblings or even for his son, William, the noted British loyalist. There are simply no two- or three-hundred-year studies of famous American families that give us heights, body builds, ages at death, and so on. Nor do we yet have detailed, long-term family data to precisely separate genetics from the effects of environment and daily lived experience.

So much for that, I assumed. But it did not end there. In 2009 I found myself the sole survivor of my mother's family line. In the Pennsylvania house where four generations of us had lived at one time or another, two floors were filled with old furniture and trunks of memorabilia and documents dating back seven generations—preserved, useful, never-before-used data.

That year, feeling alone, I visited a grave near the village of Fairchance in Fayette County, Pennsylvania. I left my business card attached to a stake driven into the earth at the grave of my great-great-grandfather, "Oliver" Densmore, born 1841, on the chance I'd find someone out there related to me. Some months later, almost miraculously, I received an unexpected telephone call from H. Thomas Densmore—an educator, a master cabinetmaker, a smart, personable guy . . . and my first cousin, three generations removed. Though we were unaware of each other's family line, our great-great-grandfathers were brothers. Tom had already done research on his family line back to a great-great-great-grandfather, Robert Dunsmore, born in 1782, who I had also discovered in the papers of an inherited trunk.

Over time the scattering of American families had separated Tom and me, just as it has separated many of you reading this. Each of us starts out with two families (one from each of our parents), then four families (from our grandparents), then eight (from our great-grandparents). The numbers stack up quickly. Among the twenty-odd families chronicled in my trunks of inherited documents, I chose to follow the three who evidenced the greatest contrast between wealth and advantage upon arrival in the developing nation of the United States, who were also intermarried. This work highlights the well-being and work histories across the centuries among the Scots-Irish Dunsmore/Densmore family (who were poorer), the Dutch Vandergrift family (who were richer), and the English Hart family, who were the early connective glue between these other two families. Anthropology at its core is both cross-cultural and diachronic. So is America . . .

ACKNOWLEDGMENTS

My research and editorial assistant of many years, Anacelie Verde-Claro, deciphered my yellow-pad handwriting, tackled research checks, and offered wise editorial suggestions. Pamela J. Nixon, a western Pennsylvania family historian, provided a fabulous summary, "Descendants of Robert Densmore," dated July 2011. Paul D. and Alice H. Densmore of California contributed family records. Archivist Gail McCormick of Crownsville, Maryland, gathered Densmore information from York, Pennsylvania, and assessed clues to Old Robert's birth family. Eden Franz created tables of Densmore, Hart, and Vandergrift heights. Amy Arner of Pittsburgh pursued the early Vandergrift business documents. Laura Holt, archivist at the School for Advanced Research (SAR) in Santa Fe, New Mexico, obtained hard-to-find nineteenth-century sources. Alexander Till, researcher at the venerable Pennsylvania Historical Society, combed eighteenth- and early nineteenth-century county tax rolls with impressive efficiency. My brother-in-law Steve Morgan of Mechanicsburg, Pennsylvania, acquired original country store account logs from the 1850s through the 1870s, which provided important real-world labor and commodity costs. Two librarians, Shirley Iscrupe and Theresa Schwab at the Pennsylvania Room of the Ligonier Valley Library absolutely amazed me with background sources on a William Page. Though he did not wind up in the book, they took less than thirty minutes to get a lock on him. "He was here from 1802 through 1803, went to Ohio in about 1804, but was co-pastor here again in 1805 and 1807. . . . Is this what you wanted?" I was impressed!

I used Ancestry.com, the Historic Pittsburgh online archives, and US Census records. I combed Uniontown Library's Pennsylvania Room and Fayette County Courthouse archives, where one of the individuals in this book was a charwoman almost a century ago. I consulted Pennsylvania's State Archives, Maryland's State Archives, West Virginia History online, and Penn State's online sources. Readers of drafts include H. T. Densmore, John Byram, Luther Wilson, and Drs. James Ayers, Rae Lee Siporin, Nicole Taylor, Stephen Beckerman, and my Pennsylvania-raised wife, Cynthia (Morgan) Stuart. She has made my books more readable, and my life a wonder.

This book was written at Limonata Café in Albuquerque, New Mexico. The owners and staff are kind and tolerant of my writing addiction, and their cappuccinos are excellent. Special thanks to my cousin Tom, who played a seminal role in gathering information for portions of this book. He did the first family historical research, so this book is dedicated to him.

NAMED INDIVIDUALS

Harts in Text

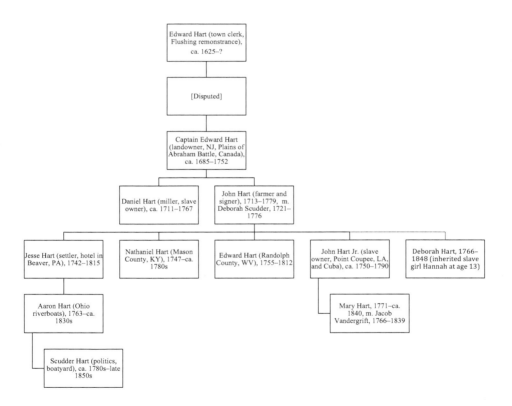

NAMED INDIVIDUALS

Dunsmores/Densmores in Text

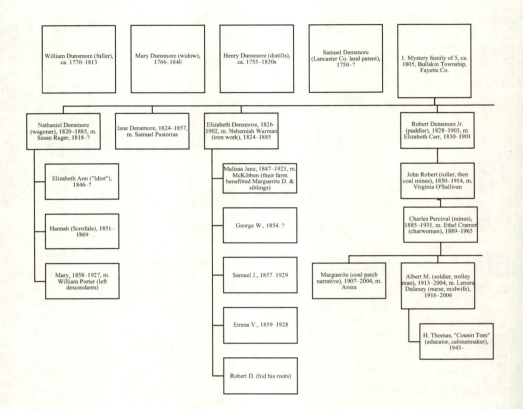

NAMED INDIVIDUALS

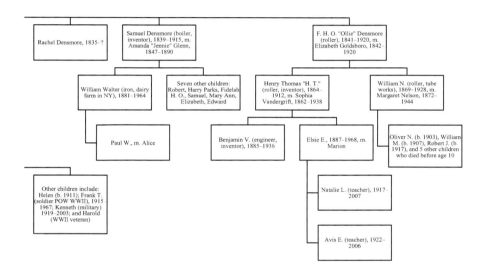

NAMED INDIVIDUALS

Vandergifts in Text

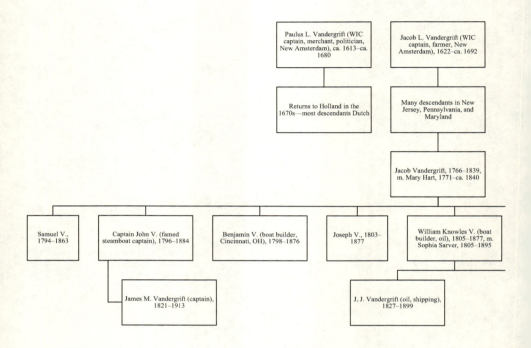

NAMED INDIVIDUALS

xxi

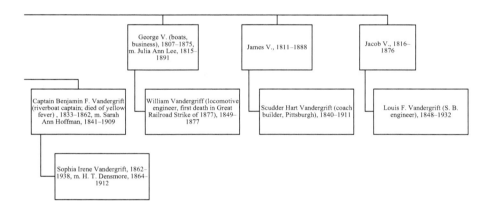

Part 1

Old Robert's America

In Colonial America self-sufficiency reigned, but not for all. Native Americans had begun to be robbed of it in the 1600s—first by imported disease then by legal chicanery and relentless trespass. In the late 1600s, many poor whites escaped hunger and homelessness in the British Isles and sold their freedom for seven to twelve years. Their new indenture contracts did not give most of them access to the self-sufficiency they craved, so this era was brief.

By the early 1700s large numbers of Africans and some Native Americans were enslaved. The descendants of those populations still have not been made whole, as evidenced by their earlier death statistics and fragile economic status as compared to white Americans. Thousands of Colonial America's Royalist families (loyal to England's King George III) were also dispossessed during the Revolution, their lands and houses confiscated, no due process involved.

Early America wasn't merely a sudden cultural and political phenomenon created by winning, at long odds, a rebellion. It was a chessboard of lands, peoples, rivers, and forests. It was a world, like most growing worlds, based in part on favorable numbers: taller heights and longer lives among American-born parents; babies born; babies who lived; age at death; acres farmed; the size of wood lots; the volume of water flow by streams and rivers, and its gradient of drop to create power for grist and saw mills; and an abundance of wild game. Most of all, it was defined by the long, intense hours of hard work that men, women, and robust children, given abundant food, were willing and able to invest in creating their own place, their own future, to leave to their children.

Early American culture and its documentary records are not only incomplete, as noted earlier, they also focused inordinately on white males—a reality that left about 60 percent of the nation's actual population, consisting of females, Native Americans, and blacks, in documentary shadow until the US Census of 1850. Thus we know the heights of men who enlisted, but we have no systematic records of their wives, the Native Americans who lived near them, nor most of the imported slave population. American culture, and its recorded data, did not further modernize until the Civil War and Reconstruction.

Documentary bias aside, the early nation's government was also rather weak, so most families continued to make do, largely on their own. Two and a half centuries later, what is amazing is how ordinary and unknown families like the Dunsmores/Dinsmores/Densmores created the ripples of what America would become. Those ripples radiated out in every direction from myriad small settlements of hopeful families until they connected to form the fabric of eighteenth- and nineteenth-century America. All the analysis, the scouring over old documents, and the calculating of biological factors comes together as one crosses the roof of the Alleghenies along the same migration routes the Dunsmores once traveled and gazes toward the valley of the Youghiogheny River. This view was Old Robert Dunsmore's America. With his stunning work ethic and outright ingenuity, coupled with a pronounced streak of stubbornness of purpose, he helped advance the job of early nation building and problem solving from the seat of a wagon and from a small forge by the river. His work output, just as it did for legions of others like him, both supported his family and generated the economic and demographic numbers that built the early nation. In a strictly formal sense, Old Robert's American world began on July 4, 1776.

Chapter 1

The American Advantage

When, on July 4, 1776, Benjamin Franklin famously commented, "Gentlemen, we must, indeed, all hang together, or most assuredly, we shall all hang separately," the odds that the Declaration's signers would indeed die at the end of a royal hangman's rope were considerable.

If contemporary Las Vegas oddsmakers had magically been in the English court to set the odds and make book, most of its aristocrats would have applied conventional wisdom and bet heavily on King George III, his navy, and his troops. Britain, of course, was clearly the more powerful.

But the reality of America was neither conventional nor comprehensible to the densely populated European worlds of the 1700s. The better part of a thousand years had passed since unclaimed open lands and rich, little-modified territory had encouraged population growth, increased farming, and the increasingly complex, aristocrat-dominated, wealth absorbing, European, socio-political structures that emerged in the centuries following the plagues of Black Death in the 1300s and 1400s.

In the England of the mid-1700s, about 1 to 2 percent of the population was rich or prosperous. That wealth derived inordinately from land holdings. Another 10 percent or so were what we would now call middle class: small merchants, small farmers, artisans, and educated professionals. As for the rest, it was not a pretty picture. Due to a toxic combination of poor diet, low wages, primitive sanitation, devastating infant mortality, and widespread child labor, the average male born in the United Kingdom when Dr. Franklin uttered his comment could expect to live about thirty-six years and attain the height of 5'4.7".[1]

In contrast, both the sons and daughters of American-born signers could expect to live about fifty-one years, and their sons would attain an average height of 5'8".[2] Most importantly, the children of their ordinary neighbors enjoyed the same benefits. Infant mortality in the American colonies was roughly half that experienced in England.[3]

The American Colonies, in short, offered a stunning biological advantage to those Colonists born in them: a 50 percent longer lifespan and much greater height and vigor. I refer to this as the American Advantage. That advantage also redounded to the benefit of immigrants who survived the Atlantic crossing and had children in the colonies. The immigrant parents also benefitted: their wages were about 20 percent higher than in the United Kingdom, and high-quality food was more plentiful and less costly.[4] Immediate economic benefits were compounded by visions of a longer life for one's self and one's children and the potential to own a plot of land. That meant an ordinary, free, white family could have a quality of life in the American colonies that was utterly unattainable in Europe or the United Kingdom when the Declaration was signed. Its oft-quoted phrase of "life, liberty, and the pursuit of happiness" takes on a new meaning in this context.

The Declaration captured the essence of American expectations in a way that the later Constitution, a procedural document, did not. The Declaration can be interpreted as a primal, cultural pushback that transformed the colonists' actual physiological and economic advantages into *rights* that their children would inherit: "We are taller, stronger, and live longer, and so shall our children! Don't spoil it with your taxes and costs of empire. Get off our backs!" it shouts quite indelicately.

Coupled with their biological and economic advantages, the American colonies were also more efficient and far less costly to sustain than were the British Isles, with its large, extensive aristocracy and military. The colonies were also much less socially and economically stratified than European societies—Colonial America's expensive aristocratic class was quite small. There was no vast bureaucracy to support and no great military gobbling up resources. Compared to Europe and the United Kingdom, a much higher proportion of families in the American colonies were self-sufficient, producing their own food, houses, and cloth. In short, the colonies could do something England could not. They could endure a conflict much longer since colonial structure cost so much less to sustain. The daily costs of the British war effort against the colonies from 1776 to 1781 were vast multiples of the daily colonies' costs. Efficient societies often win conflicts simply by outlasting their opponents. Think Vietnam.

Efficiency paired with a jaw-dropping biological advantage for ordinary families won America's freedom from British control. Modern politicians who tout the magnetic draw of the founders' ideology and their Constitution, written years after efficiency, resilience, and a realizable biological dream had already done its evolutionary work, simply do not understand what makes us American. America was founded on issues of quality of life woven into the core value of a fair playing field. That translated to decent wages, enough food, higher health standards, education, and a genuine voice in public affairs for ordinary families. So, how has this founding biological advantage fared over the ensuing 240 years?

To answer that question, this book focuses on the trajectory of American advantages in height, longevity, diet, and work calories through the narratives of three American families: the Dutch Vandergrifts of New Amsterdam, who arrived in the 1640s; the English Harts, who arrived in the Connecticut River colonies about the same time; and the Scots-Irish Dunsmores/Dinsmores/Densmores who arrived in the 1700s. By 1860 the descendant branches of all three families knew each other, had intermarried, and were participating in the fabled economic development in the Ohio River Valley centered on Pittsburgh.

Each family arrived with different cultural experiences, differing assets, and distinct skill sets. The Vandergrifts, as with many Dutch immigrants, were attracted to commerce. They were boat captains on arrival in New Amsterdam, branching out over three centuries into farming, grain mills, steamboats, oil, and gas. Some among them amassed both wealth and fame—first in New Amsterdam, then again in nineteenth-century western Pennsylvania. The Harts arrived as carpenters, craftsmen, and educated public servants. They branched out over three centuries into farming, rifle making, keelboats, and public office before eventually scattering across a wide swath of America. They also signed documents of historical note. One among them, a signer of the Declaration, was in the room to hear Franklin's famous hangman's observation.

Finally, the Scots-Irish Dunsmores, central to this narrative, arrived in several waves during the 1700s about the time Pennsylvania began to expand west of the Susquehanna. They came with few assets and were less educated. Some farmed, while others were wagoners, forgemen, coal diggers, or machinists—jacks of all trade. Four generations of them made iron, then steel. Others were inventors, ministers, distillers, and mill hands. They were a quintessentially ordinary and historically unnoticed family, which uniquely qualifies them to carry the centerpiece of this narrative. That centerpiece focuses acutely on the degree to which an ordinary family enjoyed the huge biological advantage of height and life expectancy inherited from the founders. Holding onto this edge

TABLE 1. Average Male Heights in the United States*

Year	Height (in Inches)
1710	67.5
1720	67.6
1730	67.8
1740	67.8
1750	67.8
1760	67.8
1770	68.0
1780	68.2
1790	68.1
1800	68.1
1810	68.1
1820	68.1
1830	68.3
1840	67.8
1850	67.4
1860	67.2
1870	67.4
1880	66.7
1890	66.6
1900	66.9
1910	67.8
1920	68.1
1930	69.2

* Steckel, History of the Standard of Living, table 3.

TABLE 2. Life Expectancy at Birth in the United States*

Year	Life Expectancy (in Years)
1770	51
1780	56
1850	38.3
1860	41.8
1870	44
1880	39.4
1890	45.2
1900	47.8
1910	53.1
1920	54.1
1930	59.7
1940	62.9

* Steckel, *History of the Standard of Living*, table 2.

in quality of life was no easy task. As a young America transformed and grew rapidly, the playing field's rules changed continually, as did American male heights and both genders' longevity.

Old Robert Dunsmore, born in 1782 in Ulster, Ireland, and an American wagoner in 1800, was tough as nails and worked like a demon, just like many of our great-great-great-grandfathers. His and his descendants' lines tell us much of what we need to know as we assess the trajectory of well-being in America as well as its implications for the future. Thus, we begin with him.

Chapter 2
On Braddock's Road, 1800

He rises from near the open fireplace of a low-roofed wagoner's stand alongside Braddock's Road.[1] Stretching, he shakes off fatigue, rolls up his bearskin blanket, and slings it over his shoulder after paying ten cents to the innkeeper.[2] That covers a bowl of house stew, a small, one-half-gill[3] tin cup of cheap rye whiskey, fresh water for his team, and a sleeping place to spread his bearskin before the fire. The hay for his horses costs him another six cents.[4]

It is March 10, 1800. He is a young man of about eighteen, 5'7" in height—an inch shorter than the average American-born male—lean with ropey muscles, about 130 pounds, with penetrating gray eyes and dark, shoulder-length hair.[5] His hands are already quite calloused from hard work. Dressed in the long, fringed, rust-red homespun hunting shirts and buckskin breeches that remained the freight wagoner's signature dress well into the 1840s, he slips into his moccasins, molding his toes around the drying grass he had stuffed in the bottoms for a winter shoepack. No boots for Robert, as boots were a rare luxury affordable only by gentlemen.

It has taken two grueling eighteen-hour days to cross Big Savage Mountain, both its flanks cloaked in the March 8 unexpected fall of snow that forced a small caravan of wagons and heavily laden packhorses headed west to gather and take turns pulling the wagons across the roof the Alleghenies.[6] There had been deep falls of snow in March of 1799, and again in November, but there had been no severe winter to suggest this late snow, and it has forced Robert to drive more slowly, to stop more frequently. By day's end he is exhausted. His arduous tasks of pushing, pulling, and walking in the snows are costing his body at least three hundred "work calories" an hour.[7] Before Big Savage, he had "turned out" at Sand Springs, where clear bubbling springs, the modest log wagon stand, a fenced wagon yard, and a blacksmith provided a natural stopping place for the freight wagoners and the packhorse captains headed west.

These old Sand Springs stands will be replaced somewhere between 1820 and 1830 by the Widow Ward's Wagon Yard and Tavern.[8] By then, Robert's road days will be over.

His rest stop is just one mile west of Frostburg, a hamlet founded in the 1790s. Frostburg has a small but pricier inn, so Robert rarely stops there. It caters to the sort of person he is not: the upscale wagoner from bigger towns like Baltimore and Hagerstown, and the occasional US mail stagecoach driver, both of whom are richer and better educated.

Robert's wagon is small and narrow, the box about five feet wide and ten feet long, painted gray, with two axles and four tall, red-painted, wood-spoked, iron-shod wheels. His current load is about 1,500 pounds, equivalent to the load carried by seven stout packhorses. The fact that his wagon is narrow makes it much easier to use the old, brush-choked packhorse trails that were trimmed back and widened to about eight feet by both the Maryland and Pennsylvania governments a few years before. Those "brush-outs" made wagon travel possible and generated cost efficiencies in freighting.[9] Even so, new scrub growth often required use of axe and bowie knife to clear obstacles.

He heads out to the shake-roofed horse stalls to feed his own oats and rye to his horses and water them in preparation for hitching up for another fifteen to twenty hours on the "lazy," or driver's board, he had attached two days prior so that he would not have to walk beside the wagon as it negotiated the drifts of snow. As he fills the wagon's wooden water bucket, he regrets his southern route. Three days before and several miles west of Cumberland, he could have turned north and taken the better-maintained Turkey Foot Trail[10] west to the settlement of the same name, but after a crisp and fair day at Fort Cumberland, the snows had come as a nasty surprise. The more rugged, overgrown southern route also brings higher prices for his manufactured goods than the more easily reached settlements along the Turkey Foot Trail to the settlement now known as Confluence, Pennsylvania. Besides, the northern Mount Savage / Negro Mountain district settlements like Barrelsville, Maryland, and Salisbury, Pennsylvania, are primarily German, and those folks have connections for manufactured goods brought in from Lancaster and Chester County, Pennsylvania, via the Old Raystown Traders Path to Bedford. Robert knew the competing road had been improved by the Commonwealth of Pennsylvania in the 1780s as part of Forbes Road. Both Braddock's and Forbes roads were artifacts of the British struggle for empire.

No matter, it is too late now to turn back. And much of Robert's cargo is already packaged and contracted for delivery to general stores in Uniontown, Brownsville, or Connellsville. He is too young to have much say in the trip's finances, and it rankles as he inspects the forged iron brake chain used to check the axle, which protects his horses from rear-end injuries on steep downhill descents. Robert cannot read and write, and this limits his role as a wagoner: he cannot do speculative business along the road based on written promissory notes.[11]

Robert packs his small gear into a buckskin bag: spare leather, coarse thread and needle for repairs to his leather rig, flints, tinder, a nourishing strip of "peach leather," and a pound of "jerk" for the day.[12] Last, he checks his small tin of gunpowder to make certain it is dry. With it he can start a fire or cauterize a bleeding wound. Finally he pushes his seven-inch bowie-style knife into the wide leather belt that girdles his rust-red hunting shirt, slings the bag over one shoulder, and climbs onto his wagon. In it he carries a long-handled, tomahawk-style axe, a container of bear grease to polish his leather, a bucket of homemade pine tar to lubricate his axle, and a shovel. A five-foot braided bullhide whip in hand, he is ready.

Under leaden skies and two feet of snow at the wagon stand near the foot of Little Savage Mountain, he and several others make plans to caravan across the top of the next barrier to the west. Little Savage, only 120 feet lower than Big Savage's 2,880 feet, will be nearly as difficult to cross.[13] It, too, will have four- and five-foot drifts in places. He hopes for one twenty-hour push across the top and not a repeat of the two full days over Big Savage or another night spent shivering under the wagon in his bearskins, worrying about his horses.

His target is to reach the Savage River on the western foot of Little Savage Mountain in twenty-four hours. That river crossing will be another challenge. At least the snows will deter any mounted highwaymen or Indian ambushes. Traveling with the other wagoners is wise, as the packhorse men returning west after delivering loads of ginseng, arrowroot, crystal-clear rye whiskey, and deer and bear hides to Winchester, Virginia, often own long rifles. As a small group, they can unhitch their teams in the snow to add to other teams as the group systematically wrestles carts and wagons over the mountains. "Pulling together" is common.

Beyond the Savage River, the road straightens[14] and Robert breaks his journey at an old wagon yard and log tavern.[15] The following day he reaches the most dangerous part of his journey, the long, heavily timbered swales known to the wagoners as the "Shades of Death." There, covering thousands of acres, the early nation's greatest natural stand of white pine towers up nearly two hundred feet to create an unearthly shaded twilight zone. Memories of General

Braddock's wagoners, the relentless Indian raids of the 1750s to the 1760s, and, later, the crack of highwaymen's flintlock pistols mingle with the cries of solitary panthers, the pungent scent of pine tar, the snorting of packhorses, and the creak of freezing leather to punctuate the forest's unholy aura.

Old Robert's group manages to pass through the Shades without incident. He spends the next four days crossing Red Ridge, Two-Mile Run stream, and Meadow Mountain, which divides the Little Youghiogheny's waters into west- versus east-flowing watersheds at the "Little Crossings,"[16] mapped out by George Washington in the 1750s.[17] Finally Robert arrives at dour Jesse Tomlinson's log house, tavern, and store near Stanton's Mill and Little Crossings, Maryland.[18] There he treats himself to a night accompanied by whiskey, fiddle, and Tomlinson's hearth at the extravagant cost of sixty cents. The next day he moves on north.

After Little Crossings, another two days in lighter snow brings him to Pennsylvania and a probable stop at Moses Hall's old log tavern where the Braddock Road crossed Hall's Run, just north of Markleysburg.[19] After Hall's, he reaches the Big Crossings of the Youghiogheny, also mapped by George Washington.[20] Robert passes by a water-driven mill, both grist and overhead sawmill, which he calls an "up and down," used to rip planks for clapboard, flooring, wagonbeds, and the like. He stops for the night at Andrew Flannigan's log wagon stand, built in the 1790s and tucked into a heavily wooded vale called Jockey Hollow.[21]

By day eight or nine of his snowy journey, Robert crosses Keyser's Ridge and the imposing Laurel Ridge on a portion of the road first opened up by famed frontiersman Thomas Cresap in the 1750s while he was an agent of the Virginians' Ohio Company. The road served as a gateway to Brownsville.[22] Now, in Robert's time, that section of the road branches north to Uniontown, first known as Beesonstown. By late on day ten, Robert arrives in Brownsville on the Monongahela River, a major port to the Northwest Territories. He then detours about ten miles northeast from Brownsville to visit kinsmen William and Henry Densmore and their families in Dunbar township.[23]

There is one last leg to his journey, as some of the cargo he's holding is destined for markets north on the Big Youghiogheny River and the forge and sawmill at Connellsville, in Bullskin Township. There, Trevor's General Store will purchase whatever nails and assorted goods he has left.[24] In all Robert earns about six dollars above his travel costs each direction for his haul, in which he invested about 250 work hours, or about five cents per hour. This was his version of the dreamed of "self-sufficiency" for a young, illiterate male immigrant in 1800.

Chapter 3

Family Origins and the Hunger for Self-Sufficiency

Robert the young wagoner did not, of course, pop up from nowhere. He lived and worked in the context of a young American nation, a kin network, and the cultural influences of his native Northern Ireland.

His reconstructed wagon journey connected an older, established Eastern Seaboard America to its western frontier at a time when manufacturing in the west was in its infancy and simply could not meet the demand for settlers' basic needs. The wagoners and packhorse captains who traversed into still-isolated areas like western Virginia were an important network that facilitated development in the early United States at a time when Lewis and Clark had yet to embark upon their great westward expedition.[1]

It is equally important to note that Old Robert's movements involved another network: behind him on his wagon journeys were Densmores[2] in the eastern Pennsylvania counties of Lancaster, York, Adams, and Cumberland and in the western frontier counties of Fayette, Westmoreland, Greene, Washington, Allegheny, Beaver, and Venango. Map 1 makes it clear that his early wagon routes, no matter that he started in the west or in the east, reached the farms and homesteads of other Densmores. We do not know the details of Old Robert's relationships to each of these families, but the map pattern is striking: all of them are situated at or near the juncture of improved roads with major creeks or rivers.

Old Robert was the last generation of true Pennsylvania frontiersman. He grew up when the United States was still a young, brittle constitutional republic, and he ended his life in an industrializing, centralized nation where railroads were rapidly replacing horse, wagon, and canal boats east of the Ohio River. In 1798 a wagon trip from the nation's capital in Philadelphia to the Ohio

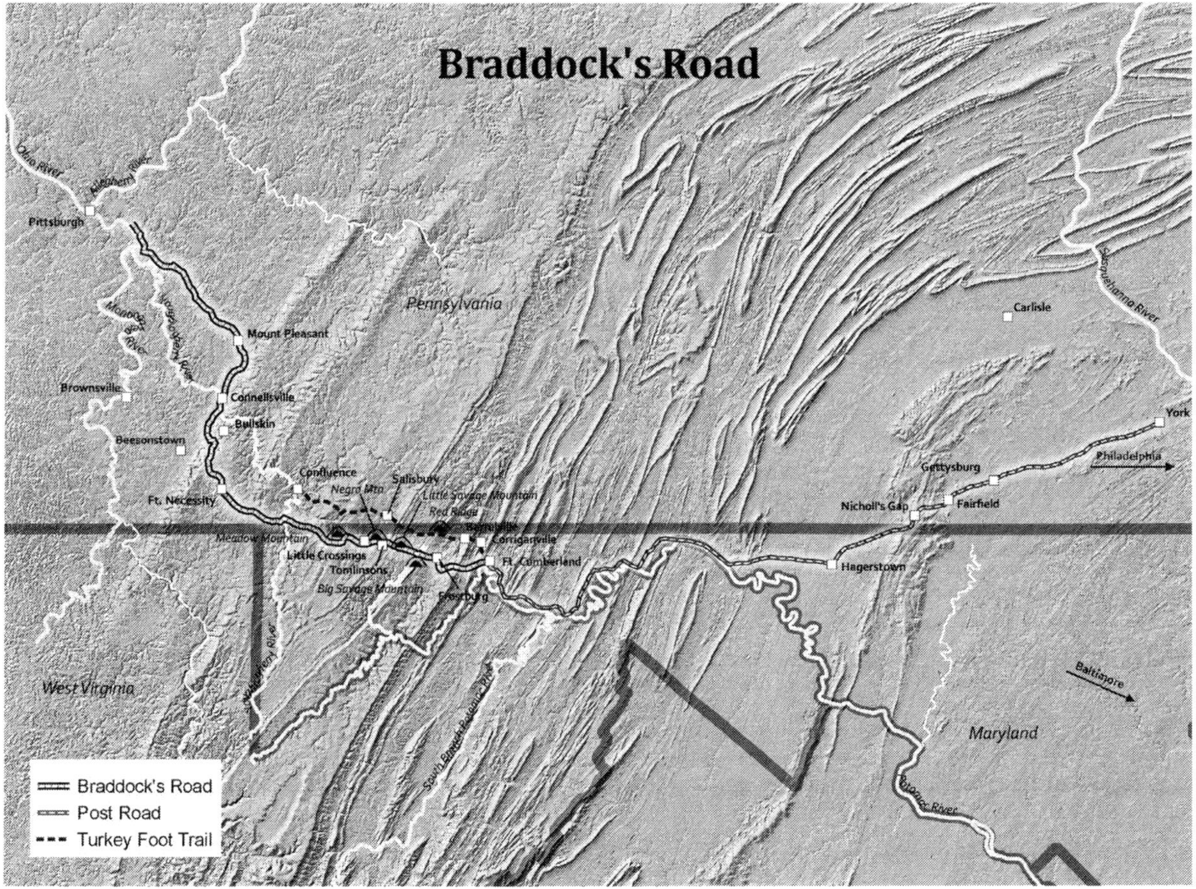

MAP 1.

River would take three weeks.³ By late 1851 that journey morphed into a canal and train ride of forty-six hours. In 1855, the year of Old Robert's death, it had become a through train ride of seventeen hours.⁴ Young America was already displaying a penchant for its eventual global reputation for "faster, better, cheaper."⁵ For good or ill, those are still signatures of our nation. "Better," of course, is under siege these days.

Old Robert was born in April 1782,⁶ likely in the Ballymoney district of County Antrim in Northern Ireland. By 1800 he was already listed on tax rolls as a single working man living in the western part of Peach Bottom Township, located in southern York County, Pennsylvania, near the Susquehanna River and the Maryland border. That contested border had finally been defined by the Mason and Dixon surveys not long before he was born.

In that region there were already other Densmores—among them another, older Robert Dunsmore, first listed as a young single man a decade earlier on York County's 1779 and 1780 tax rolls in Hamilton's Bann Township, south of Gettysburg. That area became part of new Adams County in 1800. This elder Robert was listed on the same tax roll as a single working man by the name of John Gibson, who later appears in connection with our Old Robert. By 1781 this earlier Robert had apparently moved on, replaced in the records by several newer-generation Robert Densmores, possibly sons or nephews of this elder Robert.

We may never know all the facts of Old Robert's birth. He claimed Ireland as his country of birth on five federal census rolls and on his War of 1812 enlistment roll, but he is listed with inconsistent ages on a number of official documents. That tangle of ambiguity is common in old documents.

What we do know is that prior to Old Robert, other Densmores had arrived in what is now the state of Pennsylvania. On June 5, 1751, a Samuel Dinsmore patented fifty acres of land in what was then western Lancaster County, Pennsylvania.⁷ Located on Bent Creek, west of Carlisle near the eastern foot of Kittatinny Mountain, Samuel was as far west as one could legally settle at that time.⁸ It is probable that Samuel and his sons were anchors for the later Densmores, including Old Robert's family who migrated after 1782. It is also likely that Samuel was among the wagoners and packhorse men whom Benjamin Franklin and his agents recruited from that area to accompany Braddock on his 1755 campaign to take Fort Duquesne from the French. Other Densmores were scattered about central and western Pennsylvania prior to 1800, among them several Roberts, Williams, Henrys, Samuels, an Andrew, and a James.

Of particular interest are William Dunsmore and Henry Dunsmore of German Township. Either of these men could have been Old Robert's father, uncle, or older brother. They were federally censused in 1800, first in German Township and then in Dunbar Township in Fayette County, Pennsylvania. In 1803 William petitioned for naturalization as a US citizen in Pennsylvania's western district.[9] It was granted in 1808. William and Henry Dunsmore also appear on local township tax rolls several times between 1795 and 1800. The German and Dunbar tax rolls of 1797–1799[10] list William's occupation as a fuller.[11] He appears again on the 1800 US Census in German Township and on the 1801 German Township tax roll. A notation in Henry's tax listing of 1798 notes that he "distills." At that time, the Whiskey Rebellion trials were in full swing.

In 1804, on the German Township federal enumeration, William and Henry are both noted as "gone away." In the 1808–1810 listing, William reappears as a fuller in Dunbar Township, Fayette County.[12] He also appears on the US Census of 1810 in Dunbar Township with a family of eleven. It is not clear where Henry Dunsmore moved, but he might be the Henry Densmore of Allegheny County who married Nancy Scott in 1806 and moved to nearby Ohio. William Densmore next appears on the tax rolls of Bullskin Township, Connellsville, and is again taxed as a fuller there in 1812–1813.[13] In 1813 he was living in the household of Mary Densmore, later identified in historical accounts as "old lady Densmore"[14] or simply "the widow Densmore," who would played an important role in Old Robert's life. Born in 1766 (location uncertain), she died February 15, 1840, at age seventy-four. William could have been her brother, son, or possibly her husband, and he disappears from historical records altogether after 1813. Mary might even have been Old Robert's mother.

Old Robert's Roots

To place these available fragments of information in context, we need to reach farther back in time to see a larger picture. Old Robert was part of a displaced Scots-Irish family lineage group that had been gathering in Pennsylvania since the mid-1700s. And displacement for the Densmores was not a new phenomenon. Old Robert's ancestors had originated in Scotland as long ago as the 1400s[15] on the permeable, shifting, rough-and-tumble borderlands between Northwest England and Scotland. The Densmores were among the cantankerous lowland family confederations[16] once known as "Border Reivers"—armed, independent, often uncontrollable bands of mounted men carving out a living in a military-political no-man's land at the border of Scotland and England from the late 1300s to the 1600s. The Densmores must have been among those who stood out, generating ire from both the British army and the gentrified Scottish lords in Ayrshire on the southern approaches to Glasgow. A number of them got caught up in military roundups of lowland troublemakers and sent to the emerging Ulster Plantation of Northern Ireland from the 1620s to the 1640s. Other Densmores may have joined them a bit later to escape the Church of England's persecution of Presbyterians. There, they were forced to start again.

Even if Old Robert's branch of the family had not been active Border Reivers, they likely would have been eventually dispossessed of their traditional family lands in Scotland by the 1700s. The process of dispossession had been legalized by successive "Acts of Clearance" of the country peoples in Scotland. Displacements accelerated by the mid- to late 1700s as the wool industry expanded. In response, powerful, titled landowners evicted the small farmers, called "crofters," from the open-field community farm plots and small-walled kitchen gardens that had passed to their descendants for at least five hundred years. The seventeenth century wars of the Cromwellian period over power and religion, the Church of England versus Presbyterianism versus Catholicism, were followed by the final and brutal defeat of Bonnie Prince Charlie's misguided Scots uprising of 1745–1746. Then, even more Scots fled to nearby Northern Ireland. Many Scots in those times took to the myriad of small boats that constantly plied the permeable maritime boundaries between Scotland and Ireland— another ambiguous border.

Here we see multiple forces in action: military roundups, Acts of Clearance, stable subsistence agriculture displaced by sheep, ambiguous borders, and punitive legal rules. These all combined to limit self-sufficiency, destabilize daily life, damage agricultural lands, and generate successive waves of immigration to Ulster, America, and Canada.

Life for the Densmores and other displaced Scots in Ulster in the 1620–1800 period was still very tough: famines, droughts, successive crop failures, volatile secret societies, exploitation by Loyalist Irish landlords,[17] and a new wave of transplanted Royalist Scots gentry all played roles. Worse yet, few Scots-Irish owned the new lands they farmed in Ireland. They rented small plots, and their rents only rose. Under the Ulster Plantation rules, fields were enclosed by the great landlords. That proved to be good for profits but very bad for the environment, as fallowed fields disappeared and depleted soils reduced crop yields. Rents in the early 1600s initially secured a parcel of land for thirty-eight years, which was longer than an ordinary lifetime in that era. Over the course of time between the 1630s and 1750s, the rental periods had been reduced from thirty-eight years to thirty-one, depending on the landlord, and on some estates from twenty-eight years to twenty-five. At each termination of lease, the rents went up, and the enclosed fields declined in size. The Irish and English landlords were engaging in what we now call "decontenting" in marketing practices: that new and improved bigger-sized box of cereal, for example, often contains more cardboard and less actual breakfast cereal than the old, unimproved box it replaces.

Under these realities—crop failure after crop failure and ever-rising land rents—height, vigor, and longevity declined, and infant mortality rose. These bleak conditions created three singularly pulsating raw nerves for most of the Scots-Irish. First, an obsession to obtain land that could be *owned* rather than rented or sharecropped. Second, a world in which there was enough food so that infants and children did not starve, and their fathers might eat well enough to work a full week. Third, a world in which one was relatively free from a detached and overweening landed aristocracy. A fourth and less significant raw nerve often struck was the Church of England's religious and anglophile hierarchical tyranny. A transplanted version of this subculture dominated the Eastern Shore of Maryland, coastal Virginia, and the Carolinas well into the 1800s.

In the early 1700s desperation over bleak conditions gave way to the first large wave of Scots-Irish fleeing from Northern Ireland to America. The second wave, larger than the first, came a decade later, followed by other waves in the 1740s and 1750s due to the combination of Irish famine in 1740–1741, another drought in Ulster, and upbeat reports in newspapers and pamphlets about an America blessed by "land," "food," and "better wages."

It is this wave that brought "anchor" Samuel Densmore and other Scots-Irish nose to nose with an unstable political situation and Indian wars on the Pennsylvania, Maryland, and northwestern Virginia frontiers. The early generations of Densmores were shaped by that violence and a growing sense of American identity in ways that Old Robert's later arriving generation would not be.[18]

In Ulster, more obscene land rent increases and evictions by the Marquess of Donegal in 1770 drove yet another wave of immigration to America—mainly farmers—until the Revolutionary War of 1775 to 1782 completely closed America's door to them.[19] Those who fled the famine and droughts of 1740 to 1755 most likely arrived with a single-minded hope of land, food, longer life, and children who would survive.[20] It is no surprise, then, that emigration fever swept several generations of the Densmore clan in Northern Ireland long before the 1840s when indigenous, Catholic Ireland joined the rush to America on the heels of monstrous potato famines and British managerial and political misfeasance.[21] Recurring failures to achieve well-being in Ireland had reinforced the hunger for independence and self-reliance among the Ulster Scots who immigrated to America.

But it was not the idea of America that pulled the Ulster men to American shores; it was the reality of its advantages. The average life-span of a male born in Great Britain in 1725 was a grim thirty-two years. By 1750 English male longevity had improved to thirty-seven. In the America of 1725, the average life-span was fifty. By 1750 it was fifty-two. By 1776 longevity in America had increased to range from fifty-one to fifty-five,[22] while in Britain it had eroded further into the high twenties.[23] America's longevity advantage was twenty-two years of lifespan in the 1750s of Samuel Densmore's era. By the time Old Robert's closest kinsmen arrived in the 1790s, America's male longevity had grown to about fifty-six years—almost *double* that of contemporary Great Britain. That increase in life-span was due to a combination of fewer diseases, lower infant mortality rates, access to a cheap, ample food supply, a strong demand for labor accompanied with better wages and skills, and land or tools that could be *owned*. That is what produced the young nation's sense of self-reliance.

When Old Robert arrived about 1794, he was a relative latecomer in the historic scene of Colonial America. The earliest Eastern Seaboard colonies were already more than 150 years into the job of adapting to America's ecology, climate, geography, geopolitics, unwilling Native Americans, and conflicts with other European groups. The first to arrive in what is now the United States were not, as many believe, the pilgrims of 1620 who sailed from Plymouth England to Plymouth Rock. Most of the so-called English passengers on the Mayflower actually came from an expatriate, Puritan-based Amsterdam community after a final ship change and provisioning stopover at Plymouth, England. In fact, it was the French who, in the 1500s, first created outposts from southern Newfoundland, the St. Lawrence River, and Nova Scotia at the axis of our current northern- and easternmost frontiers, as well as the Spanish, who created settlements from the southeastern most axis.[24] The Spanish had already settled St. Augustine in 1565 and New Mexico by 1598. On the Hudson, the Dutch had established trading settlements by around 1609 to 1619.

The Jamestown Colony was early but relatively short-lived. To claim *some* basis for our middle school Thanksgiving myths, Dutch, Swedish, French

Huguenots, Walloons, English, and a sprinkling of assorted Scots, Irish, and Sephardic Jews (who came from Spain and Portugal—some by way of Brazil) did begin to wade ashore in modest numbers to "found" Eastern Seaboard settlements in what were still uncontested Native American lands by the 1620s. For these "founders," life was tough. The daily realities were fraught with risk: disease on their ships, inadequate provisions, no infrastructure, understandably hostile Native Americans, and the time—and strength—needed to plant, gauge the seasons, and learn to hunt and fish in unfamiliar environments.

That first generation of diverse Mayflower-period immigrants suffered greatly—weakened by drinking brackish water, infected with dysentery-like intestinal diseases, and subjected to inadequate foods, those who arrived in a spring sailing season from English, French, and Dutch ports had often taken to their makeshift beds by the fall and perished by the anniversary of their arrival. Their imported diseases also killed a large percentage of the East Coast's Native Americans, who were not immune to them.

The generation of Swedish,[25] English, and Dutch immigrants who came from the late 1630s through the 1640s tended to do much better. They had much more information about America's geography, climate, and natural resources. European kings were granting settlement rights and land concessions to favored magnates at their courts. Attracting immigrants to risk the voyage on the promise of land that could be quickly farmed became a major business model for both aristocratic families whose ancient feudal rents had peaked and for major merchant houses in London, Bristol, and Manchester, England, all of whom were hungry to expand their markets.

The Dutch formed a chartered corporation in the 1620s, called the Dutch West India Company (WIC).[26] Its initial goal was to eject the Portuguese from their fortified West African strongholds of the slave trade and their sugar plantations in Brazil. The Dutch's forte became the "Triangle Trade" of slaves, sugar and rum, and Dutch-made textiles, which crossed and recrossed the Caribbean for more than a century. New Amsterdam (New York) was legally the WIC's company town, conveniently located to quench its appetite for ship timbers and beaver pelts. Men's beaver hats had become the aristocratic must-have item of the 1600s, and profits were huge, especially as the once-dominant Russian beaver trade had faltered due to over hunting.[27] These activities brought the Vandergrifts, the second of this narrative's families, to New Amsterdam in the 1640s.

By the 1660s great fortunes had been made in the Caribbean, first "settled" in

1493 on Santo Domingo[28] by Columbus's brother, Bartolomeo. By the late 1660s and 1670s, the British planters had rather overdone it on sugar-producing Barbados, overworking both the sugar lands and a high percentage of their slaves to death.[29] That process earned these younger sons of minor English gentry, now Caribbean slaveholders, a very dodgy reputation in their home country. To resolve their failures, many moved between 1670 and 1680[30] to the US mainland, among them the founders of Charleston, South Carolina.[31]

By the time Old Robert arrived in America around 1794 as a boy, Charleston's century-old plantation culture of large land holdings and slave labor had spread along the southern seaboard. However, his family would not likely have chosen to immigrate to the coastal south at this time, even had there been no Densmores to join up with in Pennsylvania. Its climate and ecology were alien to them. The Southern colonies' coasts were also largely owned by the plantation magnates. Many were English descendants of those who moved from Barbados, and militant Episcopalians to boot. There was also little cheap, arable coastal land to settle, and its Anglo-centric society was anathema to most of the Ulster Scots, who we now call Scots-Irish. Yet several Densmores had already trickled down the Philadelphia wagon road to North Carolina Piedmont's western margins and its forested interior, which was still "Indian country." Apparently that was preferable, as the ecology was more familiar and the land cheap.

Thus, like many of the estimated half-million Scots-Irish immigrants who arrived on American shores in the 1700s, Old Robert and his family headed west into Pennsylvania to pursue a more promising start. The Densmores would have arrived in one of three ports on the Delaware River—Philadelphia, Chester, or New Castle, Delaware—then moved west along the old and heavily traveled road to Lancaster. There they could continue due west on the roads that would later amalgamate into the Pennsylvania Road to Pittsburgh. Or they could move southwest from Lancaster on the northern trunk of the Great Philadelphia wagon road to the Pennsylvania and Maryland border, then head west where cheaper land was to be had. The Densmore map of 1790–1800 indicates that the Densmores did both in search of their new homes (see map 2).

Pennsylvania, like the South, had gentrified to a degree along the lower Delaware by the time of Old Robert's arrival, but thanks to a proprietorship awarded the powerful and, for the era, surprisingly sensible English Penn family, their

MAP 2.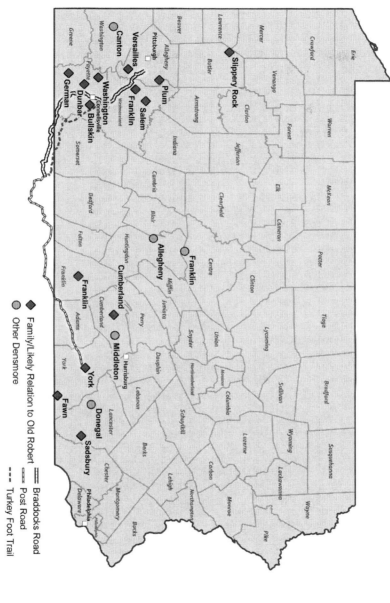

huge estates had been managed primarily through middle-of-the-road policy that nurtured small to moderate landholdings and a tolerant, laissez-faire attitude toward a person's religious practices. The Penn family, proprietors of Pennsylvania, preferred to make treaties, not war, with the Indians. At one point in 1764, Pennsylvania governor John Penn, a son of William, caved to base public pressure and did post a bounty on Indian capture or scalps, deeply staining his own moral standing.[32] Policy-wise, however, that move was an ugly outlier that was soon retracted.

By the mid-1780s, Pennsylvania began to recover from the tribulations of the Revolutionary War. Labor in demand and food plentiful, well-being did improve: longevity and height increased a bit. Cheap land was again available west of the Susquehanna. New settlers, both immigrant and American born, grew in numbers and spread west into the frontier that had been fought for with fragile success. Gone, they assumed, were the massed raids from the dispossessed, French-influenced Delaware, Mingo, and Shawnee tribes that had marked the French and Indian War.

From the 1730s to the 1750s, many Native American peoples had moved west of the Alleghenies as disease and military threats made it unsafe for them near European settlements. To limit conflict and reduce military costs, King George III had set the limits of legal settlement as the east flank of the Appalachians. This solved nothing, as new settlers simply ignored the King's decree and settled those forbidden but "vacant" trans-Allegheny lands. American Indians after the 1740s faced an epic dilemma. They became wedged between the expanding French on the north and west and the British on the east. As the jaws of an empire-driven vise closed on them, disease and hunger extracted a gnawing toll. They simply had no place to escape—so, of course, they fought for survival. Thus, as new settlers poured in, succeeding waves of brutal and even more desperate Indian raids were again staged in far western Pennsylvania and Ohio beginning in 1782.

The young nation, full of piss and vinegar after winning its revolution at such long odds, was already ignoring a critical lesson of its own history. Prior to 1794 the long series of campaigns mounted by Indian confederations were so successfully strategic and deadly that the scattered Pennsylvania German and Scots-Irish settlements established between the Susquehanna and Monongahela Rivers between the 1720s and the 1750s had been pushed eastward nearly two hundred miles to the key towns of Carlisle, York, and Lancaster. Predictably, the new push west in the late 1780s and early 1790s triggered yet another

Native American pushback. Large-scale conflict erupted in the Ohio River watershed as remnant Native peoples reorganized in the district once known as the Northwest Territories (now Ohio, Illinois, Indiana, Michigan, and parts of Minnesota).[33] These culminated in General "Mad" Anthony Wayne's military campaign and battle of Fallen Timbers in 1794, which crushed Native Americans' hopes for stability. As the well-being of new, predominantly Scots-Irish settlers improved, it declined precipitously among nearby Native Americans. The Scots-Irish carved farms out of wilderness, both changing the landscape and wearing out soil due to too many successive plantings of nitrogen-greedy corn. Thus they relied on hunting much more than had the established German farmers. Such factors would begin to change America's ecology.

In the year that gave the nation its unratified constitution, and in which Old Robert Dunsmore was born, Fort Pitt and its fragile village of "Pittsburg" were still *the* isolated, far west end of the American world. The rub was that it was also both the far *eastern* frontier of Native America's relatively intact world . . . and its most productive remaining hunting grounds.

Pennsylvania's rich land of forests, rivers, streams, runs, burns, and lovely, dark, streamside "bottoms" soil had long been a farmer's paradise—Indian raids and capricious weather notwithstanding. It was primarily Protestant Germans from the Rhine who had most efficiently developed that farming niche in the lands between what is now Chester, Pennsylvania, and the Susquehanna Valley. They practiced soil-conserving crop rotations and excelled at animal husbandry. Between the 1720s and the 1780s, the value and cost of those prime farmlands increased dramatically as newer immigrants competed to purchase farms in areas with local trails, one-lane roads, bridges, roadside inns, gristmills, fulling mills,[34] sawmills, blacksmith shops, and tanneries.[35] By the 1780s Pennsylvania lands east of the Susquehanna River located near towns sold for between twenty-five to fifty dollars an acre. In this era an ordinary working man earned an average of fifty to seventy-five cents a day. In contrast, the average value of western or wilderness lands in the 1780s averaged only two and a half dollars per acre; farther west it was even cheaper.[36]

Those prime, Susquehanna Valley lands had also spiked in value during Colonial Pennsylvania's long, grinding Native American "pushback" of the 1750–1780s period, merely because territory east of modern Carlisle was relatively safe from large Native war parties. The nation's first War College, still going strong, was in Carlisle, Pennsylvania, a legacy of mid-1700s Native American successes on the forested battlefields of the era. In that period, as noted, several Densmore families settled riskier, timbered land west of Carlisle, along the upper waters of Bent Creek, just several miles north of the soon-to-be improved Pennsylvania Road. On that risky western boundary, registered land was cheap or bought for nominal "quit rents" paid for a few years to the Penns.

By the 1780s any lands that were patented near the Susquehanna, like Samuel Densmore's in 1751, had vastly increased in value and in local community stability. But Densmore lands to the south, like those in Peach Bottom Township (modern York County) where other Densmores had settled, already had roads, wagon shops, and forges and were no longer cheap. Succeeding generations of Densmore men, like Old Robert, had to marry well, be an elder son, or move on to the West's cheaper, contested lands. The last of the Pennsylvania deeds contested by Virginia in southwestern Pennsylvania were still not settled in 1800 when wagoner Old Robert freighted on Braddock's Road.[37] In those regions, pockets of remnant Native American communities (mostly Shawnee and Delaware) sporadically contested settler movements into their prime, forested hunting territory right up to 1800. It was a familiar story to the Densmores and their Border Reiver heritage.

Old Robert and his family understood the dynamics of the mysterious, poorly defined, and dangerous boundaries they found in western Pennsylvania. They also grasped the lack of a clear legal structure, the hard scrabble way of life, the modest infrastructure, and the roving, uncontrolled bands of men of differing races and cultures trying to carve out a meaningful existence amid the whims of distant European powers. In western Pennsylvania, Old Robert had found a new, natural home—he ate better, could buy more with his wages, and was far better off than in Ireland.

Chapter 4

Transportation, Infrastructure, and Frontier Efficiencies

By 1806 or 1807, now a man of about twenty-four, his height at 5'7" (as listed on his War of 1812 Service Records), Old Robert was living in Connellsville, Fayette County, Pennsylvania, working as a wagoner.¹ At roughly 1.2 inches shorter than the average American-born male of his era, his statistical life expectancy would have been about fifty years—shorter than the average American-born male's fifty-six years, but still much longer than the average life expectancy in Ireland.

Between 1800 and 1807, Old Robert may have lived near or even with the region's only other men whose names are spelled *Dunsmore*—as opposed to *Dinsmore* or *Densmore*—on multiple US Census rolls in Washington, Fayette, Westmoreland, or Allegheny Counties, Pennsylvania. They include William Dunsmore, a fuller by trade who lived in German Township, Fayette County, in the 1790s then moved to Washington Township in the same county by the US Census of 1800. William later appeared on the Connellsville tax roll in 1811. Then there is the Henry who once distilled in German Township, moved north to Dunbar Township in the late 1790s, then again moved to Washington Township and appears on the 1800 census. His name on both the US Census of 1800 and of 1810 was carefully rendered as "Henrey Dunsmore." Living near Henrey in Washington Township was a James Dunsmore. These four men, Henrey, William, James, and Old Robert, as well as the widow Mary of Connellsville, were the only ones to appear on tax or census rolls as "Dunsmore" in the entire southwestern corner of Pennsylvania between 1795 and 1820. The US Census of 1800 documents that might formally identify Old Robert's actual birth family have not yet turned up.

As a wagoner in that era, Old Robert was engaged in one of early America's most fabled and riskiest occupations. From 1800 to 1807, comparatively few wagoners worked the southern route to Pennsylvania west of Cumberland, Maryland, as many regional roads could still be negotiated only with packhorses. In that occupation, Old Robert was a quintessential American frontiersman. This suggests a tenacious, independent spirit and a thirst for adventure mixed with a touch of flamboyance.

Wagoners of that era lived grueling, rough-and-tumble lives. Established "out west" in Connellsville by 1807, Old Robert had relatives who lived "out east" of him in both Adams County south of Gettysburg and in Peach Bottom Township, York County; northeast of him in Cumberland County; and near Carlisle. His wagon routes took him southwest of the Cumberland Road into western Maryland, where it connected to Braddock's Road west of Fort Cumberland (see map 2). The Great Philadelphia Wagon Road turned south into Maryland and western Virginia at Winchester. At times he may have traversed parts of it to connect with the Cumberland Road.

Braddock's Road was originally carved from dense, virgin forest as a twelve-foot-wide military access track to allow Braddock's army to cross the Alleghenies in 1755, with all their wagons and cannons, to siege France's Fort Duquesne. That campaign failed, so most of the road was allowed to return to forest after British General Forbes opened up a more direct northern route to Fort Duquesne in 1758. Forbes's northern military road eventually became the fabled Pennsylvania Road that would carry wave after wave of new settlers west of the Susquehanna to the Port of Pittsburgh on the Ohio.

The improved Pennsylvania Road[2] remained the primary route of trade west across Pennsylvania from the 1770s until Old Robert's era. It ran west from Carlisle, crossing no major rivers and fewer streams than Braddocks's southern route. In 1785 the Commonwealth of Pennsylvania formally took on the upkeep of the Pennsylvania Road, which reduced both road closures and local maintenance costs.[3] It connected Harris's Ferry (later Harrisburg) to the western frontier at Pittsburgh, passing through Bedford, Ligonier, and Greensburg. Forts along the way maintained security in the early days, but many languished by 1800.

Braddock's route was another matter. Though Maryland had modestly improved a section of the road in the 1780s to facilitate mail delivery to Cumberland, much of the rest was still very rugged. A regional road dipped southwest from York and Adams Counties to meet it a few miles south of the long-contested border between Maryland and Pennsylvania. That boundary, surveyed by Mason and Dixon, was settled in 1767, but the western border that separated Pennsylvania from Virginia would not be settled until the late 1790s,

Transportation, Infrastructure, and Frontier Efficiencies

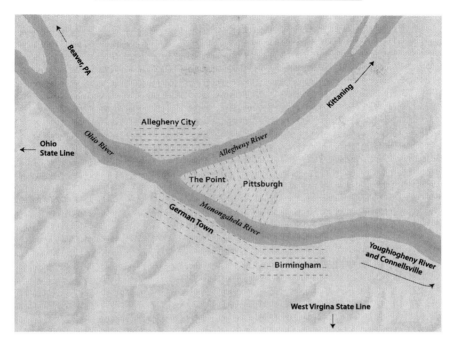

MAP 3.

after the Densmores arrived. Braddock's Road, laid out in 1754, began at Fort Cumberland in western Maryland and traversed some of the wildest, most isolated, and most beautiful country in the eastern United States. It crossed the Savage River, the Little Youghiogheny River (now called the Casselman River), and the Big Youghiogheny River multiple times. In the 1780s and 1790s, much of the route was narrow, overgrown with bushes, and studded with huge poplar stumps. During the forty-six years since General Braddock's campaign, most of those stumps had sprouted so that even packhorses had to squeeze through its narrowest stretches. The once hastily shovel-graded roadbed in places that skirted streams and hillside grades had eroded away, leaving a nightmare for any wheeled vehicle. It was easiest to pass in cold seasons when the mud was frozen stiff and the foliage was less dense.

The road dipped to the narrow Youghiogheny Valley near what is now Friendsville, Maryland, skirting the steep, once densely wooded hills to the northwest.[4] The old army path continued along the Yough[5] River's narrow valley on its path north to the wide ford known as the Great Crossing on George Washington's hand-drawn maps from the 1750s. There, settlers of the 1770s established the important town of Smithfield, later renamed Somerfield and now entirely submerged under the huge, artificial lake created by the twentieth-century US Army Corps of Engineers' dam designed to protect Pittsburgh from recurring floods.

There is no obvious way to know if Old Robert owned his own horses and wagon, but the Densmores taxed in York County owned enough farmland and livestock to have provided his means of daily labor. So did those in Cumberland County's West Pennsborough Township a few miles west-northwest of Carlisle. But William and Henry Dunsmore of Dunbar Township apparently did not, as local Fayette County tax records list no horses for either man in 1800. Whoever owned them likely claimed a share of Old Robert's earnings.

Most young wagoners in that era began their working lives at about age twelve, either as farmhands if their families owned land or as day laborers at tasks that cost many calories an hour above their basic metabolic needs. The basal metabolic cost of maintaining a ninety-five-pound boy age twelve to fourteen would have been about 1,000 calories a day **if** he spent his time sitting on a stump and daydreaming. If he worked eight hours at any of the jobs noted below, the additional food calories needed to fuel his work would have ranged from 1,600 to 3,000. In the 1700s the entire French nation still could not produce enough food for its men and boys to work full eight-hour days, five days a week. But America did!

Better yet, American food costs of the era were low, and many single, young workingmen got some board—meals and a cot—to supplement their modest wages of twenty-five to fifty cents a day engaging in any of the following: light road maintenance, a job that would amount to 300 work calories per hour; cutting and debarking fence rails, 500 work calories per hour; helping at blacksmiths or mills, 400 or more work calories per hour; working as tanners, assistants, horse groomers, or inn helpers, or chopping firewood, hauling ashes from local furnaces, or gathering/hunting the cattle and hogs from the forests each fall for slaughter, 200 to 350 work calories per hour.

In those days livestock were free-range creatures of the nearby forests. It was a very time-efficient way to have meat and hides available. Fewer acres had to be cleared of forest by hand to create paddocks that could be foraged, and no labor was invested in producing feed for much of the year, reducing overall acreage needs on a farm. Hay was cheap, but desirable orchards and gardens produced higher-priced commodities. As those forests were cut over the next fifty years, the cost of beef and pork rose, as cows and pigs needed farm-grown feed.

Young men gained experience handling farm horses and family wagons used to haul harvests to local mills or to nearby hamlets. Many managed tilling teams on family farms, much as did an adolescent Hiram Ulysses Grant in Ohio during the late 1820s.[6] When on the road wagoners could be gone weeks at a time. But packhorse trails were still the primary way that goods moved in to what is now northeastern West Virginia.[7] A packhorse trip between 1780 and 1820 from Morgantown (now West Virginia) east to Winchester, Virginia, took seven to nine days each direction.[8] Packhorses dominated in that part of West Virginia well into the 1820s.[9]

Wagoners worked year-round, regardless of ice, flooding, mud, or snowfall. Old Robert was likely on the road in 1801 the day an earthquake hit Pittsburgh and a large meteor was seen. Both alarmed the regional population and added sermon narrative for the fire-breathing itinerant preachers who traveled the back country on horseback wailing against strong drink and fornication. An eerily warm winter followed in 1802, which, for wagoners like Old Robert, meant the narrow freight roads were mired in axle-deep mud. Potholes quickly morphed into deep troughs that broke axles and taxed horses.

In the winter of 1803, it was not mud but ice that would have impeded Old Robert and his wagon. The Monongahela flooded at Brownsville, then iced up, disrupting both wagoners and Eastern Seaboard immigrants moving west to the newly opened Ohio country. In contrast, 1806 was the coldest winter weather in living memory for the residents of western Pennsylvania and Virginia. The Youghiogheny, Monongahela, Allegheny, and Ohio Rivers as far south as the Little Kanawha settlement (now Parkersburg, West Virginia) were "full of ice."[10] Wagons could operate in some places, but the rivers, which were the main way bulk goods and settlers traveled, were impassable. Old Robert's stops and detours would have been many.

The next year, when Old Robert paid his first taxes in Connellsville, the Monongahela River in Brownsville was forty feet above flood stage. Immigration as well as the supply businesses related to it must have halted for weeks on end. Crossing the Youghiogheny would have become a formidable task at both the Great Crossings in Somerfield, Pennsylvania, and at Connellsville, for Zachariah Connell's privately built and licensed toll bridge across the Yough was swept away, cutting off access to Forbes Road to the north.

In November 1810 another disastrous flood plagued the region's rivers. It was too warm to freeze the ground solid, so *both* wagoners and rivermen were stymied. In Pittsburgh the flood swept away boatyards, wooden docks, and dockside merchandise awaiting the flatboats. This was known as the "Pumpkin Flood." Tens of thousands of pumpkins ready to harvest were washed down the Allegheny to the Point[11] in Pittsburgh. It was a colorful disaster to be sure, but a hard hit for those whose crops were lost. Pumpkin meat was food for both humans and livestock, and the protein-rich seeds provided valuable oil for the local presses. Low-lying farms in the most productive upriver bottoms were obviously wiped out—pumpkin plots were typically located on *higher* riverside benches where the soil was not as rich as in the all-important silt-nourished "bottoms." Weather played a large role in daily life, and there was yet no national aid or infrastructure to soften it—self-sufficiency had both an upside and a downside.

Surprisingly, despite floods, floating pumpkins, and capricious weather patterns, markets across Pennsylvania were flourishing during Old Robert's years as a wagoner. The burgeoning markets in 1800 that he serviced were in the isolated settlements between Frostburg, Maryland, and old Fort Redstone (Brownsville, Pennsylvania) on the Monongahela. After 1803 Brownsville became a primary port and transportation node for the increasing flow of migrants heading west to snap up cheap lands across and west of the Ohio River.[12] Migrants needed the flat boats built there. They also needed salt, food, and manufactured goods: axes, hoes, shovels, pitchforks, horseshoes, iron pots, tanned leather for shoes and harnesses, rifles, powder and flints, pins, tin ware, and cloth. The isolated hamlets in between also needed many of the same items. The western markets for salt and iron proved insatiable well into the 1800s. Even so, a young wagoner's daily wages would have averaged only sixty to seventy-five cents.[13]

History, geography, culture, commerce, politics, and infrastructure all contrived to shape the district where Pennsylvania, Maryland, and modern West Virginia came together. By the early 1800s Lancaster, Pennsylvania, to the north of York County, had long been one of the nation's richest sources[14] of

Pennsylvania's "Kentucky" rifles—long, elegant, heavy-barreled flintlocks that could reliably deliver a .36 to .44 caliber ball at about 1,200 feet per second to a five-inch target one hundred yards away. Plenty enough to deal with black bears, panthers, deer, and—close up[15]—the few remaining Eastern Woodland bison.[16] The Little and Big Youghiogheny River country nurtured those animals in great abundance, along with grouse, wild turkeys, beaver, squirrels, foxes, and wolves. Human denizens included a few rugged settlers, highwaymen, runaway slaves, and small, surviving pockets of displaced Shawnee, Delaware, and Mingo Indians.

A number of the earliest European male settlers and Indian traders had married into Indian families during the 1730s and 1740s. But the turmoil of the French and Indian Wars, followed by wave after wave of new settlers hungry for Indian lands, had created a world where anger, violence, and stereotypes swallowed those old personal relationships. This created another rich stew of legal, tactical, and moral ambiguity, in which those with the most predatory personalities among both races too often set the tone for conflict.

As beautiful and as bountiful and as crowded—to Native Americans—as the country along Braddock's Road was, from 1785 to 1795 it had only just begun to be populated in earnest. Its isolated lands, broken topography, daunting winter snows, and reputation as a Shawnee stronghold had kept land values low and immigrant settler population modest through most of the mid-1700s. Its earliest European settlements (French and English) of the period from 1730 through the 1750s had been abandoned and already returned to forest. Thus, new settlements dotted the region, still awaiting local forges, gristmills, and fulling mills to produce essential metal goods and cloth. Henry and William Dunsmore of Dunbar Township served the region, distilling whiskey and making wool cloth. Old Robert was among those who served that region's market with his two-horse team, a narrow wagon, and a hunger for adventure.

Virtually all of the country Old Robert traversed in his wagon was still wilderness, as is amply documented by George Washington's 1784 ride through the area of his youthful Braddock's defeat. Most of the twelve-foot track cleared for Braddock's army in the 1750s had become *less settled*, he observed, than it was in the 1750s and 1760s when the Indian Wars pushed white squatters to the east and in the process dramatically reduced the area's Native American communities in both number and size.

What Washington noted in 1784[17] was that while the general region, absent the ecologically sound Native American practice of burning forest underbrush, had returned to even deeper wilderness than before, a growing number of infrastructure-rich settler nodes were emerging. Most were at the very places Washington himself had once stopped and rested his horses. Twenty years later, they were still the very same places Old Robert stopped to rest his horses. Washington argued that what the region most needed were maintained roads and bridges.

Washington's reports of his ride-through did have an impact—Maryland called for road projects, bridges, and such improvements to enhance western commerce in the 1780s, but many of those projects were commissioned as public-private partnerships,[18] formed between well-placed tax agents of the state, its counties, and prominent investors from eastern Maryland. Many of those investors owned major tobacco plantations in Cecil County and on the Eastern Shore. Some of the tax agents were their younger sons, sons-in-law, and so on. Few of these projects created much more than a conduit for privatizing public monies and socializing the debt from iffy cost overruns on haphazard "improvement" schemes.[19] In their wake, local occupation taxes rose. For the Densmores and other Scots-Irish, this particular situation was uncomfortably familiar. Even today it is not unusual to find the same phenomenon still redirecting public tax dollars into private bank accounts.

Then, too, George Washington did not fully separate his personal interests from the Nation's. He wanted western roads in no small part due to his own land, mills, and farming interests in western Pennsylvania. He owned extensive lands along Old Robert's 1800 route and a large plantation and grist mill complex a few miles southeast of Pittsburgh. He wanted his Braddock's Road upgraded to keep western market access profitable for eastern ports like Baltimore and Georgetown, *not* the Ohio Valley and Mississippi River trade that western Pennsylvanians favored as they sought to evade the financial and legal grip of Philadelphia, New York, and Baltimore financiers. Washington was at once President, businessman, Virginian, slave owner, and American. Those competing identities often conflicted him.

By the early 1800s pressures rose for an updated, competing road to the south of Forbes's Pennsylvania Road. That pressure intensified as Virginia land claims to the southwest quarter of Pennsylvania failed to be upheld in court case after court case. Thus, Virginian aristocrats were in the forefront of congressional efforts to build their own road. Their advocates included George Washington, then Thomas Jefferson. The goal was to capture and redirect some of the Pennsylvania trade away from the forks of the Ohio in Pittsburgh. Virginia and Maryland wanted both roads and canals built as a corridor to the west that would compete with the Philadelphia, York, and Lancaster manufacturing trade on Forbes Road and favor *their* Port of Baltimore. They wrapped their advocacy in layers of much debated "common sense," demanding a national road to the west. But the Virginians' hidden goal became crystal clear when the final route deviated from Braddock's original one near Brownsville on the Monongahela and pushed directly west through more sparsely settled lands to the banks of the Ohio at Wheeling, Virginia.[20] The new route bypassed Pittsburgh to the south by about forty miles. Self-serving or not, it proved to be the nation's first official public infrastructure project.[21] It also proved wildly successful in promoting American expansion west of the Ohio, and Virginia's financial elites met their goal: for several decades, Wheeling became the most rapidly growing city in America.

The very year Old Robert became a taxpayer in Bullskin Township-Connellsville, Thomas Jefferson, after years of Congressional wrangling, signed the act to build the road to the Ohio River on January 31, 1807. The route passed through Maryland and a strip of Pennsylvania, then the Virginia panhandle, connecting the old Virginia-owned Ohio Company store and village at Cumberland, Maryland, to the Ohio River. Formally labeled the "National Road," its primary goal was to significantly reduce the transport time for a wagon trip like Old Robert's, then eight to eleven days one way in bad weather, or six to seven days in good weather, to about half that time. That efficiency would significantly reduce the hundred-weight cost of transporting goods made in New Castle, Philadelphia, Baltimore, or Ellicott City. Shipping costs for heavy iron pots, axe-heads, and iron plow tips during Old Robert's short wagoner career often amounted to 30 percent of the delivered cost of such goods.

This drive for time-cost efficiency exemplified by the National Road has characterized one aspect of America's economy and cultural DNA for most of its history. The speed at which we could do things as a nation—make things, move things, calculate things, process things—became a signature of our nineteenth and twentieth centuries. Speeding up is characteristic of societies focused on power and economic growth. Inevitably, sustainability becomes such a society's gravest risk.

This ramping up can be conceived as a Power Phase in human society. The phenomenon often begins with technological or infrastructural efficiencies, then morphs into rapid growth as the lowered cost of energy and wages/work hours are reinvested in even more growth. In "power mode," speed, profit, and complexity increase while the efficiency that initially drove it eventually erodes. This phenomenon had already begun to enhance the nation's economic regionalism as a by-product of the Northeastern Seaboard's industrial efficiency, which conflicted with deep-seated cultural and economic patterns in the plantation South, where technological change was slow, debt margins were high, and short-term profit was used to cover the planters' recurring annual debt cycles. The rhythm, labor organization, and ecology of the South's plantation economy—though efficient in producing cotton and tobacco wealth at the expense of its slave class—never meshed well with the Northeast's business, commercial farm, and production cycles. Prior to 1810 a high percentage of the Northeast's industrial profits circulated right back into the regional economy.

In the plantation South debt cycles were primarily determined by the size of cotton and tobacco harvests as well as market price, which were controlled by trading houses in England, where planters also purchased most of their industrial and high-status goods. Thus a disproportionate stream of Southern plantation profits flowed directly offshore into the *British* economy, right up until the end of the Civil War. Ironically, the plantation aristocracy persisted in exporting much of its cash gains and importing heavily taxed British goods—one of the primary problems that had generated the Revolutionary War in the first place.

Both Washington and Jefferson were truly keen observers of their worlds, but how could they have realized that the economic and industrial forces unleashed by the nation's first real infrastructure project—the National Road—would further intensify the regional economic differences that would later distinguish "North" and "South" and play a role in the lead-up to the Civil War?

The road itself was a daunting project. Construction ground to a halt in 1816 when the Indonesian volcano Tambora erupted spectacularly, creating a winterlike spring and summer in most of the northern hemisphere.[22] Deep snows and a disastrous harvest season followed.[23] Crop failures in New England, western New York, and northwestern Pennsylvania uprooted farmers, who began to migrate west to Indiana and Illinois.[24] In spite of the urgent regional need for the National Road, grading solidly frozen soils for a road base was impossible with available technology, and funding dried up in the postwar depression of 1816. The crop failures also created an acute widespread shortage of oats to feed horses, which limited both commercial travel and the road crews that hauled rock and gravel for the new road bed in Conestoga wagons. In 1817 more oats were harvested, and the pace of construction sped up. Oats were an essential "fuel" in 1816, poured into a leather feed bucket, just as we now pour gasoline into a car's tank.

In spite of setbacks, by late 1818 the road ended at Water Street on the east bank of the Ohio River in Wheeling. Farmers ruined by Tambora's eruption and the depression it created migrated west in droves. Behind them, northwestern Virginia and southwestern Pennsylvania began to morph into a regional economy based on a rich mixture of manufacturing, farming, travel supply, and timber. Wage labor and a growing national market for manufactured goods, not slave labor and English imports, drove output and innovation in the region serviced by it.

In the same era the manufacture of machine-carded cotton cloth in East Coast factories doubled the amount of finished cloth produced per bale when compared to hand-carded cotton. Machine carding also reduced manufacturing time four- or fivefold.[25] These staggering efficiencies in cost of labor, time, and base materials created a major leap in commercial cloth production. In the north, household manufacture of cloth diminished rapidly. In parts of the Deep South, plantation slaves continued to make the coarse cotton cloth called "buckra" by hand for decades.

Forty-odd years later, the seceding slave states would pay the full price of snubbing Pittsburgh and the industrial North. By rerouting the National Road through western Virginia, the Virginians who once dreamed of co-opting Pittsburgh and had initially brought slaves into that city to change its economy and work culture between 1790 and 1825 inadvertently set it culturally and economically free to develop its own ethos based on wages, innovation, and an unquenchable hunger for industrial growth and efficiency. This cultural independence not only produced growth and huge industrial and economic benefits in the Ohio Valley but also perversely began to erode self-sufficiency as frontier settlers like Samuel Densmore (1751) and his descendants had once experienced it. What irony: the North's industrial Power Phase had begun to rob many of its skilled workers of individual self-sufficiency while the South's elite had robbed its growing population of the industrial self-sufficiency required to win the war it would start in 1861.

Chapter 5

Regional Culture, History, and Changes

It is likely that Old Robert never imagined he would be *the* generation of wagoner who connected the packhorse-dominated frontier of Western Maryland, Pennsylvania, and Western Virginia (now West Virginia) to the fast-paced demographic and technological changes that would transform the US nation's flamboyant western, trans-Appalachian frontier into a distinct region in the developing nation. It remains so even now.[1]

And what a rough, rowdy, rye-whiskey-soaked, male-focused, and cussedly stubborn frontier it had been. As noted, the hoped-for "last" major Indian peace treaty had come in 1782, the year Old Robert was born in Ulster. But the late eighteenth century's flood of new immigrants across the Ohio triggered another Native American push for survival. Thus the last major "peace" treaty east of the Mississippi was actually signed after the Battle of Fallen Timbers in 1794. Another wave of disease and aggressive displacement had further eroded the Native population, so those raids were smaller in scale than in the 1780s, but that did not matter much to the European settler victims and their surviving kin. What did matter were the forces that produced them.

Had it not been for continuous agitation of England's agents[2]—among them loyalist Virginia aristocrats like sullen Lord Dunmore,[3] who supported England's continuing post-Revolution hold on the upper Midwest—regional dynamics might have been less corrosive to both Native American and settler communities.[4] Just as the Scottish clans and their lands had once been consumed by expanding British power, so were the Indian nations of the region consumed by an insatiable, young America. The combination of large settler families and shiploads of new immigrant arrivals after the Revolution created a demographically overwhelming wave of settler competitors, disease vectors, and ecological changes that devastated the remaining regional Native American communities. Similar forces also blunted calm and stability as American-born and new European immigrant settlers competed to form public institutions and sort out land claims as former "Colonies," "Proprietorships," and "Dominions" became "States."

Ironically, the young Anglo-American government contested Native Americans on the one hand while simultaneously contesting the culture and economy of the largely Celtic Ulster Scots (Scots-Irish) who had so conveniently pushed those same Indians out of the Ohio Valley on the western frontier. Neither population was acceptable to young America's Anglophiles. Historians know the nation's Ulster Scots and Irish settler pushback as the Whiskey Rebellion of 1791–1794. Much romanticized, and tainted by politically motivated reporting of the day, it made several things clear: growing communities needed clear governmental structures and an unbiased legal system; militia movements, even when litigating valid complaints, tend to get seriously out of hand; and taxing authority is a lightning-rod issue that is adjudicated in the court of public opinion through the lens of "fair," with far greater consequences than in a court of law.

Taxing—that is, costs extracted on the value of individual labor or personal possessions—has very different consequences than taxes on profit in widely held economic combines and corporations. Taxing corporate profit has more diffuse consequences and seems far less personal. In contrast, taxing individual labor and earnings shapes parameters of daily diet, education, family accommodations, and well-being—and it gets to the universal core question of any family, community, or nation's sense of itself and its corpus: "How are we doing?" Answers to that question often depend on context—settlers in western Pennsylvania, for example, rightfully viewed the whiskey tax as a pre-meditated federal assault on their well-being and self-sufficiency. Simultaneously, surviving Native communities rightfully considered those same Ulster Scots and Irish as the primary agents actively destroying their fragile well-being and self-sufficiency.

Old Robert would have been a twelve- or thirteen-year-old working boy by the time the first whiskey tax evaders were put in chains for the three-week trip to a Philadelphia court. His heritage, and the opinion of his elders—like distiller Henry Dunsmore of German Township—undoubtedly shaped his interpretation of the Whiskey Rebellion and the mishandled trials that ended the year before his March 1800 wagon trip.

His dour if not crude interpretation would have been detested by Alexander Hamilton, the primary instigator of all those events. Since cash- and coin-poor western Pennsylvania typically used a gallon of whiskey as a basic monetary unit, just as Maryland and Virginia planters had long used a pound of tobacco, it is impossible to assume Alexander Hamilton and his financier henchmen in Philadelphia failed to realize that they were taxing whiskey in a perverse way. In the 1790s whiskey *was* currency, and punishing its use as currency among the Ulster Scots and Irish frontier settlers was intentional, especially since no similar action was taken against the seaboard planter-class tobacco growers' monetization of cured tobacco during the same era.

Further, Old Robert would likely have viewed the contested courts, Pennsylvania versus Virginia, and local governments in western Pennsylvania in the 1790s as "same old, same old," just an American version of his Scotland and Ireland no-man's-land heritage.

And therein lies another political and structural dynamic that characterized the western frontier: into small-scale legal and institutional ambiguities, political and legal forces equivalent to the ancient Border Reivers jump full force. In larger-scale societies such ambiguities create a manipulator's paradise. Contemporary "sovereign citizens," organized vote stealers, the KKK, and skinhead militias are all products of ambiguity and reactive cultural values. In short, Hamilton's exotic taxing policies on whiskey both encouraged manipulators and gave them legal cover, making western Pennsylvania and adjacent portions of northern West Virginia stubbornly skeptical of federal authority right through the chaotic and bloody Great Railroad Strikes of 1877–1878, when federal troops (and hired Pinkerton enforcers) again used lethal force on strikers in the very same region. In a number of cases, it involved the very same families only two or three generations removed. Among them were Densmores and Vandergrifts. In 1800 the American nation's young Constitutional government was still too weak to apply the golden rules of governance: make it fair, make it simple, make it clear, and make it consistent.

Old Robert Dunsmore

Though he was taxed as a wagoner from 1807 to 1811 in south Connellsville, Fayette County, by 1813, the year he enlisted in the War of 1812, Old Robert stated his occupation as a farmer. As county taxes were declared in spring, he may already have been farming in the winter of 1811, when it was so seasonably warm in western Pennsylvania that a second crop of apples was harvested in Washington Township, southeast of Pittsburgh.[5] Tax records indicate that he paid a moderate ten dollars in taxes, typical for a farm worker of that era. The slower pace of farming also suggests that Old Robert had begun to settle down.

In 2010 another researcher deduced from census records that he may have had a wife and other children *before* his eventual marriage to Hannah Glenn in 1820.[6] If so, who were they, and why can we find virtually no local record for Robert between 1800 and 1807, nor before or immediately after the War of 1812? In fact, he does not appear again in local Connellsville tax records until 1821.[7]

Eventually new information emerged, suggesting that Old Robert did have a wife and family before he met Hannah. Though there is a Connellsville tax roll for 1810 listing Old Robert's local tax of ten dollars (for two cattle), the US Census of 1810 for Fayette County showed no record of his name. Later, an entry in a tattered yellow folio containing a privately produced index of the US Census of 1810 for Fayette County, Pennsylvania, solved the mystery: "Robert Dunsmore, Bullskin, p. 1032." In a separate coded section of the index, Old Robert *is* listed. Finally, I had found him. He was *not* living alone as he was in the next US census of 1820. His 1810 household included one young boy, two little girls, and a woman—his wife, presumably, listed between sixteen and twenty-six years in age.

There he was, with the speculated family he might have had before he signed up for the War of 1812. His name had been omitted in digital online coding because the handwritten name "Dunsmore" on the original census sheet was incorrectly transcribed as "Dummore."[8]

On federal census day in the summer of 1810, Old Robert's known wife, Hannah Glenn, would have been just ten years and three months old. She can neither be a consort nor the mother of the three children listed on this census. Thus it now seems likely that Old Robert's documented children—Nathaniel, Elizabeth, Robert, Jr., Jane, Samuel, Rachel, and F. H. O.—had a half brother and two half sisters known to them during the elder children's childhood years in Connellsville, before Old Robert and Hannah moved to Fairchance in Georges Township in the late 1820s.

Though there are no irrefutable details for this newly discovered 1810 family, there are strong clues from other documentary sources in the years before and after 1810. A "John Sutton Dinsmore," farmer of Westmoreland County, died in 1854 at age forty-eight of "Asiatic cholera."[9] John S. Dinsmore's death certificate[10] lists his father as Robert Dinsmore and his mother as "Esther Sutton Dinsmore." His death certificate was registered in Greensburg, Pennsylvania, the nearest large town to John S.'s farm and the Westmoreland County seat where Old Robert actually enlisted for the War of 1812 in June of 1813. John S. left eight children,[11] among them a son William and another named Sutton.

Is John S.'s father our Old Robert? Is Esther the name of Old Robert's first wife? The timing of John S.'s birth in 1806 fits the time frame when Old Robert was settling down. He would have been twenty-four or twenty-five years old, the typical age for a man to marry. Significantly, the 1820 US Census for Fayette County included a girl and a boy in Old Robert's household, both of whom are listed between the ages of ten and fourteen. As veteran Pennsylvania researcher Pamela Nixon noted in her report dated July 2011,[12] neither of these children makes sense time-wise unless Old Robert had children from a prior marriage. His eldest son Nathaniel of formal surviving records had not yet been born as of census day in the summer of 1820. The ten- to fourteen-year-old boy in the 1820 federal census could have been a son of Old Robert's, possibly the fourteen-year-old John S. mentioned above. The girl in the same age group could be a daughter whose name is so far unknown. The last clue is a Sutton family found in the US Census of Connellsville in 1800. This could be a young Esther and her parents. Or it might be yet another tangled layer of uncertainty.

Documents establish that Old Robert lived near Connellsville, where the Sutton family lived, and that he returned to the same region after the war. Yet he enlisted in Greensburg, Pennsylvania, before he made the long march with the 22nd Pennsylvania Infantry unit to Canada's doorstep at French Mills near the St. Lawrence River. That enlistment roster is priceless: it gives us his height, eye and hair color, and occupation. It is also a testament to his relative "American" equality. There are no comparable documents for women, blacks, or Native Americans of that era, just as there were few records of poor tenant farmers in his native Ulster.

Not long after Old Robert started to settle down, it appears tragedy befell him and his young family. In that era many young wives died in childbirth, and Old Robert's first wife may have died in this way. It seems that close relative William Dunsmore, the fuller, died at this same time. Upon closer examination William was likely the husband or brother-in-law of Mary "the widow" Dunsmore, as she is later listed on the US Census rolls of 1820 and 1830 as head of her household in Connellsville—but not on the 1810 census, which lists William as head of his household in nearby Washington Township. Note that their preferred *Dunsmore* spelling often became *Densmore* in local tax rolls and historical documents. It makes sense, then, that widow Mary would take in Old Robert's children when he enlisted in 1813.

The War of 1812 offered an exit strategy for men like Old Robert. It also offered a modest salary of eight dollars a month, an enlistment bounty of thirty-one dollars cash, and, upon honorable discharge, rights to 160 acres of land in the Louisiana Purchase. Old Robert took that exit and received help with his children from his extended family.

Changes and Efficiencies

During the early 1800s Old Robert's America was changing rapidly. Both natural population growth and war generated change. Local roads improved, and many more forges, foundries, sawmills, gristmills and fulling mills were founded. Those enterprises supported more wage labor and imposed high-calorie jobs—200 to 475 calories per hour—on men earning fifty to seventy-five cents a day for nine or ten hours of work. Local bridges were improved. The National Road from Cumberland was nearing completion. In response, more state maintenance was lavished on the competing Pennsylvania Road to Pittsburgh even as the new capital in Washington feverishly repaired damages to the White House sustained during the 1812 war. But a third great driving force was the stubbornly high cost of transport from East-Coast factories to the Ohio River. Those costs created both the stimulus for more public infrastructure support and an immense appetite for the products of local and regional manufacturing.

Small forges and foundry operations throughout southwestern Pennsylvania and northwestern Virginia sprang up, most charcoal-fired, with tall stone stacks. Local laborers, often farmers' sons in slack seasons, cut huge quantities of wood (400 calories an hour) and reduced it to charcoal to fuel the furnaces. The most daring of their brothers handled the dangerous process of "jumping the pile" onto the burning wood and packing it down, feet and spade flying. This reduces oxygen intake in the pile and transforms wood, which burns at a lower temperature, into charcoal, which burns at a higher temperature. During the transformation, about 20 to 30 percent of the mass in the cut wood is lost, which means calories are lost. So, how the charcoal is used matters a great deal. If charcoal is used in a smith's small, open hearth, heat losses are high. But if the charcoal is burned in a closed furnace, heat losses are reduced. More important is the fact that charcoal burns hot enough to produce a much higher grade of iron.

Other day laborers dug the local red-stained iron ores that were then melted and shaped into "pigs," or large ingots, to be shipped to forges like the Gibson family's Yough Forge in Connellsville, where Old Robert worked after the War of 1812.

That forge manufactured some of the War of 1812's cannonballs, which were loaded onto flatboats and floated down the Youghiogheny, then the Monongahela, to "the Point" at Pittsburgh. From Pittsburgh they were reloaded onto large, locally made timber barges, then sent down the Ohio and then the Mississippi to supply US army cannoneers with the matériel of war. Well-made Pennsylvania flintlocks also played a role in the famed battle of New Orleans in 1815.[13]

As the regional western Pennsylvania tradition of producing metal goods developed, small forges prevailed. Skilled molders, catchers, and puddlers poured cannonballs, forged plow parts, and cast rough machine parts and axe-heads. Iron "heaters" or "boilers" produced the iron. Others heated and reheated ingots as "rollers" slowly squeezed them down in large presses, thinning them step by step to produce sheet iron, stove parts, plow blanks, cooking griddles, wagon-wheel treads, barrel hoops, and structural reinforcements. After 1790[14] the thinnest iron sheets were shipped on flatboats or hauled on ox-driven wagons to nail factories for cutting and finishing.[15] Small nail factories already existed in Connellsville and in Fairchance to the south. Screw blanks were forged and then tediously hand-threaded one by one with a file, a practice carried on into the 1820s. Screws were expensive, so fine wooden dovetailed joints and wooden pegs in furniture making were still the regional norm into the 1820s.

Many more important innovations were generated locally; people, manufacturing, and conveyances moved more rapidly compared to the 1700s. By 1815, given fine weather, fresh horse teams stationed every twenty miles, and improved roads, goods could be shipped via the Pennsylvania Road to Connellsville in just four or five days from Philadelphia. More bridges had been built on the National Road's southern route into western Maryland and southwestern Pennsylvania, and Old Robert's nine- or ten-day trip of 1800 was trimmed to about six days.

In 1816 a teenager named George Vandergrift, along with his brothers, helped build Pittsburgh's first wooden bridge across the Monongahela, eliminating the old ferry service's speed limitations. Most importantly, a rapidly growing base of highly skilled regional labor was created. More rapid transport of goods, more local manufacturing output of basic farm and tool necessities, and steadily increasing levels of local skill were amplified by men willing to work hard for five or six long days a week. Unlike in France, the food calories and protein from regional farms easily fueled industrial workweeks of sixty hours or more. Workers invested lavishly in dinner-table fuel to deliver the labor inputs demanded by their bosses. Coupled with incremental industrial efficiencies, that combination eventually drove down owner costs, which stabilized wages. Stable wages benefitted well-being, as is evident in the stable height and longevity of males born between 1800 and 1820. Infant mortality remained much lower than in Europe between 1810 and 1820. These factors led to both a larger regional population due to natural reproductive increase and demands for more investment in public infrastructure—schools, market stalls, and bridges. By 1820 self-sufficiency in the west meant either land, livestock, farms, tools, and children to help out, or skills, tools, well-defined muscles, and the vigor to put in sixty or more hours a week for wages.

Old Robert, like most other men in the region, had multiple skill sets by 1820. Local census data, tax rolls, and newspaper ads from the 1805 to 1820 period in Hagerstown, Cumberland, Grantsville, Somerfield, Uniontown, Bruceton Mills[16], and Connellsville list tanners, saddle makers, sawyers, molders, forgemen, wagonmakers, harness makers, cabinet makers, blacksmiths, fullers, weavers, millwrights, millers, gunsmiths, wagoners, surveyors, innkeepers, storekeepers, lawyers, doctors, and pastors. Many of these men maintained garden plots or small farms on the side at their homesteads,[17] and virtually all of them possessed secondary skills that would have garnered them "five stars" as handymen on a modern Angie's List. Skills, mind you, that are now in short supply, especially in urban America.

The Connellsville area where Old Robert settled was a world that had flowered based on two American realities. First, the trans-Appalachian districts leading to the fabled and oh-so-strategic Ohio River country were no longer primarily the violent, ambiguous domains of tough, ungovernable individualists. Second, due to a combination of population pressure and a stage of initial infrastructure improvements including roads, bridges, resolved legal land claims, and clear state and county boundaries, these "western" districts had become *every* man's lands rather than *no* man's lands.[18] From an anthropologist's perspective, that was a significant cultural step in nation building, which depends upon the perception of inclusion. One can bring his or her own chips to play at the "Big Table," but there must be a seat offered. Life was hard, but food, vigor, and opportunity allowed an increasing portion of American-born white males to play. As the 1820s unfolded, progressive states granted voting rights to many more adult white males. In the North, some black males could vote, but most blacks, women, and Native Americans would not get their voting rights for another century.

CHAPTER 5

Height, Demography, and Change

As Old Robert entered another undocumented period between late January of 1814 and the US Census of 1820 in Connellsville, the boyhood world he immigrated to had transformed in the historian's blink of an eye. That he lived farther west and had, he asserted, become a farmer by 1813 was the norm in that period. That he had a wife and family before his enlistment would have been normal as well.

Old Robert was atypical in that native-born American men of his age averaged 5'8.2" in height, whereas he was a spare 5'7". The American Advantage of our early post–Revolutionary War period that drew immigrants to these shores, at the expense of Native Americans, was clearly bolstered by the fact that American-born men living between 1770 and 1800 were the tallest and best fed in the European world.[19]

America was also exceptional in the generous length of expected life its Euro-American occupants enjoyed when compared to European countries of the time. This average longevity advantage applied to *both* genders. An average American born in 1750 just before the French and Indian Wars (the Seven Years War) could expect to live to age fifty-one. In England, Ireland, and Scotland the expected span of life was thirty-seven years. By about 1780 English longevity was eroding as industrialization increased and well-being declined. In France in 1780, life expectancy was just twenty-six years![20] As noted, the French simply could not produce the food calories needed to fuel enough labor to expand its farming enterprise—a vicious cycle that took them several generations to overcome. No wonder French farmers became a permanent, specially protected class of producers; in matters of life, death, and the specter of extinction, memories are long. A working father's age at death mattered enormously in practical terms: dead at age thirty-seven, as in the United Kingdom of the late 1700s, meant several dependent orphans for a widow or a society to deal with—hence the importance of orphan's courts. A death at between the ages of fifty and fifty-five, as in America, left far fewer dependent orphans. Of deeper consequence, biological instincts are not negotiable in the world of politics: birth, death, health, and reproduction are the crosses upon which countless empires and control-focused politicians have been crucified.

By 1800 life expectancy in England had declined by one year, to thirty-six. France had improved to thirty-three. In the young United States of 1800, native-born children's life expectancy rose to fifty-six years in spite of the Revolution's tribulations.[21] In biological terms the Revolution was a cheap war. By 1800 the average height of native-born American males had risen to a bit over 5'8", compared to England's 5'6" and France's 5'4.7".[22] In short, a European immigrant coming to America between about 1750 and 1800 could expect that they, and especially their children, might grow stronger, taller, and live twenty to twenty-five years longer *if* they could survive the ocean passage and get a spot of land or a job with prospects upon arrival. The promise of enhanced well-being was America's most crucial founding advantage.

It is also important to note that pamphlets, newspaper pieces, and even entire books on the theme of "The Best Country for a Poor Man"[23] had been saturating biologically and economically distressed European communities for more than a century before Old Robert's family came to America. Early America's profound pull on immigrants was deeply intertwined with the instinctive, biological lure of an adequate diet, a longer life, healthier children, and the increased prospect of actually owning, or at least controlling, one's means of support.

The draw of our Founding Fathers' ideologies, or the fine points of Constitutional law so frequently appealed to today by agenda-driven politicians, was likely far down the list of factors that actually motivated most immigrants to pull up stakes and risk the passage to America. In fact, the Founding Fathers did not yet exist when Samuel Dinsmore patented his land in 1751. There was no Declaration of Independence, no Constitution, and no Bill of Rights. But there were unfarmed lands and, even then, a huge biological advantage: colloquially, "well-being."

Tragically, many of our modern politicians, even those who claim to be "Constitutional originalists," do not fully understand the Declaration or the Constitution in their original cultural context. That context focused on the advantageous biological underpinnings of America's early success as articulated in the Declaration. Nor do they now apprehend the stunning quantities of hard work and food calories that it took in the century from 1720 to 1820 to achieve it for a growing population. Economic reward for hard work and measures intended to protect physical well-being played very powerful core roles in creating the United States.

As a nation, it is important for us to realize that failure to factor in the biological welfare of *all* major segments of a large population in public policy decisions virtually guarantees a fragmented society. The most straightforward way to assess modern America is to look at longevity or mortality and infant death rates in the different regions of the country, as I did some years ago in another book about the status of a society over time.[24] This helps to answer the key questions of "How am I doing?" and "How are my kids doing?" that drive any family's, community's, or nation's sense of itself and its corpus.

For example, Old Robert's somewhat short height of 5'7", when compared to the American average, might mean nothing more than a familial genetic trait. Recall that Old Robert's primary family likely arrived in Pennsylvania around 1794, when he was between ten and twelve years old—a time when America was nearing the very peak of its eighteenth-century height and longevity advantage and its striking caloric and food advantage as compared to Europe. America's food advantage during Old Robert's teen growth years may have enhanced his adult height, but it could not compensate fully for any disadvantage he suffered in his Ulster childhood.

That American food advantage—the presence of abundant, reasonably priced food—had also made ten- to eighteen-hour workdays possible for Old Robert in his occupations as wagoner, forgeman, and farmer.[25] He could work harder and much longer in Pennsylvania than in Northern Ireland, England, or France, where he simply would not have had enough food calories to fuel that many hours of work each week. England's food economy in 1800 produced just 858 work calories per capita daily, in excess of its total population's caloric demand to sustain basal metabolism. That was enough to fuel moderately intensive work for about three hours a day. In contrast, the United States produced two and a half times more work calories per capita each day.[26] Every adult in America could work at a medium work intensity for eight hours every day of the year, and their children could be well fed.

At that time, it was only in America that a man of Old Robert's family background could gain such an immense biological advantage. That work advantage, along with the high quality and low cost[27] of the available food, were the keys in generating America's early economic and demographic growth. At the crux of early American success, these two advantages were inseparable. They formed an energetic feedback loop.

Calories and Economic Efficiency

Counting simple calorie costs can clarify aspects of historic American "progress." The table below reveals a striking disparity in the number of human and horse-consumed calories involved in Old Robert's wagon trip of 1800 versus a packhorse train of that era carrying the same weight of goods.

These caloric calculations are reasonable estimates, assuming a packhorse

TABLE 3. Round Trip from Southern Adams County, Pennsylvania, to Connellsville, Winter 1800

Packhorse Train, 1400 lbs Freight, 16-Day Trip*	Calories Per Diem	Wagon Haul, 1400 lbs Freight, 19-Day Trip	Calories Per Diem
8 horses (1 spare, sometimes ridden) at a total weight of 9,000 lbs; work intensity medium	240,000	2 light draft horses at a total weight of 2,800 lbs; work intensity medium-high	56,000
1 male rider, 5'8" at 140 lbs; work intensity medium	3,100	1 male rider, 5'7" at 130 lbs; work intensity medium-high	3,100
Trip Costs/Calories		Trip Costs/Calories	
Horses = 3,840,000 calories		Horses = 1,064,000	
Rider = 49, 600 calories		Rider = 58,900	
Total Trip = 3,889,600 calories		Total Trip = 1,122,900 calories	

* The packhorses move a bit faster than the wagons through the snow and can take narrow shortcuts.

weighed 1,125 pounds and a draft horse weighed 1,400 pounds. What is clear from table 3 is that public investment in widening a narrow forest path for the passage of wagons reduced transport costs in calories by more than two-thirds, from 3.88 to 1.12 million calories. That change also meant lower breakage and damage rates of merchandise in a canvas-covered wagon bed compared to damage done when packhorse saddles shifted or when horses banged against brush and branches. As a matter of fact, horses can pull much more weight than they can carry.

In an era when a hundred weight of goods was hauled for about one to one and a half cents a mile[28] per hundred miles hauled, the reduced cost of horse feed (hay, oats, and corn) alone would have dramatically increased haulage profits for wagon freighting. The early roadside wagon stands of the late 1700s to 1800s always kept a supply of rough-milled oats (1,250 calories per pound), milled and pressed corn (1,536 calories per pound), and Timothy or other hay (804 calories per pound). On an average day, a single working horse consumed about eighteen pounds of hay, or roughly 14,500 calories, and ten pounds of oats or corn, containing about 12,500 and 15,360 calories respectively.[29]

The draft animals hauling Old Robert's wagon may also have had a bit of flax oil mixed into their oats and corn to enhance fat and protein intake while pulling through the Alleghenies. In the 1780s taverns and wagon stands in Pennsylvania sold grain, primarily corn and oats, at two and a half cents per quart,[30] and common hay plus stabling cost six pence per night, defined as a period of twenty-four hours. In Pennsylvania these were fixed, regulated prices. Old Robert would have avoided the stabling when possible, and he likely carried a hundred weight of corn or oats for his horses to start his trip. But it is essential to note that with two horses instead of eight, he spent far less in road costs to fuel his horses than did the packhorse trains.

From a broader ecological and farm-economy perspective, the shift to wagons meant that the same local hay and oat farms that had supplied the packhorses could provide the calories to fuel more than three times the weight of passing freight without expanding their farms. That meant the local farm and ecological bases were already in place to immediately support dramatic market expansion without adding more farm labor or clearing more land. Since efficiencies of this magnitude fuel rapid growth, it is easy to conjure a locustlike horde of wagons rapidly replacing regional packhorse operations in the early 1800s.

In the case of western Pennsylvania in the early 1800s, other "locusts" included thousands of weekly travelers passing through Brownsville, Uniontown, Pittsburgh, and Wheeling, intent on "consuming" the new West's resources and displacing competitors in their path. Packhorse captains and their families were left behind in the process, their way of life irretrievably displaced. Regionally powerful packhorse captains from multi-generational families had controlled the trans-Alleghenies' freight trade since the 1760s. They rued the arrival of those wagons and fought road improvements into the early 1800s to no avail.

The wagoner's impact opened up new economic opportunities for wagon makers, sawmills, timber crews, iron-chain makers, wheelwrights, whip braiders, and pine-pitch producers. But it left packhorse captains, leather pannier and bridle makers, and arrowroot and ginseng collectors at a new economic disadvantage. There was no going back.

Such efficiencies can trigger growth in human societies, just as they can in biology. In the midst of protracted famine, the most metabolically efficient humans statistically out-survive the least metabolically efficient—and wagoners like Old Robert were more efficient. The most metabolically efficient also put on weight or grow more easily. This has real implications for individual survival, as you will see in the discussion of Old Robert's descendants during World War II in chapter 18. The dynasties of packhorse captains faded away, their slow freight, its costs, and their geographic knowledge superseded by more efficient wagoners who knew less about the landscape but moved faster across it. Like fine wine, a dramatic efficiency often exhilarates on the front end and ends with a hangover.

Chapter 6
1812 and 1813
War and Its Consequences

Old Robert's radical change in lifestyle from the tough, boisterous class of wagoners to the more solitary, mundane demands of a farmer, as taxed in 1811, seems out of character for him. Between 1812 and 1813, as noted, his life apparently unraveled: his unidentified "wife" on the slash-marked census of 1810 became a documentary cipher, and by 1813 William Densmore the fuller was gone. The British had returned, and young America had also begun to unravel. In response, Old Robert enlisted for the War of 1812 in the summer of 1813.

The 22nd Pennsylvania Infantry was authorized to recruit soldiers on May 1, 1813. Its initial commander was aging General "Mad" Anthony Wayne of Revolutionary War and Fallen Timbers fame.[1] Before marching north toward the Canadian border, they mobilized at Greensburg, where Old Robert enlisted,[2] and trained at Fort Fayette—Mad Anthony's 1792 Ohio "Indian War" headquarters near Penn Avenue in what is now downtown Pittsburgh.

It was, as regiments of the era go, a smaller one. Old Robert would have known other Pennsylvanians in the ranks. Its full roll of enlistees and officers totaled 759, but only 287 of those survived to muster out. Losses were over sixty percent. Old Robert, as did the whole division, saw heavy action at French Creek, which was less than a mile from the fort at French Mills.[3] British Regulars and a large contingent of Chippewa allies engaged them on November 1 and 2, 1813. A cannon explosion maimed Old Robert during that combat, and he mustered out in January of 1814 after medical treatment in winter quarters at French Mills on the Little Salmon River near the Canadian border. His military documents recorded few details.

The 22nd went on that spring, without Old Robert and many others who had died since the fall of 1813. His brothers-in-arms took Fort Erie on July 31, 1814, from the British, decisively winning the brutal Battle of Chippewa against all odds. The 22nd's gray uniform became the adopted cadet uniform at West Point by 1815 or 1816. Every West Point cadet from then to this day wears a uniform commemorating Old Robert's unit. Among them, 180 years later, would be one of his own Fayette County Densmore great-great-great-great-grandsons.

After being discharged Old Robert, along with others wounded in the war, made his own way south to Pennsylvania from French Mills, likely on foot and in the snow. We do not know how long it took him or if any of the other men who had enlisted in Fayette or Westmoreland County, Pennsylvania, helped him or notified the Densmores who lived in rural New York, through which he passed.[4] His journey ended in Connellsville.

Connellsville

By sometime between 1814 and 1820, Old Robert was working for the iron-making Gibson family at the Yough Forge in Connellsville. Though several farms had been settled from the 1780s through the 1790s, aging Zachariah Connell had formally laid out the town in 1793. It did not attract much settlement until the period from 1799 to 1802, when a number of Connell's lots finally sold. Once they sold it quickly became a node of increasingly rich manufacturing infrastructure. By 1803 to 1805 it included a nail factory, two forges, a gristmill, a sawmill, and a cloth/fulling mill. These manufactories were nearly all powered by water or charcoal, and they tell us precisely what manufactured items were in greatest demand. Several were mule-powered during dry seasons. At least two other nearby iron furnaces, Mount Vernon and Old Laurel, were also in operation.

Several of the Gibsons—identified as originally from Chester County, Pennsylvania—had antecedents among the Scots-Irish immigrants of the 1730s. They came to Connellsville about 1793.[5] Their patriarch, John Gibson, Sr., born in 1751 in Chester County, commanded sufficient resources to purchase a tract of land in 1796 from the area's pioneering McCormick settlers.[6] The same year Gibson arrived with his sons, Zachariah McConnell laid out the charter to his town. John Gibson first teamed up with the fabled iron masters Isaac Meason and Moses Dillon to build Union Furnace, the second blast furnace west of the Alleghenies. Soon after, he built a gristmill just north of Connellsville on Mounts Creek.[7] Then came an oil press to make castor oil, then linseed oil, and by about 1805 he had built the Yough Forge. Located on the east bank of the Youghiogheny River in Connellsville, Old Robert later worked there.

That east bank at the site of the forge was low-lying ground nearly disconnected from the shore by a now diverted creek and was once known locally as Davidson's Island.[8] Not quite island and not quite riverbank, it was convenient, as pig-iron ingots could be loaded directly onto flatboats within sixty yards of the forge. Much of that iron went to Pittsburgh, then on to rapidly growing Cincinnati. Joshua had also built, in partnership, the Old Laurel furnace on Laurel Run, Dunbar Township, in or about 1797,[9] at a point in time when both William (fuller) and Henry (distiller) lived nearby. By 1815 or 1816 Gibson's surviving sons, Thomas and Joseph, inherited their father's estate, bought lands in South Connellsville, and erected Etna Furnace in 1815 on Trump's Run, several hundred yards from the Youghiogheny, near the forge. It closed down in the nation's economic meltdown of 1836 to 1837, though other sources claim 1840.[10] It is probable that Old Robert began working for them about 1815 or 1816, having had time to recuperate from his injuries of late 1813 at French Mills.

From 1795 to 1820 Connellsville became a regional manufacturing powerhouse. It is there that Old Robert morphed from wagoner to farmer to forgeman—and not just any forgeman, but one useful enough, reliable enough, and flamboyant enough to be recalled by a later descendant, Joshua Gibson, when he was interviewed by Franklin Ellis in the 1880s for his massive work, *History of Fayette County, Pennsylvania*.[11]

Injured or not, Old Robert had a presence at work; he had relatives in Connellsville, such as old Mary, the "widow Densmore," who had two sons—one named Henry, the other John.[12] It was also a time when Old Robert made new connections. Somewhere between the local furnace and the Yough Forge, he met a young, rising iron master named F. H. Oliphant, who would shape his later working life, as well as a younger fellow, Nathaniel Glenn,[13] who lived and worked at the furnace and would also shape his family life. Nathaniel's father, William Glenn, another Scots-Irish immigrant to the area, owned a small sawmill nearby and had a daughter named Hannah, born April 14, 1800.[14] Old Robert had undoubtedly been introduced to Hannah by Nathaniel, also born around 1800.[15] Injured and already worn by more than two decades of very hard work, Old Robert would have been about thirty-seven years old when he began to woo Hannah in 1818 and 1819. He was clearly still a vital man, charismatic and interesting enough to win her hand. She married him in late 1819 or 1820.

H. T. "Tom" Densmore gives their wedding as the depression year of 1819.[16] I favor 1820 since, in the 1820 Census[17] of Bullskin Township, Old Robert was still listed as living alone. Hannah likely lived with her father several doors away, as listed on a local tax roll that year.

Within a year of their wedding, a son was born to Old Robert and Hannah. They named him Nathaniel, known as "Nat," to honor Hannah's brother, as was custom of the time. Nathaniel Glenn would later become a forgeman and lay Methodist preacher, caught up in Connellsville's embrace of Methodism as a legacy of Old Zack Connell. He would spend most of his life within a few miles of the old Yough Forge, working the district's various forges and furnaces.[18]

The 1820s were biologically fruitful for Old Robert and Hannah. Their son Nat survived, and more children would be born to them. A growing family is expensive, and Old Robert's injuries apparently limited his earnings ability. In 1820 he first petitioned the federal government for a disability pension as well as for the bounty lands due him for his service and injuries in the War of 1812. Blind in his right eye and deaf in his right ear, those injuries limited the kinds of forge work he could safely do. In the world of forges and furnaces, the riskiest jobs, such as the pourers and puddlers,[19] paid much more than the safer, less-skilled jobs. One blind eye would have left Old Robert deficient in depth perception and lacking for any skill requiring fine-grained, rapid, three-dimensional hand-eye coordination. But Old Robert's petition to the war office would not be answered for many years. His army service file went missing after he entrusted it to John Reed, a young lawyer from Greensburg, in Westmoreland County. Recently widowed, Reed had remarried and abruptly moved to Carlisle, Pennsylvania, to accept a prestigious circuit judgeship. Those pension moneys would not fall into Old Robert's hands for another nineteen years.[20]

Old Robert and Hannah apparently lived in one of the log houses at the Gibson's Etna Furnace, not far from the forge. His father-in-law, William Glenn, had emigrated from Northern Ireland with several brothers in the 1790s. By 1800 Glenn relocated to Connellsville and settled near Etna Furnace, then he built his modest sawmill.[21] In July 1820 his new son-in-law was likely censused at Gibson's Etna Furnace on the east bank of the Youghiogheny. By the spring of 1821 Old Robert became a "colyer," someone who both dug coal[22] and supplied it by wagon to forge and furnace. Likely spurred to change by a young wife and infant son, in 1821 he paid a princely occupation tax of sixty dollars in Connellsville.[23]

The technology of forges and furnaces was changing rapidly—the endless supplies of hardwood trees, cut by the millions in western Pennsylvania to provide fuel for inefficient cabin fireplaces and voracious, charcoal-fired iron furnaces, had diminished. Those furnaces were being replaced by coal-fired ones, which operated at much higher temperatures and produced iron with fewer impurities and superior tensile strength. There was coal in abundance near the surface around Connellsville.

Here one sees another striking American pattern—voracious extraction of resources (timber) forcing new technological solutions, labeled in hindsight as "progress." It was progress, but only for a moment in time. The Colonial American habit was to consume without analyzing the massive impact on our environment and resource base. In modern terms, the area around Connellsville was rapidly increasing its carbon footprint and had already begun to rely on non-renewable resources (coal) as the basis for this progress. Such "progress" has a very limited shelf life in the long-term evolution of societies. And yet, as a nation, we are still addicted to it.

Community and Self-Sufficiency

Early Connellsville developed infrastructure and public services quite rapidly given that it started out with the advantage of the simple intersection of a state road and a packhorse trail, which had been widened in 1784. That widened road pushed west from the Turkey Foot settlement[24] to the Youghiogheny River. The road was maintained by tolls and Pennsylvania taxes. Virtually no other early state or federal public support was provided to Connellsville before the mid-1830s. The area's natural assets—its flowing water, forest, rich bottom soils, stone, coal, iron ore, and brick clays—were combined with huge manual labor inputs and local citizen cash "subscriptions" to meet community needs. Local businesses included Zack Connell's toll bridge across the Youghiogheny River, completed in 1801. That bridge gave access to the strategic Forbes/Pennsylvania Road.

Local "subscriptions," in Benjamin Franklin style, were America's first version of "crowd funding." Authorized in October 1806 and completed in 1810, the combination of public subscriptions, rent, and a modest local tax created Connellsville's first market house. Rented stalls accommodated many small vendors of farm produce. Beyond that, their modest rents and taxes paid "contractors" to gather and strategically place locally made ladders and oiled leather buckets for fire prevention, to fence the public graveyard, to maintain several local paths and bridges, to protect the town's public spring, and to build a log schoolhouse.[25]

The market house was built before the school and provided an immediate outlet for local farm goods, a basic necessity as more men took on public wage work. The council also commissioned gravel, sand, and brick footpaths, six to eight feet wide, to reach the market building from two directions. On April 2, 1807, the town Council directed transfer of the two schoolhouse lots set aside in Zack Connell's 1793 town charter to their active ownership. The first log schoolhouse was completed in 1807,[26] funded by a combination of local subscriptions that were to be paid back slowly to subscribers over the years from rents paid to the town council.

Those rents were assessed to the schoolteacher, who collected twelve and a half cents in tuition per student for each three-month quarter of schooling. The town council set tuition at fifty cents per year per full-time student. As a practical matter, that meant the schoolmaster had to attract the equivalent of thirty-six students who studied all four quarters and paid their full tuition just to cover his annual rent! It was not a stable arrangement. True, the tuition cost only a day or two of paid labor per child, but the Borough subscribers had not been numerous enough to cover the entire construction costs, nor the ongoing costs for upkeep and repairs to the log school: roof, chinking, broken wall slates, window glass, and so on.

Thus the school became Connellsville's ongoing bugbear. Teachers came and went, the town council alternated between lax, then excessive, oversight. No one was happy with the financial model or with this or that male teacher. The oldest teacher engaged was in his late fifties, and the youngest, James Killin in 1819, was just seventeen years old when he was hired—though he may never, for reasons unknown, have actually taught.[27] It all sounds alarmingly familiar in twenty-first-century America.

Connellsville's well-intentioned and fairly common town model was simply not sustainable. Locally, money and coinage were very scarce in Fayette County's mixed cash and barter economy of that era. Cash of any kind in early America had long been insufficient to meet public transactional needs. By 1816, in the post–War of 1812 depressed economy, money, especially coinage, was regionally so scarce that Connellsville's town council actually issued its own paper currency. Spanish "pillar" dollar coins and the "bits"[28] cut from them, French ecus of the early 1700s, English pence, and American half dollars, quarters, dimes, half dimes, cents, and half cents all circulated to compensate for the shortage of national money. As a result, local merchants had to calculate a surprising number of exchange rates.[29]

The school situation shortly became chaotic. A private "for profit" school soon competed for paying students. By 1829 the original log schoolhouse, described as "a wreck" and unusable, was put up for sale. As early as October of 1820, the Borough Council had proposed a new schoolhouse and general taxations instead of subscriptions to support it. But enough citizens opposed the new tax that Connellsville went without a public school until the fall of 1840, six years after the Commonwealth of Pennsylvania had enacted the Free Public School Act of 1834. In the nonce, some publicly "assisted" schools, which were pricier than the old fifty cents per year, operated unregulated during the 1820s and 1830s in rented rooms around town. Public and private charter schools are not a new idea; then, and now, they favored special-interest groups and/or more prosperous families.

It is a shock to realize that virtually all of the education, curriculum, staffing, cost, infrastructure, and leadership issues faced by a young Connellsville in the early 1800s were smaller-scale versions of today's national American debate, wrangling over the same educational issues. The fate of Connellsville's first log schoolhouse reflects the struggles of early America to establish a cash-based economy, a stable tax base, and street-level values of the time. Productive work and hands-on skills still mattered more for young men than did book learning. Old Robert's newborn son, Nat, would be directly affected by Connellsville's school closure in 1828 or 1829, as would other local children born in the 1820s and 1830s. Many, like Nat, never learned to read or write.

Old Robert also reflected the values of his time. Going to school was not a priority, and he himself was illiterate. On his 1820 military-pension petition, his signature was a mark for his name: a rough, triangular *R* of four pen strokes. His relatively late-arriving Northern Irish family valued work. Yet his large colyer's tax of 1821 indicates that he could work, count, and do business for himself by that time.

For generations the Densmores had been shaped by their initial, forced migration to Northern Ireland from Scotland and the legacy of the Ulster Plantation. They had adapted once before, and now in the United States they would adapt again, relying on their skills in local manufacturing, farming, and working the land in order to carve out a new life. That meant hard work for Robert from an early age and the skills and inclination to change careers as needed. These were essential elements in his adaptations to a rapidly changing America.

Old Robert and his family benefitted from the fact that skilled labor earned more in America than the equivalent of that in Ireland during the late 1700s. As noted, American housing and food costs were also lower. In Ulster in the 1790s, a smith, either in a forge or a blacksmith shop, earned between six shillings per week at the low end up to an astronomical twenty-four shillings per week in Belfast, with the average being about ten shillings, which was about two pounds per month or approximately nine US dollars. In the outskirts of Philadelphia, their wage would have been about fifty-six cents a day, bringing in about thirteen dollars in a twenty-four-day work month,[30] and on top of that the cost of living was cheaper. Even an unskilled American general laborer in 1790 could expect to earn four to five dollars a month, as compared to Ulster's equivalent of about three dollars.[31] By 1810 to 1820, those weekly American wages had increased.

As filtered through two centuries of our history, changing values, and the scale of things in modern America, Connellsville represents a small, rustic 1807 frontier outpost. But Old Robert saw a fresh, new community and job opportunity in farmsteads and wisps of smoke rising from Connellsville's hand-tended forges, which is why he made his home there by 1806 or 1807.

Nearing Connellsville, the final delivery point on his 1800 wagon trip, Old Robert would have entered the community heading north from Uniontown along a decent wagon road. As he entered what later became South Connellsville in the 1830s, he would have passed through a rolling, heavily timbered area, broken by creeks and the clearings created by scattered, early settlers. Some of them would have been awarded bounty lands averaging one hundred acres for service in the Revolutionary War.[32] The young nation, chronically short of both paper currency and specie, paid its soldiers miserably, for which it compensated by awarding land, which it owned in abundance. Fields, paddocks, wood lots, and small, recently built log houses would have come into Old Robert's view every quarter mile or so.

As Old Robert neared Zack Connell's new hamlet on the river, he'd have seen several dozen log houses, the blunt, dry-laid stone stacks and smoke plumes of several forges, a hand-dug millrace or two, a sawmill, a small tannery, and scattered livestock: oxen, cattle, pigs, sheep, and an occasional horse. One of the larger local structures in the town would have been that of the Trevor family, who had arrived about 1797. In their long log house they ran one of the region's first general stores. One bill of sale from the store, dated July 3, 1797,[33] shows that in addition to local goods and grain they carried nails, tea, cups, plates, indigo, pins, teapots, ribbon, tape, and snuff. That receipt provides insights into what a wagoner would likely have transported for delivery there in the early 1800s, except for the rough-cut nails, which were locally made in Connellsville after 1805.

Here we see a pattern, one repeated in thousands of locations during late Colonial and early Federalist America: streams, rivers, rich bottomlands, forests, and old intersecting roads or trails created and used first by buffalo, then Native Americans, then packhorses, then wagons. After the roads came locally created infrastructure: log houses, stables, blacksmiths, gristmills, sawmills, forges; then came cloth, nails, and wagon and harness shops, followed by a minister, a school teacher, a doctor, and regional entrepreneurs. Between 1780 and 1820 self-sufficiency on the frontier had scaled up beyond a simple log farmstead in an isolated clearing to a much more complex community model. Communities require complex institutions, cash, infrastructure, and properly negotiated rules to live by.

It is surprising how so much growth and change was fueled by government and commonwealth awards of lands and by abundant wood and waterpower between 1780 and 1820. Even modest road improvements fueled large economic gains. It was still a world full of low-hanging fruit, if one was willing to embrace risk and pursue a prodigious work ethic. The young federal government had played a more crucial role than most realize: by paying its soldiers in land,[34] it promoted self-sufficiency and ample food production. That supported favorable food prices and large, hardworking farm families, and it also drew in more immigrants—no small dynamic for its era.[35] Old Robert benefitted from this pattern. He did not see his world as small and rustic. In America, he saw a future that depended on his own hands, not one dominated by the grasping aristocracy of his native Ulster.

Chapter 7
Family Networks, Work, and Population Growth

Separating individual family histories from the nation's has become more difficult over time. As federal and state governments became more powerful and bureaucratic, their decisions affected daily life ever more. Or, put differently, in the 1790s Old Robert's family in western Pennsylvania was only minimally affected by what went on in the nation's capital of Philadelphia. Work and interpersonal relationships reigned, for a while.

H. T. "Tom" Densmore restored the kitchen table that first belonged to Old Robert and his wife Hannah. Rescued from the attic of matriarch Sophia Vandergrift Densmore's house near Philadelphia, it shouts "1820's Connellsville." Its use and style of hand-filed screws, lovely dovetailed joints, and an uncommon mix of woods all indicate a one-off, handmade piece dating to the early nineteenth century. As Sophia's daughter Elsie E. Densmore, Old Robert's great-granddaughter, wrote more than a century ago, it had come from Robert Densmore through his son Ollie and was made by William "Timothy" Glenn, piano maker of Connellsville. Timothy, she asserted, was a brother of Old Robert's wife Hannah.[1] I suspect the table began its life as a lovingly made wedding gift. Its unusual blend of woods, premium grade mixed with common, suggest it was made partly from scrap pieces of wood from piano or dulcimer projects. This table is proof that skills and family relationships still reigned in 1820.

The nation's depression in 1820 and 1821 marked quite a number of changes in Old Robert's life. As noted, his local 1821 Connellsville tax entry shows him in Bullskin Township, Connellsville, paying that huge sixty dollar occupation tax as a colyer. As a colyer he dug, brokered, and hauled coal to forges. Gibson's Etna Furnace could have been one of them, but so could F. H. Oliphant's Franklin Furnace at Little Falls on the Youghiogheny about ten miles west of town at

Vanderbilt, Pennsylvania.² That sixty dollar occupation tax strongly implies a crew-sized operation. If we knew whom Old Robert had recruited to his digging and hauling crew, we would know more about his 1820s family connections. If he had had sons with a first wife before Hannah, as the US Census of 1810 supports, his oldest son John S. Densmore would be about fourteen and might have worked on Old Robert's crew.

In spite of the details lost to time and illiteracy, life in 1821 was brightening for Old Robert: he had a baby boy and a vibrant young wife eighteen years his junior. Significantly, the very next entry on the 1821 Connellsville tax roll was that of kinswoman Mary, the "widow Densmore." Old Robert lived with or adjacent to her about the time little Nat was born. She probably assisted Hannah with childcare and likely had raised an earlier child or children born to Old Robert and his probable first wife, Esther Sutton. Mary's nine-year-old son Henry may have been working with Old Robert, since she was too poor in 1820 to pay his twelve and a half cent quarterly tuition to attend school in Connellsville. When Old Robert enlisted in the summer of 1813, she was probably the person to whom he sent his enlistment bounty of thirty-one dollars, to help her care for his children by his first wife.

The fact that Old Robert's federal pension papers languished may not have mattered much in 1821 given his success as a colyer—but it would matter later during the economic hard times of the late 1830s. In any case Old Robert was also in contact with another kinsman in 1821. Congress had finally authorized the issuance of deeds for War of 1812 bounty lands. Old Robert's 160 acres in White County, Arkansas, had finally become a saleable commodity. That same year, a Samuel Densmore appeared in White County, Arkansas, and the land was sold. Samuel may have bought the land from Old Robert and then resold it, or he may have served as his agent.

For Old Robert 1821 was a surprisingly good year financially, given the soft national economy. He made money from coal and from government-awarded land, and he likely invested in his coal business, purchasing a wagon and horses. He may have bought a small log house or moved in with Mary, but he apparently did not buy farmland, as no deed was recorded.³ To maintain his family on farmlands, he would have needed to own or rent about seventy acres, but he would not have been able to earn cash as a colyer or forgeman.

Thus the trajectory of his career came to depend on wages, skills, and local entrepreneurial activities, not crops. As a consequence, he became more vulnerable to cash-driven business cycles than farmers of this era, who could more easily operate in a barter economy. That uncertainty was buffered by investment of work, favors, and loans to maintain extended family connections. Old Robert's success in 1821 set the economic trajectory of his remaining life—he became tied to the erratic heartbeat of American industry, as would the four sons eventually born to him and young Hannah. It is unlikely that he perceived this, for he had endured the events that led him to enlist for the War of 1812, his physical recovery and adjustment to his disabilities, and the iffy, postwar economic years of 1816 to 1819.

At the same time, a young America was working through a similar recovery process. The nation had been through the French and Indian Wars, Lord Dunmore's War of 1774,[4] the Revolutionary War, the last Indian campaigns on the Pennsylvania, Virginia, and Ohio frontier, the Whiskey Rebellion of the 1790s, and the War of 1812.[5] All these had generated costs that diverted resources from community needs and deprived many thousands of families of their breadwinners. And all these wars had been initiated in one way or another by aristocrats—not just American ones, but also French, English, and Spanish. This fact was not lost on the common American's psyche.[6]

The perverse whiskey tax scheme imposed by Alexander Hamilton that led to the Whiskey Rebellion followed closely on the heels of a well-organized scheme to purchase the Continental Congress's "pay" bonds at pennies on the dollar from hard-up Revolutionary War veterans. Philadelphia's Robert Morris and Samuel Wharton[7] were among the upscale businessmen most involved. Interference by Virginia in Pennsylvania's proprietary government during the 1780s and 1790s also left the Ohio River Valley politically unstable. Several of the Virginian Ohio Company's aristocratic investors remained closely connected to England's royal court and parliament. They had wanted western Pennsylvania and some of their own western Virginian lands to become a new state—Yohogania—which they would own and control. To achieve this the Virginians had unleashed roving bands of militia, installed spurious judges, and even burned settlers out of their homes in Pennsylvania in the 1780s and 1790s.[8]

In response, a streak of populism spread as western Pennsylvania, southwestern New York, and a stretch of the Ohio Valley became hostile to and suspicious of federal government and Philadelphia's educated, predatory businessmen. This was enhanced by the second wave of the Great Awakening's religious fervor (1790–1820), which transformed into a movement, heightening both regional predispositions and a penchant for fiery populism. The *Lord* was in charge at the era's massive Presbyterian and Methodist church camp meetings, not those smooth, soulless, and uppity *Mammon* worshipers in Philadelphia and Boston. Populism based on the three anti-federalist *R*s of religion, region, and race intensified. And in those regions, faith in family and church networks handily trumped faith in government.

The National Road, Public Work, and Manufacturing Efficiencies

To counter this seed of populism Federalism needed to grow, and it grew, ironically, from an unlikely combination of factors: population growth, a transforming economy, and advances in manufacturing efficiencies. Whether Jefferson and others intended it or not, the National Road widened America's sense of its collective economic self and bridged the gap between regional versus national identities. But that bridge extended east to west, not north to south, generating a distinctive geographic band of migration, both cultural and genetic, that connected Pennsylvania to northern West Virginia, Ohio, Indiana, and Illinois. The distinctive genetic signature of that migration exists to this day.

After the martial conflicts ended, the United States entered a period when public resources could be redeployed to support both huge natural population increases and a constant flow of new migrants. American population had increased from 3.9 million citizens in 1790 to 9.6 million in 1820, nearly a 250 percent increase in one generation. Home manufacturing of cloth ended on all but the roughest western and deep-south interior frontiers. The age-old process of growing flax then soaking, rotting, and separating fibers before weaving, bleaching, and dying it at home involved many steps and lots of clean, hauled water just to produce one set of bed clothes, much less other clothing.[9] Hundreds of hours of labor a year had gone into this process. It was still a common task from 1800 through 1810 on the frontiers in Ohio, Kentucky, and points southwest along the Ohio River. But that changed as manufacturing efficiencies and roads reduced the cost of cloth shipped from Eastern Seaboard factories.

Other manufactured goods also reduced family labor. Small hand grinders efficiently ground daily supplies of oats, rye, barley, and buckwheat for baking, which reduced women's labor. Manufactured wool and cotton cloth freed up a frontier woman's time, allowing her to engage more actively in gardening, raising chickens, and marketing. It also meant that acreage once devoted to flax could be used to grow other market crops. Those market commodities were the equivalent of cash in local barter economies.

In 1820s and 1830s Connellsville, most market stalls were staffed by wives or daughters. Women maintained the homestead, overseeing their younger sons and daughters in garden plots, orchards, and chicken yards. Small iron stoves[10] that became common in stores, ordinaries (pubs), and schools meant less time spent woodcutting, as stoves were far more efficient than open-hearth fires, which lost most of their heat up the chimney. Durable iron plows sped up farm work, which freed many men to engage in seasonal wage work.

Public Work

Around this time, many husbands and adolescent sons took ongoing public work for the first time. *Public work*, as the Densmores termed it, meant wages paid by someone not closely related to you. In Old Robert's world, *every* capable child was valued for their work, not for their potential legal status.[11] Farm children of this era played a huge role in enhancing family farm output as regional population skyrocketed. There was no shortage of work assignments, but there was a profound shortage of hard cash to pay taxes and buy land or manufactured goods. Peach leather, jerky, eggs, apple cider, pine pitch, maple syrup, hides, etc. were all bartered or gifted to obtain necessities and lubricate family networks.

Modern sociologists have studied patterns of work—and absent male workers—that have characterized parts of Appalachia.[12] They focus on the so-called Hillbilly Highway from West Virginia and Kentucky to twentieth-century factory cities in Ohio, Illinois, and Michigan, and on the disruptive social forces it allegedly generates. But this is not a modern phenomenon. This pattern was already well established by the early 1800s, when wage work became more common in areas like Connellsville, which was still a frontier settlement. Professions like forge or foundry workers, wagoners,[13] manufacturing crews at fulling mills, gristmills, and sawmills, and even itinerant preachers provided wage opportunities and salaries for men away from home. Furnaces and forges were generally tended around the clock, demanding long shifts and shifting the men's focus from their families to their work crews. As more men earned wages from public work, they were simply absent more often,[14] diluting the former frontier closeness of daily family life. What had always been the pattern for sailors and professional military men had begun to extend to other occupations.

In general, men's work absences gave women a larger role in hearth and household management. Since childcare was a burden on young wives, multi-generational households also provided some relief, but purchasing more manufactured goods also freed up women to do and make other things. From an anthropological perspective, the emerging era of public work generated rapidly growing differences between farmers' and wage workers' calendars, family structures, authority, and daily household culture. Public wage work enhanced sociopolitical differences between farm and urban life and between household culture and work culture.

In the era before wage work dominated the western frontier,[15] family security depended on local production of nearly everything used at home (clothes, toys, wooden bowls, spoons, soap, candles, buckskins, moccasins). The home itself was usually family built. Coupled with widespread ownership of land and its tillage, frontier life relied on functioning family networks, ties to local community, and church. Public roads and public work both altered that pattern and set forces into motion that would increasingly separate many sons from their natal family circle. Many of those separated sons also married women from distant social networks.

By the 1830s the National Road connected the Port of Baltimore to Wheeling, West Virginia, to Columbus, Ohio, to Springfield, Illinois, and to Indianapolis, Indiana. It shot west like a languid arrow in flight for twenty-two years, injecting speed and transportation efficiencies to the corridor it penetrated. The road's width, sophisticated stone bridges,[16] and strategic tollbooths generated taverns, inns, and wagon yards near every toll station—not unlike the gas stations, restaurants, and motel complexes found near modern toll stops on the Pennsylvania Turnpike. Its first phase had cut travel time from Baltimore to the Ohio River in half; the second phase to Indiana did the same. These time savings piggy-backed on the huge efficiency gains first made by early western wagoners like John Hayden and Old Robert. The National Road not only reduced the cost of delivered manufacturing goods from the East Coast but also made communication of news and events move more rapidly. It also tied once isolated farmers to markets their fathers and grandfathers could not have reached—hundreds of thousands of pigs and other livestock were driven to city markets during fall slaughter seasons in the 1820s and 1830s. Common interests, both political and economic, widened in the east-west corridors it connected.

Radically reduced travel time and lower freight costs attracted both investors and new westbound immigrants. Many of those immigrants had been born on the Eastern Seaboard where family acreages could not be further divided to support yet another generation and its children. Others followed the would-be farmers, seeking higher frontier wages earned in public work.

From the 1790s to the 1820s, it had taken roughly 75 acres[17] to support a family of five. Initial farms of 150 to 200 acres could support only two to three children's families of the next generation, and the average number of children who needed land far exceeded that. In the 1820s America was on the move. By the 1830s many East Coast wood lots had been cut out, and soils had been depleted of nitrogen by overcropping corn.

Demography, Culture, and Well-Being

By the 1830s the nation's population had skyrocketed. Between Old Robert's arrival in the mid-1790s and 1830, America's counted population[18] had grown from about four million to more than twelve million, a threefold increase in one generation. In travel seasons hundreds of immigrants passed through small villages on the National Road daily on their way west. Local markets sprang up, and once-isolated farmers sold corn, barley, and rye to the hordes of pilgrims instead of transforming most of it into whiskey. On the downside, they and their children also suffered from communicable diseases carried by those travelers.

Hundreds, even thousands of people arrived in Pittsburgh daily; they came on the National and Pennsylvania Roads or were boated down the Monongahela. They stocked up and waited for boats to take them to northern Ohio or Kentucky. It was a windfall for Pittsburgh grocers and outfitters, who pooled profits to attract industry. Pittsburgh's grocers and merchants also became crucial investors in the small factories that began to make iron into axes, plow tips, nails, horseshoes, and more. No need to buy the heavy essentials *and* pay shipping from Baltimore or Philadelphia, the grocers reasoned. Pittsburgh could supply more than salt pork, bulk grains, flour, and packaged coffee. Thus Pittsburgh expanded its early, modest iron industry to outfit these immigrants and their growing families.

Demography and Regional Dynamics

Demographers have fruitfully analyzed this period, but analysis of old censuses alone does not allow them to match modern standards in rates of infant

TABLE 4. US Population, Number of Households, and Family Members, 1790–1830

Decade	Population	No. of Households	Average No. of Family Members
1790	3,929,214	558,000	7
1800	5,308,483	816,689	6.7
1810	7,239,881	1,113,827	6.3
1820	9,638,453	1,690,956	5.7
1830	12,860,302	2,338,236	5.5

mortality or the number of a woman's lifetime pregnancies. A mobile national population, isolated settlers on the western frontier, and distant record keepers all inhibited precision. But the general patterns are clear.

Early American households in 1790 averaged roughly seven individuals. Young men tended to marry at about age twenty-two to twenty-six, and they would wed young wives about eighteen or nineteen. Most women's reproductive years ended at around age forty or forty-two, and babies typically came about two years apart. Thus the average number of potential pregnancies per female in early America was roughly a dozen, with a range of six to eleven live births. Infant mortality was high by modern standards, but it was still lower than European standards of that era. Not all children lived to reach the statistically crucial age of five.[19] In the comparatively healthier northeastern states,[20] child survival rates were quite high.[21] Wills and censuses in early Federal Massachusetts suggest that a father, at death, was typically survived by five to eight children.

In stark contrast, the plantation-based societies of Maryland and coastal Virginia were, due to recurring "fever seasons," demographically fragile compared to the northeast. In British custom, men married closer to age thirty, but there were not enough marriageable women for each man.[22] Many men died young, leaving orphans—a problem that plagued the Chesapeake throughout the 1700s. Infant mortality was still high there in the 1820s and 1830s, and smaller families than in New England were the norm.

Demographic fragility, combined with Maryland's legal structure, generated dramatic historical consequences. The Chesapeake's heavily English-influenced body of law focused explicitly on primogeniture—eldest sons—and mandated a widow's 30 percent share of an estate. Yet this system also awarded unusual legal authority to any new husband *if* a widow remarried and her eldest surviving son had not yet reached the age of legal majority. In that circumstance, a new husband could dispose of 70 percent of her assets as he chose. Often, this meant that a remarried wife of a deceased plantation owner and her minor children effectively became wards of the new husband.[23] Thus in the Chesapeake region, including coastal Virginia and the Carolinas, elder sons were coddled, protected, and often sent to England for their education between age eight and ten.[24] That avoided the risks created by the region's bad food, brackish drinking water, and seasonal fevers.

Some of those sons returned from England specifically to rescue their fathers' estates in court from their mothers' new husbands.[25] Robert Goldsborough, a lawyer raised and educated in London, returned to the Eastern Shore of Maryland in the 1670s to retrieve his deceased father Nicolas's estate from his mother's rapacious second husband. Privileged Robert was up to the task: he won control of his father's land. He and his sons expanded the estate to include more than 12,000 acres, which was worked at its peak in the late 1700s by more than *six hundred* black and Native American (mostly Nanticoke) slaves. Thus, environment, health, pure seventeenth-century English legal structure, and the plantation world's social order all combined to perpetuate the privilege and cultlike power of eldest sons. Echoes of that cult have reverberated in America's political life for two centuries. Several Founding Fathers were among its members.

In health risks, law, culture, and environment, Pennsylvania was quite different. Demographically and statistically in between the national average and that of the plantation states, Pennsylvanians married younger and enjoyed much higher rates of child survival than those in the plantation states, even as it lagged behind New England. Because of the far lower risk of dying young, sons were not lavishly coddled. Most boys in the Northeast began work between ages ten and twelve as laborers or apprentices, just like Benjamin Franklin—and they were *not* sent to England for an expensive education. Some young Pennsylvania men were fortunate enough to "read the law" or attend college for a year or two, primarily to become ministers. Since widowed Pennsylvania women could legally own their deceased husband's unwilled property outright,[26] they were under much less pressure to remarry. These differing laws and demographic realities produced distinctly different regional cultures.

In America writ large, the Chesapeake and coastal Carolina region's mortality risks did not prevail. Thus the nation's dramatic spike in population between the late 1700s and 1830 was due primarily to natural increase and *not* the waves of immigration that would begin to play a huge role between the 1830s and 1850s.

In the early 1800s huge waves of land-hungry, East-Coast immigrants—primarily sons and daughters of the Northeast's large Colonial families—headed west by northwest to Ohio, Indiana, Illinois, and Michigan. Each family needed supplies: food, clothing, tools, a horse or two, cows, pigs, chickens, frying pans, Dutch ovens, needles, tin cups, and so on. Just moving those people west absorbed billions of calories, both in massive food inputs and in prodigious labor to move, manufacture, farm, and erect the infrastructure and raise animals to support it. The reward was fresh and cheaper land to farm.

It was difficult for early nineteenth century's regional economies to keep up with rapidly increasing population. In the big cities, fortunes were made. In smaller, newer communities like Connellsville, business was brisk, but small-scale manufacturing was notoriously difficult to scale up. It's one thing to manage a forge employing a hundred men with an annual output measured in hundreds of tons of raw iron, and it is quite another to establish forges annually producing tens of thousands of tons, as was the norm by the 1860s. Confounding the process of scaling up was the high initial cost of new, more efficient machinery imported from England, Wales, and Germany to New England manufactories. That machinery was simply too costly for western Pennsylvania's and Ohio's small, early iron and cloth makers. Put another way, costly technology migrated west far more slowly than did migrants.

Fuel, Work Calories, and Workweeks

Early nineteenth-century America's gains in its West's industrial output had been generated by increasing the number of hours of labor inputs and, simultaneously, the work *intensity* of those longer hours. The combination did increase production, but it also extracted biological costs from laborers. A day's labor at the small 1820s and 1830s iron works scattered across western Pennsylvania lengthened to about eleven or twelve hours a day. Of those, at least nine hours consisted of intense work at 350–450 calories per hour. In iron work of that era, most lifting, pouring, puddling (stirring), shoveling, or loading wagons was done by hand. That meant a worker had to consume 3,100–4,000 calories a day in addition to about 1,400 metabolic and body-maintenance calories—this in a nation that produced an estimated 2,000–2,800 per capita work calories per day in the 1820s and 1830s. Increasing the length and intensity of the workday to raise industrial output meant competition for the food needed to support a rapidly growing general population. In short, industrial workers' caloric needs were higher per capita than for the average American. Thus the relative cost of food began to rise in urban areas.

In the 1820s and 1830s, coal was still dug by hand by self-sufficient men like Old Robert and his neighbor Thomas Goldsboro. Shallow surface deposits were a blessing for small operators. By the 1820s many Ohio Valley forges had exhausted cheap nearby sources of firewood-derived charcoal and were modified to burn coal. Digging coal required a wagon, a horse, mule, or ox, a hardened[27] pickaxe, a hardened splitting wedge, a long-handled mallet, sharp-tipped iron pry bars, stout shovels, and long hours of intense labor. Breaking coal, then lifting or shoveling it at shoulder height to fill a wagon, was high-calorie-per-hour work.

Spring, summer, and fall were the easiest seasons to work surface coal. The deposits available to Old Robert in Connellsville were across the Yough on its right bank about a quarter mile from the river, where George Washington had noted it exposed in the 1750s.

Fall to early winter was the peak season of iron production, as completed ingots could not be barge-floated down the Youghiogheny to Pittsburgh until the spring freshets, which seasonally deepened the Youghiogheny's shallower channels. No longer a wagoner, the hourly intensity of Old Robert's physical work had increased: he needed 400–450 food calories per hour to fuel his coal digging. His daily food needs and costs as a colyer were much higher than those of his wagoner days. He owned no farm, so he purchased or bartered for most of his and his family's food.

Reconstructing his activities, let us assume he worked six-day weeks of eleven-hour days in June and July at a labor intensity level of "high" to account for the summer heat. In August, September, and October, assume he worked six-day weeks of thirteen-hour days. By November's shorter days he would again work eleven hours daily, though at a faster pace, his body burning well over 400 calories per hour as ambient temperatures cooled. By late November Old Robert ceased his coal supply activity,[28] made his deliveries, and worked the "snow season" at a nearby forge, top-loading the coal into the iron furnace's stack. Overall his annual work hours averaged 10.8 hours per day at an average work consumption of 400 calories in addition to his basal metabolism.

Comparing the total direct human caloric demands between the two jobs, one finds that a colyer needed to eat 451,180 calories a year more than a

TABLE 5. Wagoner vs. Colyer: Comparison of Old Robert's Invested Work Calories

Daily	Wagoner (1807)	Colyer (1821)
Intensity	Medium	High
Hours of work	11.5	10.8
Calories/hour	220	400
Yearly		
Hours of work	3,427	3,110
Total Work Calories	753,940	1,205,120*

* Adjusted total from 1,244,000, less twelve business days as a coal broker at 300 calories per hour × 10.8-hour workday = 38,880 calorie adjustment. Does not include basal metabolism or body maintenance.

wagoner. Those calories meant that Old Robert's personal work food costs rose over 60 percent! Animal support of two horses would have been added to his wagoner's food costs—the horses consumed another 6.4 million calories of relatively cheap food a year. Judging from one tax entry, he may have owned a slow but metabolically efficient pair of oxen at only 2.88 million extra food calories annually. Was the colyer profession worth those extra food costs? It appears so. Old Robert's occupation taxes from 1807 to 1811 as a wagoner averaged ten dollars per year, while his 1821 taxes as a colyer were sixty dollars![29] This implies a substantial increase in earnings.

Producing and brokering coal paid Old Robert more than the set wages of forgemen. But surface coal was *not* a renewable resource, and its extraction could not easily be scaled up. If he hired several younger fellows (probably the Shanabargers)[30] to wield picks and shovels, between them they might produce about three tons of wagon-loaded coal a day. Alone he could probably dig and load about a ton and a quarter. As the iron industry grew in western Pennsylvania, there simply were not enough independent coal men to meet iron furnace demands. Nor was there enough surface coal for this method of extraction to endure. The short-term advantages to being a colyer were the money, self-sufficiency, and ability to go home each night. This worked for thousands of American men for several decades before they were replaced by big money, drift mines cut into hillsides, black powder,[31] mine mules, and semi-mechanized underground baskets .

Demographics, Ecology, and Consequences

Densmore families settling across the Northeast proved statistically typical to the hundreds of thousands of ordinary families who populated the early nineteenth-century American world. In Pennsylvania in 1810 there were seven Densmore households west of the Susquehanna River that included one or two adults over age forty-five—that is, older parents and maturing families. Those seven households totaled fifty-seven persons, an average of 8.15 individuals per household. Large family size characterized the frontier environments. But thirty-six of those fifty-seven individuals were under age sixteen. Children comprised 60 percent of household members, typical of a rapidly growing population.

The eight younger Densmore families in western Pennsylvania that included no adults over age forty-five yield a smaller household size of 4.5. The aggregate population of these eight "younger marrieds" families is thirty-six individuals and includes fourteen children (39 percent) under age sixteen. In 1810 all fifteen Densmore families censused in rural western Pennsylvania included seventy-three individuals, or 6.2 members per household. As noted in table 4, the national average was 6.3.

In contrast, the 1810 US Census's thirteen Densmore families in New York State included a mix of city dwellers and rural upstate farmers; their aggregate household size was smaller, at 4.9 individuals. Smaller urban families were already a feature of American demography. Still, over 50 percent of household members were under the age of sixteen. A similar analysis of the rural Harts and Vandergrifts were almost identical. In short, all three families were demographically average—quintessential statistical households of their era.

The first US Census of 1790 recorded 3.929 million inhabitants, averaging 7.1 persons per household. By 1810 the nation had grown to 9.683 million censused—a 250 percent increase in just *one* generation! Household size declined to about six. The nation created about a million new households in just twenty years (see table 4).

By 1830 the nation's population had grown to 12,860,000, and households numbered about 2.38 million. This added yet another million households to the 1790s base. Between 1790 and 1830, national population increase was about 35 percent per decade. This rate of growth remains unmatched to this day. In a typical twenty-first-century year, native-born American population increases about 1 percent. Obviously, modern American birth rates have declined dramatically.

The early nineteenth century's natural population increase drove major economic growth: about 2.2 million log cabins and clapboard town houses were built between 1810 and 1830. New gardens and family farms consumed millions of acres of virgin trans-Allegheny lands. Clearing just one acre of forest required a work-intense month of twenty-eight days laboring from sunup to sundown. That meant more than 800,000 work calories of food energy invested to clear that single acre. Farmers struggled to keep up with the nation's demand for food. By the 1840s they would begin to fall a bit behind.

Over 90 percent of the censused population was still rural in 1830. More than two million new households established since the first census of 1790 had also required millions more horses, mules, and oxen to plow and haul, and tens of millions of pigs or hogs to supply the nation's primary meat source. Billions of food calories had been invested in labor to clear forests, shape logs, plane floorboards, build homes, tend fields, and manufacture goods. By 1820 more than a million miles of split rail fences enclosed fields and controlled livestock.[32] In cold country, firewood for each cabin's wide, dismally inefficient clay or brick fireplace consumed more board feet of firewood each year than the lumber needed to build the cabin in the first place! As huge patches of virgin forest were cut over to make farms and homes for two million new households, ancient landscapes of forest and grassland stretching from Pennsylvania to Illinois were erased. Entire local ecosystems—ten thousand years in the making—vanished in a decade or two.

All this built a national economy on a scale that would have made the New Amsterdam Dutch traders of the 1600s giddy in anticipation of the profits. In one forty-year span, young America quit counting in tens and hundreds and began counting in thousands, or millions. America was growing, but it was certainly not efficient.

The nation's population growth also put pressure on its ability to maintain the level of family and individual height and well-being inherited from the Founders. By 1830 the average native-born American male's height was 5'8.3", but life expectancy at birth was only about forty years, much lower than when the Declaration was signed. Height had held up, but in the midst of an uptick in household crowding and rising childhood disease, longevity had declined. As attendance at public schools rose in the 1830s, so did the incidents of highly communicable diseases like measles, mumps, whooping cough, tuberculosis, typhus, and poxes. Sick kids came home to crowded cabins where two or three siblings slept together. Their infant siblings were also exposed.

Trending West

Between 1790 and 1830 American-born migrants moved the frontier inexorably west. In 1790 the mean statistical center of US population was in the Eastern Shore tobacco plantation district of Kent County, Maryland. By 1800 the population center had moved to Frederick, Maryland, about forty miles west of Baltimore—just thirty-five miles south of where Old Robert started his wagon trip of 1800. By 1810 the center moved to just south of Sharpsburg (Antietam), Maryland. By 1812 the forested wilderness from which Lewis and Clark had departed in 1804 had become America's new demographic center. By 1820 or 1821, about the time of little Nathaniel Densmore's birth, it had moved southwest again, to an area just south of Cumberland, Maryland. By 1830 it had moved to a point in western Virginia,[33] due south of Connellsville, Pennsylvania.

Between 1800 and 1830 the center of Old Robert's world had moved from "out east" to the longitude and latitude of his perilous wagon route of 1800. And where the center went, so went much of the great forests, forever changing ecology, resource bases, and water flows. Those changes drove a hunger for technological alternatives to hand labor. Where once Old Robert saw scattered farm plots and paddocks carved from Bullskin Township's dense woodlands, by 1830 he instead saw scattered wood lots and many more wisps of smoke rising above Connellsville's new log houses and cleared farms. He now lived in America's statistical bull's-eye. His children would be born in it and grow up as they watched it move on to yet other frontiers to which many of their friends and cousins would depart from the 1830s through the 1850s.

Chapter 8
The Twilight of Self-Sufficiency

The years following the birth of Old Robert's son, Nat Densmore, were comprised of hard work, adjustments to the young nation's rapid business cycles, tumultuous politics,[1] and continuing population growth, both in America and in Old Robert's family. Nat's birth came on the heels of the long depression of 1815 to 1821. About the time Hannah would have weaned him, commodity prices peaked, elevating food costs. Nat's sister Jane was born in 1824, and another sister Elizabeth was born in mid-November of 1826 to twenty-six-year-old Hannah.[2] By then, food costs had risen again. The recession years from 1826 to 1828 squeezed food budgets (stagflation), and Gibson's Yough Forge reduced operations, squeezing Old Robert's income. His second son, Robert Jr., was born October 1828; he would only attain a height of 5'4", by far the shortest of Robert's four sons.

During these years Old Robert likely alternated working and living near forges in Connellsville, northwestern West Virginia, and Fairchance, Fayette County. As noted, the 1821 tax record places him in Bullskin Township, which adjoined Connellsville.[3] The 1826 tax roll lists him twenty miles south in Georges Township. Thus Old Robert was almost certainly working for F. H. Oliphant, the only regional ironmaster who smelted iron pigs in Fairchance, then freighted them north by wagon to the Youghiogheny River forges around Connellsville.

Fidelio Hughes Oliphant was born January 4, 1800, at his father John's old Fairfield Furnace on Georges Creek. When his father died he took over the family iron business around 1818 or 1819. By 1821, when Old Robert was digging coal, Oliphant purchased the Franklin Forge at Little Falls on the Yough in Westmoreland County so he could load iron onto wooden barges at riverside below the falls. That lengthened his shipping season to Pittsburgh, as he depended less on spring's high water for the "float." His iron was reloaded in

Pittsburgh onto larger barges and keelboats drifted to Cincinnati, Louisville, St. Louis, or New Orleans. Barge lumber wound up in downriver houses.[4] Some of those keelboats were built by Jacob Vandergrift's sons in Pittsburgh; others were built by Jesse Hart and his sons at Crow's Bottom north of Pittsburgh near the mouth of the Beaver River.

The northern axis of Oliphant's business centered on the Franklin Forge near the settlement of Vanderbilt,[5] on the left bank[6] of the Yough. There, he kept large storerooms to hold his profits, which were primarily in the form of bulk bartered goods such as flour, linseed oil, salt, and small manufactured goods. Oliphant's iron pigs first came from his father's Fairfield Furnace near Fairchance and were wagon-freighted from Fairchance northwest to the forge at Little Falls. Once emptied, the wagons returned through Connellsville to Fairchance laden with salt, flour, and commodities that were sold wagon-side in the settlements along the way. The remainder of goods became general store stock in Fairchance, where F. H. Oliphant had a line of credit and his workers could draw supplies. During this period, Oliphant established a large farm to further support his workers, enlarging his operations to make iron in Fairchance itself.[7]

While Old Robert worked for F. H., who was born into a rather exclusive social stratum, they likely became closer than most in business relationships. F. H. was still a teenager when his father died. Old Robert, almost twenty years his senior and a former wagoner, knew the countryside, knew horses and wagons, knew coal deposits, knew iron, and was well regarded among the area's forge hands. In the 1830s Old Robert also made an indelible impression on the iron master's young son, John, named for F. H's father. Old Robert probably taught young John more about forges, grades of charcoal, coal, and furnace efficiencies than anyone else.

F. H. Oliphant's business model also tells us much about the United States in the 1820s and 1830s. The economy had grown rapidly between 1790 and the 1820s, but the nation's money supply simply could not keep up with the exploding scale of its daily economy. On the Eastern Seaboard large banks held nearly all of the nation's silver dollars; regional banks had an insufficient supply of fifty-cent pieces and smaller coins. This scarcity accentuated erratic business cycles. Stock panics came and went, and the lands west of the Susquehanna adjusted to the return of an earlier model of economy: mixed cash and barter. Boston, Philadelphia, New York, and Baltimore formed one world, tilted toward cash. "Western" America, where barter was essential, formed another.

Chapter 8

Tracking Old Robert, 1821 to 1841

While Hannah was raising their infant children, her husband was likely hauling coal, pig iron ingots, and commodities back and forth between Little Falls, Connellsville, and Fairchance. On his 1826 tax roll in Georges Township, he was taxed for "1 cattle." That must have been a milk cow, an indication that Hannah and his children were with him.

According to Fayette County tax rolls and the US Census of 1830, Old Robert was again living in both Georges Township and Connellsville. The conflict of being censused in Connellsville by the federal government on June 1, 1830, and also taxed about twenty miles south in Fairchance isn't inexplicable. Local taxing was based on where you lived and worked. The US Census was based on where the census taker *found you* on census day. In Old Robert's census entry, there was a ten- to fourteen-year-old girl in his household who cannot be easily accounted for. She could have been Hannah's youngest sister. That year, Hannah's father had fallen to his death from the roof of a house he was building, and he had left behind several children.

A year later on local tax day in 1831 Old Robert was still in Connellsville, where he paid a substantial tax of seventy-five dollars as a "laborer." He was most likely working for F. H. Oliphant or Joshua Gibson again at the Yough Forge, where he had been employed after the War of 1812. He may also have been digging and selling coal as a sideline. Old Robert, then age forty-eight, his hard-drinking wagoner days and the War of 1812 behind him, was likely quite a storyteller. His skills were diverse; he had been a horse handler, a coal digger, a small-time coal broker, and a fixer of just about anything. Authenticated by his experiences on the "we make it ourselves" frontier of 1800 and the War of 1812, he captivated young men like Joshua Gibson, Nathaniel Glenn, and, later, young John Oliphant. He also gave them context on the meaning of "tough" times. Economically speaking, the late 1820s *were* tough and uneven. But the thrill of pure frontier had faded from the settlements in Fayette County, and cash was hard to come by. None of these young friends of Old Robert had ever made a winter walk back from the Canadian border, faced skilled Chippewa riflemen, or entered the Shades of Death on Braddock's Road when highwaymen, Shawnee, and isolated Turtle Clan Delawares still roamed its semi-darkness.

Between the birth of Robert Jr. in 1828 and that of his sister Rachel in 1835, no other living children graced Old Robert and Hannah's family. No Fayette County tax rolls have been located for Old Robert for the years 1831 to 1834. He

TABLE 6. Old Robert's Known Children with Hannah Glenn

Name	Birth Year	Economic State of the Nation
Nathaniel ("Nat")	1820–1821	Depression, 1815–1821
Jane	1824	Recession, 1825–1826
Elizabeth	1826	Recession, 1826
Robert Jr.	1828	Recession, 1828–1829
Rachel	1835	Depression, 1836–1839
Samuel	1839	Depression, 1836–1839
F. H. O. ("Ollie")	1841	Depression, 1839–1843 (deflationary)

might have been living with Hannah on Glenn family property near Connellsville. At other times, he could have been living at Oliphant's Little Falls Furnace or in Georges Township, avoiding tax assessors.

During the period from 1833 to 1839, it is likely that Old Robert worked variously in the nail factory, rolling mill, and furnace complex that F. H. Oliphant had constructed about 1832 in Fairchance. Whether Old Robert still hauled commodities, ran machinery, or was a furnace "top loader" is not known, but his multiple skills kept him employed, as tax rolls indicate, so at least some cash came to hand. He also had drawing rights on commodities at the Oliphant's company store, a long block from the mill.

As noted, in 1835—a full seven years after the birth of Robert Jr.—Rachel was born in Fairchance, where Old Robert was taxed. The nation was in the midst of another national depression. The years leading to 1835 had been chaotic for families like the Densmores. Recurring economic shocks plagued ordinary folks, and the purchasing power of wages declined. For many industrial wage earners, the nation's economic cycles trumped even the era's unpredictable weather as the most uncontrollable factor they had to face.[8] Prices were unstable. Wage workers were jerked one way, then pushed another as a wave of new immigrants from Ireland exerted downward pressure on wages. Demand for labor and the purchasing power of wages continually oscillated. Economists cite the market panic of 1837 as a key event in early American economy. For Old Robert and the Oliphant business that supported him, it was merely the culmination of an unpredictable period when costs rose then dropped, wages rose then retreated, and many adjusted yet again to a mixed cash and barter economy.[9]

Again pregnant in the midst of a national depression, Hannah bore their third son, Samuel, in 1839. Little Sam enjoyed one advantage that his two elder brothers—Nat, seventeen years his senior, and Robert Jr., eleven years his senior—did not have. Pennsylvania's public school act of 1834 meant that Fayette County schools had been built and staffed. After forty-four years in America, Sam would be the first in Old Robert's line to have full access to formal public schooling. Robert Jr. likely had several years of schooling after the age of eight, and Rachel, born in May of 1835, also received some schooling.[10] Over the next six decades, this meant that Old Robert's first four children (Nat, Jane, Elizabeth, and Robert Jr.), listed as "illiterate" on the US Census of 1850, relied on hard work and practical skills while the younger children relied somewhat more on the basic math and writing they learned as assets added to their skills and family's prodigious work ethic.

The 1840s

By the US Census of 1840,[11] there were seven members in Old Robert's family. As head of household, only Robert Dunsmore is named—the rest show up only as slash marks in age and gender boxes. The census lists four males: Nat, twenty, recorded in the "20-to-29" age group; Robert Jr., twelve, recorded as "10-to-14"; Sam, two, in the "under age 5" group; and fifty-eight-year-old Old Robert, listed as between sixty and seventy. Three females are listed: mother Hannah, marked as age "40-to-49," turned forty several months before the census; Elizabeth, listed as "10-to-14," was fourteen; and a girl, marked as "under age 5," is Rachel. Jane, then sixteen, is not listed. She had already married Samuel Pastorius, a neighbor, and would soon have a child with him.

Seven months later, on Valentine's Day in 1841, Old Robert and Hannah's youngest son, Fidelio Hughes Oliphant Densmore, named for the iron master who employed Old Robert, was born in Fairchance. Called "Oliver" for short and "Ollie" on the street, he would also attend public school, which significantly enhanced his life chances.

By 1841 Old Robert and his family were a prime example of the ordinary, working Americans of their time. Nat worked as a teamster; Jane and Elizabeth helped their mother with childcare and housekeeping; Robert Jr. was likely working as a mill "boy" at Oliphant's; Rachel and Sam were at home; and little Ollie was a babe at Hannah's breast.

From 1826 through the 1840s, every annual tax Old Robert paid in

Connellsville or Fairchance included "1 cow."[12] That cow provided essential milk for the children and crucial protein to support Hannah's pregnancies. The birth gaps between Nat and Jane (four years), and Robert Jr. and Rachel (seven years), suggest failed pregnancies or infant deaths. Each pregnancy required about 300,000 calories of *extra food* to support a birth and lactation for two years following birth.[13]

What Hannah most needed in the 1820s and 1830s was consistent intake of high-grade protein combined with enough fresh vegetables and grains to stave off malnutrition. Meat, eggs, a variety of beans, and vegetables were crucial. Without a balanced diet, over-reliance on cheaper worker's food like heavily salted fat/pork, cornmeal mush, corn syrup, cornbread, or grits could lead to low birth weight or even a pre-pellagra-metabolic syndrome induced by thiamin deficiency.[14] Such a syndrome would have lowered fertility and enhanced the likelihood of spontaneous abortion. It was first signaled by seasonal skin rashes on the face, hands, neck, and chest as protein- and vegetable-poor late-winter diets took their toll. Those seasonal rashes generally faded as fresh garden produce again became available.

Hannah and her young ones' need to consume milk from their cow also carried an element of risk. Unpasteurized milk often carried the bacteria of a form of bovine tuberculosis. That malady caused recorded infant deaths in the Georges Valley and was easily transmitted. It resulted in "scrofula," which presented in the neck as swollen and infected lymph glands. Those glands eventually ulcerated, leading to septic sores and early death.

While Hannah struggled to raise the children, Old Robert was often away working for F. H. Oliphant. In 1840 to 1841 his absence would have been partially mitigated by their son Nat's wages from wagoning as well as by twelve- or thirteen-year-old Robert Jr.'s wood chopping and part-time work as a mill boy at Oliphant's. Even with financial support, Hannah's heavy work, multiple pregnancies, uneven diet during cyclic economic reversals, and lack of a family farm all increased her risks of poor health and reproductive setbacks.

By little Ollie's birth in 1841, the nation was already two full years into a deflationary depression. The value of land, tools, and commodities like coal all declined. As Hannah's health became more fragile, childcare duties likely fell heavily on her elder daughter, Elizabeth, age fourteen. The only personal glimpse of her came from her grandniece, Elsie Elizabeth Densmore, who described her as "dark haired and steady." She had known her well. Elizabeth lived until 1902, and Elsie, born in 1887, spent a number of childhood summers in Fairchance.

"Steady" was a compliment—an adjective not used lightly. In the nineteenth century it meant calm, courageous, and dependable. And steady she was, as she cared for younger siblings both as an adolescent and again as a teenager in the mid-1840s as her mother Hannah's health failed. Elizabeth began to play a major role in family affairs during this time. Old Robert turned sixty in 1842, and he was at the height of his knowledge. But his capacity for robust work had much diminished, as evidenced by his modest twenty dollar occupation tax. It is clear that he, Nat, and possibly schoolboy Robert Jr. were all working, as the family baton passed to a new generation.

Nat took on the heavy teamster work that his father had once done, carrying pig iron and coal to Oliphant's forges, mill, and furnaces. Since Nat paid no local taxes on livestock, apart from a family cow, the horses or mules needed by Nat were probably owned by F. H. Oliphant, who had built up a regular freighting operation. Most of that freighting focused on a quadrangle: Fairchance, Connellsville, McKeesport/Pittsburgh (for trade to Cincinnati), and Brownsville. But Ellis, in his epic *History of Fayette County*, notes that Oliphant also freighted to Cumberland, Maryland, and as far west as Wheeling during the heyday of the National Road.[15]

By 1840 Fairchance rivaled Connellsville in population, largely due to iron master F. H. Oliphant's versatile business operations. Descended from an industrious family, F. H.'s great-grandfather Andrew Oliphant, from Fallowfield, Chester County, Pennsylvania, had been a young pack-train captain and Indian trader in the 1750s. Along with several hundred others, he was contracted by Benjamin Franklin to provide wagons and packhorses for Braddock's assault on Fort Duquesne in 1755.

Andrew, then about twenty, wound up being one of the men who slung mortally wounded General Braddock between his two best horses. George Washington watched, then led them out on the chaotic retreat to Great Meadows, near Farmington, Pennsylvania.[16] There, Braddock died and was buried in an unmarked grave near Fort Necessity.[17] In that packhorse and wagon train were other early Scots-Irish frontier settlers, including a contingent from the frontier districts west of Carlisle, Pennsylvania. Those recruits, local documents suggest, may have included the Densmores of Bent Creek and Kittatinny Mountain— sons and nephews of Samuel Densmore, the anchor in Pennsylvania. By the 1840s the Densmores and Oliphants had rubbed elbows for nearly a century.

In the deep depression years from 1839 to 1843, when the nation's total economic activity declined by a third, family and personal networks suddenly mattered more than at any time since the nation's founding. Working hours declined, barter rose, and boys took men's work. How tough was it? American males born in 1830 averaged 68.3 inches in height as adults, but those born in 1840 averaged 67.8 inches—a full half-inch loss in one decade! That loss of height correlates with a predicted life-span of roughly three years shorter than boys born in the previous decade.[18]

The 1840 US Census hints at the vital family network Old Robert and his family nurtured. A few doors away lived branches of the Goldsberrys,[19] Ragers, Cohenours, Carrs, and others. Next door to them lived Shadrack O'Brien, Old Robert's battlefield sergeant during the War of 1812. The bond between Shadrack and Old Robert had been forged in the brutal winter of 1813–1814 at French Mills on the Canadian border when that cannon exploded in Old Robert's face. Shadrack had drifted into Connellsville about 1806 or 1807, working as a cutler / knife maker. His employer was almost certainly Abraham Stewart, father of US Congressman Andrew Stewart, whose wife was an Oliphant. By the late 1830s O'Brien maintained a large garden; its produce likely helped to support Hannah and Old Robert's younger children, Rachel, Samuel, and F. H. O.

Self-Sufficiency and Networks

As Old Robert aged and his work capacity diminished, his family's well-being depended on the very thing that most modern Americans simply do not have—a large, nearby family network of skilled workers, farmers, and willing handymen, as well as modest pockets of cash in reserve. Old Robert's late-in-life second family made it through the economically unstable 1830s and 1840s because of its network. That is what self-sufficiency of that era looked like.

Hannah's health deteriorated rapidly in the mid-1840s, which prompted the family network, now a century in the making, into action. Hannah, about age forty-five, probably endured one last failed pregnancy. Old Robert, age sixty-two or sixty-three, had earned some money in 1844, according to the local tax roll, but it was not nearly enough to support his large family and care for an ailing Hannah. He did not own their house, and the lot they lived on was only large enough to support the one cow, if supplemented by feed purchased at

Oliphant's or Goldsboro's general store. At this point, his eighteen-year-old daughter, the "steady" Elizabeth, stepped in.

Recall that Old Robert had given his pension file to the young attorney John Reed in 1819 or 1820. Reed did act, for the pension was first approved by the US House of Representatives on February 23, 1826, as part of House Bill #118. Old Robert was formally named in the bill read on the House floor, thanks to the Honorable Andrew Stewart,[20] famed US congressman representing Fayette County. On March 3, 1827, the US Senate voted, and Bill #118 was passed into law. It authorized a pension of four dollars per month, intended to begin on January 16, 1826.[21] But no money flowed, because Old Robert's actual service record had become separated from his pension papers.

Whoever mislaid a portion of Old Robert's military file, Reed's family remained an active branch of the Densmore family network. The Reeds traced back to Middleton Township and Carlisle, Pennsylvania, where they appeared on the same mid-1700s tax rolls as the early Densmores who settled west of Harrisburg in Chanceford and Middleton Townships. Several of those tax payers descended directly from the Samuel Dinsmore who had patented Lancaster County land in 1751.[22] Between 1799 and 1810, local tax records show Reeds, Stewarts, and Densmores living near one another in what became Adams County[23] near the Maryland border. The Stewarts married into the Oliphants, and ironmaster F. H. Oliphant's grandfather, Andrew, the packhorse fellow who transported mortally wounded General Braddock, later served in the Revolutionary Army with attorney John Reed's grandfather, General William Reed. They undoubtedly also knew Samuel Densmore and his sons, Henry and John, who likely served in the Cumberland County militia during the notorious mid-1760s raid on Kittanning.

To remedy Old Robert's missing service record in 1844, Shadrack O'Brien, then about sixty-four, traveled to Greensburg, Pennsylvania, to attest to Old Robert's 1812 war service and injury. His notarized statement was crucial.[24] When Elizabeth re-filed O'Brien's affidavits to replace her father's missing 1812 service records, all of the necessary papers were finally joined with his pension file. In late 1844, on the heels of the pre–Civil War's worst economic depression, the Honorable Andrew Stewart again personally pled Old Robert's case from the US House floor, and the disability money flowed. The arrears for seventeen years at $4 per month would have been about $750, a huge sum at the time—the value of about *three* modest log houses, each on an acre or so.

On October 20, 1845, thanks to Shadrack, Elizabeth, and a family network,

Old Robert became owner of his only deeded property of record.[25] It was located in Menallen Township, three miles west of Uniontown on the north side of the National Road near Searights' legendary inn and toll stop.[26] It consisted of a lot of about three-quarters of an acre and a modest log house bought for $285. The seller was none other than the Honorable Andrew Stewart; the source of the funds was Old Robert's pension arrears. Tellingly, Old Robert deeded the entire property to Elizabeth for "one dollar and love and affection." She, in turn, legally established it as ailing Hannah's convalescent home in perpetuity. Hannah lived there near Searights until her death in the spring of 1848. Elizabeth and her brothers Nat and Robert Jr. provided support. Nat's wagon passed his mother's cottage often as he freighted on the National Road. After Hannah died, the empty house was sold in an 1849 tax sale for $120 by William Snyder, sheriff of Fayette County. Why the taxes were not paid is a mystery; that it was a sad chapter for everyone is not.

We do not know precisely why Hannah lived separately, but she was clearly too fragile to care for her younger children and her husband's household. It is clear from the deed that Elizabeth played the major role to acquire the house and move Hannah. About that same time, Elizabeth married Nehemiah Warman.[27] The couple lived next door to her father, where Elizabeth could look in on her three youngest siblings, Rachel, Sam, and Ollie. Robert Jr., then nineteen, was married and, by 1850, lived in a rented log house directly on the other side of his father's.

The once-in-a-lifetime infusion of pension cash in 1845 likely freed twenty-four-year-old eldest brother Nat to become a long-haul wagoner. With money in his father's household, he could strike out a bit. He resembled his father, and he soon married Susan Rager,[28] a neighbor's daughter, about five years older than Nat. Neither could read or write, so self-sufficiency meant a wagon; long, hard days away from home; a good woman; and immediate family nearby.

The era of homemade moccasins had begun to pass in Connellsville and Fairchance. Young men who worked around iron furnaces and mills wore locally made, thick-soled, ankle-high work boots. As a teamster, Nat probably wore boots. But the linen and wool[29] hunting shirts were still worn by many teamsters, as were a mix of buckskins and canvas pants. Nat's winter wagoner's hat was probably hand-sewn of squirrel skins. Since no military records exist for Nat, we must guess at his eye and hair color, but virtually all of the Densmore men in his line looked roughly the same: they were well-muscled and had dark brown hair and gray or gray-green eyes, long foreheads, longish noses, and hands a bit large for their height.

As noted, the mid-1830s to the mid-1840s were also the era when F. H. Oliphant, still balancing commodities, barter, and cash, outfitted a small, long-distance freighting operation to expand his regional market penetration. His iron and nails, well-known for their superior quality, sold for a premium. By 1843 or 1844, his brightly painted wagons and mule teams operated from Cumberland, Maryland, through Brownsville on the Monongahela, and thence to Wheeling on the Ohio River. The older, shorter routes of his regular pig and bar-iron transport still ran regularly between Fairchance, Connellsville, Vanderbilt, and Pittsburgh.

In one handwritten note on a scrap of yellowed tablet paper, probably dating between 1900 and 1905, Old Robert's great-granddaughter Elsie Densmore's tight, left-handed script yielded a clue: "Nat . . . wagoner—Cum. to Wheeling. N. Pike."[30] Nat is best understood as an echo of both his father and the rapidly fading frontier. Young, strong, and more traditional than his younger siblings, I envision him seated on his wagon's lazy board, behind the "wheel" (left-front) mule of Oliphant's magnificent, six-large, perfectly matched dun-colored team. His Conestoga wagon[31] is painted a pale blue, in contrast with its immense red-spoked wheels, and the sides of the wagon are neatly lettered with "Oliphant Iron Works."

Nat would have freighted manufactured goods from Cumberland to Wheeling in the fall of 1846. After delivering a load of Oliphant's iron to the forges and nails to the district's general stores, he would fill up in Cumberland with items manufactured in Philadelphia and Baltimore: new-fangled sewing needles, small handheld home grinders, gunpowder, rifle flints and fulminate percussion caps (a notable change in technology), matches, cloth, and salt. He would then transport those goods to Brownsville or to the wharfs on Wheeling's Water Street to supply the newest wave of immigrants to Indiana, Illinois, or Missouri. In Wheeling he could load up on cheap Ohio farm produce—salted pork, bull hides, deerskins, and squirrel pelts (all the rage for ordinary women's winter hand muffs)—then head northeast to Washington, Pennsylvania, then back down to Connellsville, Uniontown, and his home in Fairchance. During 1846 Oliphant also contracted to transport Mexican War recruits from Fayette and Bedford Counties west to Pittsburgh. Nat would have been one of his wagoners.

The Census of 1850, Family, Work, and Well-being

The US Census of 1850 included much more family information than earlier ones. Combined with the tables and statistics compiled by researchers like Fogel, Steckel, and Haines,[32] we see a nation that would have alarmed the Founders. The overall life expectancy at birth for American-born children had declined from about 56 in 1800 to just 38.3 years.[33] Life expectancy, as noted, is heavily influenced by nutrition and childhood diseases. The height of American-born adult males had again declined from 5'7.8" in 1840 to 5'7.4" in 1850. The level of physiological well-being upon which the nation had been founded was in clear decline. It is in this uneasy context that regionalism flowered (north-south), politics further coarsened, and the nation's first organized industrial strike—the Pittsburgh metal workers in 1849—took place. That year also saw a generation of young men head west to California seeking gold. Statistically, an average American child's life had become shorter, well-being more fragile, and self-sufficiency much harder to achieve.

The Census of 1850 also provides us a final glimpse of the Densmore family structure and status as Old Robert nears age seventy. Hannah has died in Menallen Township, but Old Robert still heads his Fairchance household and is listed as a "laborer." Living with him are Sam, thirteen; Rachel, fifteen; and Ollie, eleven. Both boys were actually two years younger than listed, but Rachel's age is correct. She may have reported for the household. On his Georges Township 1850 tax roll, he paid twenty dollars in occupation tax and is noted as "old." Even county officials knew him as "Old Robert."

Next door live his daughter Elizabeth, her husband Nehemiah, and their children, Melissa, age four, and Hannah, six months. Nehemiah's sister Sarah and her infant son John are also listed as members of the household. They both list "VA" as their birthplaces,[34] as do *both* Nehemiah and Elizabeth.[35] Robert Jr., age twenty-three, still lives on the other side of his father's place and heads his own household. He is married to eighteen-year-old Elizabeth Carr.

Nat, his wife Susan Rager, and their children, Elizabeth, age four, and Rebecca, age seven, live near ironmaster John Oliphant, a mile away to the northeast. Their household also includes Nat's twenty-three-year-old sister-in-law Mary Rager. Next door to Nat lives aging War of 1812 sergeant Shadrack O'Brien, age seventy,[36] with his wife Eliza, twenty-four years his junior. He states his occupation as "gardener" and an estate valued at one hundred dollars. As noted, he provided garden vegetables to others in his network. They, in turn, would have provided labor, cash, and firewood or coal.

The 1850 census tells us quite a lot about family support. Old Robert, well past his prime, earns little. Each of his married children has taken in kin—minors and those already widowed. Nat, who lives nearby, provides support to Shadrack. For O'Brien to make an income, Nat likely hauled his garden goods to sell at either Oliphant's pantry or Robert Goldsboro's general store in Fairchance.

Hannah lies in her grave behind Tent Presbyterian Church, which she and Old Robert joined about the time it was built in 1832. The church was constructed of locally fired brick to replace an old log structure built about 1800, which had replaced a bearskin tent once unfolded in the 1790s for visiting preachers on the small hillside grove of trees overlooking the Catawba Warrior's Trail. The bearskin tent gave Tent Church its name. The brick church still stands, overlooking the Georges Creek Valley below. Its most notable patron was ironmaster F. H. Oliphant. The church provided the Densmores with a place to worship and a stable, cultural network beyond their own family. It gave them both access to and connections with the Oliphants and others with whom they did not share blood, marriage, or class ties. It is likely that Old Robert and his son Nat made or hauled bricks, provided firewood, then hand-dug coal in lieu of cash tithes for the church through the 1830s and 1840s.

Though Old Robert was illiterate, many in the congregation at Tent Church were not. In the uncertain April of 1837, at the height of yet another national banking fiasco, F. H. Oliphant invited the fundamentalist American Tract Society to sell nearly two hundred copies of annotated scripture at the church and at his furnace in Fairchance. This suggests both many readers, and a conservative, evangelical tone among the congregation.[37]

Due to its more detailed information, the US Census of 1850 also made following others easier. In Ellis's *History of Fayette County, Pennsylvania*, he notes that Nathaniel Glenn, Old Robert's brother-in-law, "lived all his life at Etna Furnace (the Gibson's) and at other nearby works."[38] It is more accurate to say "much of his life," for in the Census of 1850 he is living on the Ohio with a younger wife and two children in Gallia County, Ohio, on the outskirts of Gallipolis[39] a few miles north of the Kentucky border. Elsie Densmore wrote in 1900 that he "migrated to Kentucky" and was known as a piano maker. In fact, Nathaniel didn't quite reach Kentucky, though he did obviously leave the

Connellsville area for a time during the 1840s. The event that most likely triggered this move was the Gibson's closure and dismantling of Etna Furnace on the banks of the Youghiogheny at Connellsville sometime in the depression years between 1837 and 1843. Having lost his first and only employer, Nathaniel struck out to the middle Ohio Valley, then developing its local iron industry.

The US Census of 1850 also provided more specific information about age, wealth, occupation, and place of birth than any of the first six censuses of the United States. It was also the first to record women's names, which were impossible to trace in the earlier censuses, and was the first to collect middle names or initials and a mother's maiden surname—all valuable kin clues. Among the Ulster Scots / Scots-Irish, an eldest son's middle name was typically his mother's surname. This census also tells us explicitly that Old Robert's younger children—Rachel, Sam, and Ollie—were all in public school in Fairchance. Old Robert, Nat, and Elizabeth were unable to read and write, but the younger ones were moving forward on literacy.

Of the working-aged men in their network, age twelve to seventy, all engaged in some form of work. The young men worked hard and long—Nat was a wagoner, Nehemiah was on Oliphant's payroll as a "day worker," and Robert Jr. also worked for Oliphant.[40] The aging men, Old Robert and Shadrack, did lighter work. There was no retirement as we now know it; neither Old Robert's four-dollar nor Shadrack's missing six-dollar monthly War of 1812 pension would have been enough to live on. Both men had already worked for nearly sixty years each, and in 1850 their work was not yet done.

A Passing

Old Robert Dunsmore was not destined to appear in the next US census. He died on April 21, 1855, after being cared for by Elizabeth, Nat, and Robert Jr. in his final days. The blessings of that Pennsylvania spring brought gentle rains, soft soil, and the season's first jonquils.

He was buried next to Hannah in the cemetery behind Tent Presbyterian Church. Both tombstones read "Dunsmore," and both offer a view of the Georges Valley. A glance to the left offers a close-up view of the simple, well-kept Tent Church, the place where they worshipped and socialized in life. The headstone names in the graveyard's oldest section represent not only a community of worshipers, but a social community spanning Old Robert's lifetime.[41] In the course of his lifetime, stunning fundamental changes took place in America:

the nation was formed; the Articles of Confederation failed; the Constitution was both written and amended; the first six censuses had been taken; the first steam-driven riverboats and a National Road were built (1811 and 1818, respectively); the first American coke and steel were made; the geographic size of the nation had expanded fourfold; and its population had grown *sixfold*. Between 1853 and 1855, as the trains came, Old Robert and his generation slipped away as if he and other men like him were simply no longer needed.

In accord with the customs of his time and place, as Old Robert failed, his family would have begun preparations. Elizabeth would have cleaned and repaired his best church clothes: home-sewn black wool pants, his best shoes, a pressed white shirt, a black ribbon tie, and a black wool jacket. When he passed the whole family would have gathered. Nat and Robert Jr., the eldest sons, would have carefully washed his body, laying it out on a long table or board between sawhorses, his corpse covered with a gauzy veil, all centered in his rented log house's front room. Word in family networks of the era spread quickly. Neighbor women and the wives and daughters of extended family would have begun to prepare food. Then would come the wake, often called the "sitting up" by Virginians and Marylanders like Nehemiah Warman and Shadrack O'Brien. His eyes would have been closed and held shut by gently placed coins. One did not enter heaven staring boldly at the Archangel. One entered humbly, gratefully.

Old Robert's body, and his soul, would have been carefully watched over every minute by his kin until the poplar wood casket arrived the next day. His sons would have lifted him into it. Nat or Robert Jr. would have already measured him, and the hand-built casket would have been made by a friend or member of the extended family. The next day, the bell at Tent Church would have tolled seventy-three strokes, one for each year of Robert Dunsmore's age, calling folks to assemble for the funeral. Then the pallbearers would have lifted Old Robert in his closed casket into a friend's or Nat's horse-drawn wagon for the trip up the Catawba Trail to Tent Church. There, Reverend Ashbel Fairchild would have read a service.

Once the grave was dug and consecrated, the pallbearers would have borne Old Robert's coffin to the grave. In turn, Nat and Robert Jr. would have taken the shovel of dirt offered them by the church's sexton. The order of shoveling dirt on the coffin would have proceeded down Old Robert's sons by age. In a slight twist on tradition, Elizabeth may have also had a turn with the shovel, as she was a force in their extended family.

Later his children would have chipped in for Robert's tombstone. In the years following Old Robert's funeral, many of his children's marriage families, which came to include Warmans, Goldsboros, Carrs, Pastoriuses, Ragers, Prices, Artises, Sullivans, Ellsworths, Wilsons, and Shanabargers, would all name sons for Old Robert. Now scattered among Fayette County and George's Township cemeteries, there is Robert Densmore Goldsboro, Robert Densmore Warman, Robert Densmore Pastorius, John Robert Densmore (Robert Jr.'s son), and other Roberts as well.[42]

In 1853 the Baltimore and Ohio Railroad, its charter enriched by Maryland's award of favorable policy and lavish tax breaks, began through service from Baltimore to Wheeling. The "palmy" days of the National Road were over. Steamboats, suspension bridges, steam-powered mills, canals, and an America now numbering thirty-one states had ended the first frontier era in America. A new frontier centered on Indiana, Illinois, and Missouri. The Densmore children were in the process of forming new family networks, ones that reflected changes to come.

Among those reflecting on all this after Old Robert's funeral would have been his employer, F. H. Oliphant, F. H.'s son John,[43] and Shadrack O'Brien. I see them, and hear them, sighing as their connection to a community of memory based on Fayette County's raw frontier of 1800 loses yet another of its quintessential witnesses. Several War of 1812 veterans survived, Shadrack among them, but who among them could describe Braddock's Road in 1800? Or its famously dour innkeeper, Jesse Tomlinson? Or the snows on Old Robert Dunsmore's long winter walk back from Canada's doorstep in 1814?

Old Robert's America had faded away. With it, measurable well-being also continued to fade, as would the kind of self-sufficiency once possible for a frontiersman with an axe, a rifle, land, and the blessings of a wife, or a young immigrant fellow with a borrowed wagon and two horses who made twelve envied American dollars crossing the Alleghenies in the snows of 1800. America's exhilarating growth and its economic/industrial changes had come with high costs and new problems to solve.

Yet Old Robert himself had won. In America he had grown two inches taller, lived twice as long, and left seven living children—all so much more than his native Ulster of 1782 could have provided. It had not been easy, and he was far from perfect, but America had given him what the Founders had promised.

Part 2
At the Forks of the Ohio
Vandergrift, Hart, and Densmore

The forks of the Ohio, now known as greater Pittsburgh, were America's most coveted real estate from 1745 to 1815. France mapped it and claimed it. George Washington mapped it, and the Virginian's Ohio Company claimed it for King George III. William Penn's son claimed it, and so did powerful, sophisticated confederations of American Indian tribes, among them the Iroquois and western Delaware. The forks consisted of the Monongahela, fed by the Youghiogheny, and the Allegheny, fed by French Creek, which emptied at Pittsburgh's Point to form the Ohio River. The Ohio rushed north, amplified by the Beaver River as it turned abruptly west, then southwest, fed by the Muskingum.

These rivers were the key to American expansion, efficient transport, and economic development after the Revolution. If, in 1810, one had casually circumscribed a seventy-mile circle with Pittsburgh's thinly populated Point as its bull's-eye, by 1860 that bull's-eye would have captured nearly thirty percent of the entire nation's pulsating industrial growth. Like moths to a flame, it drew hundreds of thousands of hopefuls to it. Among them were the Harts, Vandergrifts, and Densmores.

By 1900 economies of scale would enrich some and impoverish others. New technologies and transport efficiencies would do the same and also leave others economically displaced, just as the wagoners had once set the packhorse captains adrift. America's economic version of the Rapture took some to the heights of money and power but left many more behind to nurse their anger and disappointment. Cyclic versions of these dynamics visited the nation with alarming frequency. In each, some would become rich while others went hungry. In the end, the Civil War would render the early nation's economic trials as mere trifles.

Chapter 9
Vandergrift, Hart, and Densmore

As Old Robert's children reassessed their lives and priorities after his death, America also ruminated. Its population had skyrocketed again, dramatically enhanced and changed by more waves of immigration propelled outward from Ireland during successive potato famines in the 1830s and again in the 1840s. At risk of starvation, millions fled Ireland (though millions also remained . . . and many starved[1]). This new wave of immigration brought mostly Irish Catholics, quite unlike the Protestant Scots-Irish, Pennsylvania Germans, and Eastern Seaboard English of the previous century.

While many American citizens of the time pounced on the religious differences, the harshest daily rub was the influx of men willing to work hard for lower wages than earned by American-born men in the same age cohort. In the East, wages for everyone declined a bit and food costs went up. So more people pushed west. The rapid increase of families not possessing land and the means of their own support strained fragile, regional economies still struggling to shake off the depression of the late 1830s and 1840s, and a new one that began in June 1857.

By 1855 the nation's population, rapidly enhanced by Irish immigration, had grown to about twenty-seven million. Workingmen like wagoner Nat were frustrated as their fortunes faded even further during the new economic depression that began in June 1857. The nation grasped uneasily at new efficiencies to compensate for the costs of growth and failing commerce.

The aging transport efficiencies of the National Road could no longer keep up with the constant economic demands for "more, faster, and better." Horses and mules could only go so fast. The National Road had been completed to Vandalia, Illinois, where Abraham Lincoln's father had followed it from the east. But the oldest part of the road—the first thirty miles west of Cumberland—had already fallen into disrepair on the very stretch where Old Robert had once struggled through the snows crossing the Alleghenies.

Stung by the financial debacles of 1837 and 1839 to 1843, by the mid-1840s an investment-averse US Congress had reflexively pulled back its financial support for the National Road. That left state and local governments in Maryland, Pennsylvania, and Ohio to rely on tolls and wrangle over road maintenance with only middling success. Populist disdain for Federalism in the west, coupled with the hold that Maryland's Eastern Shore plantation elites held on their state government, meant that crucial parts of the National Road would be nearly as difficult to navigate from 1845 to 1857 as they had been from 1800 through 1810.

The net efficiency of any transport system is limited by its choke points. On the original National Road, that meant bridges were necessary at rivers and streams. So the federal government funded excellent bridges in the 1820s. But by the 1840s the governmental muddle of federal, state, and county authorities had created a quagmire. The National Road transformed into administrative fragments of regional or local transportation projects. Patchworks simply do not function efficiently when applied to large-scale projects. So how does one get faster transport without paying for it? The situation enhanced the attractiveness of more lavish state and federal railroad subsidies—the government gave land and tax breaks, and some, if not many, politicians got paid for their votes.

The National Road's early route as completed to the Ohio River in 1818 had provided notable time-cost efficiencies. These efficiencies initially redounded to the benefit of ordinary families, like that of Hannah and Old Robert, in the form of reduced household costs of manufactured goods and imported commodities. But by the peak era of the National Road, from 1845 to 1855, its second-generation time-cost efficiencies, created by highly organized freight companies, could not be scaled up again. Each infusion of new cash and resources produced just another several percent of additional efficiency—that was it.

Those efficiencies had made it profitable for F. H. Oliphant to employ Nat on the Fairchance iron work's direct delivery and sales network. Early on, Nat hauled ingots, coal, and produce between Fairchance and Connellsville. By the late 1830s he was long-distance hauling iron, nails, and forgings for Oliphant on the National Road and making good money on it, as evidenced by his Georges Township occupation tax of the depression years from 1842 to 1843, when he paid fifty dollars. From 1844 to 1847 he paid between sixty and sixty-eight dollars annually. His peak earning years were 1846 and 1847, and those earnings were undoubtedly made on the National Road. But Nat's earnings, as estimated from his Georges Township taxes, declined thereafter to an average of fifty-five dollars annually until 1855,[2] when his father died and he moved to Brownsville, Pennsylvania.

Nat's heyday as viewed in the context of his father's earnings during the same period hints at both the National Road's limits and a shift in the Densmore family. From 1842 to 1855, Old Robert was no longer the family's premier breadwinner. His annual taxes ranged from $5 to $50 and totaled $208 for those fourteen years. In contrast, Nat paid $805 in occupation taxes on his earnings for those same years.

Limits to Transport Efficiencies

In Nat's day, a full wagonload's weight on the National Road ranged between five thousand and eight thousand pounds,[3] with six to seven thousand pounds being a cited average for four horse teams. For computational purposes, consider table 7 below, and its hidden caveats.

In 1789 John Hayden was allegedly the first wagoner to make it through from Hagerstown to Brownsville on narrow but recently "brushed out"[4] stretches of the old Braddock's Road. He changed the history of regional frontier transportation with that trip. It could be done because he had done it. Old Robert was among the next wave doing it.

As you can see from the chart comparing Old Robert's 1800 trip with his son Nat's in 1845, the additional time and efficiency gains of six-horse teams and immense Conestoga wagons were simply not on a scale comparable to the original efficiencies gained by the transformation of packhorse trails to wagon roads circa 1790–1810. While the *direct* caloric costs of 1,013.14 per hundred pounds of freight hauled by Old Robert in 1800 declined to 342 calories per hundred pounds hauled by Nat in 1845, the *indirect* and uncalculated support system costs for Nat were vastly higher than for Old Robert.[5] Freight profits in Nat's National Road era were limited by the number of costly "at the ready" fresh horse or mule teams traded off every fifteen to twenty-four miles. The huge wagons that carried seven-thousand- to eight-thousand-pound payloads were expensive. So were the added costs for grooms, stables, hay, oats, and so on to support waiting horses and mules. Poorly maintained road segments also eroded efficiencies. In the 1840s Maryland, its money and politics still dominated by its coastal elite, remained cool to the idea of public investments in relatively undeveloped western Maryland.

The organized and well-funded stage and freight lines of the 1840s also undercut the independent operators. The days of independent wagoners faded quickly. Lines like the June Bug and Pioneer were fast, reliable, and efficient.[6]

TABLE 7. Individual Wagon Transport Efficiencies and Three Wagon Hauls from Hagerstown to Brownsville and Return, 1789–1845

	Trip Length	Description of Haul	Horses' Work Intensity/ Calories Spent per Day	Wagoner Physical Description	Wagoner's Work Intensity/ Calories Spent per Day	Total Trip Calories	Calories per 1lb of Freight	Freight Cost per 100lbs & per 100 miles
John Hayden, 1789	26 days*	4 light draft horses weighing a total of 5,600 lbs, hauling 2,000 lbs freight	Medium high / 112,000	5'9" / 150 lbs	Medium high / 3,200†	Horses: 2,912,000; Rider: 83,200; Combined total: 2,995,200	1,497.6	$3.00
Old Robert Densmore, 1800	24 days*	2 horses weighing a total of 2,800 lbs, hauling 1,400 lbs freight	Medium high / 56,000	5'7" / 130 lbs	Medium high / 3,100†	Horses: 1,344,000; Rider: 74,400; Combined Total: 1,418,400	1,013.14	$2.00 (Some sources say 1.5 cents per mile per hundred, but most say 2 cents)
Nat, 1845	14 days*	6 horses weighing a total of 8,400 lbs, hauling 7,000 lbs freight	Medium high/ 168,000	5'8½", 148 lbs	Medium / 3,000†	Horses: 2,352,000; Rider: 42,000; Combined Total: 2,394,000	342 (See discussion below)	$1.00

* All trip durations are estimated.
† Work calories are in excess of basal metabolism.

But by 1845 to 1850 there were no new transformative efficiencies to be got from horses/mules and wagons east of the Mississippi. As "eastern" wagoning met its limits, some wagon companies pushed west to newer frontiers where the railroad combines did not yet dominate. These transplanted wagon lines' efficiencies worked well in the far Midwest until the railroads arrived in the 1860s. The reality of the late 1840s was that Congress, in passing the buck over "who pays," had dramatically eroded the National Road's transportation advantage. Nat could not have known this in his salad days of the 1840s, even as the "Devil"[7] crept up on him and his fellow wagoners from behind. That devil had iron wheels, belched smoke, and would consume the hopes and dreams of an entire generation of teamsters. The new industry would also later consume the hopes and dreams of nearly a million railroad workers. Gain more rapid transport; lose a way of life.

Politically powerful eastern Maryland, ambivalent about federal sponsorship of the National Road as early as the 1820s, fed the new devil and chartered the Baltimore and Ohio (B&O) Railroad in 1828. Along with its immense infusions of investment-driven infrastructure—the tangle of money-driven right-of-way scandals and the prodigious amount of wood and iron consumed for tracks—the railroad both destroyed local ecosystems and increasingly overpowered local and regional public administrative entities. In matters of transportation, no single, local entrepreneur alive after 1855 would ever again have independent power over the political and financial machinery of his/her own freight and transportation enterprise east of the Ohio River. They would never again have the kind of individual control won by hard work, accepting risks, and the price of two horses and a wagon that John Hayden and Robert Dunsmore had enjoyed. The railroads operated at a financial scale that sought to crush small-scale competitors. As the wagon trade failed, more men were driven into the day labor of public work—many of them on the very railroads that had first replaced their teamster jobs. The railroad rights of way awarded by the federal and state governments should have been leased or owned by the nation. Instead, they became gifted franchises, which still limit their use to this day.

Predictably, the railroad entities that states like Maryland and Pennsylvania chartered, and to which the federal government reflexively added preferential tax and land concessions, would become totally ungovernable by those same political structures by the 1880s. In the 1870s, as historians note, both the federal government and state governors would do as told by railroad executives who disdained virtually everything except profit and power.[8] The pattern is clear: first, overwhelm local entrepreneurs, then local and county governments; next, overwhelm a state legislature; then, "buy" a few US congressmen; finally, enrich a few key senators, and make certain that a son-in-law becomes one. In this particular respect, nothing has changed in Washington since 1845.

The values represented by John Hayden, Shadrack O'Brien, and Robert Dunsmore's 1780s generation of working men—family, hard work, skill, and respect for self-sufficiency—had become "quaint folk ways" in the emerging and ever-more-powerful strata of American business. Ruthless was "in," and many were handsomely rewarded for it. No silver dimes would grace those eyes to prevent showing a "bold" or "proud" face to the Lord at death. One assumes that railroad magnates simply barked orders to Heaven's gatekeepers.

For many of the railroad titans, their creed appears to have been, "*My* will be done, both on earth *and* in heaven." Public reactions to those corporate attitudes often wound up swirling around in conversations about the rights and wrongs of de facto "work slavery" and the icy lack of empathy by the era's emerging business titans. While the railroad owners hungered for ever greater profit and power, their managers clawed for labor, fuel, and materials at the lowest possible cost. This temporarily provided a wave of new opportunities for ordinary laborers as timber and track crews, coal and ore diggers, and rolling mills all staffed up. Mechanics and engineers enjoyed new, better-paying work options. Yet it was among the common laborers that wages first suffered the most: the guy at the end of a shovel, the widowed railroad linen washerwoman down the block, the brick carrier on a station's construction crew. For them, the 1840s and 50s were tough indeed. The wages paid for unskilled public work rapidly diverged from the higher wages paid to skilled workers.

Old Robert's younger sons, blessed by some public schooling and years of adolescent experience at Oliphant's works, gravitated to the skilled-labor options opening up in metalwork beyond the confines of Georges Township. Unschooled and with the National Road's profits rapidly fading, Nat fared less well.

The Trajectory of American Well-Being Prior to the Civil War

East of the Mississippi, in both the North and the South, America's original biological advantages declined notably between 1830 and 1860. Insatiable domestic and foreign market demands for the baled cotton produced by Southern plantations created great wealth in the 1840s and 1850s. As a result, millions of African slaves lost their freedom and their dignity. But the plantations they worked were efficient enough that the "market" value of strong, healthy male slaves rose disproportionately; thus, they were better fed than the South's large, under-censused population of uneducated, unskilled, often landless white males.[9] Between the 1820s and 1850s black male slaves' heights rose, even as height among a rapidly growing class of unemployed and underemployed white males declined. Those white males and their families were to the large slave population as wagoners had been to the underclass of trans-Appalachian packhorse captains of the 1790s—redundant, poor, and defeated. Far fewer of them had the right to vote than in the North. Keri

Leigh Merritt's *Masterless Men* provides a rich, illuminating source on this Ante-bellum "poor white" world.[10]

Simultaneously, unregulated Northern businesses were just as unaccountable as the Southern plantation magnates. As unanticipated waves of immigration (Ireland) suddenly provided cheap labor to American industry, the labor windfall combined with unregulated working conditions to generate huge profits. Those profits transformed America, but that transformation extracted increasing biological costs from its workers as long shifts and higher work intensity skyrocketed in manufacturing. The biological consequences are fairly easy to document.

Biological, demographic, and economic facts are often at odds with the alleged "facts" presented in politicians' "historical" narratives about America and its status. Yet when scholars analyze the available documentary data, a much clearer picture of American dynamics emerges. In fact, America's original Advantage, its magnetic attraction, its "pocket ace," *was* the height, robustness, longer life-span, and far lower infant mortality for its era when compared to Europe. Yes, part of that advantage was built on cheap land once taken from Native Americans, then traded, sold, or conquered by the French, British, and Spanish empires before the United States followed suit. But the early American nation's strong demand for skilled labor, reasonable food prices, lower exposure to epidemic diseases, and much lower inequality of wealth than in European nations of that era were all seminal in supporting that physiological advantage.

The promise of a longer, healthier life for one's children than in the countries from which the immigrants came was powerful. George Washington represented this "Exceptionalism."[11] He was idolized as much for his height of 6'3"[12] as for his actual military and political accomplishments. He was America's aspirational portrait of biological and economic success personified in a well-dressed, walking billboard.

In 1780, about the time of Old Robert's birth in Ulster, the average native-born American adult male attained a height of 5'8". Most soldiers of the War of 1812 were a bit taller, their adult height averaging 5'8.2". Many of them were born between 1780 and 1790. Those born twenty years later in 1810 could expect to attain an average height of 5'8.1".[13] As already noted, native-born Union soldiers born about 1840, when measured at enlistment, averaged 5'7.8", a half-inch shorter than soldiers born in 1830, who measured 5'8.3".[14] What had happened to the American Advantage in the span of Old Robert's lifetime? Native-born male heights had actually *decreased*. Not a lot, mind you, but enough to raise a flag, and enough to statistically reduce predicted life expectancy. The loss of one half-inch in height correlates statistically with rising epidemic disease, higher infant mortality, and a life expectancy roughly three years shorter. This downward trajectory in well-being accelerated during the 1840s. Recurring economic crises, massive immigration, increased food costs, lack of public sanitation, a larger urban population, and growing inequality in wealth all factor into the era's decline in adult male height and all American-born children's longevity.

Even more alarming data reveal that, by 1850, American-born children's life expectancy had declined to 38.3 years[15] from the 1780–1800 bellwether era of 51–56 years![16] This was both stunning and complicated. A larger, more crowded population is more susceptible to communicable disease vectors. Public schools with bucket-drawn wells and outhouses enhanced children's disease risk. Tuberculosis, cholera, typhus, and diphtheria swept through cities like Pittsburgh in rolling waves throughout the 1840s and 1850s. Riverboats and stage lines carried those epidemics to places never before affected. Increased public school attendance combined with more rapid public transportation and large influxes of new, overseas immigrants expanded the reach of once isolated epidemics. One can still walk through the special section of Allegheny Cemetery near Pittsburgh where hundreds of cholera victims of the 1850s were buried.

The decline in male height and longevity, I suggest, was also negatively influenced by increasing work inputs: because more efficient European industrial machinery was very expensive, many American factories pushed workers to work harder—and longer—hours to compensate for aging equipment. Such workers needed to eat more to support longer work days and harder physical labor. But the nation's production of per-capita food calories available for work[17] had declined from 2,313 calories a day, based on data from pre-revolutionary Virginia, to 1,810 calories a day in 1840.[18] A decline of 403 per-capita daily calories available to do work meant a loss of food energy equivalent to two hours of medium intensity work at a semi-mechanized loom or carding machine. For the iron and steel men doing their extraordinary, taxing work, costing over four hundred work calories an hour, it meant the loss of food fuel to "buy" a full work hour daily on the mill floor. In short, those who worked the hardest during the 1870s and 1880s disadvantaged their children the most when wages declined.

But the already long American workweek of fifty to sixty hours was *lengthening* at the demand of industrial employers. This decline in America's available work calories provided an upper limit to economic output based on body-generated calories. Where to get these demanded work calories? The father and the eldest working son often ate first, and separately, and consumed a greater portion of the household's daily protein calories. Simply put, the mother and the younger kids ate less, especially of the costly proteins.

Food costs rose relative to wages in the 1840s and 1850s,[19] but then, as now, much of the profit went to wholesalers and grocers—not to farmers. America's era of stunning successive population increases, decade after decade, coupled with ever more work hours and bigger doses of hard, muscle-tiring work and an overwhelming wave of new immigrants (from 1835 to 1855) finally outpaced the national farm industry's ability to *cheaply* produce enough fresh, unspoiled food for America's growing population. That formula extracted the non-negotiable biological costs of muscle work to balance out nature's zero-sum game of "energy in must equal energy out." By the time of Old Robert's death in 1855, some of those energetic debts had already been collected in the form of a noticeable height and longevity loss among American-born workers and their children.

In the heavily populated Northeast of 1835 to 1855, it was primarily the rise of urban, nonfarm labor that had first unbalanced the founding era's equation of cheap, plentiful food and strong wages. Though the majority of American families were still rural and farm based in 1850, the rising cost of land east of the Mississippi, ever-smaller farms, declining farm profits, and the recurring weather-related crop failures had done severe damage. In short, the clearest case to be made for deterioration in nutritional status falls on the nation's increasing ratio of public work in mills, foundries, and other manufacturing sites, which still relied heavily on semi-mechanized labor. Food-wise, those industrial workers had grown to be the most costly per-hour economic sector of America's available caloric investments. Farmers exported calories and protein on modest profit margins. They were then disproportionately consumed on factory and shop floors to create more generous owner profits.

While farmers and old-fashioned artisans still outnumbered wage workers, the rapidly increasing length and intensity of that industrial wage work required work calories far out of proportion to the sheer number of those wage workers. By the 1850s American workers without regular access to family farms or large gardens both spent a much larger portion of their wage income on store-bought food than had their parents and consumed more per-capita daily work calories than those parents. Worse yet, those wage earners' pay envelopes were disproportionally—and increasingly—invested in their *own* dinner plates, to meet dietary needs at work. That need increasingly consigned the rest of the family to lower-protein, higher-carbohydrate meals. In short, stagnant wages in the 1840s and 1850s, coupled with longer work hours and wages lower in purchasing power than those from 1800 to 1810, typically deprived industrial workers' children and spouses. Thus many jobs in the narrative that follows are labeled in "calories per hour" to give the reader a rough clue to the proportion of food dollars needed to support a family's heavy laborers.

By 1850 to 1855, America's life expectancy gains over France and England, for both sexes combined, had declined significantly. In 1800 an American could expect to live twenty-three years longer than in France and twenty years longer than in England; by 1850 that advantage over France had been reduced to just *one* year, and it was just *three* years longer than in England.[20] American men were no longer taller than British men! Those biological givebacks would shape the lives of children born in that era and contribute to growing tensions in America. These factors, though rarely acknowledged by historians, generated a protracted contest over the value, control, and quantity of labor, which remains a national issue to this day.

The rich body of literature about American labor history is essential in showing us the connection between biological and economic tensions. In the nineteenth century, the often ignored issues were the height, weight, and length of life of a worker, as well as his or her children's vitality. History suggests that the question of "How are we doing?" means more than "How much money do we have?" Underneath economic and labor history and historical narrations of wages and work conditions lies the pith of our nation's biological status: a worker's human condition, or well-being, if you will.

The dynamics of reduced height and longevity are complex. In the first place, height once attained is not lost due to inadequate diet or overwork. If you are 5'8" and starve to death, you are still 5'8" at death.[21] But in an era when adult men and teenaged sons expended enormous calories in hard work, as was common from the 1830s through the 1850s, the cost of the calories and protein in their households meant they ate more premium foods—meat and eggs—and their wives and children economized, often subsisting on milk, cornbread, grits, cornmeal mush, and corn syrup, when wages did not keep pace with the combination of growing family size or rising food costs.

Uncertainty and Income

We know from broad economic studies that analysis of wages from 1800 to 1850 suggests a general upward trend in household income. But there were huge economic setbacks in the 1830s and mid-1840s. In other words, the unstable national economy that characterized the era had a greater impact on wage-dependent urban household incomes than on the numerically more common rural family's economy, which was based on production from their own farms and gardens and barter or seasonal wage work. In short, the price of food commodities impacted both kinds of families, but quite differently. Farmers lost wealth in certain cycles, but nutrition became the biggest impact in married, urban workers' households.

Merchant George W. Smith's "Ledger and Day Log" notes that a day's wages in 1858–1859 in Cumberland County, Pennsylvania, just west of Harrisburg, paid seventy-five cents to one dollar per day for heavy work. The large group of day laborers of the 1850s era were not gaining economic ground. Most only made ten to twenty cents per day more than Old Robert did on his wagon trip of 1800.[22] Large-scale nineteenth-century studies aside, wages had not risen everywhere.

In the mid-1830s to 1850s, the magnitude of these economic/wage dislocations altered many families' behavior and sense of well-being. Protracted uncertainty creates medically corrosive stress; it also leads to obsessive overwork in periods of high labor demands merely to catch up after a layoff, a sudden drop in wages, or rising grocery costs. Economic dislocations in the era's unstable national economy and unregulated bank shenanigans likely exacerbated nutritional deficiencies among children ages two to five and young workers ages twelve to seventeen. Between 1835 and 1849 American-born children show the statistical effects of a less beneficial nutritional status in the midst of superficial economic progress as measured in raw dollars of income.[23] It matters, evolutionarily, *how*, *when*, and *where* protein, nutrients, and calories are invested. In short, a young American economy made out as best it could through the economic unpredictability of the 1830s to the 1850s. At the household level, dietary decisions were made based on limited options and information by legions of twenty-year-old mothers just like Hannah Glenn Dunsmore, who could not read or write.[24]

Mothers like Hannah faced a succession of extraordinarily difficult economic episodes following the War of 1812; those include the depression of 1815 to 1821; the recessions of 1822 to 1823, 1825 to 1826, 1833 to 1834, and 1836 to 1838; the deep four-year depression of 1839 to 1843; and a short yet deep recession again from 1847 to 1848. It is no accident that many American families considered the decades that followed the War of 1812 as "the hard years." At the household level, they were replete with stress and uncertainty. In addition to affecting health, high stress levels deeply impact mood, attitudes, and reactions to events. Though America's measurable well-being in height and longevity marched in place from about 1800 to the mid-1820s, the moderate President John Quincy Adams—his term in office beginning and ending in recessions— had led to a heightened yearning for Populist control. That yearning was fueled by ordinary white males' expanding rights to vote, which brought to office a president who promised to fulfill a false dream. The flamboyant rule breaker, Indian hater, slave holder, and financially corrupt President Andrew Jackson gave them the illusion of control but not the reality. Uncertainty, angst, worry, a vacillating economy, and an eroding sense of self-sufficiency all play significant roles in history, politics, belief systems, and well-being.

If intensity and duration of labor, the purchasing power of wages, the cost of food calories, and community and household stability are among the factors that shape body size, health, child survival, and longevity, then these factors are about *us*—our identities, our culture, our politics, our organizations, and our goals—the "American dream." That dream to be taller, to be healthier, to live longer, and to be blessed with the means of our own support—"happiness" as voiced in the Declaration—meant that from the 1840s on there was growing angst to recapture the remembered advantages that America's first citizen generations of grandparents and great-grandparents had enjoyed when censused in 1790 and 1800.

———

Height and life expectancy continued to inch downward as Old Robert and Hannah's sons entered the full-time workforce between 1834 and the 1850s. Both of those statistics reached a new low in 1860—American-born males that year attained a height of 5'7.2", a loss of 1.1 inches since 1830.[25] By 1860 the life expectancy for American-born children had deteriorated from the 56 years of 1800 to about 41.8 years.[26] Biological losses are a powerful component of "How are we doing?" and these played out at millions of kitchen tables.[27] By 1860 the answer among many was, "Not as well as our fathers and grandfathers." These reversals contributed to an uneasy nation that quarreled over culture, slavery, regionalism, class, and identity. War was only months away.

Chapter 10
Angst, Iron, and the Drumbeats of War

The US Census of 1860 for Fayette County, Pennsylvania, offers clues as to how the Densmore children adapted to their father's passing and dealt with their own daily realities. Their generation struggled both to hold onto a share of that shrinking American biological advantage for their children and to retain the same economic freedoms and self-sufficiency that their father and his contemporaries had enjoyed.

By 1860 Nat had moved to Brownsville, Pennsylvania, on the Monongahela and was still working as a wagoner. The heyday of National Road commerce had waned, so he freighted locally. His work consisted of short runs to and from local mills, hauling metal and coal. He also hauled general cargo to the big river barges lined up on the Monongahela. Those timber barges were towed behind the many steam tugs that plied the river. Among those steam towboats were ones owned and operated by brothers John, William, George, and J. J. Vandergrift of Pittsburgh. Their family would soon become formally intertwined with the Densmores. Nat would also have hauled ingots from Oliphant's in Fairchance to Brownsville's forges and rolling mills. By then F. H. Oliphant's son, John, sought market penetration upriver on the Monongahela as Monongalia County and Morgantown, West Virginia, industrialized.

Living with Nat was his wife, Susan, and their daughters, Elizabeth, age thirteen; Hannah, age nine; and Mary, age two.[1] Both Elizabeth and Hannah[2] were in school. Nat was surrounded in the neighborhood not by kin but by other households in which the breadwinners were carpenters, nailers, molders, puddlers, steamship stewards, and the like.

Back in Fairchance, Nehemiah Warman and steady Elizabeth had many family responsibilities. Both are listed as age thirty-four, though Nehemiah was actually thirty-six. Living with them are their children, Melissa J., thirteen; Hannah L., ten; Mary E., eight; George W., six; Samuel J., four; Sarah A., two;

and Emma V., just one month old. Had Melissa been a son, she would also have been a wage worker at age thirteen. They also housed Nehemiah's widowed mother, Mary Warman, age seventy-four and Elizabeth's youngest brother, Ollie Densmore, then age nineteen.

Nehemiah and Ollie were the primary breadwinners for this composite family of eleven members living near the Fairchance Iron Works. Ollie took up full-time work when his father died in 1855—it was the "manly" thing to do. Both men were listed as "day laborers" on the 1860 census, and their work involved iron making. Together their wages provided good nutritional status to the household. Both Ollie and Nehemiah worked for the Oliphants in their Fairchance works, which produced top-quality iron pigs. Some were squeezed and rolled thin on site to produce very-high-quality nails. But many were also shipped out north to Connellsville or southwest to Brownsville.

The precise house they lived in is not now identifiable, but Nehemiah stated that he owned it. It may have been part of a large lot that Ollie later purchased in 1868. Nehemiah's house and its grounds[3] were valued at three hundred dollars on the 1860 census. Nehemiah lists additional property valued at four hundred dollars, which was a combination likely composed of a milk cow, cash, tools, furniture, and a sheep or pig. He and Elizabeth may also have owned a spot of land in the surrounding countryside.

Ever-faithful Shadrack O'Brien, age eighty, still lived just two doors away from Elizabeth and Nehemiah. In August 1860 he was censused with his wife Elizabeth, listed as "Eliza," and their youngest son, George W., age seventeen, who was born in Pennsylvania, literate, and also working as a day laborer for the Fairchance Iron Works. Nehemiah's neighbor and brother-in-law, Robert Densmore Jr., was on Oliphant's payroll as a highly skilled puddler, and he had likely played a role in getting young George coveted work at Oliphant's. Like Nat, Robert Jr. still interacted with Shadrack O'Brien, who had helped his father financially in the dark days of the mid-1840s, when Shadrack's affidavit led to receipt of Old Robert's pension arrears. Shadrack listed his occupation as day laborer. His house and garden were valued at $150. He also listed his estate at $400: tools, furniture, cash, chickens, and a cow are suggested by his earlier Georges Township tax records of 1855.[4]

Like Old Robert, Shadrack had been wounded in the War of 1812 at Lundy's Lane on the Canadian frontier. He was noted as a "good soldier." After recovery he was ordered to Pittsburgh in October of 1814, where he served as a recruiter until he was detailed to Sackets Harbor on February 2, 1815. He was discharged there on April 2, 1816, with the notation "*Fistula in Ano*.[5] See pension case." As with Old Robert, it seems years passed before any federal action was taken. Shadrack again filed for a War of 1812 pension in 1858, as noted in the Annals of the US Congress for that year.[6] No payout entry was found for him, but a federal index listed two pension numbers.[7] It took his widow Eliza until January of 1879 before the federal government finally paid nearly six hundred dollars in arrears.

At the 1858 filing, Shadrack was seventy-eight years old. Born June 18, 1780,[8] most likely in Harrison County, West Virginia, he gave his occupation as "cutler" at his enlistment in Connellstown, Pennsylvania,[9] on March 6, 1813, at age thirty-two. After the war he married, or perhaps remarried, a much younger Eliza. They had a daughter, Dorcas, and a son, George W.[10] By the 1860 census the old couple—he was eighty and she was fifty-six—lived alone. He still gardened. As Shadrack's health failed in the spring of 1866, Eliza again re-filed for his 1812 war pension with the US Congress, and she petitioned for another from Pennsylvania's General Assembly, as he had served in the famed 22nd Pennsylvania Infantry. The Pennsylvania filing was dated March 16, 1866, and is listed as Bill No. 1179. It resulted in a seal-clad certificate issued on April 25 for a sixty dollar gratuity and six months annuity due July 1, 1866. In contrast, the processing of the federal pension was bogged down, just as it had been for Old Robert.

The enigma of conflicting records intrudes again, for Eliza tendered his Pennsylvania annuity petition in 1866, yet his gravestone at Tent Cemetery reads "Oct 22, 1865." Other sources claim varying death dates.[11] On November 2, 1865, *The Genius of Liberty*, a regional newspaper in Uniontown, Pennsylvania, published his obituary. It reads:

> O'Brian, Shadrack, Georges Township, Fayette Co. on Oct. 22, 1865. Age 86 years, 4 mos., 4 days. Born Harrison County, Va. Lived some years in the West Indian Islands, fought in Battles of Fort George, Chippewa, Lundy's Lane.

Whatever the details, Shadrack had died, and his widow received at least sixty dollars ex post facto. By the 1870 US Census, aging Eliza lived with George W., his wife, and their children.

When Shadrack died, Ollie Densmore, then working in Pittsburgh as an iron roller, returned to Fairchance for his funeral. In fact, each of Old Robert's sons would have helped George W. dig his father's grave and participate in another somber ceremony at the Tent Presbyterian graveyard. No longer the fair-complected, blue-eyed, 5'7" tall, and light-haired young man described in his discharge papers on April 2, 1816, from the War of 1812, the church bell would have rung for him an amazing eighty-five times. Or was it actually eighty-six, as described in the newspaper's obituary? And how did a fellow who once claimed to hail from Montgomery County, Maryland, wind up listed as born in Harrison County, Virginia?[12] And did the years spent in the West Indies really happen? More documentary tangles.[13]

Born 1779 or 1780 into an America that no longer existed, faithful Shadrack was another irreplaceable loss. His life spanned the American Revolution, the War of 1812, the great years of the National Road, the Mexican War, and the Civil War. Who was left in Georges Township to recount the brutal winter of 1813–1814 on Canada's doorstep, or the epic battle of Chippewa, or the wounded British General Riall's capture at the Battle of Lundy's Lane? Shadrack fought there under the young, sharp-tongued General Winfield Scott, who had thrown himself and his company straight ahead into the teeth of the British regulars. How does one replace someone who saw, smelled, tasted, and lived such events? And just how does one repay such a man?

Birmingham and Iron

There were other surprises on US census day in June 1860. Sam Densmore, then age twenty-one, had already gone to Pittsburgh's South Side to make iron.[14] East Birmingham, as it was then known,[15] was the lower right ventricle of Pittsburgh's industrial heart, pumping out iron for railroads and bridges that was sold as fast as it could be produced. That move put him closer to the national tensions that brewed over politics, wages, the role of paid labor, industry versus aristocracy, and slavery and plantation culture versus wage-based production. Slavery had been a central theme in the debates between Lincoln and Douglas in Illinois, which took place between August and October of 1858. Lincoln lost his Illinois Senate race but published the famous senatorial text of those debates in April of 1860.[16] Widely read, the issue of whether or not to abolish slavery was at the forefront of talk in the 1860 presidential election. Newspaper reporting was breathless and immoderate. While many small-town folks eschewed getting tangled up in urban America's increasingly complicated social and political changes, instead clinging tightly to local networks, young Sam saw both opportunity and freedom in Pittsburgh.

Sam's elder brother, Robert Jr., remained in Fairchance where, at age twenty, he married eighteen-year-old Elizabeth Carr, on March 16, 1848. Their wedding ceremony, officiated by his eldest brother Nat's next-door neighbor John R. Means, was held just a month prior to their mother Hannah's death in April of 1848. When Nat moved to Brownsville after Old Robert's death in 1855, Robert Jr. became the titular head of the Densmore family in Georges Township.

On census day in August of 1860, Robert Jr., age thirty-one, and Elizabeth, age twenty-eight, lived with their children, John Robert, age nine; Elizabeth, age eight; Mary Jane, age five; and Sallie, age one.[17] They lived several doors from the Warmans in Fairchance. Robert Jr. continued his employ as a highly skilled puddler[18] (a 460-work-calories-an-hour job) at the Fairchance Iron Works. He would have begun regular wage work as a twelve- or thirteen-year-old forge boy around 1840. By 1849, just a year after his marriage, he would have had a front-row seat to the theater of American labor history when the first nasty iron workers' strike started in Pittsburgh, then spread outward to provincial Georges Township.

Robert Jr. listed no owned real estate on the 1860 census, renting his house near the west end of the Fairchance settlement. Work was but a five or ten minute walk away. Robert Jr. did, however, list an estate of four hundred dollars. Again, any cows, horses, tools, wagons, cash, an out-of-town house plot, or a share in the Jordan lot would have been included in this rough estimate.

Robert Jr., head of household, was listed as unable to read and write. But his wife could read, and their school-aged children were in public school. His primary responsibility was to provide for his family on his weekly pay, which was about twenty-eight dollars a week. His second priority was to ensure his children attended school. Although in later censuses Robert Jr. would be recorded as literate, Connellsville's public school was closed from 1830 until 1837 or 1838, so he would have missed schooling before age ten. Then, during the Panic of 1837, paying work as a water boy or helper at Oliphant's would have trumped all else. What Robert Jr. may have lacked in public education, however, he clearly made up for as a highly skilled iron worker, a reliable father, and a Civil War soldier.

The thing Robert Jr. could not compensate for in adulthood was his father's or his brothers' adult heights. His Civil War enlistment records tell us that he was only 5'4",[19] with dark hair and the typical Densmore family's gray eyes. Robert Jr.'s birth in 1828 falls in one of the most complicated periods in his birth family's life. His birth year of 1828 came after the punishing recession of 1825 to 1826, at a time when tax rolls suggest that his father moved frequently, seeking work.

His father moved back and forth on work assignments between Fairchance/Georges Township, Connellsville, and northern West Virginia during the mid- to late 1820s. In the summer of 1830, when Robert Jr. was two and a half years old, Hannah's father, William Glenn, fell to his death. Recall also that in the 1830 US Census of Connellsville there were three children listed in the household who were not fathered with Hannah. Death, grief, and uncertain income do not make for a healthy, well-fed mother of twenty-eight with four children. Robert Jr. would have been nursing still when Hannah's father died, and we know from tax records that the family cow was in Georges—*not* in Connellsville with Hannah and her baby where she grieved for her father.

Robert Jr. was already in his critical early teenage growth spurt, engaged in hard labor around the Fairchance Iron Works, when the family again fell on hard times in the deep depression years of 1839 to 1843, which followed the recession years of 1836 to 1838. In short family struggles came during Robert Jr.'s two most biologically crucial growth stages, from ages one to five and ten to fifteen, and likely shaped Robert Jr.'s adult height. Economy and environmental situational factors had trumped young Robert Jr.'s inherited genes.

While Robert Jr.'s childhood and teen growth years appear to have physically shaped him, they did not shape his grand engagement with America. Nor did his height of 5'4" render him a weakling. He daily tossed white-hot 160–180 pound ingots and puddled/formed 150–200 pound balls of molten iron by hand before depositing them on a pushcart to go to the mechanical squeezer in preparation for rolling. His core body strength was prodigious, and his muscle to fat index was extraordinarily high. Even at rest he burned many more calories per hour than an ordinary man of his size. Much shorter than his male siblings, Robert Jr. illustrates demographic findings that the economic, nutritional, and dietary status of a family can generate a combination of forces that really do shape the expression of inherited genetics. Most scholars refer to such forces in their general published statements about the influence of "environmental factors" on height and longevity.

As noted, family circumstances improved in 1844 and 1845 when Old Robert's pension arrears started flowing. Thus Robert Jr.'s younger siblings Sam and Ollie must have enjoyed a better childhood diet than their older brother had experienced. Genes are only a piece of each child's story: place, time, family economy, diet, love, physical contact, childhood diseases, and vagaries of chance all shape a child.

1860 in Perspective: The Run-Up to a War

Rapid population growth, an era of substantial foreign immigration, and America's aborted attempt to pump up economic and farm output between 1840 and 1860 had run headlong into the nation's declining ecological and biological advantages. It was a frustrating period. Firewood was becoming expensive. In some areas it was scarce. The cost of meat, especially beef, was increasing faster than daily wages. To top it all off, fifty-four-hour workweeks had often become sixty-to-seventy-two-hour ones as waves of immigrants drove down the wages for unskilled labor and encouraged industrial management's rush to demand more of workers . . . or else. Management by fear became more common. "My kids don't have enough milk," "Mommy, can we please have an egg or bacon for dinner?" and "The water is dirty—I can't drink it!" often followed months of unpaid layoffs as factories and forges shut down on short notice. These tensions, coupled with increasingly strident disputes over the spread of slavery, combined to create a very brittle national environment.

In the wake of census questions of 1860, millions of workers compared how many months that year they had not worked. Ten years later in 1870, the US Census would include that very question. Worse yet, whoever controlled those erratic work, business, and banking cycles could not be easily identified by laborers with modest educations. Were these work interruptions real? Or were they just a game that owners played on them? Ambiguities piled up as family leisure time eroded, and far too many children settled for a breakfast of cornmeal mush—or, if they were lucky, corncakes fried in lard and topped with corn syrup.

The constant cultural epithets flung from newspapers and pulpits, both Northern and Southern, also took their toll; the nation was one immense, emotional powder keg as the presidential election unfolded in the fall of 1860. The South's elite worked incessantly to radicalize its white population. Paid "Secession Commissioners" traveled the South from 1860 to 1861, drumming up support for a separate nation[20] even if it meant a battlefield solution. Specifically, those Secession Commissioners and many Southern newspapers worked tirelessly to sell Southern whites on the fantasy that a black Republican horde, marshaled by Lincoln himself, would descend upon the South, violate their women, and destroy the status, freedoms, and gene pool that whites stridently protected.

Again it is important to understand that part of the nation's susceptibility to a regional culture war was that its actual biological well-being, as evidenced by longevity and height, really had eroded. The year 1850 saw the nation's all-time shortest life-span of 38.3 years for male and female native-born children. In 1850 American-born males would attain a height averaging only 5'7.4". A statistical majority of the nation's sons were significantly shorter than their fathers. American children born in 1860 could expect a longevity of forty-one years, but it was the shortest male birth cohort, at 5'7.2", since long before the nation was founded.[21] Even the earliest analyzed cohort of boys born in 1710 were taller! The Founders' coveted advantage had simply vanished.

In the rural South, white male heights declined between 1830 and 1860. There simply were not enough tall, well-fed male members of the elite plantation class to elevate, and thus mask, the white underclass's unfolding biological and economic disaster.[22] In both the North and the South, ordinary families' angst over household well-being and eroding self-sufficiency added fuel to the fear that things were headed in the wrong direction.

Lincoln was elected, but the Secession Commissioners had done an excellent job of selling their myths, and core Southern states prepared to secede even before he was sworn into office. On April 12, 1861, impetuous South Carolina elites put match to cannon, shelled Fort Sumpter, and signaled their intent to blow up the Union, forming a new, separate government of Confederate States explicitly designed to protect slavery. "Slavery," of course, also meant the lion's share of tangible wealth held by the South's small class of plantation elites.

It was left to hundreds of thousands of ordinary men like Robert Densmore Jr. to see the mess through. And he did see it through, along with legions of others quite like him. But, among those legions, most, like Robert Jr., were an inch or two shorter than their American-born grandfathers. More than two million of them, North and South, would die or be wounded in a great, unneeded "sorting" generated by a small cadre of racial, social, and economic elitists. The Civil War was not merely an economic or culture war—it was also a well-defined class war.

Chapter 11

The 1860s
Whose War Was It?

As the nation unraveled and slipped into civil war, the average soldier on either side faced more than moral and political issues. For most of the privates, in both the North and the South, the 1830s to 1850s had made for harder, riskier childhoods than their grandfathers had known. Many were also caught up in the manipulated political sloganeering that peaks in most run-ups to war, then and now. Many ordinary Union soldiers thought they were protecting "the Union." Others, perhaps like Old Robert in 1813, may have simply needed an escape.

The South's ruling hierarchy had a long history of pointedly insulting white Northern working men. Its flamboyantly contemptuous attitude toward those men is captured in this 1856 quote from Alabama's *Muscogee Herald*:

> Free society! We sicken at the name. What is it but a conglomeration of greasy mechanics, filthy operatives, small-fisted farmers, and moonstruck theorists? *All* the Northern men and especially the New England states are devoid of society fitted for well-bred gentlemen. The prevailing class one meets with is that of mechanics struggling to be genteel, and small farmers who do their own drudgery, and yet are hardly fit for association with a Southern gentleman's [black] body servant. This is your free society which Northern hordes are endeavoring to extend into Kansas.[1]

Neither side in this war could quite fathom the other, for they were, in the evolutionary sense, very different species of society. The North was becoming a huge, complex, fast-paced, multifaceted amalgam of industry and constant change where identity, for most, had come to depend on work and skills. The South, in contrast, was a society that, for most, depended on the fortunes of birth. The Southern gentility who started the war in 1861 simply did not understand young Northern men who believed in hard work done with their own hands. The very idea of manual labor for a Southern gentleman of the mid-1800s was anathema. Indeed, the South's contempt for men of any race who worked for a living was profound, as the following indicates:

> Slavery is the natural and normal condition of the laboring man, whether *white* or *black*. The great evil of northern society is that it is burdened with a servile class of mechanics and laborers unfit for self government, yet clothed with the attitudes and powers of [voting rights] citizens.[2]

Ordinary Northern working men simply could not fathom a cultural world based on such attitudes. The Civil War was, as historians note, a contest about industrialism and wage work versus agrarianism and bonded/slave labor. But to an anthropologist it goes much deeper, to a battle over the definition of "personhood," not just for blacks but also for white male workers as asserted in the newspaper quote above.

The South's economy and formal legal structures militantly supported their restrictive cultural definition of personhood. A cadre of the South's planter class enforced the region's rigid caste system. Landed white males and their eldest sons tightly controlled access to happiness and well-being as the Founders had first defined it; the planter class had definitively rejected the Declaration's credo that "All men are created equal." That rejection included blacks, poor Southern whites, and Northern white men who worked for a living.

As the war dragged on, staying power became the most crucial element, just as it was in the Revolution. The North won, not merely because of its superior manpower and industry, but because of its greater adaptive flexibility in the face of adversity. The South's long reliance on agriculture, British imports, and traditional plantation-style production became its Achilles' heel. It was virtually impossible to rapidly scale up and transform competing, family-held agrarian enterprises into interconnected ones repurposed to support war. And, as important, the Southern coastal elites' 150-year-old habit of importing manufactured goods from England—cloth, guns, clothes, china, wine, even salted meat—not only blunted local manufacturing capacity, it left them cash poor. Planters typically ran up huge debts to British trading houses and had to pay off the debts when the next cotton or tobacco crop sold.

In short, the vast majority of the South's wealth could not be deployed quickly to prosecute their war. That wealth was inordinately tied up in the value of slaves who, if armed, might support the North. By the last year of the war, four out of five Southern white men had served. Planters in uniform typically left plantations in their wives' control. By the third year of the war, even the elites' white overseers had been drafted. Once the overseers were gone, most remaining slaves simply did not fear the women as they had previously feared their male counterparts. The South's economy suffered as cotton cops declined and Union blockades took their toll. Even basic food became scarce in many districts by late 1864. Culturally and organizationally, the South's decision-makers were still a relict variant of seventeenth- and eighteenth-century landed English gentry, so fantasies of rescue by Great Britain were common. But, contrary to Southern expectations, Great Britain did not enter the war on their behalf.

For the seriously disadvantaged white males trapped in the South's rigid underclass, the idea of a victory and a grateful Confederacy likely fed hopes of a new and more powerful personal identity—one in which merely being white would automatically move them up a notch. Scorned in daily Southern civilian life, they were finally needed on the battlefield. The defeat and surrender at Appomattox ended that. After Reconstruction had been successfully torpedoed in the 1870s by Southern politicians in Congress,[3] the South's farm-boy foot soldiers and their male progeny returned to their redundant, land-poor, under-employed, and seasonally undernourished status. But the dream did not die—for a moment they had been more valuable than black males. We still see it expressed today in the visions of "Alt-Right," Klan,[4] and white nationalist movements. The chants of "We will not be *replaced*" in Charlottesville in 2017 suggest cultural memories of an era when black male slaves had been more essential and far more valuable to the upper echelons of Southern society than their own great-great-grandfathers.

In sum, the Civil War was initiated in an era of rapidly declining well-being by those least affected by such decline, but it was fought primarily by those who had experienced it. Multiple American subcultures had become trapped in and harmed by the fantasies of a small elite. How eerily similar to England's seventeenth-century schisms!

Pennsylvania, Land of Racial Ambivalence

The 1860s had their impact on western Pennsylvania's sub-culture as well. None of the great battles occurred there, save Gettysburg, but a staggering 690,000 of

Pennsylvania's sons had served. There had been a Confederate raid on Mechanicsburg in Cumberland County, just south of Harrisburg. That expedition had been based on the Confederacy's notion that south-central Pennsylvania's farmers would join their cause en masse and regain the right to own slaves prohibited by Pennsylvania statutes of 1780, 1788, and 1827. Thus, the raid won little support among Pennsylvanians, even though abolition sentiment and street-level racism thrived side by side. But most of Pennsylvania's elite and determined slaveholders had already emigrated to the region around Natchez, Mississippi, between the 1820s and the 1840s.[5]

A complicated 1790 Pennsylvania statute had established that children born to slaves would be free citizens, ending slavery over the span of a generation or so. In fact, those children were subject to indenture until age twenty-eight, then they would be freed. Old Robert, Henrey, and William Dunsmore undoubtedly worked alongside a few of those skilled black indentures at wagon stands, forges, or in fulling mills in the early 1800s. But, aided by constant moral pressure from the state's Quakers and Abolitionists, many Pennsylvania slave owners honored that overturned law and manumitted their slaves. By 1820 there were fewer than two hundred slaves in all of Pennsylvania.[6]

A second law enacted in 1827 outlawed all slavery and ended the indenture clause of the 1790 law, but it was overturned by a Southern-dominated US Supreme Court in 1842 as tensions over race, immigration, and citizenship swept the nation.[7] Free black males had enjoyed the right to vote[8] in Pennsylvania since the early post–Revolutionary War period.[9] But in 1838 the state's General Assembly reacted to both a large increase in the number of free black voters[10] and an ever more conflicted national conversation about race and ethnicity. They abruptly reversed course and amended the Pennsylvania Constitution in the depression year of 1838 to prohibit free blacks from voting in the Commonwealth.[11] The percentage of both free and runaway blacks in Pennsylvania's cities had risen rapidly. Coupled with a rising wave of Irish immigration, competition over jobs and wages had created new dynamics.

Uniontown and Brownsville had been stops on the Underground Railroad since the late 1840s.[12] A network of abolitionist sympathizers transported runaway slaves from Monongalia County (Morgantown), Virginia, north to Uniontown. From Uniontown, the runaways were escorted northwest to Washington, Pennsylvania, then to Beaver County, where they were sheltered by a combination of Quaker farmers and several old-line Presbyterian "covenanter" clans.[13] Though most white Pennsylvania working men in the 1850s believed "on paper" in blacks' freedom to work and live as they chose, it remained a classic case of, "Just don't live near me or take my son's job as a water boy."

After Maryland's "runaway slave" law of 1850–1851 was enacted, chasing slaves who had fled to Pennsylvania turned into an often violent business operation that violated Pennsylvania Statute. As a consequence, tensions along the Mason-Dixon Line rose dramatically and the Underground Railroad went into overdrive.[14]

Skin in the Game

Nationwide, 490 Densmores[15] served in the Civil War.[16] Those 490 Densmores are evidence of the demographic/reproductive power of their large, early-American families and the benefits of early American well-being. Simply put, many more Densmore infants survived to reproduce than would have in Scotland or Ulster. Of those 490, 29 Densmores served in the Confederacy. The other 461 served in the Union army, and an estimated 90 Union Densmore soldiers died.[17] Many others were wounded. Among them, the Pennsylvania Densmores had "skin in the game": about 51 of them served. Their average height is not definitively known, for muster rolls became sloppy as the Union frantically processed draftees after battles like Gettysburg. A smallish sample of Densmore enlistees, most born in the late 1830s, indicates an average of about 5'8" for their era and reflects the wage benefits of skilled labor and the nutritional/environmental advantage on northwestern Pennsylvania farms. In contrast, a small sample of Vandergrifts who married into the Densmores yields 5'9", a loss of almost two inches in height when compared to their 5'11" of the War of 1812 era.[18]

By the 1860s the Densmores had spread throughout the upper Midwest. Some Vandergrifts had also gone west, as had a number of the Pennsylvania and New Jersey Harts.

In broader perspective, the Civil War's historical narratives are many and rich, addressing themes like slavery, honor, a "good death," and why men on both sides served. Factors like religion, culture, status, economy, and identity of "place" are all discussed. Missing from those histories are the factors that define well-being: height, life expectancy, infant mortality, nutrition, and degree of self-sufficiency. The declining well-being of the 1830s to the 1860s in

America matters as an important and understated backdrop to rising national tensions.

Wars are primarily fought by ordinary soldiers. The Civil War's regular troops (both sides) averaged age twenty-six, with a weight of around 140 pounds and a height of roughly 5'8". In contrast, wars are directed by generals. The South's generals, most born into elite families, were extraordinarily tall for their era.[19] They were also older than the average enlistee. Most were born between 1805 and 1830. The North's generals were also taller and older than their average trooper. But they came from several tiers of society, so they represented a broader range of backgrounds than their Southern counterparts.

Many tomes have been written in hindsight about the Civil War's causes and consequences. One of the best is Robert Penn Warren's *The Legacy of the Civil War*.[20] But far fewer questions have been raised about well-being, height, and longevity as background issues that must have influenced an entire era. In the 1850s run-up to war, American-born males had lost about sixteen years of longevity and more than an inch of average height from the halcyon days of their great-grandfathers in the 1780s.

The war had huge consequences. More than 750,000 boys and men died before the war music faded away. More than another million were wounded. Hundreds of thousands of orphans' lives were changed, and "orphan trains" became a phenomenon. A generation of women lost loved ones or were unable to find a husband. Yet memories, especially the peculiarly virulent ones created by the defeated South to blame the North, still shape political, social, economic, and attitudinal behaviors daily in modern America and in the halls of Congress. But if we look beyond our own borders, we see that modern European countries once riven by horrendous war and hatred are now among the nations where citizens claim to be most "happy." Those happier nations are ones that have invested most heavily in healthcare, education, and well-being. That is also what the Founders sought to highlight in the Declaration.

One can argue that among the reasons the Civil War's echoes still have power is precisely that the initial job of spreading happiness and well-being to all sectors of American society remains unfinished.

The Densmores: Sam and Robert Jr.'s Civil War

On July 11, 1863, Sam Densmore, the twenty-four-year-old iron worker from Georges Township, was corralled and drafted at or near Anchor Nail and

Tack,[21] where he and his younger brother Ollie had been working in Pittsburgh. Trained at Oliphant's in Fairchance by their elder brother, Robert Jr., and their brother-in-law Nehemiah Warman, he and Ollie had just begun to make serious money at Anchor when fate jerked the rug from under Sam.

Two days later he and several hundred others were shipped by train to Philadelphia. There he was assigned to Captain Humphrey's Company E of the 82nd Pennsylvania Infantry Regiment. Company E was desperate to refill its ranks in compensation for the staggering slaughter of Pennsylvania men lost exactly one week before at Gettysburg.

By late July Sam and Company E were detailed to the pursuit of Lee's army in northern Maryland and western Virginia. August and September were spent patrolling from bases in Culpepper and Warrenton, Virginia. From October 9 through 22, the 82nd was engaged with the Briscoe Campaign, then marched to the Rappahannock in November to launch the Mine Run Campaign in late November and December.[22]

By January 6, 1864, Sam and the 82nd had been moved, partly by rail, to the federal military prison at Johnson's Island in Lake Erie to guard Confederate prisoners there until May 6. The 82nd was then transported to Washington, DC, to join the army of the Potomac in the field. They fought in the Rapidan Campaign and the grotesque Wilderness engagements, then at Spotsylvania Courthouse, joining the assault on the Confederate salient on the May 12. By May 23 they were at the North Anna River; by May 26 they were in the front line at Pamunkey; on May 28 they were engulfed in the haze of blood and black powder at Totopotomoy.

Then from June 1 to 12 came more fierce fighting at Cold Harbor. From June 22 to 23 they marched to Petersburg, Virginia, faced Confederate General P. G. T. Beauregard, then moved forward to the Jerusalem Plank Road. These were major, brutal engagements for Sam and his company. The siege action near Petersburg, Virginia, lasted until July 9, at which time the 82nd was drawn back to Washington, DC, to bolster defenses as Confederate General Jubal Early attempted to capture the nation's capitol.

The 82nd and Company E were then detailed to the Snicker's Gap Expedition in the Appalachian foothills, after which their goal was to join Union General Phil Sheridan's Shenandoah Valley campaign.[23] However, Sam never made it to the Shenandoah that fall. As his company marched west through Maryland, he, his record states, took an unauthorized turn north, back into Pennsylvania. That right turn to the north would have taken Sam straight back toward the old 1790s Densmore territory near Gettysburg, Adams County. On a fragile, yellowed muster roll dated July 24, 1864, Sam is listed as "Deserted." But on another document his Civil War profile indicates, "Mustered out on 24 Jul. 1864."[24] Another tangle of enigma.

A document I read a few years ago (and now cannot find) noted that Sam had left the ranks to attend to his dying wife in Pittsburgh. He was never subject to military justice, even though he had apparently re-contacted his captain after going AWOL and rejoined his unit. So that deathbed story could have been true. Yet even the hint of temporary desertion must have been a pretty touchy subject among friends and family back in Georges Township. Sam never again lived in Georges after the war. And in a Densmore genealogical abstract[25] of "H. O. Densmore," aka Ollie, Sam is breezily dismissed: "Samuel is retired from business affairs and lives in Youngstown, Ohio."[26] In fact, Sam was physically failing in Girard, Ohio, a suburb of Youngstown about seventy miles northwest of Pittsburgh,[27] when the piece was published.

By the fall of 1864,[28] Sam was back in Pittsburgh as an iron worker. Living near him was Ollie, who was a laborer. Both he and Sam would become legendary among the skilled iron workers of Western Pennsylvania—and in very different ways. Ollie, the youngest male child of the family, would become the lynch pin of their late nineteenth-century family economy and the dynamics among Old Robert's descendants. Ollie, just a seven-year-old boy when his mother died, had not been an actor in the family crosscurrents and tensions leading up to their father's death. He was a neutral party, so he became the family broker.

Unlike most of the era's ordinary families who can only be known from census and tax records, we know Ollie and his children in striking detail from family records, notes, and stories. In fact, Ollie's life became a fiber around which the later Densmore story would be entwined. In the summer of 1905, his granddaughter Elsie spent about five weeks at the Densmore homestead in Fairchance, Georges Township, with him and Elizabeth. The fold-over paper on which she wrote as her grandfather dictated to her at the dining-room table has survived.

In Elsie's distinctive hand it notes, "Oliphant D. and Elizabeth G. were married, November 1, 1860." Ollie was nineteen years and seven and a half months of age, and his compact, dark-eyed Elizabeth Goldsboro, born February 5, 1842, was eighteen years and seven months. She was the daughter of Elizabeth Ryland and Thomas Goldsboro,[29] a minor partner in his brother Robert's general store and primarily a coal miner/broker.[30] Ollie and Elizabeth were married[31] by her great uncle, Reverend Ryland.

Elizabeth had come from one of western Maryland's early frontier families. Elizabeth's great-grandfather, born in Holland, England, or Ireland, depending on whose account is given, had settled on the untamed Pennsylvania/Maryland border by the 1770s. Elizabeth's first child with Ollie, Charles Henry Densmore, born October 19, 1861, in Fayette County, tragically died three weeks later on November 1.[32] On February 5, 1863, a daughter, unnamed, was born in Pittsburgh and died the same day.[33]

After the death of their first child, the young couple had moved to the East Birmingham industrial district of South Side Pittsburgh sometime between late 1861 and the spring of 1862. A year later Ollie and Sam appear together on an army roster of "draftables" from Lower St. Claire Township dated June 1863.[34] Just four or five weeks later, Sam got drafted at work. It is likely that the drafting detail tried to take Ollie, too, but since Elizabeth was pregnant at the time the recruiters showed up, Sam may have stepped forward, as a deep bond between the two brothers endured.

Meanwhile, in Fairchance, thirty-five-year-old Robert Jr., the well-paid puddler at Oliphant's, despite his children and obligations, made a decision that smacks of atonement for Sam's presumed desertion. On September 3, 1864, five weeks after Sam's disappearance from Company E south of Pennsylvania's border, Robert Jr. enlisted in the Union army's cavalry.[35]

Robert Densmore Jr.'s Civil War service in Company E of the Pennsylvania 14th's Cavalry Unit, the 159th Volunteers, also proved dramatic. His unit's mounted battlefield service included close encounters of the dangerous kind with Confederate General Jubal Early's corps as well as Jeb Stuart's cavalry in the Shenandoah Valley campaign in the fall of 1864. By the early spring of 1865, his unit was defending Washington, DC, and Robert Jr. was in Washington for the Grand Review of the victorious Union army after Lee's surrender at Appomattox.[36] The irony is that Robert Jr. had actually served less time than Sam, just over eight months, yet was honorably discharged in May of 1865.

Like his father, Robert Jr. would later get a military pension. He also joined the GAR,[37] an important community of memory among Union Veterans. After his discharge, Robert Jr. returned to his wife and children in Fairchance, and to his role as puddler at Oliphant's. Changes in postwar American industry would soon affect him and his brothers in Pittsburgh, but it was good to be home and at work again. During his service he had earned two hundred dollars in enlistment bounties and eight dollars a month. Upon his return, he would earn about four dollars per day in Fairchance.

In 1864 Robert Jr.'s twenty-three-year-old younger brother Ollie appeared in Thurston's city directory listed as "Denzemore, Oliver, Roller, Perry near Carson," in East Birmingham.[38] With him, but *not* listed, is Sam,[39] whose idea it may have been to spell their surname as *Denzemore* and maintain a low profile after his "I made a right turn near Hancock, Maryland," decision.

Sam may or may not have been married during this time; there is that poignant suggestion in his military records that he had a gravely ill wife in Pittsburgh in 1863–1864. What is clearer is that on January 4, 1865, he married seventeen-year-old Amanda Jennie Glenn, known as Jennie. She was born on June 7, 1847,[40] to William and Elizabeth Glenn of Kittanning. Her father, William, was almost certainly a nephew or grand nephew of Hannah Glenn Densmore's father, William, who died from that fall near Connellsville in 1830. Jennie was not just Sam's wife—she was also a cousin.

Baptismal documents in Kittanning, Pennsylvania,[41] indicate that Sam and Jennie's first son of record, Robert Densmore, was born on August 15, 1865. That suggests her pregnancy began in late 1864. Young Robert was named for Sam's father and elder brother, who had mustered out of his cavalry service only nine weeks prior to his namesake's arrival. The church records indicate that this third generation Robert Densmore was born in Manor Township. Other sources support his birthplace as Pittsburgh. It is probable that he was born in East Birmingham and later baptized in Kittanning.

By the 1860s several members of the extensive Glenn family in or near Kittanning were farmers. Others became iron rollers and puddlers during Kittanning's early industrial stage. Kittanning was just a four-hour paddle wheeler's trip up the Allegheny. It would have been easy for Sam to work alongside Ollie at Anchor Nail and Tack, then slip away to Kittanning to visit Jennie and their child during the frequent iron-work shutdowns of the 1860s postwar recessions.

Post–Civil War recession, combined with the early 1860–1865 war time's dramatic inflation in cost of food and fuel, continued to limit working America's level of well-being and household security in the 1860s. Recall that the adult height of American-born males had declined more than one full inch since the Declaration was signed. The average life-span in 1860 was 41.8 years (both sexes), a loss of fifteen years since 1800. By 1870 male height had only gained two-tenths of an inch since the war, but life-span had increased a bit to 44 years. Those gains came from somewhat lower infant mortality (partly due to lower foreign migration during the war, thus diminished disease vectors) and more medical knowledge/innovation gained during the Civil War. For a moment in time, it looked as if America's measurable well-being might again be on an upward path. If so, would it hold?

Chapter 12

Cousins in the Nation's Industrial Bull's-Eye

Sporadic steamboat service had begun on the Allegheny River in the early 1830s, but regular service did not blossom until oil was discovered in the late 1850s. One of the early steamboat operations on the Allegheny River was in the hands of a branch of the venerable Vandergrift family who had migrated from Bucks County, Philadelphia, and the adjacent Delaware River to the Pittsburgh area around the time of the War of 1812.

The deep depression of 1815 to 1821 that followed that war had limited work opportunities and sucked a number of Vandergrift cousins into both the war and postwar military service. The eight for whom I found Pennsylvania and Delaware War of 1812 records were all born between 1768 and 1799. They averaged an impressive height of 5'10.78". All had blue eyes and either sandy or dark hair. Obviously they were well fed in childhood.

The sons of a Jacob Vandergrift born in the Delaware Valley about 1770, however, chose to move west to the Forks of the Ohio. By the late 1820s his sons, Captains John, Joseph, and Benjamin B. Vandergrift, all had keelboats on the Ohio. By the 1830s and 1840s, they were on the Allegheny with their steamers *Prairie Bird* and *Thomas Scott*.[1] They were upwardly mobile, bold, no-nonsense entrepreneurs. Blue or blue-gray eyes, well built, and broad faced, this branch of the Vandergrift men exuded the distinctive impression of a pack of bulldogs. Three decades on the Ohio had enhanced their wealth, and their influence. In the rough-and-tumble business of steamboats, which cost about fifty thousand to seventy-five thousand dollars each in 1860, the bulldogs and their family network had done rather well.

Unlike most of Pittsburgh's movers and shakers in the 1860s, Jacob's sons, John and William Knowles Vandergrift, lived just four blocks from Ollie and Sam in the gritty bowels of East Birmingham. Brother George Vandergrift lived a mile or so northeast in Allegheny City overlooking the Point at the mouth of the Allegheny River. Pittsburgh in the 1860s was rather unlike most other American industrial cities. Its concentration of skilled labor was higher than in any other. Iron and steel dominated as in no other American industrial center of that era, so its workforce included far fewer women than other eastern manufacturing towns.

If Pittsburgh proper was different, its smoke-belching South Side across the Monongahela was downright exotic. Birmingham in 1860 was a mélange of German, Prussian, Dutch, English, Welsh, Scots, Scots-Irish, Jewish, and Catholic-Irish, all mashed together in high density home and boarding houses along the Monongahela. Several squares, two small parks, and about a hundred pubs and small businesses—from gun makers to tailors, shoemakers, grocers,[2] and cabinetmakers—were mixed in to the mostly solid street fronts. In and among that jumble of houses, shops, horse-pulled streetcars, and merchants there were huge lots housing large glassworks, nail factories, tube works, rolling mills, forges, shipyards, and, yes, several proprietors' houses. Smoke, heat, sewage, and noise all exceeded common experience elsewhere. It was *the* most industrially productive five square miles in 1860s America.

The Vandergrift Dutch Connection: History, Culture, and Commerce

This branch of the Vandergrifts, who had first squeezed into the decrepit palisade walls surrounding 1640s New Amsterdam, before it became New York, found themselves at home in the busy and tightly spaced industrial buzz of Pittsburgh. The Vandergrifts[3] of record trace back to the 1580s in Charlois, Holland, now part of greater Amsterdam. Their progenitor, Leendert Evert van der Grist, born in 1587, was Dutch but had married Maritje Pauwelse of Prussian ancestry, born in the city of Aachen. As was common in their era, they married young and reared a large family of seven children, including Paulus Leendertsen[4] Vandergrift, their third child, born in Amsterdam on June 27, 1609. His younger brother, Jacob, was born there on or about October 20, 1613.

After serving as mates and ships' captains for the Dutch West India Company (WIC) in the 1630s and 1640s, these two sons forged their American experience in New Amsterdam. The WIC, as noted earlier, was created in 1621 as a public-private Dutch trading corporation. It sought to corner the African slave trade and South American / Caribbean sugar production, then dominated by the Portuguese. It carved out new markets in Africa, the Caribbean, and the Americas for Dutch-manufactured goods.

CHAPTER 12

The WIC chose the location of New Amsterdam as a small but strategically located mainland hub. New Amsterdam was not only an ice-free port, but it controlled the mouth of the Hudson and East Rivers. It also had potential control of the upper Delaware River. It was Holland's main entrepôt in North America, surrounded on three sides by established English settlements, which would come to create trouble for the Dutch. The official administrative heart of the WIC's New World operations was situated on Curaçao in the Caribbean. In Holland, which included several old "departments," the WIC was managed in Amsterdam—the most liberal and most cosmopolitan department of Holland.

Dutch power in that era was two pronged: a relatively sophisticated domestic manufacturing capacity was enhanced by an orderly civil and economic environment; and its sea power was both merchant and military. Levels of education in old Amsterdam were high for the time, and almost everything was regulated by some statute or institutionalized custom. The legal, jurisdictional, governmental, and property-right ambiguities first experienced by the Densmores in Scotland, then in Ulster, and again in Western Pennsylvania, simply did not exist in the Dutch homeland. Everyone was accountable—even, to a degree, the commercial magnates.

The WIC projected its Dutch power by combining its fleet's heavily armed brigs and yachts with commercial activities. Thus, even the 1637 conquest of the great Portuguese slave castles, like that of Elmina on the Gold Coast of West Africa, were franchised and regulated from Amsterdam, where slavery did not exist. Slavery was not "normal" in Holland. Instead it became a distant profit center, an abnormality practiced in lesser, therefore "abnormal" parts of the world. Out of sight and out of mind.

In the mid- to late 1630s, the WIC also tried to drive the Portuguese out of their settlements in Brazil during their successive naval sieges of Olinda in Pernambuco. The goal was to take over the Portuguese sugar industry and claim the sugar-producing districts for Holland. The Dutch fleet was sizeable—about twenty heavily armed ships. In 1637, the year of the second raid on Porto Calvo, elder brother Paulus Van der Grift, a burly, dark-haired, imposing fellow of about age twenty-eight, was first mate and pilot of the warship *Neptune*.[5] He maneuvered the ship into place to deliver a broadside cannonade from sixteen of its thirty-two guns. Those cannonballs sailed into the coastal fort at Porto Calvo that protected access to Olinda and Recife.

I imagine Paulus waving the signal to the captain for the ship's gunners to fire. Grinning ear to ear, he watches the iron balls whirr across the water in an acrid haze of smoke and sulfurous mist from black powder. Alive, energized, and thrilled at the mayhem, he had a taste for aggression and chaos—and the mercurial temper to match. He may have been a member of a shore party, one of those who observed the local Portuguese planter elites fleeing on their brightly caparisoned horses, their favorite mulatto mistresses in the saddle behind them, while the grandees' actual wives struggled afoot behind.[6] He may have gotten his first glimpse of New Amsterdam when the *Neptune* dropped anchor at the southern tip of Manhattan on July 16, 1640.[7] Twenty of its crew were quickly requisitioned to pursue raiding Indians by New Amsterdam's hot-headed, and often inebriated, director, Willem Kieft.

Paulus's usefulness had not gone unnoticed by the WIC. On May 26, 1644, he was appointed "skipper"[8] of the *Neptune* by Peter Stuyvesant. It also seems that Paulus acquired a waterfront warehouse lot in New Amsterdam sometime between 1640 and his promotion in 1644.[9] On May 18, Stuyvesant, then the WIC director in Curaçao and still recovering from his wounds at Saint Martin's, had issued a resolution to "send recent troop arrivals to Curaçao to New Netherland to support Kieft, again entangled there in an Indian war of his own making."[10] It appears that Paulus and his *Neptune* carried those new WIC sailors and soldiers to Manhattan, which is when he might also have purchased his lot.[11]

Three years later his ship and crew served as the escort and bodyguard in the small fleet that transported Peter Stuyvesant to New Amsterdam in May of 1647 as the replacement WIC director to oversee the New Amsterdam colony.[12] Stuyvesant had largely recovered from his famous leg amputation, a result of the botched St. Martin siege that was intended to dislodge the Spanish from that Caribbean island.[13] Once Stuyvesant settled in, he named Paulus to serve on his council of "Nine Men" (1647–1664).[14] Paulus's flinty intensity can be assessed by an opinion he rendered as a member of the Council of Nine on a criminal case, dated September 30, 1647: "That the prisoner must first be brought to the rack (tortured) and confess. Otherwise, he cannot be condemned to death. He can only be banished."[15]

Paulus's alleged dark hair and sun-leathered, ruddy complexion may have complemented his ruthless, narcissistic inner essence. He would also grow rich as Burgomaster/mayor of New Amsterdam (1657–1658 and 1661–1664) and become the subject of more local court cases than all but two other members of the burgeoning community on Manhattan Island. Those legal cases focused on debts, alleged misuse of his public powers, disputes over contracts, land sales, and so on. He drank with gusto, drew his sword as it pleased him, engaged in fisticuffs on off days, and imported a surprising number of young, female, Dutch "house servants" over his decades in New Amsterdam. In 1660 one of those servants arrived on the WIC ship *Bönte Couw*,[16] which four yeas later also brought the first of the Vorhees family to New Amsterdam. A century later those two families would later intermarry near Philadelphia. His far less mercurial younger brother, fair-haired, blue-eyed Jacob, also a WIC ship's officer, had come to New Amsterdam with him to settle.

From time to time Paulus captained WIC ships on special Caribbean assignments, as did Jacob. In the mid-1640s Paulus had already begun to build a warehouse on his waterfront lot on Pearl Street. His pier was just southeast of Fort Amsterdam.

Both Paulus and Jacob also maintained several smaller coastal freighting ships that worked out of their dock and warehouse complex. In addition to being a member of Stuyvesant's Council of Nine, by the late 1650s Paulus was also in charge of New Amsterdam's defenses. By the mid-1600s Dutch ascendancy in the Caribbean and their stronghold on Curaçao had ruffled highly placed feathers in England, France, Spain, and Portugal. Several of these countries licensed privateers[17] to push back. In the 1600s "market penetration" often included military tactics. Thus "market competition" often involved ships, swords, and black powder.

Paulus's brother Jacob also became a WIC captain of a ship called the *Swöl*.[18] He was a much milder sort. Trapped partly by the blowbacks from his brother's brash shenanigans in New Amsterdam, Jacob, often in debt, struggled to find success and avoid controversial entanglements. At times he was a minor owner in Paulus's large, conflict-prone storehouse operations at what is now #21 Pearl Street. There all kinds of wheeling and dealing, licit and illicit, attracted official WIC attention. Overshadowed by Paulus, Jacob was variously licensed as a bottler (liquor or beer) and a grain-measurer, among other trades. In 1657 he was listed as a small (ordinary) citizen of New Amsterdam. In that document his name was rendered "Jacob Leendertsen Vandiegrist."[19] Later in life he farmed part-time on Manhattan Island's East River strand near the Dutch and English settlements around Vlissingen (Flushing) and Newtown. Like his brother he was also occasionally assigned to captain a WIC ship, the *Neptune II*. His legal record in the colony's courts was as placid as his brother's was turbulent.

Paulus married in New Amsterdam and raised a largish family. But in 1664 his job of mayor and advisor on the colony's defenses went terribly wrong. He had pushed Stuyvesant for years to demand that the WIC invest more in fortifications and cannon and to increase the number of military personnel in the settlement. But the WIC was, first and foremost, a profit-focused business operation that was actually losing money in the 1660s. True, it avidly pursued its nation's interest in dominating trade in the Atlantic and the Caribbean, but New Amsterdam itself was no longer a true major profit center.

The young colony often operated at a loss. Supplying its livestock, smoothbore firearms, cloth, tea, nails, and new citizens all cost a lot. Labor was scarce, the beaver trade had its ups and downs, and because of its small size New Amsterdam was only a modest purchaser of Dutch cloth, luxury items, and other manufactured goods. Even the cost of its government and courts, core Dutch institutions, were a profit burden. The colony simply had to make do with a Sear's Roebuck version of "good" rather than "better" or the "best" defenses.

That worked when the issue was an occasional Indian raid or unruly privateer out in Long Island Sound, but it failed on a particularly hazy August morning in 1664. As the morning mists burned off Manhattan's southern tip, the British attack fleet that had been rumored for months was revealed.

Suddenly Paulus was not in control. His bluster was of no use. Already fifty-five years old, he and Stuyvesant negotiated, then signed, the Articles of Capitulation[20] that the British offered in order to save the town from almost certain total destruction. It was, given the circumstances, the right and prudent thing to do. The British promptly renamed the town of approximately 1,600 residents "New York" in honor of the Duke of York.[21] About 8,500 other citizens, including some English, populated the rest of New Amsterdam's territory.[22]

Five years later, in 1670 or 1671,[23] a much richer Paulus reassessed his situation. Both unable to manipulate British Governors Nicolls or Lovelace as he had Stuyvesant and stung by the colony's rapidly declining commerce due to the perverse British Navigation Acts, he sold his house on Broadway. Over the next months he wrapped up his diverse business affairs and returned to old Amsterdam with most of his family. The fact that British taxes caused a rapid decline in the value of Dutch New Amsterdam trade in the late 1660s likely fueled his exit.[24]

His great-great-great-grandson, the flashy J. J. Vandergrift, pursued the very same business model that Paulus and his colleague Gillis van Hoornbeeck pioneered in New Amsterdam of the 1650s. That was a business model described as, "a distributor, ship owner, financier, freighter, insurance broker, and retail . . . distributor."[25] Nothing had changed in Pittsburgh for three hundred years.

Brother Jacob stayed on in America, living variously on Staten Island (near the Flushing/Newtown settlements on Long Island, which is now part of the Elmhurst section of Queens) and later across the Hudson in what is now coastal New Jersey. Thus most of the Van der Grists, Vandegrifts, Vander Grifts, Vandegriffs, and Vandergrifts in America descend from Jacob. He and his sons and sons-in-law farmed, engaged in ordinary coastal trading, and held occupations such as carpenter or stonemason in several localities around a growing English New York until the early 1700s when Jacob's widow and sons began to migrate south along the Delaware.[26]

In order to understand the worldview of Jacob and his descendants, one needs to understand both old Amsterdam and New Amsterdam's cultural legacy. First and foremost, liberal old Amsterdam placed high values on religious freedom, well-organized laws, and courts—due process. Holland also tolerated cultural, religious, and racial diversity in an era when that was uncommon; however, just as important to the Dutch world was business, commerce, and organized efficiency.

The Dutch citizens of New Amsterdam had regularly appealed to their home land's social values, citizens' rights, and legal system to counterbalance the episodically excessive power and regulations imposed on them by the various WIC directors in the colony. However, New Amsterdam on Manhattan Island was never *exactly* like old Amsterdam in Holland; it was a continual tug-of-war between sophisticated Amsterdam and its obsession with "normal" versus the commercial and social realities of frontier empire. That tug-of-war would eventually have a direct influence on early Anglo-America's own conflicted desires for business prosperity and personal freedoms on the one hand, and neat, orderly, regulated society on the other.

Flushing and "Culture Wars"

In the 1650s, before the Capitulation, emerging English settlements had begun to expand on the end of Long Island nearest Manhattan. This created both civil and corporate malaise on the part of Stuyvesant and his Council. Stuyvesant and Paulus attempted to push the English settlers back toward their Connecticut River colonies and deny them the privilege of any religious affiliation other than in the Dutch church. The initial pushback focused on the nearest English settlement at Newtown, where the irritatingly different English inhabitants were living within the chartered boundaries of New Amsterdam lands.

Peter Stuyvesant, history amply records, detested Jews, Quakers, Puritans, and Baptists. He also loathed the English, especially those creeping in from the far end of Long Island and the Connecticut colony beyond. So openly abusive was Stuyvesant that the WIC directors in old Amsterdam reined him in time and again to enforce at least some of the homeland's more generous cultural norms in New Amsterdam.[27]

Stuyvesant's religious animosity against the English was at its peak in the mid-1650s as he went witch-hunting for Quakers and Baptists. As a consequence, the English-dominated town council of Flushing/Newtown drafted a formal complaint requesting an end to religious persecution and delivered the petition to Stuyvesant's office at the end of December 1657. Stuyvesant erupted, hauling in and imprisoning both the Newtown sheriff who had delivered the letter *and* the town clerk who had drafted it and signed it. Other arrests followed. Known as the Flushing Remonstrance, some scholars argue that this document played a role in shaping ideas about religious freedom as codified more than a century later in the American Constitution. Stuyvesant was again chastised by his directors in Holland and forced to free those he had jailed and control his hostility to religious differences.

The town clerk who had drafted and signed the petition was Edward Hart of Newtown, a descendant of earlier Harts who likely arrived in the late 1630s to settle the Connecticut River Valley. Edward Hart, the town clerk, was the great-grandfather of John Hart, signer of the Declaration of Independence (NJ), and he undoubtedly knew the younger Vandergrift brother, Jacob, who had farmed and lived several miles away on the shore of Manhattan's East River.

The America that the Dutch Vandergrift brothers experienced was one populated largely by those who could read and write. They lived on rich and diverse lands, forests, and incredibly productive salt grass marshes among stunningly bountiful bird and marine life. Oysters by the millions were consumed as poor man's food. Crabs, fish, birds' eggs, seals, sturgeon, herring, and limpets also abounded. On a fall day when great flocks of ducks and geese filled the sky in migration to the south, one had but to poke the barrel of a flint blunderbuss at the center of the flight to bring down several fat birds at one discharge.

In the colony's early days of the 1620s and 1630s, Indians mostly watched and waited, but by the 1640s and 1650s, dislocation, disease, and new immigrants brought relations to a boiling point. As Indian families asked themselves, "How are we doing?," an instinctive nightmare of deep biological and potential demographic catastrophe (including smallpox and other diseases) must have begun to haunt them. They pushed back. Recurring conflicts ensued. Each side fashioned conflicting responses to protect its economy, and most cherished cultural values. For Indian peoples these values included access to land and resources that they did not live on year-round and the ability to continue ancient customs of mobile, seasonal resource utilization.

The Dutch desired to assert their view of land and resources as surveyed, owned, and recorded and to maintain a world that reflected Dutch norms of tidy organization and legal process. In New Amsterdam even cutting the abundant reeds from another Dutchman's salt marsh was formally adjudicated. That these two completely different worlds—Native American and Dutch—could each successfully cohabit the same real estate in harmony was both an ecological and cultural impossibility. Recurring raids and counter raids peaked in the mid-1640s, and again in 1656 when Paulus Vandergrift suffered a deep upper-leg wound from an Esopus warrior's tomahawk in what would be labeled the "Yellow Tomahawk War." More Indian raids followed in 1661.

Indian raids began again in early 1664. Stuyvesant and Paulus Vandergrift unsuccessfully attempted to simultaneously deal with the Indian threat and enhance town defenses against the rumored English assault fleet. It is tempting to suggest that, were it not for the need to defend against the desperate and angry Native communities, New Amsterdam might not have capitulated to the English in late 1664. But it did capitulate, and, as noted, Paulus Leendertsen Vandergrift did return to Holland with his family. He opened a large mercantile business in old Amsterdam, built a large townhouse on old Amsterdam's fabled Herrengracht (Gentleman's Canal), prospered, and died there in 1679. He was buried at the Old Zijds Chapel on October 10, leaving a family of sailors and businessmen who continued to do business with New York.

Jacob, as stated, never left. After he died in 1697, he was buried in New Amsterdam's Old Dutch Reformed Church cemetery. He left a family of farmers, coastal mariners, traders, and a master carpenter. His widow and children moved farther south into New Jersey around 1700, bought land in what was then Hunterdon County, then expanded south again to Bucks County, Pennsylvania, between 1710 and 1720, as did a number of other second- and third-generation Dutch New Amsterdam families. There, Jacob's sons and grandsons bought lands in Bensalem, a farming community composed of mixed Dutch, Scots, and English.

By 1713 Jacob's sons, grandsons, and in-laws had patented land in Bensalem along Neshaminy Creek.[28] There they became members of the Dutch church. In all, the descendant brothers and daughters' husbands owned at least a thousand acres along the creek. One grandson, Abraham Vandergrift, and a sister or aunt Maritje, were identified in Bucks County tax records as "on the river." That was the Delaware River, known in the first Dutch settlements as South River. On that river several of Jacob's grandsons still maintained river yachts, carrying farm produce down to Philadelphia for the growing settlements at Germantown and Frankford.

By the 1750s the Vandergrifts were well versed in the Delaware Valley's diverse cultural scene. They had married into several of the Philadelphia area's upscale and historically prominent families, among them the Biddles, Vanzandts, Nolls (Knolls or Knowles), Ellsworths, Kings, Cloessens, Vorhees, Van Arsdalens, and Corsens. But by the early 1750s, the Neshaminy Creek's community had come to be dominated by recent Scots and Scots-Irish Presbyterian immigrants.[29] Wanting some of their religious autonomy back, a number of Vandergrift grandchildren and great-grandchildren moved south again, to the Frankford and Germantown settlements in Philadelphia. Several other branches moved even further south into the lower Delaware—the very region from which their great-grandfathers had once pushed the seventeenth-century Swedes' settlement out by force of arms.

The Harts

One of these later great-grandchildren, Jacob Vandergrift, born about 1767 and named for New Amsterdam's old Jacob, married into another upscale family—the Harts. In 1791 at Christ Church in Frankford, Philadelphia County, Jacob married Mary Hart, born around January 14, 1771, in Hunterdon County, New Jersey—only four miles from where young Jacob's grandfather had purchased land after the death of his father, the patriarch and WIC captain. Mary was a great-great-granddaughter of Edward Hart, drafter of the Flushing Remonstrance, and a granddaughter of Declaration signer John Hart, born in Hunterdon County, New Jersey, in 1713. In the 1650s these two families had once represented polar factions among European settlers in New Amsterdam—Dutch WIC company men, Dutch Reformed Church, Dutch speaking, and "normal," versus Protestant, Baptist, Quaker, Puritan, English speakers loyal to Britain's unfocused ideas of "normalcy," quite unlike the Dutch definition of it.

I see a twenty-four-year-old Jacob and a twenty-year-old Mary at the altar of

Christ Church, the son and daughter of an early Colonial America that each one's family had shaped and was to be shaped by. That marriage brought Mary some of the constancy she must have yearned for. Her father, John Hart Jr., the signer's youngest son and spoiled namesake, had left Mary in his father's care while he pursued adventure and sought wealth as a slaveholder and planter in Pointe Coupee, Louisiana. He was, at one point, in partnership with Isaac Monsanto[30] in a land/slave venture. John Jr. was the family's "problem child," born in 1748 when his father, the signer, was already politically powerful. Young John was also heavily influenced by his father's brother, Daniel, a slave owner who ran their jointly owned mill complex at Scudder's Falls on the upper Schuylkill River.

Signer John Hart is described in common narratives as "Honest John, a simple farmer of modest education," or with similar tropes. The reality is much more complex. He had a long career in New Jersey's County and Colonial governments, signed several issues of the colony's paper bank notes, was the largest landowner in Hunterdon for a time, and owned, with his brother Daniel and others, several mills and shares in other enterprises.[31] He was literate and prosperous for his time and place. But given the easy comparisons to far richer and more powerful aristocrats like Thomas Jefferson and George Washington, it was natural that the American fascination with wealth and power would overshadow him. There were, of course, many other overshadowed signers like him in the famous Continental Congress that produced the Declaration of Independence. Elsie Elizabeth Densmore adored the idea that signer John—her mother's great-grandfather—was a simple farmer, the fluffy stuff of an appealing rags-to-riches American saga.

On the other hand, in strict Darwinian evolutionary terms, "Honest John" was *the* biologically most successful member of that Continental Congress. A review of the membership rolls of the society, Descendants of the Signers of the Declaration of Independence (the DSDI), makes it abundantly clear that signer John and his children generated more descendants than any other signer.[32] In evolution, those with the most surviving offspring and descendants win the statistical contest of shaping future gene pools.

Toward the Ohio: A Riverboat Dynasty

Old Robert Dunsmore the wagoner was nine when Mary Hart and Jacob Vandergrift married. That marriage would produce eleven living children, eight of them sons. Mary and Jacob's elder Vandergrift sons, led by twenty-year-old

Samuel, moved west to the Ohio Valley about the time Old Robert was marching back from Canada in the spring of 1814. The pursuit of multiple economic strategies was deeply ingrained in the Vandergrifts. The family's traditional combination of river commerce, farming, grain mills, and food processing[33] that Old Jacob had once pursued in his flamboyant brother's shadow on Manhattan Island in the 1600s still prevailed in their Bucks County, Frankford, and Philadelphia enterprises. Those were the same enterprises they would eventually establish in the Ohio Valley. But the deep, postwar depression that began in 1815 displaced a number among the large, extended Vandergrift clan spread out along the Delaware, from New Jersey to northern Maryland. Tall, strong, and blue eyed, they had eaten well as children, but the crowded Eastern Seaboard had been flat-out hammered by the 1815 economic collapse.

Jacob Vandergrift and his sons Samuel, George, and John headed to the forks of the Ohio River at Pittsburgh. It is unclear just where the still young patriarch Jacob and Mary first made their home at that time. They maintained some property and had many kin in the Philadelphia area. Some sources say that they lived south of Pittsburgh in Washington County. Others assert they lived in Pittsburgh and died there. There is a grave some allege to be Mary's in Allegheny Cemetery, Pittsburgh, and another with the same name in Beallsville, south of "little" Washington, Pennsylvania, on Pike Run. There was a Jacob Vandergrift censused on the Pike Run division of Washington County's 1810 US Census, but too few male sons are listed to confirm beyond doubt that it was the correct Jacob.[34] The Jacob we want had six living sons by 1810, but such a census record cannot be found in Allegheny County—in document records he is everywhere and nowhere. His date of death is listed on a number of DAR, SAR, and DSDI[35] applications and ranges from "after 1816" to as late as 1850. His place of death ranges from Washington County to Pittsburgh's North Side to Philadelphia. A combination of factors had surrounded the move west: Mary's health, a postwar depression, fractured family connections, and declining postwar markets for agricultural product as postwar food prices collapsed. Around Philadelphia, farmlands were also being consumed by the expanding city.

It is alleged by some that Mary died about February 4, 1816,[36] possibly in childbirth with her youngest son, James M. A gavestone in Beallsville, Pennsylvania, and another in Allegheny Cemetery suggests that she died in 1840. Her younger sons would soon follow their older brothers to Pittsburgh. Other branches of the Vandergrifts remained in Bensalem, Philadelphia, Delaware, and northern Maryland as home anchors.

CHAPTER 12

For the Vandergrift brothers the Point at the storied forks of the Ohio was as natural a home for them as once wild and ambiguous western Pennsylvania had been for the Densmore Border Reiver descendants. Their great-great-grandfathers had begun their American saga at the south point of Manhattan island, where the waters of the Hudson and East Rivers mingled and lapped against the pilings of their family wharf. Pittsburgh's Point offered the city three rivers for commerce—the Allegheny and the Monongahela meet there to form the Ohio. The Point also offered nearby farms, riverside warehouses, a burgeoning legal community focused on maritime law,[37] and a newly opened, American-owned river path of commerce from those warehouses to New Orleans, Mexico, and the Caribbean. The Battle of New Orleans in 1815 had stimulated an end to the War of 1812. Much to the chagrin of Southern Seaboard planters in Virginia and the Carolinas, the Ohio and Mississippi were finally "open for business" to Americans. The Louisiana Purchase was in administrative process—the sky was the limit.

The Forks of the Ohio were already rich in resources and infrastructure. Small boatyards had been scattered along all three rivers to build flatboats and wooden cargo barges since the early 1780s. Several larger, more sophisticated barge/flatboat yards were already operating in Brownsville and Elizabeth, Pennsylvania, both on the Monongahela.[38] North of Pittsburgh was the flatboat yard of Jesse Hart and his associates on the Ohio at the mouth of its tributary, the Beaver River. Jesse Hart, eldest son of signer John Hart, was Mary Hart Vandergrift's uncle. Among Jesse's family was his younger brother, Scudder.

Even before the Vandergrifts had made their way west, Jesse Hart, with Scudder, had headed to western Pennsylvania a few years after his father's death in late 1779. A sheriff's sale of signer John's property in New Jersey to settle debts had encouraged a new start. Jesse first moved to Washington, Pennsylvania, south of Pittsburgh, then moved on. Jesse was among those who chartered Beaver Township north of Pittsburgh in the late 1790s. He built an inn near the mouth of Beaver Creek, and the boatyard he and others shared was nearby. In most early records his location is identified as "Crow's Bottom." Those bottoms later became part of the town of Beaver.

By 1816, the year in which their youngest brother, James, was born, John Vandergrift and his older brother Samuel, both young, single fellows, were actively working on the first permanent bridge across the Monongahela near the Point. Both young men had some engineering skills, placing them within the younger, semiskilled labor category. All of Jacob and Mary's children had been raised around the family's grain and cloth mills near Frankford, and several of the boys likely worked on boats as deckhands for an uncle, Abraham Vandergrift, a descendant of the first Abraham and a sailor born in Bensalem from the "on the (Delaware) river" Vandergrifts. His Seaman's Citizenship Warrant of 1800 is available.[39]

In Pittsburgh, brother John focused on river commerce, as did brother George and their younger brother William Knowles[40] Vandergrift, whose keelboats would carry cargo from Pittsburgh to Louisville by the 1830s.[41] The first real western steamboat, the *New Orleans* side-wheeler, had departed the Point for the Mississippi in October 1811. It paused in Louisville, waiting for high water, then continued on to St. Louis, Vicksburg, and New Orleans, reaching that town's fabled "Algiers Bend" on January 10, 1812, to great fanfare. It had passed old Jesse Hart's place in Beaver en route. Its engine, a large, single cylinder driven at low pressure, was not particularly sophisticated, so while the downriver trip past Wheeling, Marietta, and Cincinnati went well, the upriver return against the Mississippi and Ohio's currents had been a long, slow struggle.

The age of classic steamboats with large cabins and rear paddle wheels had not yet arrived. Even so, John Vandergrift began buying shares in riverboats as early as the late 1820s. He is explicitly credited as devising the propulsion linkages that permitted rear-paddle, as opposed to side-wheel, propulsion on his steamboat, *Beaver*,[42] built in 1832.[43] By the early 1840s he was known as "Captain John Vandergrift" from Pittsburgh to St. Louis. By the late 1840s he owned all, or shares in, a half-dozen boats.[44]

During the early riverboat era, roughly 1820 to 1850, most boats had multiple owners. A single investor like John might own, in aggregate, the equivalent of one or two entire boats, but those shares would be spread over six to eight named boats on the water—the very same ownership model that their Manhattan Island progenitors had depended upon in the 1640s to 1660s. Self-insurance through limited partnerships also ruled the early Ohio River era. The value of a particular boat's shares was a complex derivative based on build cost, cargo capacity, engine type, draft, captains' and pilots' skills, and integrity of the pursers.[45] The risks were many: blown boilers, fire aboard, great log snags, heavy fog, and especially dammed-up icepacks.[46] Ice sometimes froze boats in place, and surrounding ice dams often squeezed them like a boa constrictor.[47] On a good day, an ice flow might merely punch a leak in the side at the waterline, giving time to make shore and affect *ad hoc* repairs. On a bad day . . . well, that's what the partnership shares were all about.

Documents about early Vandergrift investments in Allegheny County, boat and otherwise, are scarce. One has to wonder where, or if, many were ever formally recorded. Document scarcity makes it nearly impossible to identify specifics of the Vandergrift family's growing wealth and influence on commerce and transportation. It is possible that at least some of their early steamboat records were in one or another of the local attorney's offices that burned in Pittsburgh's great fire of 1846. That fire also consumed several Vandergrift houses built within sight of the surviving colonial era Blockhouse on the Point. Thus the best surviving reference on Captain John's early career comes from a memoir published by his son-in-law, Captain C. W. Batchelor,[48] after Batchelor became the director of Pittsburgh's huge US Customs House.

We can also get a sense of the Vandergrift wealth another way. In the 1860s a riverboat captain earned $250 a month. This adds up to $3,000 a year, a princely salary when compared to the national average of $800–900.[49] The envied upper-middle-class captains earned roughly three and a half times as much salary as did the solid, skilled working class.

By the time Ollie and Sam Densmore, or "Denzemore," were in Pittsburgh working iron at Anchor Nail and Tack in the early Civil War era, the Vandergrifts were already huge players in steamboats, boatyards, boat repair, coal, land, transport innovations, and banking. They were also branching out into natural gas, and within a few years they would be heavily involved in oil. Though the Vandergrifts were movers and shakers on the eve of the Civil War, most of them were still rather private about their influence. Their horsepower was rather like that hidden under the hood of an old Hudson Hornet straight eight—smooth and quiet, but plenty of torque.

There is one exception to the Vandergrift modesty—Jacob Jay Vandergrift, called "J. J.," whose life was flashy like a Corvette. Members of America's Densmore clan would become instrumental to his fast and flashy rise to the pinnacle of Pittsburgh industry.

In the meantime, the first open, public record of the Vandergrifts so far found in Allegheny County was a listing in an 1841 business directory of Pittsburgh and Allegheny City: "Vandergrift, George, steam boat carpenter Water b.[50] Wood and Smithfield."[51] This was a Vandergrift-owned boatyard on the waterfront of Pittsburgh. The next public listings appear in Samuel Fahnestock's *Pittsburgh Directory* of 1850. It lists: "Vandergrift, George, carpenter, 12 Clarke; Vandergrift, James, ship carp., Water, Bir;[52] Vandergrift, John, carp. 8 Colwell; Vandergrift, Joseph, 105 Ross; Vandergrift, Samuel, carp., 33 Duquesne; and, [William Knowles] Vandergrift, fisherman, Water, Bir."[53]

Six of Mary and Jacob's living sons are listed here in 1850; only Benjamin B. Vandergrift, born in Frankford 1807, is missing. All of those listed, and those not, were involved in building and owning steamboats—or, more accurately, owning shares in steamboats. Legal records aside, most of the Vandergrift steam boats are documented in *Way's Steamboat Directories* of both "packet" (passenger) and "tow" (freight) boats.[54]

Several Vandergrift deeds have been recovered, one dated 1849: "For purchase of land transferred to Joseph Vandergrift in 1847, a lot in Manchester Borough (Sampson St. and Alley) toward Jackson Street, then to Beaver Street to property already belonging to said Vandergrift." It had been the previous property of Hugh Davis. Joseph was adding to prior land he owned in the village of Manchester, later part of greater Pittsburgh.[55]

By 1862–1863, Thurston's Directory of Pittsburgh lists two former steamboat captains as "Gentlemen," meaning they were retired with income. They are Samuel, Jacob and Mary Hart's first son (born 1794), age sixty-nine; and Captain John (born 1798), of wide fame. Combined with the recent death of their nephew Benjamin F. Vandergrift due to yellow fever contracted when his crew was put off the *Red Fox*[56] by the Union Navy, the Civil War years of 1862 to 1864 saw three Vandergrift captains "off the river." Still, as "gentlemen," a rare status, both Samuel and John quietly continued to partner in some family river ventures.

Civil War and the Vandergrift Rivermen

The Civil War changed many lives in the Vandergrift family. In March 1862 the family lost J. J.'s son, eighteen-year-old George Vandergrift, engineer of the *Grey Fox*. He drowned in a boat accident on the Allegheny as he was hauling freight for the Union.[57] It also cut short the life of twenty-nine-year-old Benjamin F. Vandergrift, the *Red Fox*'s master.[58] Benjamin had married Sarah Ann Hoffman (born in Birmingham, Allegheny County, September 30, 1841) on Christmas Eve of 1861, in the Civil War's first year. She was the daughter of Catharine Page and master machinist Joseph Hoffman, he of Prussian descent. Benjamin died in the house of his father, William Knowles Vandergrift, on "Joseph Nr. Sidney" Street in East Birmingham on November 5, 1862. Benjamin's little daughter, Sophia Irene Vandergrift, was born on November 2, three days before his death. Orphaned by her father, she had to settle for her mother's assurance that she had been placed in her father's arms and he had awakened and smiled at her before he died. Business connections aside, little Sophia would later become the first genetic connection between the Vandergrifts and Densmores.

Benjamin's death was tied into the Vandergrift's business ventures, which were deeply affected by the Civil War. From 1861 to 1862 the Confederate Navy closed the Mississippi to shipping in an attempt to damage the huge river trade from Pittsburgh, Wheeling, Cincinnati, and St. Louis. They imagined the Union quickly caving in. This strategy, combined with their refusal to ship cotton to English textile mills, was simultaneously intended to blackmail both the Union and the English Parliament. While financial "blackmail" clearly persists in modern American politics,[59] overreaching—then and now—often backfires.

In response to the river's closure below St. Louis, the Union quickly authorized, funded, and organized a "Western Water's Navy." The Union Quartermaster began to pressure commercial boat owners to lease or sell steamboats outright in order to put a steamboat Navy on the western rivers. Amid the rush and chaos, Union Naval officers bungled the care of several of the Vandergrift's leased boats. They abruptly replaced a number of veteran civilian crews with uniformed naval personnel accustomed to seagoing vessels.

The lease of the *Red Fox* was one such messy example. Built in 1855 at Pringle's Yard in Brownsville on the Monongahela, the *Red Fox*[60] had been in service towing coal and brick to Cairo, Illinois, for several years before the war broke out.[61] When Captain Benjamin F. Vandergrift and his crew were ordered ashore by Union Admiral Foote in the early fall of 1862, at or on Island No. 10, he and a number of his own crew were abandoned, stranded, and contracted yellow fever. That yellow fever ended young Benjamin's life. The Vandergrift family was not amused.

It didn't help that the *Red Fox*'s other owner, flashy older brother J. J., had prevailed on his nephew Benjamin to master her when she was leased. Benjamin was still in the first year of his marriage to Sarah Ann, and she was already pregnant. His younger brother's death stoked both J. J.'s guilt and his extended family's anger. Benjamin's death was especially bittersweet since the *Red Fox* was famed as the first steamboat to *push* a tow of barges to St. Louis instead of dragging "a tow" behind it. It was the idea of Daniel Bushnell, another river man and business partner of J. J.'s, to try it, but it was J. J.'s gumption as a young captain that made it happen. It succeeded wildly and remains the way river barges are moved worldwide to this day.[62] J. J. and his *Red Fox* were the world's first to do it successfully.

In 1861–62, not only was the river closed to the Vandergrift combine's twice-weekly freight runs to New Orleans, but an iconic boat and crew were lost. To top that off, the Confederates had attacked and destroyed recently established, Vandergrift-owned, natural gas wells east of Wheeling in what was still Confederate western Virginia. The Confederates had also requisitioned several smaller Vandergrift boats docked at Wheeling earlier in the war. Six of the Vandergrift boats, worth at least $50,000[63] each, got tangled up in the Union war effort. They are listed in Table 8. In 2018 dollars, each of those boats cost about $1,374,000 to build.

Acting on both anger and necessity, J. J. and his brothers moved their smaller

TABLE 8. Vandergrift Boats Sold, Commandeered, Lost, or Leased in the Civil War[*]

The Volunteer, built 1862	Owned by Captain Lewis F. L. Vandergrift et al. Leased to Union Navy December 1862.[†] On November 25, 1863, was declared a prize of war by the US government. Sold at Mound City, Illinois, on November 25, 1865, for $9,000. (Way's Packet #5608)
The Conestoga, built 1859	Owned by J. J. Vandergrift and Daniel Bushnell. "Sold" May 7, 1861, and converted to timber clad gunboat renamed the USS Conestoga on October 1, 1862. Ran the cannons at Vicksburg. Sunk at Grand Gulf, Mississippi, on March 8, 1864.[‡] (Way's Packet #1286)
The Empire City, built 1854	Owned by Captain James Vandergrift et al. Leased as a US transport, 1862–1865. Lost in ice dam at St. Louis in private troop service on January 12, 1866. (Way's Packet #1852)
The Argosy, built 1862	Owned by Captain G. W. Reed and Captain Lewis Vandergrift et al. Taken over by US government at Cairo, Illinois, in March 1863. Converted to tin clad, #27, and sold to private owner by the US in 1865. (Way's Packet #0329)
The Argosy 2, built 1863	Owned by Captain G. W. Reed, Lewis, and James Vandergrift, minor partners. Bought by the US at Cincinnati on November 14, 1863. Renamed *The Wave*, a six-gun tin-clad. Captured by the Confederates on May 6, 1864, at Calcasieu Pass, Texas. (Way's Packet #0330)
The Red Fox,[§] built 1855	Refitted 1858–59 and owned in 1859 by J. J. Vandergrift. It was captained by Benjamin F. Vandergrift[**] when chartered by the US in November 1861. Sunk at Island No. 10 in 1862. As of 1880 J. J. Vandergrift had not been compensated for the loss. (Way's Tow #T2126)

[*] Way, Way's Packet Directory, 616.
[†] Three weeks after the death of Captain Benjamin F. Vandergrift of The Red Fox.
[‡] J. J. Vandergrift later named one of his buildings in Pittsburgh "The Conestoga" to commemorate this boat.
[§] Way and Rutter, Way's Steam Towboat Directory, 189, 290.
[**] A major error in Way's Red Fox entry had Benjamin F. incorrectly listed as Benjamin B., who was his and J. J.'s uncle.

boats up from Vincennes, Indiana, and Cincinnati, put them on the Allegheny and Monongahela in Union territory, and, depending on whose story one chooses to believe, either gave or sold the sturdy side-wheeler *Conestoga* to the Union. Built at Brownsville[64] in 1859, it was personally delivered by J. J. to St. Louis in early 1861, where he stayed with it until it was converted to a timber-clad man-o-war and became the USS *Conestoga*. It was one of the first three Union gunboats to successfully "run the batteries" under the cliffs at Vicksburg on April 16, 1863, and break the Confederate blockade of the Mississippi. Several issues of *Harper's Weekly* carried prints of the *Conestoga*,[65] seen both in Europe and America.

Oil and Natural Gas

The Vandergrifts would recover their gas fields in 1864 and 1865, soon after West Virginia became a Union state (1862–1863). This business would outlive them and eventually transform into the company that became West Virginia Gas and Power.[66] Several Vandergrift brothers would continue as rivermen into the 1880s and 1890s, running both passenger and cargo boats out of Pittsburgh, Wheeling, Parkersburg, Brownsville, Cincinnati, and Covington. Several of their larger boats reestablished their trade to the lower Mississippi, docking at Governor Nicholl's wharf in postbellum New Orleans. In all, as recorded in Way's Packet and Tug Riverboat directories, the Vandergrifts would be identified as owners of twenty-five to thirty steamboats between 1842 and 1885. The number of unnamed skiffs and keelboats they built between 1828 and 1880 may have approached a thousand.

In contrast, after the Civil War J. J., his sons, several nephews, and his father, William Knowles Vandergrift of Pittsburgh's South Side, would refocus and pursue the emerging oil business in Venango County. They had dabbled in oil as early as 1859. In fact, the *Conestoga* had originally been refitted for towing barges filled with wooden barrels of oil for the Pittsburgh trade. Shipping losses had been high—the narrower upper Allegheny and its tributaries, like Oil Creek, were prone to icing, marked changes in water levels, and congested river traffic. Those risks cut deeply into profits, but the Civil War had gutted the Vandergrifts' established trading patterns. They needed those new markets up the Allegheny.

The solution to Oil Creek shipping losses would require innovation to render the oil trade profitable in northwestern Pennsylvania. To generate those innovations, J. J. and William Knowles Vandergrift, with Daniel Bushnell, commissioned brothers Amos and James Densmore[67] of Meadville, Pennsylvania[68] to build "bulk boats"[69] so that oil could be pumped directly into the barge hulls, lowering the load's center of gravity.[70] That eliminated both the cost of barrels and precious oil bobbing in the Allegheny when ice, abrupt maneuvers, or dockside collisions bumped the barrels overboard. The Densmore inventors got the job done, and the Vandergrifts again revolutionized shipping efficiencies on the western rivers.[71] Oil profits rose dramatically as shipping losses declined.

The next transport innovations came as the Densmore brothers applied the bulk transport concept to railroads and patented prototypes of true railroad tank cars. The first tank cars employed two huge, upright wooden barrels that could haul about 3,400 gallons per flatbed rail car. Their first trial run, petroleum from Oil Creek shipped to New York City by tank car in September of 1865, resulted in *no* losses. By 1869 their cars had morphed into hump-domed metal ones somewhat more reminiscent of today's tank cars.

Vandergrift money was regularly invested in this experimentation as well. The Vandergrifts and the Densmores from Meadesville, Pennsylvania, worked together, developing a history of innovation leading to profit-building incremental transport efficiencies. News of these innovations was headlined in newspapers and trade journals. Of course, other Densmore workingmen in Pittsburgh, Fayette County, and Kittanning took note. Old Robert's third-born son, Sam Densmore, of complex Civil War record, was a lover of machinery and innovation. From his base in Kittanning and a family farm fronting the Allegheny, he knew the Densmore brothers from Meadesville, just eighty miles away on French Creek, a tributary of the Allegheny. But he would also have run into them in Pittsburgh. By 1867 Amos and James Densmore had moved on from tank cars to other inventions. This inventive streak among branches of the Densmores is explored below.

As shipping to New Orleans became impossible, the Vandergrifts had helped to create a new American industrial enterprise: oil production, shipped by water or by rail. By the late 1860s J. J.'s Corvette-like flash blossomed when he attracted newspaper attention as the public face of the Vandergrift combine. Well tailored, well spoken, well connected, and richer by the month, J. J. nurtured his image as a man of commerce, of the Presbyterian church (a legacy of the mid-1700s Neshaminy Creek Church), and of an urbane version of, "I made it up from the ranks of a cabin boy on the river." Built like a Boston bulldog with a wide, flat face to match and nicely turned out in his three-piece suit, he smiled often, shook many hands, relied on cordiality, drank but little, treated his close associates as equals, and, like a superb bantam-weight fighter, danced the ring of business and commerce and punched way above his weight.

At this point, and still in his early forties, he began to gravitate to the finer things in life: a large house, club memberships, a fine carriage and matched horses, bespoke woolen suits, and house servants, including a butler.

He and his partners would go on to incorporate the Union Pipeline Company, the Union Tank Car Lines, Keystone Bank, Forrest Oil Company, and dozens of other commodity enterprises. Old Paulus Vandergrift, the one-time New Amsterdam mayor once described as "the opulent merchant,"[72] would have been proud.

By 1864 the Vandergrift listings in that year's *Thurston's Directory of Pittsburgh and Allegheny Cities*[73] were much expanded. They included

Benjamin, Capt. [The Red Fox—deceased by the time this edition hit the street]
George, boat carpenter, #2 Clark
George W. engineer, #6 Wilkinson's Row, residence #60 Stevenson
Jacob J. steamboat capt; McKee nr corner of Bingham B (Birmingham)
James, laborer, #70 First
James M., clerk—US Customs House, #21 Clark
Louis, steamboat captain, #61 Robinson—Allegheny City
Samuel W., watchman, US Custom's House, boards #21 Clark
Scudder, coachman [builder], #70 First[74]
William [Knowles], Sidney nr Joseph, East Birmingham[75]
William, carpenter [son of above] Sidney nr. Joseph, East Birmingham

East Birmingham

As 1864 came to a close, ship carpenter and engineer William K. Vandergrift,[76] his young, widowed daughter-in-law Sarah Ann Hoffman Vandergrift, and his three-year-old orphaned granddaughter Sophia Irene were the subject of a family council. Sarah Ann, three years a widow, had met a boat carpenter in her father-in-law's boat and engine shops, Samuel Wheaton, born in Maine in 1836.[77] Sam was as fine a man as ever laid hands on a steamboat's hull, engine, or mangled paddle wheels. Tallish, reliable, reserved, and taken with Sarah Ann, they married in 1866 and made a new home.

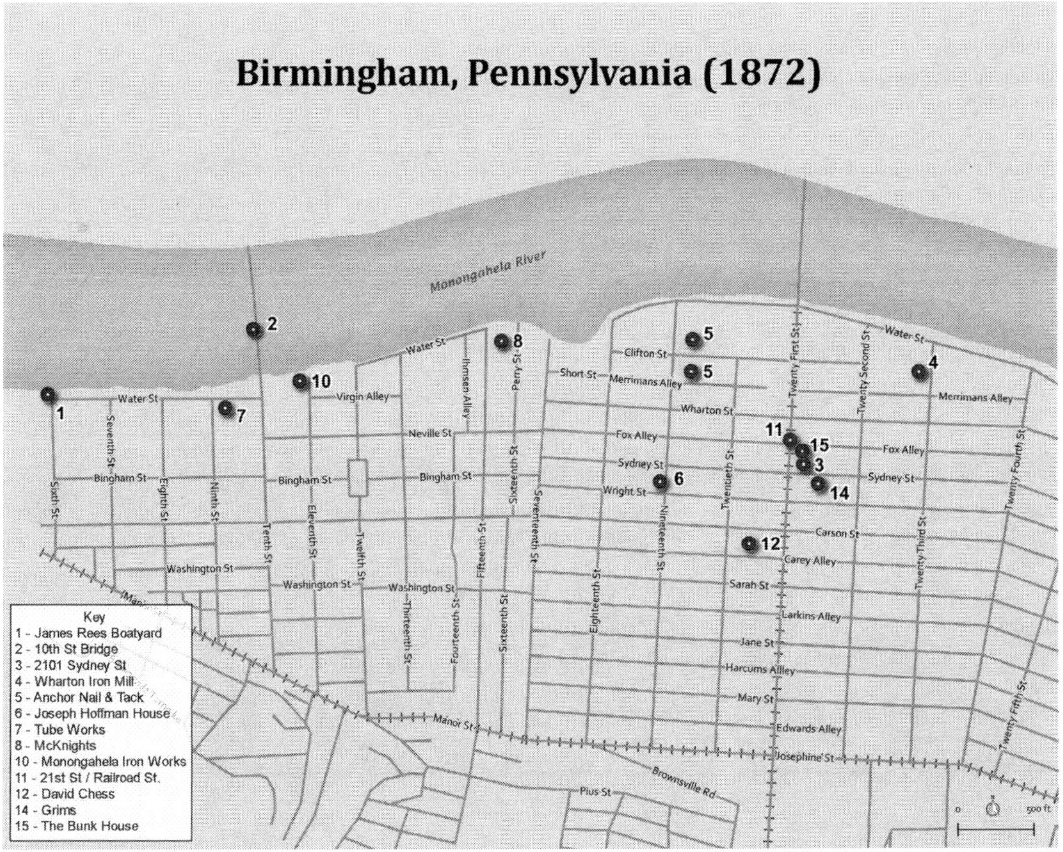
Birmingham, Pennsylvania (1872)
Monongahela River
Key
1 - James Rees Boatyard
2 - 10th St Bridge
3 - 2101 Sydney St
4 - Wharton Iron Mill
5 - Anchor Nail & Tack
6 - Joseph Hoffman House
7 - Tube Works
8 - McKnights
10 - Monongahela Iron Works
11 - 21st St / Railroad St.
12 - David Chess
14 - Grims
15 - The Bunk House
Water St
Sixth St
Seventh St
Eighth St
Ninth St
Tenth St
Eleventh St
Twelfth St
Thirteenth St
Fourteenth St
Fifteenth St
Sixteenth St
Seventeenth St
Eighteenth St
Nineteenth St
Twentieth St
Twenty First St
Twenty Second St
Twenty Third St
Twenty Fourth St
Twenty Fifth St
Bingham St
Washington St
Virgin Alley
Neville St
Ihmsen Alley
Perry St
Clifton St
Short St
Merrimans Alley
Wharton St
Fox Alley
Sydney St
Wright St
Carson St
Carey Alley
Sarah St
Larkins Alley
Jane St
Harcums Allley
Mary St
Edwards Alley
Josephine St
Manor St
Brownsville Rd
Pius St
0
500 ft

MAP 4.

Several blocks away from William Knowles, who was still living in the house where Sarah Ann was born and his son Captain Benjamin F. had died, Ollie Densmore lived on "Perry Nr. Carson" in East Birmingham.[78] He worked at Anchor Nail and Tack as an iron Roller. Recall that his peripatetic older brother Sam came and went according to work demands and wages—which remained high since iron railroad track that was destroyed as the Civil War raged was continually being replaced. The inevitable postwar recession was yet to come.

War generates a peak in Power Phase –related behaviors. Production is sped up, materials of war are destroyed nearly as quickly as they are produced, and men at war are not in the civilian labor force. That means work and, temporarily, more propitious wage conditions for the men and women who do not serve. It is also why lengthy wars unsettle a society—the extravagant costs of high-output war production, loss of life, and disruptions to daily normalcy and street-level economy are all deeply corrosive.

Sam had already started a family with his wife, Amanda "Jennie" Glenn. His precise comings and goings between Kittanning and Pittsburgh are unknown. He likely bunked with Ollie and Elizabeth while working in Birmingham. To get home he had only to cross the river on the Monongahela River Bridge at the foot of Tenth Street above Sidney Street and take a horse-drawn streetcar to the Allegheny Valley Railroad terminal in Lawrenceville. The train had only three stops before reaching the Kittanning station forty-four miles northeast of Pittsburgh. On that same train would pass more than a million barrels of Vandergrift oil between 1867 and 1878, in tank cars patented by the upstate Densmore brothers.

In the fall of 1864, Ollie and Elizabeth had their third child, baptized Henry Thomas Densmore.[79] Though "H. T." was the third child born to them, he was the first to live. Recall that their first child Charles had lived only three weeks, and their second, an unnamed daughter born in Birmingham, lived only a few hours. In fact, H. T. was one of only two children to survive to adulthood of the nine children born to them. America's once-low infant mortality bypassed them, probably due to a combination of environmental and genetic factors.

The wages were good at Anchor, but a fire closed part of the shop in mid-1864, so Ollie would have taken temporary work at McKnight's Birmingham Rolling Mill and Nail Works a few blocks northwest up Sidney Street, or at Wharton's Furnace a few blocks southeast. The combination of continuing wartime conscriptions and rising wartime orders meant the larger works needed all the skilled labor they could get. Both those larger works turned out iron rail during the Civil War. Anchor, in contrast, turned out shoe tacks and military hardware.

Meanwhile, East Birmingham had grown so rapidly as a consequence of the metal-production demands imposed by the Civil War that it is fair to characterize it as having rapidly morphed into a densely populated industrial ghetto cum toxic chemical waste dump. Birmingham's sewers were inadequate and, in places, non-existent. Unskilled workers lived in conditions similar to the deadliest of England's classic mill towns of the 1830s and 1840s. Clean water was a challenge. The smoke was so consuming that grim jokes of the time made reference to South Side's Birmingham and the Shades of Purgatory as one and the same.

But no sidewalk joke could compensate for the observable decline in every parent's dream—to see their children live, grow, and thrive. If America's original biological advantage, as had reigned from 1770 to 1830, had been sorely tested from the 1840s to the 1860s, it had gone straight to hell in South Side Pittsburgh between the mid-1860s and the late 1880s.

At What Cost?

South Side Pittsburgh and Birmingham were bounded on the east and northeast by the Monongahela and separated from farms and orchards six miles south toward Canonsburg by steep hills and a prominent ridgeline.[80] Its five square miles of unrivaled industrial might and residential crush in the mid-1860s and 1870s contained the highest concentration of highly skilled laborers of any place in the western hemisphere. It was the belly of New World iron-steel production, and virtually no other local industry rivaled it, with the possible exception of glass working. Neither was easy work. Most boat building had moved out to nearby areas where timber was closer and the riverfront less choked by lines of moored steamboats. In order to expand, several of the newer, huge mill complexes[81] had also exited Birmingham's crush.

If you were a good iron roller or puddler, characterized by labor historians as America's "princes" of skilled labor, the 1860s in Birmingham was the place to be.[82] Between 1850 and 1880 the population of Pittsburgh tripled. This far surpassed the growth of the nation, which had roughly doubled during that period.

It was already a struggle for the nation to provide basic infrastructure, water, and other essentials to a population that had grown from 23.2 million in 1850 to 38.5 million in 1870, a 70 percent increase. As population skyrocketed[83] the confined South Side "flats" district of Pittsburgh found it virtually impossible to keep up with public services.[84] Fresh, untainted water was a pressing problem. A safe sewage system was a dream. Deadly heavy metal waste was already an environmental reality. Chemicals like sulfur and cyanide seeped into the ground. Markets sold out of fresh food and produce by 8:00 a.m., and clean air was vanishing almost as quickly. Pittsburgh wasn't called "Old Smokey" for nothing.

In what had been East Birmingham,[85] all these practical problems intensified under explosive industrial output. Tuberculosis (consumption) became common, and typhus and cholera epidemics swept through with alarming regularity, disproportionately killing children and the elderly. House fires were frequent. Raw sewage flowed in the alleys. Altogether, the intense industrial noise and thick haze also contributed to a stressful environment. That stress wore people down. One could only rarely look up at night and see the stars or the northern lights. Those who fared best were rich or had country homes away from the city. The Densmore men bunked together in the bowels of South Side, but unlike many they had country refuges in Fairchance or Kittanning with in-laws.

In 1850 about 90 percent of Pittsburgh and South Side's population was native born. By 1880 that had dropped to about 68 percent as more immigrants moved to the city.[86] Immigration raised cultural issues, including animosity between Catholics and Protestants, (Slavic) language communication difficulties at work, and a flood of cheaper labor, enhancing competition for the less-skilled jobs. Over time this trend lowered wages for the less-skilled iron workers and made it much harder for longtime skilled employees to get their young sons placed in odd jobs around the mills.

An early-morning sidewalk view of Sidney Street in August of 1865 is grayer and darker than the summer world out there beyond the smoke and haze.[87] Coal ash from the mills leaves streaks on windows and grit on sidewalks, renders red brick facades a crusty mahogany, and creeps into every fold of clothing worn by the quiet, sweat-soaked men who pass by in loose groups. These men are not antisocial; they are simply bone tired, hungry, and dehydrated after their twelve-hour overnight shifts in the heat and noise of the mills. There is no after-work escape from the mills' relentless cacophony—it dominates Birmingham's daily life. The sharp sound of horseshoes on cobbles penetrates the background din. But normal conversation does not.

The veteran rollers and puddlers are easy to identify by the leathery, burnt-orange skin on their hands and faces—attributes peculiar to those who stand before furnace mouths and glowing ingots for years on end. Through the morning's August heat and billowing clouds of steam and ash pass horse-drawn carts full of produce, an occasional horse-powered streetcar, and dozens of handcarts making deliveries to the storefronts along Sidney Street. The scents of sulfur and horse manure mix with the yeasty aroma of fresh bread, cheap Conestoga cigars, and souring milk. Some men stop to purchase a "stogie" cigar with the new two-cent coins minted to accommodate Civil War inflation. Others, craving fluid and sugar, stop for lemonade. But most go directly to their nail-holed boardinghouses to strip off their sleeveless "work blues," take a quick "bucket" shower, then eat—ham, eggs, cornbread, fried potatoes, and fruit pies. Breakfast ends with tin tankards of cool water, lemonade, or coffee. Many decline the caffeine but refuel and chat with others at the table while their food settles. Then comes sleep . . . blessed sleep.

The boarding house veterans who pay on time get the quieter rear rooms. As they sleep, children spill into the streets when school lets out at 2:30 p.m. They yell, squeal, chase each other, and play at marbles, mumblety-peg, stick hoop, and hopscotch, oblivious to the adult world. After a few hours the children vanish and the men with bulging muscles, orange faces, leathery hands, and no sleeves return to the noise on the street. Within months the postwar depression will make these men remember this as their gloried "salad" days.

Chapter 13

Iron, Industrial Efficiencies, and Consequences

As the Civil War dawned, the North's industrial production ramped up the pace of output in anticipation. Workplaces became more dangerous, and new technologies began to drive daily wages downward. Recession-generated layoffs and shutdowns in 1860 and 1861 muted industrial output. Then, in April 1861, Fort Sumter fell, and the nation reversed course, demanding iron for rails, cannons, ship fittings, wagon axles, rifle barrels, and elaborate cannon balls. In short, the nation's core industries went from reverse gear to high gear—"pedal to the metal"—in a heartbeat. Production speed and long hours skyrocketed until technological efficiencies caught up. The rapid transition from reverse to a pedal-down, forward gear can blow an auto's transmission. In 1861 Birmingham's workers *were* that transmission. They and their families suffered in the 1860s from deteriorating work conditions, skyrocketing food costs, and ever larger, more efficient, less personal iron manufactories. War and its profits generated investments in more efficient industrial infrastructure, but it also led to declining investments in public infrastructure.

Age-wise, Pittsburgh as a whole was demographically young due to the "constant infusion of young men into the city and the dangerous nature of its dominant occupations."[1] In 1860 only 2.3 percent of Pittsburgh's residents were over the age of sixty-five, making the over-sixty-five population one-half to one-third of that found in other American cities. This was due to a combination of unaddressed public health issues: contagion, chemical toxicity, pulmonary ailments, and an alarming rate of work accidents in the mills.

When the war ended in the summer of 1865, industrial demand tanked, and a long period of deflation ensued. Food scarcity and its skyrocketing costs as well as absent breadwinners early in the war had impacted American-born babies in

1860. Many died in infancy. Those baby boys who did live to adulthood attained an average height of only 5'7.2", more than an inch shorter than boys born in 1830. As noted, the combined life expectancy of all American babies born in 1860 was 41.8 years—a bit better than the 38.3 years of 1850, but *fourteen years* shorter than children born in the 1790s.

Working life was both demanding and risky in the city's rolling mills, forges, metal shops, and glassworks. The dangers of industrial accidents and physical stress on the bodies of iron workers were stratospheric when compared to most other American industries. In one older, established working-class neighborhood across the river from Birmingham, widows headed 19 percent of households in 1870. In the mill districts, including Birmingham, widows headed 22 percent of households. In contrast, widows comprised only 10 percent of Pittsburgh's suburban households, home to the middle and professional classes. Those most likely to be maimed or killed were the mills' poorly paid, unskilled workers.[2] Their increasing presence on work floors from the 1860s through the 1890s actually made iron and glass work more dangerous for veteran and neophyte alike.

S. J. Kleinberg's impressive work *In the Shadow of the Mills*[3] makes the important inference that the higher rate of widows in the newer downtown was due primarily to natural aging given the older age structure of the upscale central business district near the Point. In contrast, the much younger overall average age of the population in Birmingham and other mill districts leads to Kleinberg's conclusion of untimely death for many mill workers as an explanation for the 22 percent of relatively young widows.[4]

Daily iron work risks included splattered molten steel, which was guaranteed to burn or blind, falling or shifting piles of coal, cooling ingots still hot enough to spit oxide crust that stuck to the skin and produced deep burns, and in-motion accidents, as when a "tosser" miscalculated a throw, hitting a helper with hot iron. Stacks of pig iron often fell, crushing nearby workers. Then there were the mechanical risks: the era's steam boilers powered machinery but often exploded—shrapnel and scalding water flying in every direction. The rolling presses also jammed at times, trapping extended arms and hands.

Astoundingly high noise levels led to destroyed hearing, which added huge risk, as warnings or commands might not be heard. Simply getting enough cool water to drink was also a daily challenge. Brigades of seven- and eight-year-old boys circulated constantly, carrying water buckets and ladles.[5] During the postwar depression, traditional "helper" jobs filled by grown men would be replaced with ten- to twelve-year-olds whose growth spurts, as the era's statistics suggest, were compromised.[6] The mills also exuded enormous quantities of uncaptured heat, a signature phenomenon of a Power Phase when efficiency has not caught up with the scalar increases in production or when technology lags. "Do not make heat" is the first rule of efficiency, as lost heat is useful and valuable energy lost.

"Efficiency," of course, is a formulaic construct requiring that whatever is being measured is specified. Efficiency and power are ratios of one to the other. They are not separate phenomena. Thus far we have looked at horses, wagons, and total calories needed to move a hundred-weight of cargo (simplified on table 7 to cost per pound) over a specified distance. However, in the case of the Pittsburgh mills of the 1860s, it's virtually impossible to calculate heat losses during the 1860s and 1870s in works like Anchor Nail and Tack. The data on daily coal consumption, net furnace efficiency, and temperature and weight of the "melt" that became iron simply do not exist. The data currently available are far too general to be useful, as known iron outputs are usually lumped into "Pennsylvania" or "Ohio" production reports published for the 1860s and 1870s.

Yet enough is known about the numbers of furnaces operating in Pittsburgh in the 1860s to estimate that stated daily furnace capacity was at least 20–25 percent higher than actual iron output. But well-defined annual efficiencies based on fuel, heat waste, and human labor calorie inputs, compared to tons of iron output, would have been much lower. No foundry or mill of that period managed to evade the realities of broken machinery, seasonally frozen coal that would not burn, boiler blowouts, missing crews, and so on. There were also macro-impediments: cyclic national markets, unstable order volume, and confined shipping seasons due to river ice or flood.[7] What we do know is that the frantic wartime rhythm of production during the Civil War was inefficient enough to extract costs in physical well-being from workers, their wives, and their children and also to waste huge quantities of heat. In Birmingham that waste heat contributed to its own deeply unhealthy microclimate.

Iron versus Steel: Higher Temperature and Faster Output

Iron railroad track proved not durable enough once wartime locomotives and their freight loads increased in size and tonnage. Under constant pounding, battering, compression, and hot-cold seasonal cycles, iron rails became brittle and failed quickly. In the 1860s a section of heavily used iron track often had to be replaced in a year or less. By the early 1870s it was clear that steel track lasted at least ten times longer than iron. This wear factor was a major stimulus in the nation's near-universal postwar adoption of steel track.

But Birmingham primarily made iron. Thus from 1865 to 1867, when the postwar recession struck and Birmingham's iron makers most needed work, the Pennsylvania Railroad built its own dedicated steel-track plant, drawing desperate longtime workers away from the traditional iron shops. Their proprietary Cambria Iron Works cut deeply into the postwar iron business in Pittsburgh, and the railroad's wage scale was much lower. Gearing up to produce steel track had also set the stage for huge new works on Pittsburgh's outskirts. Those works employed thousands of men, not the dozens or hundreds typical of Pittsburgh's traditional iron industry.

Raw data about large-scale industrial input and output in the iron and steel industry during the second half of the nineteenth century improved to a degree, but no one quite got past the furnace capacity versus actual furnace usage with enough detail to be definitive.[8] But a very rough estimate would show furnaces, nationally, producing at about 75–80 percent capacity when market demands were highest.

As the 1860s bore on, traditional iron works struggled to survive. The move to large-scale works required larger, more modern furnaces—often one hundred to two hundred in a single complex, as opposed to the typical Birmingham works of ten to thirty furnaces. Older specialty works faded in number as the capital needed to retool and scale up to enter Pittsburgh's new, high-grade iron and steel production, which spiraled upward at a breathtaking pace.

The Anchor Works and Ollie Densmore

Anchor Nail and Tack was among the specialty shops that got pushed around in the postwar economy. The Chess family founded it in 1842 while Old Robert Dunsmore was still alive.[9] The Oliphants of Georges Township were among the Chess brothers' first pig-iron suppliers to its first half-block-long, brick-walled works located on South Nineteenth Street in Birmingham. Those works were later moved a few blocks north to the Monongahela. Like most of the Vandergrifts, the prominent Chess family downplayed their wealth. They maintained their comfortable family residence and surrounding garden near the corner of John and Carson Street in Birmingham through most of the factory's life.[10]

Anchor Nail and Tack's brand was a circled anchor. Later it streamlined and modernized its name to "Anchor." It specialized in nails and tacks from the 1840s through the 1860s, when wartime specialties were also produced. By the 1870s and 1880s, it had already reorganized several times to bring in capital and upgrade machinery. It branched out into angle irons, industrial hinges, thin-rolled corrugated plates for interior factory walls, and many specialty items for builders, cabinet makers, and carpenters. Among the latter were ships carpenters like the Vandergrifts. Anchor brand nails and tacks were held in nearly as high a regard in the market of the 1850s and 1860s as were Oliphant's nails. That is no surprise, as Oliphant's Fairchance works supplied some of the pig iron used at Anchor. The Chess family did not cut quality on raw materials. But it was their smaller tacks that absolutely dominated shoe repair and manufacture in the Ohio Valley markets. Those tack heads did not snap off under the stresses of walking like those made of inferior, more brittle iron.

Anchor was one of the smaller works to survive the post–Civil War era. It was agile in adapting to competition from massive operations like Jones and Laughlin. It carefully judged its markets—nails, tacks, and specialty-pressed sheet iron or tin-plated iron—and declined to take on the giants. High-quality, precision-made products, the most efficient and experienced workmen, and frugality in recirculating scrap metal all combined to see it through. In short, it successfully exploited a production niche from which the emerging "Big Boys" and their unskilled labor could not make a profit. Those massive combines were all about efficiencies of large scale and cheap labor. Anchor could not scale up easily, so it exploited a niche theoretically too small to matter to the "bigger and cheaper" crowd, initially paying higher wages to its rollers and puddlers. Ironically, this strategy did matter to the big-box iron and steel manufacturers, who continually bullied and manipulated small shops to pay ever-lower industry wage scales.

On Anchor's factory floor, for nearly thirty-eight years, in good times and in bad, sweating, lifting, pulling, and carefully easing ingots of hot iron through the massive roll trains, stood Old Robert's youngest son, F. H. O. Densmore. Ollie stood a bit over 5'9" and in his prime weighed a bear-like 185–195 pounds, much of it upper-body muscle. Erect bearing, dark-brown hair, penetrating gray eyes, and a quiet confidence all added to his presence.

Already an experienced young roller when he arrived in late 1861,[11] Ollie was a stalwart fellow quite like many others who came to Pittsburgh from many of the long-established countryside iron works. What he did not know about rolling out nail and tack sheets from Fidelio Hughes Oliphant's operation in

Fairchance, he learned quickly at Anchor. And he must have been highly reliable, for in the ensuing decades when business slowed down, the Chess family usually kept him on the payroll as a "laborer," even when the roll trains were shut down.

Ollie's solid status is easily evaluated from Thurston's Pittsburgh city directories of the era. In 1864 Ollie was a roller at Anchor Nail and Tack, living at Perry near Carson; in 1865 he was a catcher, living at Centre below Bingham. In 1866 he was a recession-era "laborer,"[12] living at Sarah near John.[13] This tells us that Ollie rented or boarded near Anchor. Elizabeth and their son H. T. might or might not have lived with him. H. T. was born in Allegheny County, but his mother likely took him to healthier Fairchance. If they did not live with Ollie full-time, he could work more of the fabled overnight "long-turn" shifts.

During the Civil War, demand for Anchor's products was high. From 1861 to 1865 the US quartermaster bought immense quantities of shoe tacks from Anchor for Union troops. The government also bought special fittings and hinges for cannon caissons, horse-drawn ambulances, and the like.

Then the postwar slump took hold. In 1866 Ollie worked only two-thirds of the year at Anchor. Many of his shifts were at lower pay, and not all of them were on the roll trains. Many veterans were furloughed, and a machinery revamp was in process. Military needs were "out." Rebuilding factories, railroad stations, storehouses, and mills destroyed in the border states during the war were "in." Ollie returned to Fairchance in late fall of 1866, most likely to find alternative employment at Oliphant's. By March of 1867 Elizabeth was pregnant again, and a fourth child was born to them. Her name was Jane, after Ollie's older sister. Born December 14, 1867, Jane lived only six weeks and died January 28, 1868.

Ollie returned to a newly equipped and reenergized Anchor, taking longer shifts. The ordinary work shift in this era was six days a week for eleven to twelve hours a day—a basic sixty- to seventy-hour week. Demanding, but not considered extraordinary in that era.

It is not known if Elizabeth remained in Fairchance or returned to Birmingham with him that winter. Four children had been born to her, and only one still remained alive—H. T., now age three and a half. Ollie and Elizabeth must have blamed their lost children on poor conditions in Pittsburgh, else an aged Ollie would not have insisted his granddaughter, Elsie Elizabeth Densmore, record every child born, with dates *and* place of birth in Fayette or Allegheny County.[14]

Ollie, like many men from unknowns to a young Teddy Roosevelt, drowned his sorrows in work, taking every shift he could get, including the eighteen- to twenty-hour "long turns" once a week as crews rotated in and out of the works. The Anchor works included puddling furnaces: heating furnaces used to bring iron up to a temperature where it could be worked. The work floor also contained about 160 nail and tack cutting/forming machines. There were twenty-four single puddling furnaces, four heating and two annealing furnaces, and five roll trains. Four of those roll trains were for hot-rolled iron; the other was for cold-rolled iron.[15]

These rolling presses operated rather like old-fashioned washing machines with the hard rubber rollers atop the washing drum. Those household rolls pressed most of the water out of the freshly washed clothes before they were hung outside to dry. In the iron roller's press, the rolls, made of heat-treated steel, both thinned and shaped the metal passing through and squeezed out any remaining impurities.

Estimating from an output capacity noted in a steel and iron trade newspaper of 1901, the Anchor plant, at full tilt, likely produced about twenty-five thousand large boxes of nails and tacks annually in the 1860s. After the war nail production likely increased while shoe tack production likely decreased.[16]

While Ollie obviously operated a nail-cutting machine when work slowdowns reduced the need for the thin sheet iron from which those machines cut the nails, his main job as a roller was to form the iron sheets—literally slide them through the huge mechanical presses and their hardened "rolls" hour after hour, day after day, week after week. Sweating, lifting, pushing, and using sound and feel, he relied on experience gained since age fourteen when his father, Old Robert, had died. By the 1860s he knew how to do it perfectly, safely, and rhythmically.

Those huge, chilled-steel overhead rolls had a heartbeat, a pulse, a presence of their own. If one listened for that heartbeat, perfect sheets emerged, no one got hurt, and no fanfare was made. One had but to match the rhythm of the machinery. Trusted helpers oiled them. Water boys carried fresh buckets of water to the rolling lines. Those rolling lines at Anchor were each fed by four furnaces. From them, the puddler's long tongs pulled balls of molten iron, working them tediously to homogenize the forming metal's components according to the characteristics of the ore being melted and the quality of the coal.

The puddler's assistant then passed the hot, worked iron to the "bloom boys," who operated mechanical squeezers. Then they were tossed into the rolls, where massive pressure and pass after pass gradually flattened them. These skilled iron men were like doctors with a stethoscope, a thermometer, and lab samples. They listened, felt, checked color and density, and took the pulse of the iron they were making. Healthy iron cooled to cherry red, with low surface scaling and a cohesive consistency. At this stage in the industrial evolution of iron making, all players were irreplaceable: furnace loaders, puddlers, bloom boys, roughers, rollers, then catchers, who tossed the sheets of rolled iron back to the roller for more thinning. If your goal in America was to work hard, work smart, be rewarded for your skills, and have the autonomy to use those skills to make genuine production decisions for an owner who you actually knew, a place like the Anchor works on Birmingham's South Nineteenth Street was where you wanted to work.

In the 1860s Anchor, now located on the Monongahela, still had only two roll trains. One was a "three high, twenty-four incher," and while Anchor employed about two hundred men and boys regularly, there were at most a dozen rollers on their contract list to run the roll trains. Steadfastly reliable and work-obsessed, twenty-four-year-old Ollie remained on the payroll in the lean times from 1867 to 1868. During that recession he bought more land in Fairchance at a favorable price.

In 1867, during the even more deeply depressed iron market, Ollie branched out into other factory roles: nailing machines, cold-rolled plate, catcher, and heater. He likely took shifts at other nearby works as they were offered. His early years at Oliphant's Works in Fairchance had made him quite versatile.

During one of the traditional work breaks—the "spells" between "heats"—I see Ollie dressed in his faded canvas Levi's and work-blue shirt. He leans against the shop's long north wall, chugging water and munching on homemade jerky or peach leather. The Monongahela, muddy and slow like a stubborn ox in the summer's dry season, now runs fast just thirty yards away. Over his left shoulder he can see the Tenth Street Bridge straddling the Monongahela. Beyond, just visible in the haze, are the iron arches of Roebling's steel chain suspension bridge. It had replaced the first Smithfield Street bridge, which was made of wood and completed in 1818—the same bridge project that had employed several of the Vandergrift boys, now aging men, living in Birmingham.

The early evening's gentle April breeze momentarily parts the haze, and he can observe the work going on in William Knowles Vandergrift's skiffyard just two long blocks away to his left, but his mind is on Elizabeth and his son H. T.—life seems so fragile. A steamboat's horn jolts him out of the moment. The shore in front of Ollie is crowded with a dozen riverboats tied up, most belching smoke. He pulls his brass-cased watch from his jeans' watch pocket, sighs, and returns to the cold-roll train awaiting its evening dinner of mild steel.

Ollie's whole world is comprised of noise, heat, smoke, and work. He burns about 4,000 calories per day in pure work, and another 1,400 calories are needed to maintain his metabolism and body weight. The price of meat has risen, even though most commodities have fallen in price. Still, he has no complaints. He is earning about three dollars per day.

This wage was much lower than the $4.50 a day of 1866 and the $5 a day during the early 1860s. But Ollie is a saver. Whatever the job assignment, however long his shift, Ollie draws his pay and saves much of it. Not a big drinker, perhaps even close to a teetotaler, and no girlfriend on the side, he saves. And works. And saves. *Work, eat, sleep, save* has become the anthem of his life. Ollie has a second child on the way with his beloved Elizabeth.

Elizabeth Goldsboro Densmore

About 4'10" tall and roughly ninety-five pounds, Elizabeth (Goldsboro) Densmore had high cheekbones and a regal quality, as described by Elsie Densmore. And, Elsie often noted, she "looked like an Indian." Whispers of Elizabeth's Indian blood passed back and forth across four generations in this line of Densmores. Ollie made certain that his granddaughter noted elements of Elizabeth's life, too, and that of Elizabeth's father, Old Thomas Goldsboro, who had eloped with her mother in 1829 when they were nineteen and fourteen years old, respectively.

That branch of the Goldsboros had settled on the Potomac near Harper's Ferry in the 1750s, and descendants had drifted south to the Youghiogheny in the Friendsville and Selbysport area by 1800. Elizabeth's mother, Elizabeth Ryland, was born in 1815 to John Ryland, son of a legendary Sylvester Ryland who, in the 1770s, had settled in the geopolitical tangle that is now western Maryland, far northern West Virginia, and southern Pennsylvania.[17] Their enclosed world, centered on the Youghiogheny River, had been encircled by the Allegheny Mountains and virgin forests, as well as displaced Shawnee and Delaware, who had been successively agitated by the French or English since the 1730s.

It is entirely possible that Ollie's Elizabeth carried some Native American genes acquired when one or another of the Ryland women were carried off as prisoners of war in the late 1700s. Ollie's Elizabeth was born either in Confluence, Pennsylvania,[18] or in Selbysport, Maryland.[19] Another source says she was born on Ryland's Hill about two miles northwest of Friendsville, Maryland, though it's most likely that it was Elizabeth's mother, also named Elizabeth, who was born on Ryland's Hill.

What mattered most to Ollie was that his Elizabeth was calm, warm, and steady, just like his own older sister Elizabeth, who, with her husband Nehemiah, had raised him. Ollie was only five when Elizabeth spent nearly half of Old Robert's pension money to buy their mother a house on the National Road. There she could convalesce, relieved of the burden of caring for others or enduring another pregnancy. For Ollie, his sister Elizabeth must have been the mother figure he actually bonded with.

Ollie retained a strong sense of family obligation his whole life. He attended to the history of his in-laws as carefully as if they had been Densmores, dictating names, places, locations of the forges and furnaces where the Goldsboro men had once worked, and details of Old Thomas Goldsboro's elopement with his wife's mother in 1829. His granddaughter Elsie took that dictation and wrote down the elements. Family letters also filled in some details.

The Rylands were a force in the Youghiogheny River district, as were the Friends, Frazees, Listons, Coddingtons, Lowdermilks, and other early settlers. They had settled in a land of tall timber, ginseng, snakeroot, black bear, panther, and eastern woodlands buffalo. They farmed, tanned buckskin, rolled peach leather, and tended maple sugar camps on a frontier that lingered until the National Road project began in 1811.[20] By 1818 the road had finally begun to open their southern perimeter to an outside world.

The Rylands' homeland had still not fully opened when Old Robert drove his wagon through the snows in 1800. The packhorse captains still reigned there until the early 1820s, when it began to transform. Many wagons, and huge herds of pigs, sheep, and cattle, passed along the National Road. Numerous wagon stands, blacksmith shops, and inns opened from the 1820s through the 1840s, bringing in newcomers, more cash and barter business, and new diseases.

When Ollie's father-in-law Thomas Goldsboro took a shine to his Elizabeth Ryland, he was working at the forge on Bear Creek, which empties into the Youghiogheny at Friendsville. She was just a girl of about fourteen with little formal schooling, but they were in love, and Elizabeth Ryland proved to be the Youghiogheny River version of a southern "Steel Magnolia." When they ran off together, her father, John Ryland, was mightily vexed. To say that Thomas and Elizabeth were merely in "hot water" would be an epic understatement.

First they fled Maryland, heading into western Virginia. There Thomas worked at Muddy Creek Forge near Albright, now West Virginia, where it empties into the Cheat River. Three and a half years later, in the early fall of 1832, and two forges later, Elizabeth and Thomas felt it was time to return to her family. With her infant at her breast, she mounted a horse provided by Thomas's brothers. Thomas, then twenty-two or twenty-three years old, walked behind the brightly beribboned horse, as was the custom in old-time marriages. He carried no rifle, no tomahawk or belt knife. Together they made their way along the old Morgantown Road and back to the Ryland homestead near the Youghiogheny. Thomas was subdued, if not nervous. As they approached John Ryland's porched cabin, word spread quickly of their impending arrival. John, well-known as a sharpshooter, a Pennsylvania rifle cradled in the crook of his arm, spied his daughter holding his grandchild and set the rifle down, nodding for them to approach the porch.

Some oral versions of this event assert that they were forgiven by the family and "remarried" in the little Methodist church at Selbysport by a Ryland or Glenn pastor. That church still stands on the left side of the road as one drives north from Friendsville toward the Pennsylvania border. Thomas, it is said, wore his black Sunday coat and matching pants. Elizabeth wore a russet gingham dress and moccasins, ribbons in her hair.

When Ollie married their daughter Elizabeth in 1860, he did not marry merely a woman. He married a tradition and a family, and an old frontier one at that, for even George Washington had stayed several times with a "Goldsberry" ancestor on the Potomac[21] in the 1780s.

This branch of the Goldsboros also knew and made iron. They even knew and traded with the younger sons of John Hart, signer, who had moved to the Maryland / western Virginia frontier in the 1790s. Several of John Hart's younger sons had settled down in what is now Randolph County, West Virginia, a few miles and a thousand feet above Philippi, where a number of them still live. Just eighteen months after Ollie's marriage to Elizabeth in 1860, the Hart brothers, astride the narrow mountain road to Winchester and Baltimore, on July 11, 1861, warned the Union troops of a possible ambush from Confederate forces. Their farm, established about 1795 on the slopes of Rich Mountain, became part of the first battleground of the Civil War.

Birmingham—Making Iron

Back at the Anchor works, the remainder of Ollie's long turns pass in a swirl of noise and heat as the night wears on. Hot iron and huge overhead rolls groan.

"Stay alert," he tells himself. In later days he would repeatedly admonish his sons and grandsons likewise: "The alert avoid injury"; "No injury means no break in pay, son." At 7:00 a.m. the dangerous turn that so often injured the drowsy, unskilled helpers is over, and Ollie makes his sweat-soaked way back to his rented room on Fox Alley, East Birmingham. We do not know the actual alley address, but the narrower alleyways behind the row houses facing major streets teemed with rental rooms where iron workers boarded. The room comes with a boarding house breakfast—usually pork, eggs, potatoes, and either corn or buckwheat cakes. Boardinghouse commodes consisted of pottery bedpans and a reeking outhouse tucked into a corner of what had once been a backyard garden in the 1840s and 1850s. On this early April morning, it is chilly enough to subdue the scent of close quarters.

Recent spring rains have temporarily washed the worst of human and industrial wastes into the Monongahela. Winter and spring are Birmingham's consumption season,[22] when tubercular lungs often give out. It is also the season of domestic fires, as the heat of winter's continuous coal hearths and stoves slowly transform roofs, floor joists, and timbers abutting chimneys from wood into more flammable, low-grade charcoal. At least there is no cholera or yellow fever,[23] which thrive in warmer weather.

Ending the long turn, Ollie eats to prevent the shakes,[24] drinks more water, then sleeps eight to nine hours. On rising he will eat heavily, grab his food pail, then walk back to Anchor for the new week's evening turn of twelve hours, from 5:00 p.m. to 5:00 a.m.—easy physically, but harder emotionally as it gives him more time to think. It has only been nine weeks since little Jane died in Fairchance. Three of four babies have not lived. "Why?" he asks himself. Is it this damned smoking furnace called Birmingham? Or is something wrong with me? With Elizabeth?

It is unlikely that Elizabeth was with him in Birmingham that April. She was likely with her parents in Fairchance, where the Goldsboros ran a general store[25] and had built up savings as sutlers to the Union army during the Civil War.[26] Elizabeth was again worn out and depressed by the loss of another child. Unlike Birmingham, in Fairchance she had a wide network of friends and family, among them the Warmans, Carrs, Prices, Wilsons, Artises, Pastoriuses, and Goldsboros, to ease her way. She also had her one living son, little H. T., then three and a half years old, to care for. Best to keep him in Fairchance where the air was fresher, the water cleaner, and diphtheria infrequent.

In the spring of 1868, Anchor had rebuilt after the devastating fire that consumed much of the works in 1867. Running full-tilt after taking on new partners and an infusion of investor cash, the works began rolling thin iron panels used to roof factories and warehouses destroyed in the South during the war. Ollie's elder brother Sam, already a familiar figure at Anchor, had again come down from Kittanning. He bunked with Ollie long enough to wind up in Diffenbacher's Pittsburgh directory.[27] His address is listed as Fox Alley, East Birmingham. His wife, Jennie Glenn, remained on the family place near Kittanning, an outlying settlement of primarily Scots-Irish residents known as Slabtown. Their family, unlike Ollie's, was growing, and Sam needed more work at better pay than in Kittanning. He lists his occupation as "laborer." But above all else his true mete was as a master fixer, innovator, and assembler of complex machinery. In this postwar period, Anchor Nail and Tack was reorganizing and replacing machinery to diversify its products as an antidote to the loss of large military orders. Sam's primary role would have involved modifications to Anchor's machinery.

On weeks when Anchor did not need him, Sam likely worked at Birmingham Iron and Steel, McKee's Works, or Wharton's Rolling Mill, all just blocks away. Sam's work in Birmingham brought in enough money to support his well-fed family near Kittanning. Other cash and food came from the family farm there.[28] Ollie's wages also covered his typical room and board of about $4.50 per week, and he, too, would have sent household money to Elizabeth. The rest went into the bank.

The Roller

By the end of 1869, just six weeks shy of his twenty-ninth birthday, Ollie had already worked at least 1,600 shifts at Anchor, which adds up to about 17,400 hours.[29] About $450[30] of his wages resided in the bank. The post–Civil War depression eased up a bit, so his earnings had gone up again by about fifty cents a day. As a roller, Ollie was a semi-independent contractor. He had control of his rolling line, and he chose his crew from among those accepted by the Chess brothers and others for whom he lobbied to be added to Anchor's roster. The roller not only selected the crew but was paid, as was the puddler, by Anchor for the volume, in tons, of rolled product produced: nail sheets, specialty plates, and hinge and hanger stock. The roller then paid his crew, each according to a negotiated scale approved by Anchor, a growing union movement, and the increasingly intrusive Big Boys of iron steel.

As paymaster Ollie occasionally also made short-term loans to regular members of his crew. They usually returned about twenty-five to fifty cents as interest if the payback lingered past a pay period. Such extras obsessively went into Ollie's special fund in the bank. Maintaining a formal log of work and pay was his obligation as a roller, but this habit of keeping weekly records and recording household costs would be passed to several more generations of his direct descendants.[31]

Meanwhile life was beginning to look up in other ways. On April 7, 1869, another son named William[32] had been born in Fayette County to Ollie and Elizabeth. As of Christmas 1869, little "Will" was thriving. For safety's sake Elizabeth and her two boys mostly remained in Fairchance. In late fall of 1870, both boys were still doing well, and Elizabeth was pregnant again. For his growing family, Ollie had purchased more rural land in the depression market of 1867 to 1868 and built or enlarged a home[33] in Fairchance near the Oliphant's Works.

On the much-referenced 1872 map of Fayette County, Pennsylvania, Ollie's house is marked clearly as that of "O. Densmore." Nearby lived their friends and families, the Carrs, Prices, Warmans, and Goldsboros. Ollie and Elizabeth had become homeowners, a milestone for workingmen of that era. A two-story place in Fairchance, it came to be known as "the homestead." Likely built about 1840, its massive log innards had been covered by locally planed "weatherboard," and a pretty front porch was added later. It had started as a squared log house, so its rooms were wide but shallow. Tall and lean captures the essence. It may have been the very house that Old Robert and his sons once rented in the 1840s and 1850s.

Finally, Elizabeth had a permanent place, a relief, as her father Tom Goldsboro's house was full with three generations under its roof. Now she and her two boys had more than an acre to spread out on. The grassy areas were dotted with an outhouse, a large shed, one cow, and one sheep to keep the grass under control. Two apple and two peach trees graced the side yard (see photo).

The 1870 Census

Though the image of a house and garden in the village of Fairchance surrounded by supportive kinfolk is warm and pleasing, that scene is contested by the content of several hard, cold documents. The 1860s had exacted a very dear price on the families of Old Robert's children. Ollie and Elizabeth were not the only ones to lose children to early deaths.

Nat and his wife Susan (Rager) lost their daughter Hannah in October 1869. Born 1851 and barely eighteen years old, young Hannah died of scrofula from infected milk drunk in childhood. That meant she had spent a childhood and adolescence scarred by disfigurement and fragile health. If she had been able to attend a barn dance in her early teens, it would likely have been a Warman, Goldsboro, or Carr male cousin who invited her to dance. Hopefully the fiddle and banjo music and a partner, even an uncle, would have given her some moments of delight. Her death is registered on a Fayette County roll dated October 1870. On that yellowed sheet she endures as merely an entry, another small footnote in an era when child death rates increased.

There are other footnotes, surprises, and mysteries yielded up in the US Census rolls of 1870 for the Densmores, as well as for the Harts and Vandergrifts. In Allegheny County in 1870, it appears that some recorders either got a very early start on the census visits or misunderstood some of the Census Bureau's instructions on whom to count. They were supposed to count family members who had not died by January 1870, but it was a complex two-sentence instruction that some recorders may have misunderstood: "The name of every person whose place of abode on the first day of June, 1870, was in this family."[34]

In contrast, the June 1870 Census of Georges Township went smoothly. Former cavalry man Robert Jr., forty-one; his wife, Elizabeth Carr,[35] thirty-seven; and their children, John Robert, nineteen, Mary, fourteen, Elizabeth, thirteen, and Sallie, eleven, are living on the outskirts of Fairchance, about a half mile or so from Oliphant's Works. Robert Jr. worked there as a roller, as did his son John Robert. That meant their family earned two decent daily wages, which made them fortunate in that era, especially with the "down" weeks on account of the rudderless postwar national economy. Robert Jr. is still listed as unable to read and write, but his wife and children are listed as able to do both. The Commonwealth's public school law of the 1830s had begun to accomplish its intended mission.

Ollie and his family were not censused in Birmingham, nor is Ollie listed in the 1870 Pittsburgh directory. Instead he is censused in Fairchance with Elizabeth and their three children: Harry T., born 1864; William, born 1869; and, mysteriously, Jane, listed as age four despite the fact that she died in late 1868 or 1869. Also surprising is Ollie's granddaughter Elsie's handwritten death date for her as January 28, 1868. So, why was a deceased child listed on the 1870 census?[36]

Perhaps the census taker scrambled his info, or a depressed Elizabeth and Ollie could not concede the loss of another daughter they so badly wanted. To add even more mystery, no record of Jane's grave, or a headstone, has been located. She is the only child of Ollie and Elizabeth who survived a month or more for whom a grave has not turned up.

Ollie's sister Elizabeth and her husband Nehemiah Warman were no longer living three doors away that summer. Instead they appear in the 1870 Census of East Birmingham, Allegheny County. Nehemiah's name in that census has been mangled rather impressively, for he is listed as "Nicolas Wornom."[37] On that page the census taker did not note the street being censused, so their precise residence cannot be pinpointed. A reasonable guess would be in the Fox Alley area where Ollie had previously roomed.

Nehemiah, listed as age forty-eight, was working as an iron "heater" (puddler). His sons, George, age sixteen, and Samuel, age thirteen, are both working in the "W . . . Rolling mill."[38] This "W" mill is almost certainly Wharton Brothers Rolling Mill near the intersection of Caroline Street and the Monongahela waterfront in Birmingham. His wife, the "steady" Elizabeth Densmore, is forty-four. Their daughters Hannah, twenty-four, and Mary, eighteen, both live with them. Several blocks away live Nehemiah's brother, Bartholomew, and his family from the Morgantown, West Virginia, area. He was also working in an iron mill, likely alongside Nehemiah at Wharton's.

Ollie's brother Sam is also listed in Thurston's 1870 city directory as a laborer in East Birmingham,[39] though no explicit address is noted. His family—Jennie and their children—were still in Kittanning; they were recorded there that year as having attended services at St. Paul's Lutheran Church. The oldest Densmore brother, Nat, still resided in Brownsville, mourning over his daughter Hannah's passing. As urban crowding, public schools, and widely used public transport continued to increase, so did infant deaths due to childhood diseases. By the late 1870s postpartum childhood health risks were actually higher than in the 1770s.

Well-Being and Worldviews

As surprising as it is that Ollie was back in Fairchance on census day while the Warmans were in Birmingham, there were complex currents at work in 1870. And those currents flowed in the direction of increasingly rapid change. In 1870 America's traditional family network and local church-based society was again being tested by the ever-greater scale of things, increasingly diverging wealth, and declining well-being. Citizens at opposite ends of the nation's rapidly diverging spectrum of prosperity lived very different daily realities of personal autonomy and well-being. That fueled dramatically different worldviews. Traditional communities of memory were fragmenting, and mutual interests became a bit less mutual among different segments of society. "Belonging" to a family, city, or community took on new contexts.

As noted, the 1870 Census places Ollie in Fairchance. That, coupled with the fact that traditional iron mills were going through rapid changes, contests the published family record[40] of Ollie's thirty-eight years of unbroken work at Anchor Nail and Tack.[41] Based on census documents and city directories, Ollie was not at Anchor during part of 1870. In addition, business abstracts appearing in iron and steel reports clearly stated that the Anchor works was twice almost entirely destroyed by fire, once in 1864[42] and again in 1866 or 1867.[43]

It is possible that Ollie worked at Anchor in each of those thirty-eight years, but not year-round every year. Living in Fairchance in 1870, or part of 1870, he likely worked for Oliphant at a lower, countryside wage, while Nehemiah and his brothers Robert Jr. and Sam worked Pittsburgh for every cent they could get. This was not a new phenomenon. Fayette, Greene, Westmoreland, Washington, Beaver, and Armstrong counties had already been sending its men seasonally to Pittsburgh and Youngstown for most of the century.

The wage benefits of the 1870 work year in Pittsburgh for Robert Jr., Sam, and the Warmans appears to have enabled them to buy or build houses in Fairchance or up the Monongahela in nearby West Virginia. That work would also have dramatically enhanced their home communities' perception of their skills, for in the world of iron they had played their chips at the Big Table in "Old Smokey." Among skilled workingmen they had become players.

Sam Densmore's work with machines, rolls, presses, industrial vent fans, and every type of steam-driven engine imaginable would take him to a new personal pinnacle by 1880. In that year he is advertised in trade magazines as the manager of the repair shop for Connellsville Coke and Iron Works, supporting the massive coke-oven operations opened up at Leisenring, near Connellsville.[44] He was one of only six employees named in those notices, the others being the senior officers of the company. He had likely earned some of those street credits revamping machinery at works like Anchor after fires in the 1860s, and again in 1870 and 1871, as Anchor shifted to a new product mix, added another roll train, and took on new partners. By the 1880s he was also well-known in Youngstown, Ohio, and Celoron, New York.

While in Fairchance during part of 1870, Ollie may have helped the Oliphant Works make the impending transition to new ownership under Henry C. Frick and associates as the iron-steel magnates waited like vultures to capture the brand's legendary quality and bully its highly skilled local laborers into ever lower wages. Whatever the details, within several years the new owners of Oliphant's Fairchance Iron Works had both lowered wages and doubled production outputs from ten tons a day to twenty.[45]

On March 16, 1870, about a hundred employees requested the Oliphants' presence in the mill's main workroom to honor the aging iron master, Fidelio Hughes Oliphant.[46] His namesake, Ollie Densmore, was there for the legendary iron man's retirement. Spiced apple punch flowed freely as lubricant for the formal toasts offered. F. H. Oliphant had long forbidden whiskey or apple jack in or around his forge and furnace. He not only detested alcohol and tobacco, he thought them dangerous in the work places. Alcohol led to lethargic reactions, so it was dangerous. A lit stogie[47] distracted a man catching iron, he claimed. How a man lived off-shift was never considered the Oliphants' business, but once in the Oliphant yard, there were rules: no drinking, no smoking, and no fighting. Chew and snuff were also discouraged, though the men were free to cuss—so long as religious figures were omitted.[48]

In spite of these strict rules, F. H. and his sons John and Bert were loved by the crews. They produced a quality product, played fairly by imposing no brutal shifts, used the "long turn" only when essential, and provided huge quantities of food and necessities at discount to retail through the Works's own farm several miles up the Georges Valley. Those commodities had been delivered in lieu of wages at a modest discount when there was no cash in the region during the economic miseries of the 1830s and 1840s, and again during the late 1860s when inflation, followed by recession, upended family food budgets. One can only imagine the jolting changes to come once the sociopathically grasping Henry C. Frick became owner of Oliphant's Works in 1870 or 1871. In fact, he far surpassed the reputation of merely a bad boss to become one of the most hated men in America. By 1892 that hatred, as we shall see, was well earned.

By mid-1870 many mills and furnaces were being revamped in the iron capitols. In 1867, as noted, the Pennsylvania Railroad Company, already an economic and political behemoth, had reacted to the steel- versus iron-track longevity issue by demanding *only* steel track. The railroad's own in-house Cambria plant near Johnstown and another near Harrisburg would soon pass into the combine that became Bethlehem Steel. Other massive conglomerates were forming at the same time.

The hunger for steel had meant a sudden depression in the sale of iron pigs and ingots, despite the fact that steel simply could not be produced fast enough. Many smaller, family-owned iron mills in western Pennsylvania found themselves disadvantaged by both new financial stresses and aging technology. The value of their pig iron was in the doldrums, and high-grade steel was in short supply. They needed money to retool. Anchor took on new Manhattan-based investors and morphed into Chess, Smythe, & Co. around 1880.

The rapid speed at which steel could be produced in newer Bessemer and open-hearth furnaces ran counter to a century of existing work culture. These factors gave the emerging big-box steel combines enormous power that they abused in every way imaginable. They bought large quantities of iron pigs well below production costs, then "dumped" them in flamboyant market fixing. Their obedient bankers denied credit to the small shops, and expensive worker "skills" were engineered out of their production lines. The world of iron and steel was rapidly bifurcating into massive combines and works staffed by 500 to 2,500 workers and a fading world of smaller family or partner-owned specialty works employing 25 to 200 workers. As intended, the capital needed to fund upgrades was simply not available to most of the smaller owners.

Like the mid- to late 1860s, the 1870s were yet another era of cash and coin scarcity on main streets nearly everywhere. Economists know this as the Long Depression of 1873 to 1879. As virtually every coin collector knows, US coinage with dates in the 1872–1879 period are scarce, and that was precisely the coinage needed by main street America. As in the 1830s the lion's share of it was held in big East Coast banks.

A major family food dilemma had been created when the Union Army's massive consumption drove pork and beef prices through the roof. The nation's price of a pound of pork had spiked 170 percent by 1865. After the war, its price gradually declined through the 1870s depression, but it was still 10 percent more expensive in depressed 1880 than it had been in 1860. The price trends for a pound of beef were almost identical. Many households, priced out of generous portions of pork and beef, turned to chicken, beans, and buckwheat meal. Thus, those commodities also rose in price and stayed comparatively expensive throughout the Long Depression, even as daily wages declined. Despite depression, overall food prices rose about 13 percent between 1864 and 1880. In short, the percentage of total family income spent on food rose significantly in the midst of depression, and the cost of protein rose the most.[49]

The Long Depression and its trajectory of declining wages but stubbornly high food prices throughout the 1870s contributed to measurable consequences. American-born boys born in 1870 attained an adult height of 5'7.4", a two-tenths of an inch gain from 1860, possibly because the depression of October 1873 did not impinge on their first several years of childhood. Boys born in 1880, at the end of the depression and its deeply declining wages, would only grow up to attain an average adult height of 5'6.7", more than *two* full inches shorter than American-born boys when the Declaration was signed, and 2.5 inches shorter than their grandfathers born in 1830. Their sisters and their life expectancies at birth were only 39.4 years—not the fifty-six years of American children born in 1790. Again, multiple factors were involved—urbanization, rising infant diseases, negative wage trends, crowding, industrial environments, immigrant-imparted disease vectors, and food costs. As we shall see in a later chapter, these challenges led to substantial unrest.

The Vandergrifts, 1870s

In 1870, change of a different sort was also afoot in western Pennsylvania's Vandergrift family. When William Knowles Vandergrift and his sons J. J. and James did not appear in East Birmingham on the US Census of 1870, most of Birmingham's teeming population probably did not notice their absence. Their seasoned foremen kept the Vandergrift boatyards and repair shops running as normal. But Pittsburgh's big shots in Shadyside and on the city's expanding "Millionaire's Row" definitely noticed.

The Vandergrifts had become involved in both oil and in developing commodities like natural gas since 1860, when the Confederacy closed the Mississippi. No longer able to ship coal, pig iron, and finished iron to New Orleans, they refocused on resources to the north of Pittsburgh along the Allegheny and Kiskiminetas Rivers. Oil Creek, of Edwin Drake's first oil well fame (1859), was a tributary of the Allegheny. Recall that they had started shipping barreled oil in the early 1860s, and by 1865 they were working with Meadville's Densmore brothers, James and Amos, who patented the "Densmore Tank Car." By 1865 or 1866, the Vandergrifts began to ship oil down to Pittsburgh by rail, while the Densmore brothers began shipping oil to New York City in September of 1865.[50]

CHAPTER 13

Captain J. J. Vandergrift, former majority owner of the *Red Fox* and the *Conestoga*, bought his first oil land and rights near Oil Creek in 1862. As prices for land and drilling rights skyrocketed, J. J. and his favorite business partner, Daniel Bushnell, kept buying.[51] In early 1859 potential oil land was worth four dollars an acre, compared to four thousand dollars in 1870. As the price of drilling skyrocketed, the Vandergrifts quit buying land and branched out into producing, refining, shipping, and brokering oil.[52] Oil City in Venango County, Pennsylvania, was the place to be in 1870, and flashy J. J. jumped onto the ground floor there like a bullfrog on a grasshopper.

The 1870 US Census[53] of Venango borough, just outside Oil City's boundary, lists Sophia (Sarver) "Vandergriff," age sixty-four,[54] and her husband, "William (Knowles) Vandergriff,"[55] age sixty-three, occupation, boat builder, with no value listed for real estate but a personal estate of three hundred dollars. Considering the wealth that he and his family had, J. J.'s father, William K., appears amusingly and consistently sedate. Always shy of the limelight, or of disclosing his business details, the three hundred dollars was probably what happened to be in his pocket on census day.

Next on the census list is William's younger son, James, age thirty-four; his wife, Martha, age twenty-seven; and their daughters, Etta, age nine, Victoria, age three, and Susan, nine months. James's occupation is listed as "oil dealer," which he would pursue to the end of his life.[56] Young James, his wife, and one or another of his girls would maintain contact, primarily by letter, with their Aunt Sophia, the daughter of deceased *Red Fox* captain Benjamin F. Vandergrift, into the early 1930s.

On page seven of the 1870 US Census for Oil City, Venango County, Pennsylvania, J. J. Vandergrift was listed as forty-eight years of age, though he was actually forty-five. With him are his wife, Henrietta (Morrow), age thirty-seven, and his children: Kate, sixteen; Bennie, fourteen; Jacob, twelve; Kitty (Catherine), seven; Maggie (Margaret), six; Harry, four, and Joseph, two. Also living with them is Henrietta's widowed father, R. P. Morrow, age fifty-nine. J. J.'s occupation is "oil dealer," his real estate is listed at twenty-two thousand, and his personal estate is twenty thousand. Not afraid to show his wealth, J. J. presents a wondrous contrast to his father. Though flashy, J. J. was disposed to look out for close family members, as is clear from the composition of his household on the 1870 census.

Back in Pittsburgh, the other Vandergrifts carried on by adapting to the era's brittle economic circumstances in smaller ways. Thurston's city directories for 1869–1870[57] indicate that elder Vandergrift brother Captain John,[58] once owner of the steamships *Pinta, Prairie Bird, Black Diamond*, and co-owner of many others, had finally retired from the western waters. Already in his seventies, he had become a regional road commissioner and moved with his wife to a home on the Greensburg Pike in Liberty Township several miles from Pittsburgh. The Greensburg Pike was once part of Forbes Road, the "Pennsylvania highway," and is now Pennsylvania Route 30.

Two of the younger Vandergrift boys, John C. and James S., were both working as clerks in the US Customs office, which was directed by their uncle-in-law, renowned former river man Captain C. W. Batchelor. Another younger Vandergrift, Samuel W., was a travel agent at Rogers & Vandergrift, a company that promoted convenient railway and steamship travel packages. Its clients ranged from newly arrived immigrants headed to the Midwest to businessmen hustling most anywhere. Still "on the waters" were Captain James Vandergrift, living at 21 Clark Street, and Lewis F. Vandergrift, engineer[59] at 853 Penn Street. Two other Vandergrift males were listed in the 1870 city directory as "foreman" and "laborer." George senior, who had first worked as a helper on construction of the Smithfield Street Bridge from 1816 to 1818, was in his sixties and winding down his riverboat activities.

In the Vandergrift family the founding Pittsburgh generation was passing. Like many others of the era, their family was also fragmenting into diverging lineages based on wealth and occupation. The skiff-building continued on the Monongahela waterfront, but no Vandergrifts were living in Birmingham or nearby on Pittsburgh's gritty South Side in 1870. In 1871 that may have changed, as both Lewis the steamboat engineer and his son Lewis Jr. were listed in Thurston's Directory at #93 14th Street, Birmingham.[60]

Echoes of the Civil War

In the post–Civil War world, an urge to sort out national identity and forget its unfixable realities consumed much of America. By 1870 the nation's population had grown to 38.6 million, up from 31.5 million in 1860. That meant about 1.5 million more new households, many still rural or in the new West.[61] These households needed the basics: plows, axes, hand mills, shovels, nails, sawn boards, iron pans, Dutch ovens, tin cups, hinges, fireplace hangers and "frogs,"[62] and shoe tacks. About half of those households also needed horses, mules, livestock, and firewood. The raw frontier had moved a thousand miles west of Pittsburgh's Point. In the East's industrial centers, new households needed homes and home furnishings. Parts of Philadelphia below South Street had remained in cornfield until about 1870 to 1872, when brick row houses rapidly replaced crops. It was the same on the fringes of Boston, New York, and Baltimore. As more immigrants arrived, crowding and attendant communicable diseases impacted well-being in the urbanizing Eastern Seaboard.

It should have been a peaceful, constructive time in America, but large numbers of Union troops were still deployed to parts of the defeated Confederacy and the contested sectors of border states like Missouri and Kansas. Mayhem generated by the five-year-old, rapidly growing Ku Klux Klan and local "regulators" had spiraled out of control. Among those ne'er do wells was William Quantrill and his raiders, including Frank and Jesse James. There were also less well-known ones, like southern West Virginia's John McNeill and his two-hundred-odd hate-driven rangers. Die-hard "East" Virginians, they were not content with the majority of the state's residents who had voted for separation from Virginia in 1862 and 1863. Then there were the fanatics on both sides acting out in the ambiguous spaces between victory and defeat, war and peace, right and wrong. The North's John Brown had been one such early agitator; Tennessee's bloody Bill Anderson was his 1870 southern counterpart. So systematic were these widespread, militia-style atrocities that Congress passed the KKK Act of 1871 to rein them in.

The Reconstruction era was not the first time that an uneasy calm in American society reignited into regional conflict. Pennsylvania's Whiskey Rebellion of the 1790s began as civil meetings and roadhouse discussions among local settlers in the Ohio Valley about federal tax agents and the distant big shots in Philadelphia who imposed new taxes they could not pay. Thus the Philadelphia Federalists came to be perceived as adversaries who neither respected nor understood the locals' way of life and economy.

The grievances of the 1790s had morphed rapidly from spirited public debates to strident conflicts. Based on imaginary legal powers, local militias were conscripted. First conducted in an orderly way, the loudest, angriest, most aggressive voices soon drowned out the calmer ones at meetings, and aggrieved, western Pennsylvania quickly spiraled out of control. The stubbornly authoritarian and avaricious Virginia plantation–born federal tax collector, General John Neville, played an outsized role in unleashing the years of chaos that followed. What had started as a citizens' protest ended in rebellion.[63]

Similar dynamics were unleashed by Reconstruction and the deployment of federal troops to the South from 1865 to 1872. The deployment of federal troops had been necessary after a series of stunning massacres of recently freed blacks.

But that military presence also fueled new cultural grievances as the defeated planter class shifted blame from themselves to the Yankee troops as the explanation for harsh postwar daily realities. The shattered Southern caste system, a poor economy, insufficient food supply, and ruined infrastructure were real.

Wide swaths of the South were already devastated, infrastructure-wise. That loss of infrastructure held back the Southern regional economy for decades. So did the loss of slave labor. Southern plantations and many small shop or factory business models, originally based on seasonally "hired-out" slave labor, were simply not structured to pay wages. Many of the most skilled blacks headed north. As a consequence skilled labor, though it temporarily paid quite well regionally, remained in short supply compared to in the North.

Southern women had suddenly lost most of their men folk, temporarily or permanently, to a war in which four-fifths of white males served. Husbands killed and young, single men taken to the slaughter changed the social and economic roles that Southern women played. The prosperous ones were left to manage plantations, making do in circumstances they had never before faced. Many had never cooked a meal, swept the carpets, or patched worn clothing, and their servants were suddenly gone. Who managed the remaining slaves? Who made the farm decisions? Who was left to protect them? In reality, Southern women's world had turned upside-down. The Confederate government repeatedly failed them on promises of food and protection, and when their defeated men came home, they were no longer the hallowed, invincible men they had once known.[64]

As for hundreds of thousands of poor, rural Southern women struggling on forty acres, cultural grievances didn't count. They were hungry, tired, and heartbroken that their young sons and husbands had not come home. Many, if not most, could not even read or write. In many dirt-poor districts, local ministers, both black and white, were their most reliable and empathetic supporters.

The North, burdened by policing the aftermath of its victory, and the South, burdened by destruction and tangible loss, both struggled to move forward. While the war aborted complete regional factionalism, it unleashed unfamiliar economic, cultural, and political currents that created new waves of divisive forces on both sides' Main Streets. Those forces continue to this day.

The nation had lost more than 20 percent of an entire generation of young men—over 750,000 dead, and hundreds of thousands seriously wounded. In what had been the Confederacy, the percentage of that lost generation was much higher. In both the North and the South, hundreds of thousands had lost an arm, a leg, an eye, a hand, a foot, and even their "manhood," as testicles had been shot away by canister shot or a musket ball. In some locales morphine-addicted soldiers were suddenly as common as stray dogs. Frightened orphans were left in virtually every community. The "lucky" wives of survivors faced long odds of making new and happy lives with wounded, defeated, or stress-afflicted husbands. What researchers now call "despair deaths" due to drug or alcohol addiction, suicide, and chronic stress rose everywhere, but especially in the South. Hundreds of thousands of widows grieved and struggled to feed their children while a generation of young single women lost hope of finding a husband. For the first time since the Declaration, there were not enough young men to go around, especially in the South.[65]

The postwar politics and posturing on both sides were simply not effective at helping families on farms and on main streets to negotiate the daily aftermath of war. Government aid was limited. Public health depended primarily on emerging volunteer groups.[66] Among veterans, such groups offered rehabilitation for lost limbs, therapy for addiction, or re-training for new work. But that support network was inadequate. Veterans' disability pensions were far too modest to sustain a family whose main breadwinner had been maimed.

A rudderless, reactive federal government struggled under feckless President Andrew Johnson. In response, the North's civilian society tried to forget much of what happened during the war. The civilian North turned away from the imponderable issues of government, war, and slavery, focusing instead on the here and now.

In an attempt to forget, hordes of loners and drifters among the veterans on both sides headed west, even as other men became joiners. Lodges like Lulu, the Masons, and the Odd Fellows expanded explosively as men sought the company of like-minded men and the small insurance and burial benefits of the lodge movements. Women gravitated to the more practical self-help organizations focused on medicine, diet, and aid to indigents. They protested against strong drink and for the female right to vote. Blacks, hungry for self-determined forms of community, hunted for kin who had been sold away prior to Appomattox or who had fled plantations in the Confederacy's waning days. They bought land, built new communities, and founded thousands of their own churches.

In these churches their children first learned to read and write. Their ministers wrote letters and reviewed legal documents to which they might affix their mark and often negotiated the sale of tobacco and cotton from their small farms. Those churches sought good, and so they remain culturally and socially powerful to this day.

In response, prominent Southerners deployed scarce public resources to support strategies countering a cohesive black community. They rigged voting rules against freed blacks, denied them access to public schools, and pretended helplessness to find those who burned black churches in the dead of night. In Southern aristocratic minds, the idea that blacks could now vote and hold public office had to be nullified at all costs. Several Southern states still actively and artfully try to minimize minority access to the ballot box.[67]

In evolutionary and energetic terms, such detours are costly. Resources—cash, human life, human work, military material, and good will—consumed in controlling the fringes of postwar Southern society diverted much of both regions' remaining resources that might have been made available to rebuild the South's core and move it forward more quickly to higher levels of diversified economic productivity. Among the outcomes, this postbellum detour cost legions of Southern children—both black and white—high levels of measurable well-being and public education right into the 1950s. Had the prevailing federal government treated the defeated South in 1866 as George C. Marshall of Uniontown, Pennsylvania, later treated a defeated Germany in 1946, the postwar era might have gone much better for everyone. But why would the nation's Congress fund it, given Lincoln's assassination and the failed Confederation assassination attempts on his vice president and cabinet? In the affairs of a nation, impulsive petulance can be a very expensive indulgence. The Civil War, triggered by impulsive petulance in the spring of 1861, ended just as it had begun.

The Densmores and the Hard, Gritty 1870s

The Densmore families were tested by many of the same postbellum issues as the rest of the country. Working at Pittsburgh, Kittanning, and Fairchance iron mills, Ollie, Sam, and Robert Jr. experienced major challenges in wages, family costs, and work assignments. They faced wage competition both from newly freed and skilled Southern blacks who were crossing the "Cotton Curtain" to Union states as well as from yet another influx of European immigrants. Unskilled rural blacks also escaped Southern postwar hostility and competed with their sons and nephews for jobs as helpers or mill boys. The Densmores were acutely aware that, among their cousins, a number had died at places like Gettysburg or in one or another notorious Southern stockaded POW camp.[68] They had also lost many skilled work-crew members to the maw of war. Among them were close friends they had worked beside for thousands of hours in the heat and haze at Anchor, Wharton's, or Oliphant's.

On the positive side, Ollie had not served in the war, and his two elder brothers mustered out physically unharmed. Even more, they had steady jobs—that is, as steady as could be expected while the nation's prodigious wartime expenditures of energy and material declined to a more normal trajectory. The peak of wartime's frantic Power Phase had passed, its energy crashing down and spreading out like a wave hitting a wide, sandy beach. Unprotected by great wealth, the Densmores, unlike the oil-producing branch of Vandergrifts, were as grains of sand on that beach.

The Densmores' financial reality experienced before the war versus after it is typical of most 1870s American families. In 1861 Ollie's average weekly earnings as a plate roller would have been at least $12.75 a week, and about $14.25 for each week he worked the long turn. As a machinist, Sam would also have earned an average of $12 a week, and Robert Jr., a puddler, would have earned an average of $13.37 a week. By early spring of 1867, Ollie's wage would have temporarily increased to about $21 a week, but Anchor closed for repairs. Sam's wage rose to $18.11 and Robert Jr.'s to $23.17.[69] But rapidly rising wartime inflation had trumped most of those wage gains. Food purchased for one dollar in 1860 had risen in cost to $1.87 by 1865.[70] Only Ollie, with one living child, could consistently save money in the face of shutdowns. With four children, Robert Jr. could not.

These wage increases sound great until one considers the realities of work schedules and family maintenance costs. Let's take Ollie's situation as an example, since his work life and schedule were not interrupted by service in the Civil War. We can reasonably suppose that only Ollie worked in Pittsburgh nearly full-time from 1862 to 1867.[71] In the winter of 1861 to 1862, Ollie's average wage of $12.75 a week[72] covered average family costs of $5.10 for Ollie and Elizabeth. This calculation is based on data prepared by the US Department of Revenue for Congress in 1868[73] and includes basic, fundamental costs like rent and food. Incidentals, clothing, and so on probably ate up another $2 per week. Thus, Ollie's savings potential was about $5 a week.

By early 1867 Ollie's wage of $21 a month was ample. But the Civil War had dramatically inflated basic food and commodity prices. In 1867 Ollie and Elizabeth had one living child, H. T. Their average household costs had doubled to $10.24 and incidentals to about $4 a week. Little H. T. created additional costs, yet even so Ollie's savings potential had increased to about $6.75 per week. If his three children who died—Charles in 1861, a daughter in 1863, and Jane in

1869⁷⁴—had lived, Ollie's savings potential would have been near *zero*. Two to three months out of work on account of the 1864 and 1866–1867 fires at Anchor Nail and Tack did not trigger an emergency because Ollie had *only* H. T. to support, as well as access to cheap lodging, garden crops, and smoked meat in Fairchance. Ollie purchased land in Fairchance during 1867 and 1868, so it is obvious that he had savings.

It is not certain just when, where, and how much Sam, Robert Jr., and Nehemiah worked in Pittsburgh and in their outlying hometowns during the 1860s, because the two Densmore brothers each served about a year in the war, and all three of the iron makers moved around quite a bit. In spite of that we do have enough information about their whereabouts to estimate their capacities to save money during this time. It is likely that Sam, Robert Jr., and Nehemiah temporarily went to Pittsburgh now and again when their outlying mills closed down on account of fires, furnace repairs, or slack orders. But their regular wages were largely provincial ones, which averaged about 5 percent lower than in Pittsburgh, so we can intelligently estimate their capacities to save money.

The US Census of 1860 indicates that Nehemiah was an iron heater[75] at Oliphant's Works. This was highly skilled work, requiring great strength and judgment. Heaters actually made slightly higher wages in the 1860s than did the rollers. Though they did not control the full production process to the extent that the rollers did, they did control an important portion of the daily rhythm and speed of molten iron output. An average Pittsburgh weekly wage for a heater in 1867 and 1868, about the time Nehemiah moved there with his family, was $23.36.[76] One as skilled as Nehemiah, with fifteen years or more of experience, could have earned as much as $28 a week at Birmingham Iron and Steel or Wharton's Mill. This was a fine wage, yielding an enviable income of about $1,400 yearly, *if* one worked six days a week year-round—most unlikely.

But in 1868 Nehemiah and Elizabeth were supporting a family of *ten* in Pittsburgh: mom, dad, and children Hannah, Mary, George (who works), Samuel (who also works), Sarah, Emma, and Robert.[77] Boarding with them was none other than one "Oliver Gerishmier"[78] (Densmore), age twenty-eight. In 1868 Ollie was censused both in Georges Township and in Birmingham. He obviously engaged in some work in both Birmingham and Fairchance. We know this is Ollie Densmore in spite of the egregious spelling error on the census record because he is in his sister's household, is the correct age, and is listed as an iron worker.

Nehemiah is supporting himself, his wife, five dependent children, two working sons, and a working brother-in-law. According to the Congressional report of 1868, a two-parent and seven-child household cost $23.78 a week for food, rent, and basic clothing in 1867 and 1868. In Fairchance Nehemiah would have just broken even at a wage of $24 or $25 a week,[79] without paying for incidentals like treats, clothing, and the like. But in Pittsburgh his salary would have allowed him to save about $3 a week at sixty-four hours a week from his own wages and also claim half his sons' wages as board, fixed at $2.80 a week each for full-time, fifty-four-hour workweeks as an apprentice or forge "boy." With Ollie paying a typical $5 per week for his board (meals and a bed), $3 of which was Nehemiah's actual cost for boarding him, Nehemiah could potentially save $5 or $6 a week in Pittsburgh. Though this does not seem like much, in 2018 dollars its purchase power was about $80.

Two years later, the US Census of 1870 lists few details for Nehemiah in Georges Township, though we can safely calculate that his savings were in the range of $50 to $100 in cash plus tools, furniture, and a squirrel rifle. His listed real estate value of $1,200, plus $500 in personal assets seems high.[80] He may have inherited some land in West Virginia or built a house in Fairchance on a portion of the Jordan lot. He and Elizabeth had already been married more than twenty years and he, like Ollie, had been in iron work throughout.

During the 1860s Robert Jr. was employed as a puddler at Oliphant's in Fairchance, and he was occasionally on Anchor's payroll in Pittsburgh whenever the Oliphant Works was down. He supported a family of four children through the 1860s and earned about $13.37 a week as of 1860 to 1861. He could meet his family's basic needs of rent and food in Fairchance for about $10.07, leaving a $3.20 margin for clothes, incidentals, and savings. He'd have been lucky to put aside more than a dollar or two a week. By 1867 to 1868, when wages and costs had inflated, his weekly wage in Fairchance would have risen to about $23.17, and his basic necessities—if he maintained access to local gardens and meat—would have gone up to an average of $17.79. Incidentals with four children and a wife would have eaten up at least $2 a week, leaving him capable of saving at most $3 a week. Robert Jr.'s family spent less than the average in Fairchance, as he had access to cheaper food through Oliphant's farm and Shadrack O'Brien's garden, but his theoretical annual capacity to save was at best $80 to $100 a year, most of which would have been erased by a month or six weeks of annual shutdowns.

In short, inflation and interrupted work schedules made saving very hard, if not impossible, for all but Ollie. Notably, the 1868 government report of household food costs (from which the above data derive) appears to understate inflated food costs, a crucial factor in childhood nutrition and well-being.

Chapter 14

Postwar Culture
Class, Labels, and Consequences, 1861–1879

In the North, ordinary folks systematically began to forget the war, move to new cities, and take new jobs. This erased some of the war-generated pain from its community of memory and allowed them to disengage from the plight of both freed slaves and free blacks in the South. In stark contrast, a large segment of Southerners invested heavily in remembering—obsessively so—and also in revising history to create their own fantasized narrative of events.[1] The "War of Secession" or "War Between the States" became the "War of Northern Aggression." Southern legislators invested enormous efforts to prevent freed blacks from receiving any real-world benefits from their formal freedom. Meanwhile, in Washington, DC, enraged Northern republicans sought legislative and military revenge for the Southern plot that killed Lincoln and attempted to murder the rest of his Cabinet. Neither the North nor the South's psychological and social responses to the Civil War's aftermath were optimal. The well-being of the nation's diverse citizens and vast amounts of destruction should have been the focus on both sides.

As already mentioned, much of the South had long practiced *minority rule*; the planter class's political artistry at dominating the majority of its own population began in the 1670s but flowered in the mid-1700s. An increasingly rigid and privileged view of full citizenship still ruled right up to the Civil War, and it continued in modified form through Reconstruction and Jim Crow, which lasted in modified form into the 1960s. Stealing elections and other procedural cunning long characterized Southern politics. Prior to the Civil War, South Carolina did not even allow the male public to vote in presidential elections. Only their legislature—mostly planters and their sons—voted. Not one ordinary South Carolinian male was permitted a vote in the crucial presidential election of 1860, which triggered the Civil War. Thus history cannot tell us what the average white male South Carolinian thought of the 1860 election. Only the narrowly defined elites could vote.[2]

The echoes of such tensions still play out in the halls of the United States Congress and in daily American life: sovereign citizens imagine rights that exceed those of ordinary US citizens; "States' Rights" are claimed to trump federal "overreach"; Union members demand the right to bargain for wages while magnates claim that such a right unfairly constrains owners' rights to set wages and work conditions at whim.

The Original Legal Sin

From an anthropological perspective, the racial, cultural, economic, and structural issues litigated between the North and the South on Civil War battlefields remain largely unresolved. In Constitutional terms, a number of those issues were intertwined in the oddity first created when a compromise in the 1780s Constitution codified enslaved blacks as three-fifths of a "person"[3] for purposes of computing a state's population, and simultaneously limited each state to just two senators regardless of population. This "deal" was necessary to induce Southern states to ratify the Constitution.[4] It was a double-barreled counting formula that gave the Southern states a substantial overrepresentation in Congress compared to its actual voting population and allowed the South to stack the Supreme Court, guaranteeing a majority in the House of Representatives until after the Civil War. The South used its built-in representational advantage to both direct disproportionate federal tax dollars to support Southern needs as well as to stifle any national legislative attempt to end slavery. "Democracy" was—and is—one thing on paper and quite another in daily practice. At the end of the day, it is the daily practice that counts.

Many other of the American nation's basic identity issues are still being contested. In the process of defining who we are, labels like *voter, resident, citizen, immigrant, DACA, liberal, conservative, black, white, straight, gay, trans, Protestant, Jew, Muslim*, and so on are all tossed about. As in the Constitution, when blacks were counted as three-fifths of a person, such labels often become legal definitions. *And definitions have consequences*. Labels can trigger—or withhold—deployment of public resources, and therefore become coupled with often-powerful selective agents in both biological and cultural evolution. Definitions of personhood and citizenship have obvious socioeconomic consequences: green cards, work permits, visas, driver's licenses, voter registrations, Social Security cards, Medicare cards, and licenses to practice medicine, cut hair, drive a commercial truck, or hold a federal job requiring a security clearance. Such labels can also determine marriage rights. The consequences of such labels feed directly into family income, diet, and healthcare. These factors influence one's "class," which is clearly reflected in longevity, infant mortality, life-span, height of children, and general health status. How our tiers of government define each of us matters at the kitchen table, the ballot box, in our bedrooms, in our churches, and in each of our own life chances. For instance, a change to advance the official Social Security retirement age would create real, measurable changes in well-being—mostly negative for those age sixty-two to sixty-eight.

One's position or "class" in America comes down to the amount of money, energy, goods, and services an individual or family controls and the labels it claims. We often talk about poverty and public education in America, but few of us realize we are speaking the language of data-based evolutionary factors. It is a fact that blacks in America, both before and after the Civil War, do not live as long as whites. As a group, poor white men in America do not live as long as more prosperous white males. Females of all races live longer than men. Yet all American females, regardless of race, have less access to healthcare than in any European nation. In fact, their healthcare and outcomes is like that of Turkey—not France or Germany. Class, status, gender, work opportunities, education, and access (or lack thereof) to the full benefits of the Big Table are all measurable—a data reality that exists apart from the need to talk politics.

Each of us is responsible for putting our chips in play. But the nation is responsible for having clear conditions and rules for reaching that Big Table: an effective, *efficient* military; disaster management; public infrastructure; good, fact-based public education; equal access to healthcare; due process under the law; and a fair, clear tax code—we need no more Whiskey Rebellion- style fiascos. Of the factors above, access to good, healthy diet and preventative healthcare matters most to us and our children. For the skeptic, please note: a healthy population costs far less of a nation's wealth than a sick, stressed-out citizenry. Our total national healthcare costs *doubled* between 1980 and 2017, from 8.9 percent of our gross domestic product to 18 percent—the most of any industrial nation.[5] But that massive investment does not match results: in 2016, 2017, and 2018 our life-spans have been declining, and diseases once thought to be eradicated, like measles, are returning. So just where has that money gone?

Fantasies of the "Good Ol' Days"

Many tomes have been written on slavery, its conditions, its consequences, and its economics. Again, as with human height issues and biological status, Robert Fogel wrote one of the standard-setting books on the underlying economic realities once built into the American South's style of slavery.[6] Many others have written detailed economic analyses of the post–Civil War era's voracious industrialism and its transformation into an enterprise owned by too few at the expense of too many. Others have written extensively about the great wealth of the Golden Age and the Robber Barons. We have fairly well documented portraits of American extremes. We do know that the North created more wealth and higher education levels for a broader spectrum of its occupants than did the highly class-stratified Southern world from 1808 to 1960.[7] But neither managed to create a truly level playing field for its citizens. In Mississippi delta country, nineteenth-century infant mortality was nearly double that in agrarian Pennsylvania—and it remains that way to this day.

In contrast, we have fewer narratives about the middle ranges of American society, because much of history and news focuses on extremes. That is precisely why the Densmores, Harts, and Vandergrifts matter—none of them managed to keep their entire extended families at the pinnacle, nor tolerated the entire clan stuck in the darkest cellar of American economic society. In the face of changing realities over the generations, these families continually adapted and adjusted their goals. Some of those adaptations were gritty enough to create a longing for the "good ol' days" when life was simpler and a skilled working man enjoyed both respect and earnings sufficient to support his family.

Cultural Rigidity

As a society grows, cultural rigidity does not work for either a nation or its individual families over long historical spans. Time does not stand still. Climate, environment, and resources are not static. Neither are the needs of growing populations. The larger and more complex a society becomes, the greater the volume of caloric energy that flows through it—food, fuel, and resources—and the more rapidly it morphs. The more it changes, the more it risks creating its own unanticipated logistic and structural problems. Think "climate change." As growth accelerates and troubles pile up, many ask, "Who did this to us?" The best answer is often, "Nearly everyone." But that reality leaves no one to blame, so politicians and their backers typically step in to explain. Rapid change confounds most societies.

One can live partially frozen in time if a smallish socioeconomic subculture remains largely independent of its complex, surrounding society's infrastructure and benefits. I consider that akin to micro-niche separation in biology. The Amish community in America between 1750 and 2000 offers us a reasonable example of this. It still relies primarily on late eighteenth- and nineteenth-century technology, energy sources, and agricultural practices (though that, too, is changing). The core Amish world is very different from current mainstream America in fundamental ways. The scale of society is small. The rules are the rules—they are not continually and casually renegotiated. Ambiguity is minimal. And, notably, the Amish world consumes far less energy per capita—caloric, renewable, or fossil fuel, including coal—than the rest of us. They do not waste food and energy as most of us do. The average American consumer tosses out, or allows to spoil, a *third* of all the food sold in the United States. Nor are the Amish technologically dependent on the huge electric energy and agricultural food combines that confine our choices and extract profit from the rest of us. Their society changes much more slowly. Wealth-wise, it is not as highly stratified. Their farm, home, and carpentry work is hard, but they are in control of the immediate means of their survival, as was Old Robert in 1800. These are all signatures of classic efficiency-focused societies.

In contrast, most of the rest of us are absolutely not in control. Gasoline shortages, weather, closed airports, trucking strikes, and dependence on the grid leave most Americans living rather uncomfortably dependent lives. We struggle merely to understand what the rules *really* are, and just what is actually expected of us. Contemporary mainstream America is a head-exploding exercise in processing near-constant change and dealing with the near-constant stress of adapting, performing, and staying ahead of the game. Most of us deal with ambiguity daily. Why does a crime committed in one jurisdiction result in a ten-year prison sentence, yet the same crime committed fifty miles away in another district results in probation and monitoring? Why is the public gas or electric franchise/company from which you *must* purchase energy actually owned by private shareholders and not by the body of its customers? Why is that company guaranteed a monopoly and also a fixed profit percentage no matter how poorly it may be managed? Why does it also enjoy preferential tax rates? Lack of choice and self-sufficiency is a large, complex society's Achilles heel . . . legions of ordinary citizens, but especially those most biologically prone to intense fear responses, suffer enormous stress and bewilderment. Protracted stress is a notable factor in negatively impacting a person's long-term well-being. It also generates anger, as the nightly news so often demonstrates.

Western Pennsylvania and More Echoes of War: 1863–1896

In the postwar North, most of the general population accepted that they were part and parcel of the nation and its economy. But that acceptance was nuanced. Sam Densmore initially wanted to forget the Civil War, his older brother Robert Jr. wanted to celebrate his role in it, and the youngest in each household didn't give a rip about it beyond the occasional dramatic rye whiskey– fueled battlefield stories, as it was an otherwise unremembered event from their childhood years. How could they have understood that those meaningless war years had already shaped their heights and shaved the statistics of their predicted longevity?

Ollie would have had little to say about the war, since he did not get inducted in the general draft of 1863, possibly due to Sam's selflessness on draft day in July 1863. He and Sam were certainly not the only "no thanks" guys in the North. There had been violent anti-draft riots in Boston and New York City in the summer of 1863. And thousands of northern middle-class fathers ponied up the $350 to pay a stand-in to serve in place of their sons. But talk or not, having served or not, for or against slavery, the Civil War still shaped lives on a daily basis long after Appomattox. The most deeply affected were in the states from which the largest numbers of men served: New York and Pennsylvania in the North, and North Carolina in the South.

As noted, more than 750,000 men had died—the 2018 statistical equivalent of seven million. As many as a million children were orphaned—the modern equivalent of eight million. Many of the men who died were guided by aspects of morality and religious beliefs. Many believed in the cultural notion of a "good death"—a life lost in support of a great and worthy cause. But that notion did little on a daily basis for the widows and children they left behind. Impoverished widows and orphaned children were taken in by thousands of related families, both genetic and in-law. As extended-family food budgets were squeezed to accommodate those taken in, food portions—especially the cost-inflated meat proteins—shrank. And with that shrinkage, crowding, and stress of mourning, the components of well-being arced downward.

In Pittsburgh the desperation of young widows was compounded by so few female factory jobs. Many became private washerwomen who traveled each day to middle-class homes on the north side to mend and do laundry, while a niece or eldest daughter watched the little ones. In such households it was no longer just the twelve- to fourteen-year-old sons who ended their educations—both they and their younger brothers of six and seven took unskilled factory or mill work, often lobbied for by a skilled uncle, older brother, or father-in-law. During this period many postwar families fell back into an American version of the world as described in *David Copperfield*.

The crowding in doubled-up households enhanced disease vectors and infant mortality and sent boys to work who might have otherwise made it to eighth grade or even finished high school. Marriages of necessity took place, and everywhere there were broken veterans, begging, picking trash, or tucked against an alley wall, sleeping off the laudanum, whiskey, or morphine. A wave of skilled black men from Southern industrial cities like Birmingham, Alabama, also made their way north and were willing to work cheap. Riverboat stewards and captains who accepted passage from blacks[8] sometimes had to protect them from embittered Southern contingents aboard. This was tense, messy stuff.[9] The reminders were everywhere. Like the Vandergrifts, many other steamboat owners had lost boats; others had entire cargoes seized, most by Confederate operatives but some also by undisciplined Northern units operating along the middle Mississippi River.[10]

The small mill owners in Pittsburgh continued to retool and to test new markets throughout the early 1870s. Others were swallowed up by the growing steel and transportation combines. Nearly everyone had to lower prices, including those for steel rails, which were still in strong demand. Steel track prices stuttered, due to rapid overproduction at the expense of widely needed lower profit margin commodities. Those included tacks, nails, iron skillets, pans, and iron plate for wood stoves, horseshoes, and carriage axles—the list was endless. And with not enough hard cash in circulation, the consequences of the Civil War bounced around city streets as stridently as the never-ending din of the mills and forges. The nation had entered a thirty-year era of deflation that did not end until 1896. This long economic cycle robbed value from hard assets: homes, land, tools, livestock, furniture sold to make ends meet, and wages, especially those of the most highly skilled workers.

Adaptations

As already noted, the Ninth US Census of 1870 indicates Fairchance/Oliphant's most skilled were working in Birmingham—Robert Jr. and the Warman brothers—while Ollie, one of Birmingham's best, resides in Fairchance sorting out his children's deaths and waiting for Anchor to reopen once it retooled and restructured. Everywhere in the region both workingmen and businessmen were trying to decode the signals of change as they sensed transformation in the industrial heartbeat of the nation. Nervous and stressed, they tried to anticipate the "new normal." But the new normal was a rapidly moving target.

As some of the Vandergrifts moved toward the source of oil up the Allegheny, others doubled down on their riverboats and moved boats west to the Missouri and Wabash rivers. How could they have known that instead of fading away, the economic and social trials of the late 1860s and early 1870s would only intensify. By 1875 and 1876 William Knowles Vandergrift's health was failing. He died in Venango Township a year later on February 18, 1877. His oldest brother Samuel had died in 1863, and another brother, Captain George, who had worked on the bridge in 1816, had recently died in Pittsburgh. The industrial candle fueled by old Jacob Vandergrift and his wife Mary Hart's sons began to gutter as affairs passed to their grandsons.

Grandsons J. J. and James had become rich, having successfully negotiated petroleum and natural gas as new sources of energy. J. J.'s father, William K., had lived long enough to see J. J. triumph at being the first to ever transport natural gas by pipeline in the fall of 1875. That gas fed streetlights, gas flames in the glassworks, and gas-fired forges.

The other new source of industrial energy that came of age in the 1860s and 1870s was coke. It was the high-temperature fuel needed to make enough heat to produce the more durable steel demanded for railroad track during the Civil War. Coke quickly became a prime industrial driver of iron and steel production. The simplest analogy to explain coke is that coke is to coal as charcoal is to wood. Coke is heat-reduced coal—some mass is lost in production as carbon content is raised. It, like charcoal, burns hotter than its parent raw resource. That heat is an essential factor in making steel from iron.

The move toward steel and large-scale production of coke to accomplish it directly affected three of Old Robert's four sons—Robert Jr., Sam, and Ollie. Coke transformed the industrial technology and markets that provided their wages and shaped their daily tasks. Nat, the teamster/wagoner, was less directly affected in the nature of his tasks. But hauling coke on short hauls from Fayette County ovens to nearby furnaces also contributed to his earnings. Most coke in that era was transported by train or riverboat, but two- to five-mile hauls to small, low-volume local specialty forges didn't work with the high marginal costs of adding dedicated rail spurs. High infrastructure costs left modest, low-tech, low-paying economic niches open to men like Nat. Meanwhile, the women at home also had household puzzles to solve.

Diet, Calories, Economy, and the Trajectory of Well-being

Among the consequences of the Civil War and its aftermath was the rising cost of commodities, especially meat and eggs. As noted, in 1861 and 1862 both armies bought meat in huge quantities, reducing domestic supply. Beef, the working man's preferred staple, shot up by roughly 20 percent in Pennsylvania that year. By the winter of 1868, beef that had cost twelve cents a pound in the winter of 1860 cost twenty-two cents a pound, an increase of 85 percent. There were no cheap alternatives—ham and even beans[11] had also doubled in price.[12] Though overall wages for skilled iron workers rose 40–50 percent between 1860 and 1865, when a generation of young men went to war, those increases in wages simply did not offset the increased retail costs of daily diet and clothing. These striking price increases in beef, eggs, and ham meant that children ate less meat and eggs. In households where men were engaged in the heaviest labor, that impact was amplified. In the several hundred thousand households from which twenty-ish wage-earning sons had been summarily drafted in the summer of 1863, the loss of that working son's paid board immediately eroded food, clothing, and school budgets, impacting his younger siblings.

During the decades between 1840 and 1870, America's per-capita food calories available to devote to work had declined from the colonial standard of 2,313 to about 1,800 calories per day.[13] It has already been made clear that this decline, sharpest by 1860, had contributed to a reduction in male height and longevity.[14] The inflated commodity prices of the Civil War era directly added to the biological stress placed on working breadwinners' families. The lower a civilian breadwinner's wages, the greater the impact. The height of American males born in 1860 was, at maturity, a spare 5'7.2", the shortest since 1710.[15] As food costs skyrocketed and several million men were deployed on battlefields, the nation's native-born children paid a price in declining nutrition, rising household stress, and increased levels of childhood disease. This trend was made worse by declining access to physicians who had been called to the battlefield in great number. Acute shortage of medicines was another consequence of the war. Diminished physical development during their wartime toddler years

(1861–1865) translated into shorter heights as adults and statistically correlated with a briefer life than in the late 1700s.

Recall that, if one was born in England in 1750, life expectancy was thirty-seven years. In France it was twenty-six years, and in the American colonies it was fifty-one years. In the 1790s American male longevity rose to fifty-six years. But by 1850 life expectancy had risen to forty years in England and forty-two years in France, while in the United States it had *declined* to 38.3 years.[16] The decade from 1850 to 1860 was also the period of the shortest life expectancy for American males, North and South.[17] American men in 1860 had about the same height and life-spans as the French and British and had fallen behind men in Norway and Sweden. By the dawn of the Civil War, America's physiologically based advantage in well-being had been erased. Statistically, that life expectancy was temporarily dented further by the appalling male mortality of the war between the spring of 1861 and mid-summer of 1865.

By 1870 the nation's vaunted per-capita gross domestic product, a universal measure of economic output, had been eclipsed by Belgium, the Netherlands, and the United Kingdom. The Civil War and the changes it generated cost the nation a biological and economic edge that it would not fully regain for nearly half a century.[18]

But the Civil War's side effects were not ethereal. Its effects on towns and families' daily lives were both personal and myriad. Every one of this narrative's families—the Densmores, the Vandergrifts, and the Harts—had lost someone, at home or on the battlefield. Mass movements of soldiers on trains enhanced disease vectors. This meant that many carried home diseases like typhus, diphtheria, pneumonia, tuberculosis, and cholera. Burials of the war dead and transport of their bodies for burial suddenly became huge cost factors for hundreds of thousands of families.

Although Congress had readmitted Georgia, the last "Confederate" state, to the Union in 1870, the 1870s proved a far more complicated transition than anyone could have predicted. Things were slowly moving in the right direction until October 1871, when unexpected and unrelated events energized wide public fear. Chicago's great fire destroyed much of that growing city and its surroundings. The fire caused millions of dollars in damages, destroyed 17,450 buildings, killed 250 people, and left another 90,000 homeless.[19] On the same day in Wisconsin, another massive fire erupted, wiping out towns in six counties and killing between 1,000 and 2,000 people.[20]

These catastrophes raised nationwide anxiety. The specter of a world out of control took on a life of its own, and responses varied from depression to anger and overreaction. Mobs in Midwest cities like Detroit and Columbus protested the state and federal governments' slow responses to the disasters. Millions of ordinary workers snarled about rising food prices and falling wages. In Congress, the North's most reactionary Republican Confederacy haters wanted to extract yet more revenge. In the South, Night Riders of several ilks also sought revenge.[21]

In 1872, hoping to assuage continuing regional social tensions, Congress passed and President U. S. Grant signed the Amnesty Act, restoring citizenship to all Southerners, save about five hundred Confederate leaders. But in 1873 some of Quantrill's former rangers, among them Jesse and Frank James, morphed into railroad bandits in the Midwest, and Union General Custer and his 7th Cavalry began engaging the Sioux tribes. This created more wasteful trouble and directed more resources away from basic community needs. The motives, too, were complicated: businessmen wanted railroad expansion; settlers were hungry for land, roads, and bridges; and, at the expense of Native Americans, millions held out hope for gold in the Black Hills to fix the nation's problem of too little hard coinage in circulation.

Finally, in the fall of 1873, a combination of greed and dodgy Northern business practices created a tipping point, and the New York Stock Market buckled under the weight of bad debts. This was primarily due to overexpansion of the railroads and the era's value-inflated derivative bonds[22] issued by the railroads for sale to the public. History was repeating itself—ninety years earlier, federal bonds issued to Revolutionary War veterans by the Continental Congress had been manipulated by associates of Alexander Hamilton in Philadelphia. That remembered episode had been America's first version of the "Big Short," which had sucked assets from impoverished veterans into Philadelphia's elite hustler class. In contrast to the manufactured, pre–Whiskey Rebellion bond devaluations, the railroad's bankers also got stung in 1873. Bank after bank collapsed, deepening the economic crisis.

The depression did not ease until early 1879. It affected this book's subject families in quite different ways. Flashy J. J. Vandergrift weathered the first round of depressed prices. He was brilliant at agilely dodging economic bullets. His sense of risks versus opportunity was as refined as a watchmaker's most complicated movements. He and his associates organized America's first formal Oil Trader's Exchange in Pittsburgh on July 21, 1878. J. J. also founded its successor, the Pittsburgh Petroleum Exchange, in 1882. Four or five years before that exchange opened, Vandergrifts and allied oilmen had operated a small exchange out of Oil City, Pennsylvania, and had created enough competition for Rockefeller, who was based in Cleveland, to buy out J. J.'s own oil operations. It was not a pure love match, but by late 1875 J. J. was both a vice president of Rockefeller's Standard Oil *and* on its board of directors.[23] By 1881 his holdings in his own limited Union pipeline company also merged with Standard Oil.[24]

Even as J. J. became a Rockefeller man in the 1870s, Pittsburgh's first oil exchange allowed about three hundred member traders,[25] most from western Pennsylvania, western New York, and Ohio, to retain just enough independence to operate for another five to six years as Rockefeller's combine gathered financial steam and political power. During that interlude, J. J. and his sons and partners also branched out, as noted, creating new enterprises outside of Standard Oil, including piping natural gas, creating large-grain commodity combines, and venturing into the business of travel, transport, and banking.

Family Matters

Just like his uncle six generations before, the aforementioned "opulent merchant" Paulus Vandergrift of New Amsterdam in the 1650s, J. J. scooped up fruits too small for the emerging Rockefeller machine to focus on in northwestern Pennsylvania and northwestern West Virginia. To top it off, J. J. was better diversified—he knew oil, gas, transport by rail and river, grain and meat commodities, refining, and travel, and he collected franchise income from low-risk, exchange-house brokerage fees. By the time he joined Standard Oil, he was already one of western Pennsylvania's half dozen most powerful men. But unlike many of his competitors, he had few enemies and thus avoided a ruthless businessman's costly battles to counter constant espionage from rage-obsessed competitors. As a businessman, J. J. was able to avoid policing costs similar to those that had consumed significant Union resources during the South's Reconstruction era.

By the mid-1870s J. J. was no longer a working river man. Like Paulus Vandergrift he had become the merchant, entrepreneur, and founder of multiple enterprises that spanned wide sectors of the American economy.[26] He was positioned to win big when the Long Depression of 1872 to 1879 lifted. None of his enterprises were forced into bankruptcy. He always sensed the limits and sold or restructured, ever agile and aware. He took risks and rewards in balance.

The mid-1870s found J. J.'s sister-in-law, Sarah Ann Hoffman, now Mrs. Samuel Wheaton, living on Water Street in Wheeling, West Virginia. Samuel was a master carpenter and the foreman in a steamboat repair dockyard. That business's major partners and shareholders included J. J., his father; William Knowles Vandergrift, his uncle; the legendary Captain John Vandergrift of early riverboat fame; and others. Sarah Ann and her daughter, Sophia Irene Vandergrift, and Sophia's young half brothers, John and Joseph Wheaton, were provided for through constant employment during that period. Their repair shops did make money, but family obligations were met without fanfare. Wheaton's constant employ throughout the brutal 1870s was both rare and precious. But it wasn't condescending charity—as one of the nation's most skilled steamboat paddle-wheel builders, Samuel Wheaton was a very valuable employee in a highly competitive business.

In contrast, the 1870s were much harder on western Pennsylvania's Densmores. The iron business was tense and turbulent, especially for the smaller, family-owned operations. Many highly skilled iron workers preferred work at such mills simply because the human connection and conditions were sunnier than in the emerging big-box operations with work rolls of thousands. All of the Densmore iron men struggled to one degree or another in the 1870s, especially between 1873 and 1876, when few managed a full fifty- to sixty-hour week's work. They and their employers faced shop fires, growing labor-union tensions, market rigging, and the transition to high-speed steel production to feed the ever-expanding railroads. On the shop floor, changes in manufacturing technology also began to limit the role and wages of the old-style puddlers.

Nat the teamster likely struggled the most—during the 1870s his wages stuck somewhere between nine to eleven dollars a week, when work was to be had. With four growing children, Nat had only a modest chance of amassing savings. He had returned to Georges Township from Brownsville. His entry on the 1870 US Census places his residence some distance from Fairchance's center. His daughter Hannah had died in 1869, and he and his wife, Susan, may have moved to another house farther from Oliphant's Works.

Nat had banked on his father's former occupation as a wagoner, which held great promise when he made his choice in the mid-1830s. But a wagoner's work had stagnated into a low-wage, low-education sideline to canal boats and railroads by the time he was thirty-five years old. Trapped in his father Old Robert's world, he had retreated from the world of his youngest brothers, Sam and Ollie, when he moved to Brownsville in the late 1850s. His brothers, in contrast, moved out of Fairchance to take on the changing world with jaws set.

By the mid-1870s Sam was farming in Slabtown near Kittanning[27] and also working variously as an iron heater, or "boiler." In the technology of the 1860s and 1870s, a boiler oversaw the heat and status of molten iron forming in a puddling furnace that held 500 to 600 pounds of iron ore.[28] Judging the moment at which it began to crystallize and form solid material was learned through long experience and was a highly valued skill. As the slag and ore transformed, the right moment for puddling was chosen with care. The puddler reached in with long tongs to form a mass, or ball, of the firming melt—usually weighing 150 to 200 pounds—working it with his tongs until it was ready to be pulled out, tossed on a cart, then moved to a mechanical squeezer, which compressed it, releasing impurities. If those steps went as planned, well-mixed, tough, fracture-resistant wrought[29] iron was the product delivered to the roller. The roller then pressed it between massive circular drums, the roll trains, until it was sized properly for the finished product it would become. The catchers caught the hot sheet and returned it for further thinning in the rolls. Then came more steps of forming or finishing by other work crews.

All of these daily jobs consumed at least 3,500 to 4,500 work calories per ten- to twelve-hour shift. All required superb skills, great strength, and endurance to dangerous, prolonged heat and ear-damaging noise. There were no schools to teach this in the 1800s. One signed on as a young man of thirteen to seventeen years of age and, for two to three dollars a week, learned it as cheap labor, helpers, or apprentices. Once trained, respect among other workingmen was a bonus on the wages. So were good employers who focused on safety, fresh water, and sane shifts. None of these benefits, however, were guaranteed.

Sam's work as a boiler had paid about twenty-five dollars a week in Pittsburgh in 1868, and it probably paid twenty-two or twenty-three dollars in Kittanning. He and his wife, Jennie, had four children at that time,[30] and they also often took in widowed or orphaned Glenn relatives. Densmores from both Uniontown/Fayette and Beaver Counties, Pennsylvania, also showed up in Kittanning as the Long Depression deepened. Sam worked mostly in Pittsburgh during 1868, 1869, and 1870, and he was listed in Thurston's directories of Birmingham. He might have been able to save about four or five dollars a week. By 1871 or 1872 he was likely working primarily in Kittanning, where his wife and children resided.

The most refined of Old Robert's sons, Sam dressed a bit more formally than the others when not at work in the mills. He was tallish for his era at 5'9.5", lean, and quite handsome. His neatly cut brown hair, carefully trimmed sideburns, high forehead, and striking gray eyes all added to his mystique. Sam, as he is dressed in a family photo, could walk into a room today in any American university: dark charcoal, single-button suit, neatly pressed white shirt, and hand-knotted black bowtie. Heads would turn.

Only one fragment of a letter he wrote has come to light—it is smoothly written in neat, flowing hand. Even in his photographs he exudes a confident presence. In his well-tailored Sunday suit, he looked for all the world like a successful young businessman. And he was a genius at designing, repairing, altering, and tweaking machinery. But Sam lived in two worlds. He was also a consummate puddler and roller. In those work moments he would be standing at the mouth of a heating furnace, stripped to the waist, sweating, dirt-streaked, and smelling like a football locker room.

That is how Sam spent two hundred days or more each year. Since an engineer or machinist was paid only fourteen to eighteen dollars a week from 1867 to 1868, he listed himself in directories simply as a laborer, but he worked most often as a heater, which paid 30 percent higher wages than his engineering skills normally brought in. As machinists and engineers were quite respected occupations, he may have minimized his yearly occupational taxes in Allegheny or Armstrong County by identifying himself as in a lower wage scale.

Sam interacted on a far wider level than did Nat, Ollie, or Robert Jr. He was a joiner, networking other businessmen and professionals in groups like the Odd Fellows and the Society of Red Men[31] in Connellsville.[32] Recall that by 1880 or 1881 his networking paid off in spades with the best job of his life—in the huge Trotter Coke Works a few miles northwest of Connellsville, owned by the Connellsville Gas-Coal Company,[33] as foreman of Trotter's machinery repair shop. The machinery included the mechanicals for over two hundred coke ovens in 1881, with another two hundred under construction in 1882. There were also furnaces, mineshaft fans, pumps, engines, and the complex's various waterworks and tool-making forges. It paid Sam a princely fifty dollars a week, precisely the same wage his great niece, college-educated Avis Densmore, would earn as a public schoolteacher in Westchester, Pennsylvania, seventy years later.

Sam had reached his pinnacle, and merely advertising his name was a business asset. The coke works knew it had hired *the* best machinist, engineer, foreman, and hands-on iron man it could find. And the men working under him approved. His fire-roughened and permanently bent left hand, which had held the puddler's iron stirring rod, was living proof that he was no ordinary management slicker—he had done the same jobs as they did, shift after shift, and in "Old Smokey" to boot. Then there were the tales of his father, Old Robert, kneeling to watch the color and heat of the charcoal flame at Gibson's Etna forge just eight miles away from Trotter's during the legendary early days of Fayette County iron making. There was also the Oliphant connection for both Sam and his father. It had, after all, been Fidelio Hughes Oliphant who had made some of the earliest blast-furnace coke in the 1830s.

Oliphant's early experiments with coke were just that. His small-scale use of coke turned out some very fine iron, but coke was not yet ready for prime time, given the inefficient furnace technology of the 1830s. By 1880 coke was indispensable to the Age of Steel. The railroad's demands for more durable steel rails in the mid-1860s had also led to greater use of steel in machines, building construction, gears, ball bearings, bolts, bridge supports, and hardened roll trains. As the economy shook off the Depression of the 1870s and the turbulent, riot-laced years of 1876 and 1877, the industrial appetite for coke was insatiable. But, as in all things American, that too would evolve.

For Ollie and Elizabeth, this period was an excruciating series of ups and downs. So far in the 1860s they had two healthy young sons and three infant deaths. The demographic curse had visited them a fourth time, but once again it was lifted on November 15, 1873, when Ellen, called "Ella," was born as the Long Depression began. Coincidentally, this was just about the time the New York Stock Exchange crumbled. Two years later, another son, Frederick, was born on December 7, 1875. Little Freddie[34] died on June 29, 1877, in Allegheny County in the midst of one of the most disturbing summers in American history. As the harsh economy and the host of worsening environmental factors in the 1870s claimed more children, Ollie again retreated into his anthem of work, eat, sweat, and save. There was likely a good dose of silent prayer tossed into the mix. Elizabeth again retreated to Fairchance.

Turbulence and the Nation's Centennial

The nation's centennial year of 1876 was an odd mix of celebratory fantasy and treacherous politics. One would have thought—after a century of hands-on experience at governing, and the Civil War to clear everyone's heads—that the centennial-year presidential election of 1876 would have been handled more carefully. The national election's public vote count went, by a small margin, to Samuel J. Tilden, a Democrat.[35] The Republican candidate, Rutherford B. Hayes, lost the popular vote but eventually won the presidency by *one* vote in the Electoral College.[36] Hung up in uncertainty, behind-the-scenes bargaining began almost immediately. Votes were traded and principles abandoned. Souls were bought and sold in the ensuing four months after the election. On March 2, 1877, Rutherford B. Hayes was elected president by the "bargained" Electoral College. By the merest thread, the presidency was retained by the Civil War's party of Lincoln, but the bargain made with Southern Democratic delegates was for disputed votes in Florida, Louisiana, South Carolina, and Oregon in return for a "back hallway" presidential promise to end enforcement of Reconstruction in the South. Had there been no Depression of 1873 to further distract the public, it seems less likely that such a crass election bargain could have been concluded.

The biggest losers of the election were Southern blacks. Others were the down and out everywhere—victims of the Long Depression. Ordinary citizens continued to lose trust in the federal government, partly because the voting majority's intent had been again nullified by Southern strategists. Southern blacks quickly lost their Reconstruction-era gains of the vote, equal citizenship, and their fleeting place at the Big Table of Congressional elective office.

North, South, and Midwest, the economics of the 1870s had also hurt farmers badly. The Indian Wars in the "New West" drug on—embarrassing, unprincipled throwbacks to an earlier America. On June 25 and 26, 1876, General Custer learned the hard way just how Sitting Bull and his allies at the Little Big Horn felt about cavalry raids on unarmed women and children asleep in their tipis. Overlooked by historians was the fact that Custer's Plains Indian adversaries, among the best-fed (they ate bison), strongest, and tallest men in the world,[37] easily overpowered many cavalry troopers in hand-to-hand combat. No "American," of course, could outride them. The demise of handsome, headline-hungry George Armstrong Custer deeply unsettled Eastern society. In 1876 the growing myth of Union Cavalry invincibility quickly deflated like a balloon.

Given the deal they negotiated with moderate Republicans for their electoral votes, Southern Democrats in Congress smirked, then moved quickly to rid their states of Republican organizations, newspapers, "carpet baggers," and elected officials.[38] The emerging Republican Party in the South vanished within months. Northern newspapers sounded off about President Hayes's dreadful "Southern Policy." One Ohio paper decried Hayes's obvious "compact with the

Master Class of the South."[39] Eventually Hayes obediently pressed the South's three lonely Republican governors[40] to resign their offices. On April 10, 1877, he ordered the removal of Union troops from the South. The South promptly mounted a reign of terror targeting blacks, Republicans, and others who irritated the ruling white class.[41] After Union troops exited, the list of cultural irritants continued to grow.

Southern sharecroppers, both black and white, were already in distress from the Depression that began in 1873. Many poor white farmers who came of age just after the war harbored deeply troubling memories of a Confederate government that had let their families starve while their forcibly conscripted fathers and older brothers did the dirty battlefield work of 1864 to 1865.

In just eight weeks the North would also go through upheavals based on both epic corporate misbehavior and rapidly deteriorating conditions of work, wages, and well-being. Greedy corporate authoritarians in the North, coupled with Southern race, class, and religious authoritarians, managed between them to upset the fragilely reunited nation's apple cart.

While the South's poor, rural families suffered, Northern workers also suffered sudden and arbitrarily reduced wages, increased shift hours, and rising cost of staples. Bankrupt farmers sold out, further lowering national food production. These trials led to an increasingly angry labor environment focused on one version or another of "fairness." The Depression of 1873 had financially destroyed wide segments of America's workers. Historian Michael Bellesiles points this out in reference to the first great American wave of tramps, later called "hobos."

> That the tramps appeared so suddenly on the American scene is easily explained. The Depression that started in 1873 devastated the American working class. Those lucky enough not to lose their jobs saw their wages cut. Those who lost their jobs enjoyed no safety net beyond the generosity of some churches.... Not surprisingly, many jobless workers took to the road and rails in search of work.[42]

The Densmores, Harts, and several third-generation branches of Vandergrifts in western Pennsylvania, West Virginia, and Ohio also found their wages eroding. Part of that third generation of younger sons moved west to Indiana, Illinois, Kansas, and Iowa. A number of young Vandergrifts who stayed took on ordinary jobs in Pittsburgh, like "clerk," "laborer," "waiter," and "carpenter's apprentice."[43] The military, economic, and cultural dislocations that had exploded in April 1861 continued to roll like nighttime thunder across America's angry, lightning-ridden skies.

While solid middle- and upper-middle class Americans trimmed their household servants and shortened seaside vacations to "make do," millions of others reduced their food intake, darned worn-out socks, and patched hand-me-down clothing for the nth time. Another wave of seven- and eight-year-olds became water boys in mills or labored in seaboard textile sweatshops. Fathers re-soled their kids' winter shoes. In summer many went barefoot. More breakfasts consisted of corn meal mush.

On Birmingham's Monongahela waterfront, the Vandergrift skiff builders—James, his sons, and his sons-in-law—saw their orders drop sharply in 1873. The same had happened to Scudder Vandergrift, named for Scudder Hart, the well-known river man of Beaver, Pennsylvania, and a grandson of John Hart, signer. As a coach builder in Pittsburgh, Scudder and his extended family had done handsomely well during the Civil War, as the Union Army Quartermaster for the Pittsburgh district issued a constant stream of orders for wagons. Scudder paid more in federal taxes on those orders in the mid-1860s[44] than unskilled laborers earned in a year. But that level of business was gone by 1876. Some of the Vandergrift boys took work on the railroads, as did some of their second and third cousins who moved into Northeastern West Virginia.

The Vandergrifts who continued to retain wealth were James and Lewis Vandergrift, boat owners and captains. But it was J. J. Vandergrift, his invested but ailing father William Knowles, and J. J.'s son, young oil dealer William Vandergrift, who most profited from their new energy business and its diversified spin-offs. By 1876 and 1877 the Pittsburgh Vandergrifts were clearly fragmenting into "rich" (oil, gas, banking), "pleasantly prosperous" (riverboats), and "losing ground" (public wage work) sub-branches of their clan.

Simultaneously, the Densmore brothers of Fayette County were also fragmenting into financially stable, skilled working-class Ollie, the best at saving due to his small family; at-risk, skilled working-class Sam and Robert Jr., who had to deal with growing families and unpredictable bosses; and struggling, less-skilled Nat, increasingly at the mercy of day-to-day hauling jobs. These dynamics—work identity, self-sufficiency, and self-judgment about success and failure—are powerful agents that can enhance or destroy family networks. Nat's core family role was shrinking, Ollie's was expanding, Robert Jr.'s was static as the titular head, and Sam's life was split between his home in Kittanning and his various work sites.

In ways sometimes overlooked in modern academic anthropology, men of the era were under immense societal pressure to be successful providers. For most ordinary American men, it wasn't quite the neatly structured "men can do anything" rules of carefree patriarchy some academicians imagine to have existed. Ordinary workingmen of the 1870s were often ruled as ruthlessly by the owner class of American industry as by any hated monarch. And they were just as trapped by sixty to eighty hours of work a week as were women with frequent pregnancies. If one accepts the statistics published in S. J. Kleinberg's work, Pittsburgh male factory workers of the 1870s and 1880s were more likely to die prematurely from workplace factors than their wives were from pregnancies.[45]

Whatever one currently thinks of gender roles, it was *not* an idyllic world in the 1870s for a clear majority of ordinary American men *and* women. The appalling loss of marriageable young men to the Civil War had upended the male/female sex ratio and impacted female worldviews. An unstable economy also amplified social changes. In this lived reality, the urge for reforms blossomed. Women wanted the vote, access to high school and college education, opportunities for nursing or teaching professions, and clearer property rights.[46] Many women lobbied for temperance. Two dollars a week for cigars and taproom rye whiskey with beer chasers was one thing in the boom days of the North's 1860s war economy. After 1873 a husband's cigar and whiskey consumption stepped hard on food and rent budgets at that once common one- or two-dollar-a-week male "allowance."

For their part, men wanted the weekly wages of the late 1860s and their work shifts trimmed from seventy-two to eighty-four hours a week back to the fifty-four hours a week of the late 1850s. An evening and a full Sunday off would allow them to see their kids or attend a church picnic. Anything was better than their current reality of constant sleep, eat, work, eat, sleep. They also wanted safer working conditions. But business tycoons shunned the cost of safety features and demanded ever-faster output. Injury rates and accidental deaths began skyrocketing at the larger works, where the proportion of unskilled labor rose as former skilled jobs and re-engineered manufacturing processes began to reduce or eliminate the best earning veterans.

After 1870 unskilled workers in Pittsburgh suffered five times as many workplace accidents as white-collar workers and two and a half times the on-the-job accident rates of the skilled veterans.[47] The city's post–Civil War flood of unskilled workers—many of them recently arrived immigrants—died at *twice* the rate of white-collar workers from all causes. Death rates from all causes among skilled workers fell neatly between the rates among white-collar workers and the unskilled.[48] In the 1870s negative changes in Pittsburgh's working conditions were clearly killing and injuring more men.

As the number of veteran puddlers declined on shop floors, catastrophic burn rates rose alarmingly among the unskilled. A man could be splashed by hot iron in the face and blinded, his ears or nose burned off in seconds, or a hand could be lost in one fatigued moment at the mechanical ingot squeezer. One could easily be killed by core body shock from splatter burns on the chest and upper arms. In any of these cases, a worker's career was over in an instant. Instead of thirteen to fifteen dollars a week, an injured survivor would become a common day laborer, earning a dollar or so a day for three or four days a week. His children hungry, his twelve-year-old son would have to quit school and go to work as a mill helper at $2.60 to $2.80 a week. His wife would "make do," taking in laundry or boarders. And if he went crazy and took to the road, a broken tramp, what would happen to his family? There was no publicly funded social agency to step in during the 1870s. There was no unemployment compensation. Just hunger and a sense of failure. This was *not* the America of their grandfathers!

Naturally, veteran laborers formed unions to press for a measure of sanity in the dramatic change from "valued skilled worker" in a medium-sized works to just another expendable iron juggler on a roll of two thousand men. At that cue the emerging business titans pushed back.

The Great Strike of 1877

For five years the Pennsylvania and B&O railroads had been systematically reducing their workers' pay rates. Railroad men had been asking for restoration of former pay rates, saner work schedules, and safety improvements. But messing with the all-powerful railroads that owned US congressmen and senators by the dozen was like pulling the hammer back on a loaded rifle pointed directly at the upset workers, not at the railroads.

It was 1877. By early summer tensions over wages and an increasingly out-of-control wave of violence in the South were at a peak. Hundreds of thousands of increasingly desperate wage workers began to join unions and push for changes. The first trainman's union was organized on June 2, 1877, in Allegheny City in northwest Pittsburgh, near the locale where George Vandergrift, recently deceased, had added to his lot in 1849.

Elsewhere, large rallies of angry, summarily laid-off workers began to pop up. Those "dangerous" worker reactions had already been reported in foreboding tones for several years by a number of the nation's major newspapers. Several of those newspapers had sensationally conflated, perhaps intentionally, the nation's growing labor unrest with Russia's growing communist movement. And there *was* just enough of a thread of ideological interest in socialism among some American workers to puff up the alleged dangers. That, along with the increased number of tramps, had much of inconvenienced middle-class America terrified. Many of the urban middle class imagined an imminent Russian-style communist revolt led by the poor, lazy, uneducated, and heavy-drinking working classes. They believed that labor's intent was to take over, then destroy, America.[49]

The small but violent group of "Molly Maguires" in Pennsylvania's Reading area and their spectacularly reported trials[50] had further convinced millions of white-collar Americans that the working classes, replete with immigrants, were in fact demanding something for nothing—and if most of the tattered and worn tramps moving about the country really wanted to better themselves, there were jobs aplenty if only they would wash up and apply for one. Most Americans now recognize the fantasy in this conversation—except for politicians' buzz phrases like "makers" versus "takers," it has not changed one whit in the last 150 years.

As urban middle-class and owner-class fears of Communism and of the "great unwashed" rose, programs to feed and help the poor were actually closed down. This made circumstances even worse. As Michael Bellesiles puts it, "The tramp scare and the Molly Maguire trials presaged the collapse of the ideal of American Exceptionalism. No longer could the United States boast to be free from the danger of class warfare."[51]

Well-Being—Lived Definitions and Realities

White middle- and upper-class Americans had already redefined the Founders' 1776 declaration of freedom to pursue "happiness," then understood as basic physical security, unregulated self-sufficiency, and well-being, into a headier type of success based on comforts derived from income, education, and class status. Of course, most of that middle and upper class did not comprehend the working class's worldviews or their problems. Huge swaths of America already lived in parallel universes, as much of America still does. One worldview embraced the American economic dream of its era. The other approximated the American worker's worst nightmare: a nation that would become like the Europe or British isles of their forefathers—a world in which the working, wage-earning majority once again lost all control over land, resources, and the value of their labor to overlords, losses that would again doom them to helplessness, hungry children, and much shorter lives.

In contrast, working- and farming-class America still calculated its lot—"How are we doing?"—primarily on the original version of freedom to pursue America's physiological advantage. They were in the numerical majority. But in urban centers of the Northeast and upper Midwest, the middle and upper classes were large enough, and their social worlds small enough, that they actually believed they were in the majority and that their worldview was the norm. The well off in 1877 may have been formally better educated, but they certainly were not well informed about the other two thirds of America's polity. Many middle- and upper-class wives practiced some form of contraception; two- and three-children families were becoming the norm. Their nutrition was ample, and their houses were cleaner and far less crowded than in blue-collar, working-class households. They experienced fewer infant deaths and lower disease rates, and they had much less fear of economic insecurity. They assumed the rest of the world was the same.

Their primary concerns and sense of financial "sacrifices" generally consisted of giving up a housekeeper, wearing two-year-old clothes, or not being able to purchase an insulated ice chest or a piece of George Eastlake's expensive new style of furniture. For them, "disappointment" meant selling their private carriage and riding a horse-drawn public trolley or passing on a seaside New Jersey vacation. In contrast, for millions of wage workers, "disappointment" meant no eggs and milk for their children, a much higher rate of child mortality, constant fear, and a veritable sea of corn meal mush. At the core of each worldview in 1877 were two dramatically different definitions of American success.

In fairness, those who identified with the warnings of a communist insurrection in major newspapers' editorial pages did not know that the big railroads, at once the largest employers in the United States *and* the most generous business to their shareholders, kept their premiums[52] at 6 percent to 10 percent a year throughout the entire Depression of 1873 to 1879. Stockholders, many of them middle and upper-middle class, were naturally overjoyed. Behind the scenes, the Pennsylvania Railroad and the Baltimore & Ohio had paid those stock and bond holders boom-time earnings in the midst of a depression by systematically and repetitively lowering their workers' wages by fiat—often unannounced. The fight among wage earners was for a pay envelope that they had agreed to—not one cagily reduced behind closed doors and handed them *after* they had done the work.

Historian Bellesiles lays it out for the B&O Railroad firemen, who shoveled the coal in train engines.[53] They "saw their wages fall from $55 a month in 1873 to $30 in 1877."[54] That was more than a 40 percent cut, even as the B&O paid out record dividends to unsuspecting shareholders. The wages of brakemen, a crucial and skilled job in the era before young George Westinghouse's air brakes took the industry by storm, fell from seventy dollars a month in 1873 to thirty dollars a month in 1877. That was not only a 60 percent cut in pay but a series of de facto cash transfers from the food and household budgets of their workers to bond holders and company profits. These shenanigans put direct downward pressure on the physiological well-being of more than a million railroad workers' children born between 1870 and 1880. The sons of those railroaders—and millions of other working men like them—would average only 5'6.7" in adult height, a loss of seven-tenths of an inch, and a lifespan reduced by about another four years, all in just one greed-soaked decade.[55] In 1877 America's railroad Robber Barons were actively engaged in the direct theft of promised wages and measurable diminishment of the nation's well-being.

The railroad's salary reductions also began to erase the pay and work-identity distinctions between skilled (brakeman) and less skilled (fireman), whose high manual work intensity meant higher food costs. The men shoveling coal had to eat many more calories than the brakemen or engineers, and as their wages declined they consumed a steadily increasing share of the weekly food budget. Those corporate strategies intentionally targeted wages and their workers' self-sufficiency. The Pennsylvania Railroad employed about two hundred thousand workers at that time. If we add in an average of four family members supported by each worker, those directly damaged included a million citizens in all. In regional economies their severe, unannounced pay cuts in the summer of 1877 were equal in impact to a thousand Anchor Nail and Tack companies lowering wages all at once, or outright shutting down. The B&O, smaller by about half, held viselike power over more than one hundred thousand wage-earning families—all told, a half-million people. The two railroads controlled the lives of 1.5 million people in a nation of about 50 million—about 3 percent of the total population. In late 2018 and early 2019, a crippling government shutdown of thirty-two days directly affected eight hundred thousand federal workers and about one hundred thousand contractors; using a generous additional family size of 2.5, 2.25 million workers and their dependents were affected directly—about seven-tenths of a percent of the population in a nation of 330 million. The statistical power of the railroad strikes had an impact on life in 1877 that was four to five magnitudes greater than the 2018 to 2019 shutdown.

The Great Strike, 1877

Pent-up emotions over pay cuts and unfair treatment finally erupted in the B&O Railroad's Camden Junction yard several miles from Baltimore around noon on July 16, 1877.[56] That morning, the Baltimore morning newspaper reported yet another surprise wage cut directed by smug, arrogant John Garrett, president of the B&O. That is when trouble hit the fan.[57] The era's caricatures of illiterate, common workingmen notwithstanding, surprising numbers of disgusted B&O workingmen could read the morning papers. Dozens gathered spontaneously at Camden Junction Station to complain among themselves. In response, a fireman on one train in the yard stepped off, refusing to shovel more coal. Then another fireman followed.

By two o'clock in the afternoon, there were more than one hundred seriously upset B&O men in the yard, blocking outgoing trains. B&O managers at the Camden junction demanded city police help. Baltimore's mayor was a big B&O stockholder, and he tried to accommodate, but a local judge balked at the legality of using city police out in the county, beyond their jurisdiction. Garrett[58] then summarily deputized the local police as "special railway police." Meanwhile, his son-in-law John King hastily gathered a mob of paid strikebreakers. All striking employees at the yard were fired on the spot. The trains moved again.

But the strike was already spreading like wildfire. Its next locus was Martinsburg, West Virginia, a strategic train yard and round house complex on the main B&O track west to the Ohio Valley. The strikers at Martinsburg lived in a different world than that of Baltimore. Theirs was a world of coal mines, timber crews, forgemen, and local artisans and merchants in all the basics: blacksmiths, saddles, rifle makers, farm equipment, wagons, and shoes. It was a world of skills, contracts by handshake, and the sacrament of hard work. A high proportion of the Martinsburg area's citizens turned out at the yard and along the track to support the strike. It was their worldview—their values and culture—that men like Garrett most hated.

Enraged, Garrett's son-in-law, King, telegrammed the governor of West Virginia, *directing* him to break the strike. The governor quickly ordered out the Berkeley County militia[59] based on King's fabricated claim of extensive violent rioting and mayhem in Martinburg.

Not long after arriving in Martinsburg, a twenty-eight-year-old striker named William Vandergriff, revolver in hand, fired a warning shot toward the militia unit as he tried to hold closed a track switch. Some accounts claim his bullet grazed a soldier. Two militiamen responded with a volley of rifle fire and grievously wounded William. Described by big city newspapers at the time as a "local railroad hand," William was, in fact, an experienced locomotive engineer. He was the railroad world's equivalent to the princely skilled working status enjoyed by iron puddlers and rollers like Ollie, Robert Jr., and Sam Densmore. Yet William Vandergriff was anything but a "local railroad hand." Born in Pittsburgh's 6th Ward in 1849, he was the only living son of George Vandergrift,[60] boat builder and brother of William Knowles Vandergrift. That made William a first cousin of the now rich and powerful J. J. Vandergrift, vice president of Standard Oil. Young William was not only a son of one of the most powerful families in Western Pennsylvania, he, like the Harts in Randolph County, West Virginia, was a great-great-grandson of John Hart, signer.

I can find no historical account that identifies William in an accurate context during the railroad strikes. The Martinsburg *Statesman* carried the most authoritative account:

> The militia company was deployed on both sides of a train which was about starting, an engineer and fireman having volunteered to work. As the train reached the switch one of the strikers, William Vandergriff, seized the switch ball to run the train on the side of the track. John Poisal, a member of the militia company, jumped from the pilot of the engine and attempted to replace the switch so that the train should go on. Vandergriff fired two shots at Poisal,[61] one causing a slight flesh wound in the side of the head. Poisal returned the fire, shooting Vandergriff through the hip. Several other shots were fired at Vandergriff, striking him in the hand and arm.[62]

It seems the news outlets of the day preferred to cast the first striker to die in what would come to be known as the Great Railroad Strike of 1877 as an unknown rabble-rouser from somewhere in West "By God" Virginia rather than a well-placed victim of the nation's structural and class problems. William was living proof of diverging worldviews and the competition between different definitions of American well-being, "Exceptionalism," and "Dream" held among differently situated branches of the Vandergrift clan. It had taken only forty years of asymmetrical Vandergrift wealth building, an erratic economy, and one additional doubling of the nation's population to generate those family rifts.

William's father, George, had died two years earlier in 1875, so William was grieved by his widowed mother, Julia, his in-laws, and his twenty-one-year-old wife, Ida, whom he had married in Martinsburg thirteen months prior. She was then pregnant with their first child.

One cannot help but wonder if one of the rounds to hit William came from a third or fourth Hart or Chenowith cousin's rifle. He was carried to the house of his father-in-law, Jacob B. Dock, at 689 Queen Street, Martinsburg. The poor fellow had his arm amputated and lingered nine days in deep pain. Despite elaborate efforts to save him, he died. As no Pittsburgh Vandergrifts showed up, Ida[63] buried William in Green Hill Cemetery in Martinsburg. It was a fine marker, to which many local strikers contributed. William's West Virginia death certificate informant was Jacob Dock. That certificate confirms William's parentage:

28 July 1877 Died—Martinsburg, Berkeley, Wva.
Age 28/white/married/male
Fath. Geo. Vandergriff
Mother Julia Vandergriff.[64]

Later that year Ida delivered his son, whom she named William. The fact that locomotive engineer William was never connected by the press to the Pittsburgh Vandergrifts and that he was not buried in Allegheny Cemetery with his extended Vandergrift family could signal that his involvement in the strike branded him as a traitor to his class. A few months later, Thomas Scott, the Pennsylvania Railroad's president, dedicated the first formal toast to exchange founder J. J. Vandergrift in the ceremony that opened the newly built Oil Exchange. B&O president Garrett attended and also raised his glass. I rest the case.

Despite this treatment of William, the Vandergrifts had been one of those rare families that provided some of the glue that kept separate tiers of society connected. They had come to Pittsburgh in late frontier days, had worked hard, and had risen. And with them had risen local sons-in-law and daughters-in-law and many of their best workers.

Most of the Vandergrift brothers had always lived in proximity to their work. They were known widely. As a family-networked enterprise, they had been employers for two to three generations. No telling how many hundreds, even thousands, of workingmen and their fathers, brothers, uncles, or grandfathers had worked for one Vandergrift or another over the previous forty-five years. A number of their sons and grandsons had married the daughters of skilled workers, just as Captain Benjamin Franklin Vandergrift of the *Red Fox* had married the daughter of master machinist Joseph Hoffman. Sadly, the era of inclusion was fading, replaced by the very kind of class/caste system based on wealth and breeding that William's great-great-grandfather, John Hart, and the other more famous Founders had contested in their Declaration 101 years earlier, to the month.

FIGURE 1. Old Robert Densmore.

FIGURE 2. Old Robert's wife, Hannah Glenn Dunsmore, Tent Church Cemetery.

FIGURE 3. The National Road east of Uniontown, ca. 1900.

FIGURE 4. Flashy J. J. Vandergrift, ca. 1890.

FIGURE 5. Riverboat near the Point, Pittsburgh, Pennsylvania, ca 1880.

FIGURE 6. Robert Jr., puddler and Civil War veteran, ca. 1870.

FIGURE 7. Robert Jr. and Elizabeth Carr Densmore in Fairchance, Pennsylvania, ca. 1900.

FIGURE 8. F. H. O. "Ollie" Densmore, ca. 1910.

FIGURE 9. F. H. O. Densmore's payroll and account book cover.

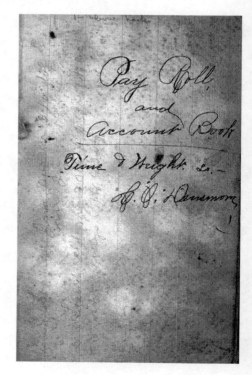

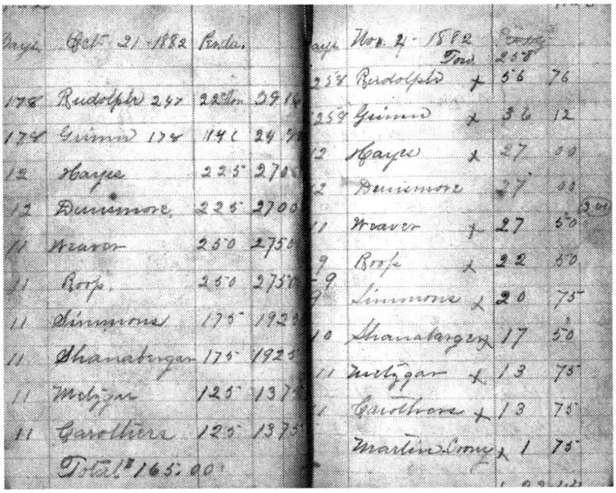

Days | Oct 21 1882 | Rate
178 Rudolph 247 | 22 1/2 ton | 39 1[illegible]
178 Grimm 178 | 1 1/2 c | 24 [illegible]
12 Hayes | 2 25 | 27 00
12 Densmore | 2 25 | 27 00
11 Weaver | 2 50 | 27 50
11 Roop | 2 50 | 27 50
11 Simmons | 1 75 | 19 25
11 Shanabarger | 1 75 | 19 25
11 Metzger | 1 25 | 13 75
11 Carothers | 1 25 | 13 75
Total $165.00

Days | Nov 4 1882 | Tons 258
258 Rudolph x 56 76
258 Grimm x 36 12
12 Hayes x 27 00
12 Densmore 27 00
11 Weaver x 27 50
9 Roop x 22 50
9 Simmons x 20 75
10 Shanabarger x 17 50
11 Metzgar x 13 75
11 Carothers x 13 75
Martin Crony x 1 75

FIGURE 10. Pages from F. H. O. Densmore's payroll and account book.

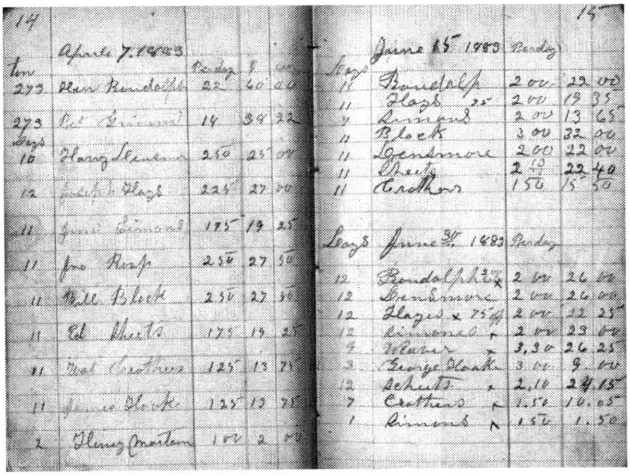

14
April 7 1883 | Per day | $
Ton
273 Han Rundolph 22 60 00
273 Pet Grimm 14 38 22
Days
10 Harry Simmons 2 50 25 00
12 Joseph Flags 2 25 27 00
11 Jim Simons 1 75 19 25
11 Jno Roop 2 50 27 50
11 Bill Block 2 50 27 50
11 Ed Sheets 1 75 19 25
11 Nat Crothers 1 25 13 75
11 James Hoake 1 25 13 75
2 Henry Martin 1 00 2 00

15
Days | June 15 1883 | Per day
11 Rondolph 2 00 22 00
11 Flags 25 2 00 19 35
Simons 2 00 13 65
11 Block 3 00 32 00
11 Densmore 2 00 22 00
11 Sheets 2 10 22 40
11 Crothers 1 50 15 50

Days | June 30 1883 | Per day
12 Rondolph 2 00 26 00
12 Densmore 2 00 26 00
12 Flags x 75 2 00 22 25
12 Simons x 2 00 23 00
9 Weaver x 3.30 26 25
3 George Hoake 3 00 9 00
12 Scheets x 2.10 24.15
7 Crothers x 1.50 10.05
1 Simons x 1.50 1.50

FIGURE 11. Pages from F. H. O. Densmore's payroll and account book.

FIGURE 12. Ollie and Elizabeth Densmore's early-death children, Minnie, Freddie, and Ellie.

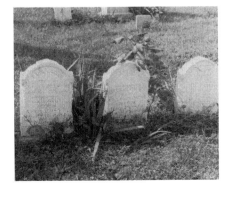

FIGURE 13. H. T. Densmore, young roller, 1883.

FIGURE 14. Sophia Vandergrift Densmore, wife of H. T. Densmore, ca. 1883.

213

FIGURE 15. 1035 Brownsville Road.

FIGURE 16. H. T., Sophia, and Elsie Densmore with John Wheaton at 2101 Sidney, ca. 1895.

FIGURE 17. The Densmore "Homestead" in Fairchance, ca. 1880s.

FIGURE 18. Elsie Densmore at 1035 Brownsville, ca. 1910.

FIGURE 19. Benjamin V. Densmore, inventor, ca. 1915.

FIGURE 20. Natalie Densmore, ca. 1923.

FIGURE 21. Samuel Densmore's eldest son, Robert, in Alaska, ca. 1900.

FIGURE 22. Ethel Cramer Densmore, charwoman, ca. 1920.

FIGURE 23. Marguerite Densmore Avera, 1980s.

FIGURE 24. Lenora Dulaney Densmore.

Chapter 15

Continuing Unrest
The 1870s

Whatever the Vandergrift family dynamics, the broader repercussions of William's shooting and subsequent death would be just one among many. The Berkeley militia was furious at the governor for using them in such a role and refused to serve further. News of a railroad worker being shot by militia sparked more protests. Like a lit black-powder fuse, the strike quickly made it all the way to San Francisco.

In response, the CEOs and presidents of all the big railroads leaned on mayors, governors, army generals, congressmen, then on President Rutherford B. Hayes. At every level of government, elected officials turned into de facto railroad-police recruiters. Most of Western Pennsylvania's industrial pockets saw brutal assaults by both Alan Pinkerton's gun-happy "railroad police" and poorly trained local militias. The severity varied from place to place, but Pittsburgh, Youngstown, Cleveland, Canton, Detroit, and Chicago were all strike targets.

By July 20, just four days after the shooting incident in Martinsburg, the railroad strike had grown into a national worker's strike across multiple industries. Big strike trouble was brewing in Pittsburgh, too, as William Vandergriff lay in agony from gunshot wounds, his name ringing like a bell in the city's working-class districts. Working-class America had plain had it with huge corporate salaries, untouchable business titans, and the politicians whose souls and principles those titans appeared to own outright. In the large body politic of America, now numbering nearly fifty million, those with calloused palms and work-bent fingers understood how things really operated in working-class society. Those with smooth palms did not.

The alarming news of William's condition was merely a factor, not the root cause of working-class Pittsburgh's explosive anger. That William Vander*griff* was William Vander*grift* was never openly acknowledged among Pittsburgh's upper classes. William, then, was merely the canary in the mine in one very crucial dimension: "Holy Ghost! If they can shoot down Will Vandergrift, what the hell will they do to *us*?"

The answer to that question, coupled with the controversial behavior of inexperienced militia and railroad police thugs, left no doubt that talks would not work. The historical Pennsylvania marker at Pittsburgh's modern 28th Street at Liberty Avenue includes this telegram in its background information: "Situation in Pittsburg becoming dangerous. Troops are in sympathy, in some instances, with the strikers. Can you rely on yours [troops]?"[1]

For two days large crowds of striking workers in iron, steel, glass, railroad, and their sympathizers fought with rocks, bottles, and some guns against heavily armed units of railroad police, contracted Pinkerton "detectives," and federally activated National Guard units imported from Philadelphia.[2] Then, on the night of July 21, the skies lit up glowing with fire along the Allegheny riverfront, not five full blocks from the home of mortally wounded William's widowed mother, Julia.

This fire was larger than any iron works in full blast or fire from a furnace blowout. The blocks-long Pennsylvania railroad station, engine house, repair shops, and bunk houses along the waterfront all fed the massive blaze. Mobs of strikers had stormed the station that afternoon, taking control of the property.

Earlier in the day, bayonets fixed on their rifle barrels, the Philadelphia units of National Guard had unwisely poured rifle fire straight into mixed civilian crowds gathered on the streets surrounding the Pennsylvania station. More than twenty civilians were killed, including one woman and three children. Hundreds of others were wounded. As it turned out, the Pennsylvania Railroad's president Scott had explicitly demanded the Pennsylvania governor John F. Hartranft to order "a rifle diet for a few days" to the strikers.[3]

It was those horrific tactics on July 21 that finally brought out the iron and steel workers from South Side's Birmingham. More than a thousand crossed the Monongahela, a huge wave announced by the steam shift whistles of the iron mills along the Birmingham waterfront.[4] According to the Pennsylvania Historical Commission, the iron and steel strikers first engaged the railroad police and US Army, then soon took over most of the railway stations and yards along the Allegheny river. By the early dawn of July 23, they had destroyed 39 buildings, 104 locomotives, 46 passenger cars, and 506 freight cars. Twenty civilians and five National Guardsmen were killed. There is no accurate account of the wounded.[5]

By July 28, the day William Vandergriff died in Martinsburg, Pennsylvania governor Hartranft arrived in Pittsburgh. He not only had called out all the state's National Guard but had control of seven hundred regular US troops, fourteen artillery companies, and two regular US infantry companies. Together, he had 3,200 troops. When it was all over, Allegheny County was actually forced by a lawsuit to pay the Pennsylvania Railroad $1.6 million in damages! The funds to pay Allegheny County's legal settlement came primarily from local workers' wage taxes and property taxes. In spite of the massive damages and train stoppages in the summer of 1877, the Pennsylvania Railroad still made a profit of $2.3 million that year!

Sometime that summer, while working at Anchor Nail and Tack, iron roller Ollie Densmore acquired a Hopkins and Allen No. 4 XL spur trigger revolver, which had been factory converted from percussion to .38 rimfire caliber. Now worn and unused for some 140 years,[6] it was likely the first civilian revolver owned in the entire Densmore clan.

The Myth of Classless Society

The pattern of events in Baltimore, Martinsburg, Cumberland, and Pittsburgh was repeated again and again in Pennsylvania over the next few weeks. Protests, strikes, and fires were met with police, militia, National Guard, and US troops, all deployed to serve pure corporate interests. Their visitations left a wake of dead civilians in Reading, Scranton, and Shamokin. In short order, similar events spread to Youngstown, Cleveland, Chicago, St. Louis, and places in between.

In the first month of the strike, *none* of the big railroad, oil, or iron-steel combines that were struck offered to negotiate with their workers. Instead, they fired striking workers by the thousands. As the damage and body count piled up, some storefront merchants and shocked middle-class citizens'[7] attitudes began to shift toward the strikers and away from men like Scott, Garrett, and King, whose increasingly overt public contempt for their own most skilled workers began to run up against ordinary America's cultural definition of "fairness." Just why *were* these companies earning record profits while also systematically cutting wages in what citizens had been assured was a deep, lingering depression? How could much of the nation have been reduced to poverty and hard times in this endless Long Depression of 1873, while others became stunningly richer?

The lessons of Pittsburgh had first begun to sink in when more than a thousand iron and steel workers had abandoned their roll trains, furnaces, and squeezers in Birmingham, then crossed the Monongahela to join the striking railroaders. The militia and National Guard quickly lost all control. These workingmen, virtually all able to toss 150 to 200 pound loads around for ten hours a day, were simply not intimidated in the face of a street fight. Clubs and bayonets did not work. When the US troops poured heavy fire into their ranks, a few strikers died. A few others were wounded.[8] But the majority of them disengaged, moved a few blocks down Liberty Avenue, and looted several gun shops, in particular the showroom of the Great Western Gunworks Company.[9] That company manufactured or carried a wide variety of rifles, pistols, and shotguns and dealt in tarted-up surplus military rifles. The strikers would have gone for the army rifles and any .38 to .41 caliber pocket-sized rim fire revolvers. The strikers then returned and regrouped. Among them were a number of Civil War veterans and a few veterans of the Mexican War. The notion that one large corporation or national industry could seriously cheat its employees and *not* cause ripples among workers in other industries died on Pittsburgh's Liberty Avenue in July of 1877.

The working classes, though rendered noticeably shorter and less long-lived than their American-born grandparents, survived and pressed on with their struggle for stable wages, bargaining rights, and safer workplaces. State militias, Pinkertons, and federal forces broke, jailed, and killed strikers right into the 1920s. Finally, the cultural and legal consequences of F. D. R.'s presidency, the New Deal, and World War II left most of corporate America without state and federal troops to litigate its wage/work disputes.

In the late 1870s professional middle-class, white-collar America and working-class, blue-collar America eventually established a cultural truce, albeit an uneasy one. As the seriously depressed home real-estate crisis of the 1870s lifted, so did the middle class's mood. But hatred of their workers among the titans of iron, steel, and the railroad industry did not abate. Their response was to invest even more rapidly in manufacturing processes that were more "efficient." Too often, "efficiency" was defined merely as success in eliminating entire categories of highly skilled jobs. The tong-wielding puddlers were already on the road to redundancy in steel shops by the 1870s. Between 1877 and 1900, many more job titles and their pay scales would be downgraded. Job-hungry, unskilled immigrants and hastily filled trainloads of Southern black workers made strikes and work slowdowns much easier for owners to combat in the late 1800s.

The arc of tensions between labor and corporations waxed and waned in rough concert with the nation's complicated phases of both long and short business cycles.[10] The strikes of 1877 had imposed the first fragile behavioral limits on the rising business barons and exposed America's growing class differences. Those limits were supported by state and county militiamen's widespread distaste for killing their fellow citizens over a strike, and the main-street, small-business community's broad cries of excess brutality. Because of the public's pointed disgust at the use of lethal force by federal troops to protect private profits, Rutherford B. Hayes suffered more broadly from negative public opinion for his deployment of federal troops at "corporate command" in 1877 than he did for betraying Reconstruction and millions of blacks. The strike-supporting crowds into which those militia troops had fired were, of course, predominantly white.

Echoes of 1877: The Hidden Factors of Well-Being

By the end of summer of 1877, even the nation's more prosperous classes had also begun to burn out on the specter of federal troops shooting into mixed crowds. Gatling guns and stacked rifles faded away. The summer of 1877's unexpected turmoil must have seemed incomprehensible to most Americans at the time. First the tramps, then the rioters. But the underlying malaise among millions of Americans is made comprehensible by exploring the physical challenges that faced the general population in the aftermath of the 1860s. The Civil War left its ugly mark on mortality rates. What many Americans currently do not realize is that post–Civil War corporate America had squeezed its workers hard enough to leave indelible statistical impacts on the height of American-born children by the late 1870s.[11] Due to the male-focused bias of the era, we only have the height data for American-born adult males. Their height, as interpolated from the records of the Ohio National Guard and other enrollment and draft lists, contributed to Steckel's widely cited height tables. American-born-male heights had bottomed out in 1860, risen slightly by 1870, then declined precipitously to 5'6.7" by 1880.

When the Civil War deaths ceased, general life expectancy improved statistically. Life expectancy at birth for the nation's civilian population rose from 38.3 years in the nadir of 1850 to about 44 years in 1870,[12] still thirteen years shorter than it had been in 1800! Yet by 1880, thirty months after the 1877 riots, life expectancy for both sexes had declined again to 39.4 years.[13]

The Great Railroad Strikes of 1877 took place in an era of economic deflation, rising infant mortality, pronounced devaluation of skilled labor, wage pullbacks, lengthening work weeks, rising unemployment, and the dangerously declining self-sufficiency that was imposed on millions of ordinary workers by an unfettered and cancerously greedy business elite. Fear and hopelessness had put tramps on the rails and rendered working men and women reactive and distrustful of the increasingly hostile business world that had entrapped them.

Did *any* of the era's business elites understand that both their greed and dreadful safety records were impacting workers? Did they know that their demands for longer hours at lower wages were impacting children? Did they care? They should have cared, for they played a direct role in stripping working families of the biological advantage inherited from the Founders.

At millions of blue-collar family tables, there were few leavening answers to the "How are we doing?" or the "fairness" triggers in the 1870s. The guilt a worker felt from watching his or her children cry because they were still hungry was not quenchable with platitudes, nor was it remedied by social shaming. For a sizable number of working folk, daily life had become a stressful biological dilemma. Ancient instincts were in operation: "If I eat the meat and eggs needed to work my shift, my children will have only cornmeal and syrup. What can I do? I do not even know what they will *choose* to pay me next week."

As humans we are, first and foremost, stuck with the realities of age, health, gender, body image, and access to energy—that is, calories. We eat calories. We pump them into the tanks of our cars. We switch on the TV and it "eats" electricity and makes heat. So do our light bulbs. Our modern stoves "eat" gas or electricity—their versions of calories. And we nowadays buy almost all those calories with dollars—not bartered labor or mason jars of canned food. Sixty- to seventy-hours-per-week workers in the 1870s also bought their calories, food and fuel, with dollars. In urban settings they had neither the time nor the garden plots to farm on the side. In 1877 workers held their breath, fearing the next unannounced reduction in their pay envelopes. For millions, that was their American reality.

In the court of public opinion, the railroads and big-box manufacturers had overplayed their hands by the fall of 1877. In short, the public finally discovered that it was too often greed, not actual worker efficiencies, that drove the contents of weekly pay envelopes. The Depression of 1873 had given plausible cover to the need for repetitive reductions in wages. In fact, many of the large corporations reducing wages were making large profits. So were their shareholders.

When the riots ended, steel and iron men in Birmingham went back to work for as many weeks as company orders would allow. The strikes had brought disparate workers together, and industrial workers began to take collective bargaining more seriously.

The huge number of railroad freight cars destroyed in the Pittsburgh strikes, as elsewhere, generated large orders for replacements. This created temporary work for casters, forgers, and machinists as well as lumber dealers and carpenters. Pittsburgh Locomotive and Car Works had orders for nearly a hundred locomotives.[14] Baldwin Locomotive in Philadelphia had a number of orders for its heavy freight locomotives. That meant employ for even more skilled workers—polishers, finishers, boilermakers, welders, and rivet men. Pittsburgh Locomotive Company's rail car division added many workers as they hustled to replace the five hundred riot-destroyed rail cars. Suddenly skilled carpenters and iron workers temporarily had full work weeks, but at Depression-era wages. In terms of sustained gains in well-being, it was a pyrrhic victory.

Chapter 16
Pittsburgh's Symphony of Iron
The Densmores

We know from Thurston's Pittsburgh directories for 1876 that Ollie Densmore, listed as "Oliphant Dinsmore, Roller," was living at #48 15th Street near the Birmingham rolling mills owned by the McKnights.[1] He may have been temporarily working there, but it was only a five-block walk to Anchor. He undoubtedly rented, and that address only appears once. It is unlikely that Elizabeth was with him, as little Freddie had been born in Fairchance in December of 1875. By early 1877 Ollie was living at "2114 Sidney SS,"[2] listed as a laborer.[3] He was apparently back at Anchor Nail and Tack, which had again brought in new investors and was operating under the style of Chess, Cooke & Co.[4]

In 1879 Ollie was again listed at 2114 Sidney.[5] He had been working every possible shift through the Long Depression. And saving. During the late 1870s Ollie appears to have focused his riverside work breaks at Anchor on how best to organize his and his family's life.

That same year, he completed the purchase of an empty lot in Birmingham from the Ormsby Estate. It was the northeast corner lot on Sidney Street at Twenty-First—also known as Railroad Street—in the less crowded Southeast end of Birmingham. This lot, when built out, would become #2101 Sidney Street, a home for Ollie and his entire family. The US Census of 1880 would show them all living there: Ollie, age forty; Elizabeth, age thirty-nine; H. T., age fourteen; William, age eleven; and Ellen, age seven.

It is easy to underestimate just how hard the 1870s were for families like Ollie's. Between 1871 and 1879 Ollie and Elizabeth lost three children: an unnamed son (1871), little Freddie (1877), and Minnie, who lived only five weeks and died on November 13, 1879. The new house, a possible antidote to these sorrows, was just a few blocks from the Presbyterian church they would attend, four blocks from Anchor Nail and Tack, and three long blocks from the Chess's family mansion. A new public school was under construction several blocks away. Across Sidney Street and five doors to the left, Ollie's front stoop offered a view of the porch at the Grimm family boardinghouse at 2114 Sidney,[6] where he and his brothers had bunked for several years.

Ollie commissioned construction plans for a four-bedroom brick house at 2101 of about 2,100 square feet, plus a bunkhouse facing Fox Alley at the rear of his lot. Both Ollie and H. T. were employed in iron work that year, Ollie as a laborer/roller and H. T. as an apprentice at Anchor, earning about $3.20 a week. Both indicated on the 1880 US Census that they had been out of work for seven months that year.[7] Perhaps they were trying to save on local wage taxes and make time to work on the new house.

Family letters, photos, a deed, and both 1872 and 1901 survey maps[8] give us a clear picture of the lot and house. The lot measured 39 feet wide by 120 feet deep. The brick residence on the front of the lot measured 22 feet wide by 56 feet deep on the ground floor, and its second story was 910 square feet.

Upstairs was a hallway, a water closet, a sink, and a built-in linen closet. One large bedroom, sixteen feet wide by twelve feet deep, faced Fox Alley to the rear. It was the master bedroom with a pedestal sink and two large windows. The water closet was adjacent. Two small bedrooms faced the front, with a view of bustling Sidney Street. Approximately ten by eleven feet, those bedrooms belonged to H. T. and Will. H. T.'s left-front bedroom had a second window facing Twenty-first Street.[9] The room, assumed to have been Ellen's, measured nine by thirteen feet. It was on the other side of the water closet from the master bedroom, facing the stairwell, its windows opening to Twenty-First Street. There was attic storage in the peaked roof.

Downstairs, to the right of the front door, was a large front parlor with a fireplace. Only partially walled, its rear archway opened to a dining area. The left side of the house was taken up by the stairwell, closets, another small parlor about ten by twelve feet, used as an office or spare bedroom, and a large kitchen. Out back was an extension that included a shower room with a short clawfoot tub and an overhead shower. The basement housed a tool workbench, storage, and a modern coal-fired furnace. The Twenty-First Street side of the house sported a tall brick wall to diminish noise from the Birmingham and Whitehall railway that ran down the median.[10] Several years later the Trinity Lutheran Church was built next door at 2107 Sidney Street.

This was an impressive house for a self-made working man of that era. Ollie kept some records that hint at how he managed to pull it off. His savings and the sale of a lot in Fairchance bought this lot, and some money was left over for materials and plans. The work his son H. T. happened to be doing at Anchor at the time was laying bricks, a useful skill in building their new brick home. In fact, H. T.'s earliest job at age thirteen or fourteen was as a bricklayer. He started work at the end of his eighth-grade year, which is what most public schools offered at the time. Ollie also had bricklaying skills and would later become co-owner of a brickyard in his Fairchance "retirement" years. Between Ollie and H. T., they had the brick situation under control.

It would have been quite Densmore-like for Ollie to have made the bricks at one of the old brickyards three quarters of a mile south of Sidney in Upper St. Claire Borough and accepted his wages in untaxable bricks to build his house. That strategy may well have been the one he used to get the house and project moving in a slack working environment.

In the Densmore world of the era, skills and labor typically materialized through family connections. Ollie's younger son Will, then eleven or twelve years old, probably helped carry and lay brick at 2101, along with one or more of Sam's sons from Kittanning and Nehemiah and Elizabeth's sons. Ollie's old stomping grounds in Fairchance and the Georges Valley played a role by producing lumber, hinges, and window fittings cheaper than in Pittsburgh. Smoked country ham, salted pork, and garden crops were also cheaper there than in Old Smokey, allowing the family to save money.

One of the most important elements in Ollie's home-owning coup was the fact that he had become a landlord. On the lot's rear corner, Ollie built a second brick house, right out to the property boundaries facing Twenty-First Street and Fox Alley.[11] It may even have been the first structure erected on the lot. It began life as a working man's boarding house, which Ollie and Elizabeth called the "Bunkhouse" and rented out on a weekly basis. It consisted of a large parlor/dining area and beadboard-walled bunkrooms. A rear extension included the kitchen and a tiny shower room. The bunkhouse and the main house were separated by a shared courtyard and small backyard garden.

Six renters paying two dollars per week for a room, or four dollars weekly for full board—breakfast, dinner, ham-and-potato-stuffed lunch pail, bed, linens, and personal laundry—would have brought in about twelve to fourteen dollars per week in profit, the equivalent of a younger skilled wage earner's salary. Over the next several years, other Densmore men such as Sam, Robert Jr., and their sons, would occasionally give their address as "2101 Sidney" or "Fox Alley near

Twenty-First Street," on the boundary between the South Side's 25th and 26th Wards. All of these meant the bunkhouse.

By the mid-1880s a residential second story had been added to the bunkhouse. Its downstairs eventually became a bar and taproom that Will would run as a long-term sideline into the 1900s. The taproom specialized in boilermakers—beer and a shot of good Monongahela rye whiskey from Overholt's or the historic Large family's distilleries.[12] The core clientele, of course, were iron workers and the real-life boilermakers who worked in Birmingham. While the extended Densmore family in South Side Pittsburgh, Fairchance, and Uniontown did not approve of the taproom, their discomfort was softened by Ollie and his sons' capacity to support extended family members who came into the taproom when luck had run out or finances had gone awry.

The bunkhouse rental, combined with rents from their Fairchance house, allowed Ollie to realize his dream. Finally he had enticed Elizabeth and his family to full-time life in Pittsburgh. Two important family events would occur soon after the family was established in their new house. First, on October 21, 1881, Ellen, just weeks short of her ninth birthday, died at 2101 Sidney.[13] None of them ever completely got over it—the tragedy of her death was still discussed in the late 1950s. Much of the nation experienced similar losses as the environment in which children were raised deteriorated dramatically. When the iron and steel industry recovered, Ollie reprised his anthem of work, sweat, eat, sleep, and save. This time, however, the Fairchance house had been leased to help pay for 2101 Sidney. There was no immediate retreat for Elizabeth.

Not long after Ellen's death, a young woman came into their lives, who perhaps created a bright spot in the midst of their grief. Two and a half blocks away at #70 Joseph Street stood the house of Joseph Hoffman, a sixty-four-year-old master machinist.[14] He was the father of Sarah Ann Hoffman, who, please recall, was the widow of Captain Benjamin F. Vandergrift and the mother of their only child, Sophia Irene Vandergrift. In 1879, when Ollie purchased his lot, eighteen-year-old Sophia had come of age, departed her stepfather Sam Wheaton's house in Wheeling, West Virginia, and returned to her mother's hometown of Pittsburgh to reconnect with her grandfather and other extended family. By mid-1880 Sophia temporarily moved into 30 Forbes Avenue in downtown Pittsburgh as a guest of a female Vandergrift cousin who had married one of the locally powerful Darragh clan. Another Vandergrift hostess married a Blackstone.

No longer mired in the rough-and-tumble, unruly waterfront life of river towns like Wheeling and Parkersburg, Sophia was "introduced" to Pittsburgh society by the Vandergrift women. By 1881, social rounds over, Sophia was back in Birmingham with her grandfather and Hoffman cousins at #70 Joseph Street. Meanwhile, just a few blocks away, Ollie's seventeen-year-old son H. T. was already working at Anchor as a mill hand. At some point, the two met and hit it off.

H. T., a bit over 5'8.3" in height, was well built, arrow straight, and hazel eyed. He had what women of that time considered a "sensitive" mouth. Well-mannered and well-spoken, he kept his chestnut-brown hair brushed back and liked to dress up. Sophia was a fine-looking young woman, sturdy and striking, and had the reputation of a fabulous cook. She had done much of the cooking for the two generations of Hoffmans living at #70 Joseph Street. The couple began to go to church and church socials together. Ollie's house was another place where they met.

The main house at 2101 Sidney is now gone, pulled down to create a parking lot. Ollie and Elizabeth lived there until 1895 or 1896, when they returned to the homestead in Fairchance. The house passed to H. T. and Sophia, who lived in it until the spring of 1900, when they built a new house for themselves on the Old Brownsville Road.

The Vandergrifts and the 1880s

As the 1880s deeply impacted family well-being, wage, and work identity among the Densmore working men, some among the Vandergrifts were also impacted. Captain J. J. and his son William, oil brokers, returned to Pittsburgh in 1880 or 1881. But J. J. and his family did not return to Birmingham. Their social world had both elevated and narrowed as Pittsburgh's elites became more enclaved and socially selective. J. J. never wavered on his cordiality, but his close associates no longer knew the price of cornmeal, bread, or a gill of rye. J. J.'s social world gathered on Pittsburgh's inner North Side and on the trendy East End of Forbes Avenue.

J. J. was likely already worth more than a million dollars in 1880 when his eldest daughter was married. This is the era during which he, his sons, and several of his sons-in-law opened or expanded banks (Keystone), oil companies (Forrest), transport (Union Tank Line Company), natural gas pipelines (United Pipelines Company in western Pennsylvania and northwestern West Virginia), a farm-commodities operation, and a "package" travel agency, which connected the B&O and Pennsylvania railroad trains to riverboat schedules. Some of those riverboats belonged to his brothers and cousins. In the midst of the recession of

1882 to 1885, when the nation's business activity declined by a third, he and his associates bought low and held long, fabulously enriching themselves.

In the 1883/1884 edition of *Diffenbacher's Directory of Pittsburgh and Allegheny Cities*, entries document some of these operations: "Vandergrift, B.W. of Vandergrift and Sowers,[15] Walnut nr. Hiland; Vandergrift, E., clerk Masonic Bank, 139 Wylie Ave; Vandergrift, J.J., Pres. United Pipe Lines, 113 4th Ave; Vandergrift & Sowers, oil brokers, 115 4th Ave."[16]

Large ads in the same publication list J. J. as a director of Allegheny National Bank. He also incorporated the Keystone Bank in 1884. But there are also contrasting Vandergrift listings in 1884: "Vandegrift, J.A., wid. George, 103 Colwell." This is Julia Vandergrift, bereaved wife of George, who died in 1875, and mother of William, shot at Martinsburg in 1877. Within a year she had been taken in by her daughter and son-in-law. Another entry reads, "Vandergrift, M., wid. John, 139 Wylie." This is Mary, widow of Captain John Vandergrift. And there were others: "Vandergrift, Robt. F., laborer, 271 Preble, A;"[17] "Vandergrift, S. H.,[18] coach builder, 59½ Grantham, A;" "Vandergrift, Wm, waiter, 8 Townsend." By the nation's economic meltdown of 1882 to 1885, death, time, and circumstance had socially and economically enhanced the separation between descendants of the sons born to Jacob Vandergrift and Mary Hart. Was there no middle ground? Yes, as noted, two Vandergrift rivermen continued to pursue the 250 years of family maritime tradition.[19]

Still operating "on the waters" in 1884 Pittsburgh were Captain James M. Vandergrift and Louis Vandergrift, who benefitted from the golden age of the large packet steamboats. In this era they captained boats and repaired them. Each was also a minority shareholder in other packet boats. They were the upper-middle-class members of the Vandergrift clan. One of their repair shops in Wheeling had been overseen by Sam Wheaton, who later moved on to oversee a Point Pleasant, West Virginia, dock and shop.

The Vandergrifts were no longer one cohesive, well-oiled family machine. Evidence of this can be found in the graveyards of Allegheny County. At the upscale Allegheny Cemetery in northwest Pittsburgh, burial home to icons like songwriter Stephen Foster, J. J. Vandergrift had gathered the most privileged portion of his clan for their eternal rests. The Vandergrift working stiffs of the 1870s to 1890s, waiters, laborers, and clerks, did not make it to Lawrenceville's eternal family table. They are found in ordinary cemeteries like the South Side Cemetery on the Brownsville Road, Green Hill at Martinsburg, West Virginia, and at other cemeteries in Millvale and Allegheny City. It was not time and geographic distance that separated the great-grandsons of Mary Hart and Jacob Vandergrift into different cemeteries—it was wealth, wages, well-being, and the iconic cultural capital of their job titles.

American Well-Being in 1880

As noted earlier, the adult height of American males born in 1880 had shrunk again to a new low of 5'6.7", even as the pace of social, economic, and technological change reaccelerated in America. The economy expanded, wages temporarily gained a bit of buying power from 1880 to 1882, but the adult height of American-born males did not increase. By 1890 white American males were *even shorter*, at 5'6.6".[20] That adult height did not even match the birth cohorts of 1710 to 1730 when American-born men averaged 5'7"![21] Among the causes of this decline were enhanced childhood disease vectors, cyclically unstable national markets, continued downward pressure on wages (due, in part, to a flood of new immigrants willing to work cheap), the erosion of skilled labor due to major changes in manufacturing technology, and a more toxic industrializing landscape.

Poorly maintained water and sewer systems and the crowded tenements surrounding urban industrial districts amplified public health problems, as did the growing problem of toxic industrial waste. Increasingly dramatic inequality in the distribution of wealth also characterized the era, as did the deeply corrosive financial and political power of the Robber Barons and unregulated bankers.

The deep South had also begun to industrialize in urban pockets like Birmingham, Alabama. Some of their largest industrial projects were quietly co-owned or partnered by northern corporations such as US Steel, which found the South's cheap labor environment quite profitable. In a number of cases both convicts and blacks indentured by bogus debts or flimsy vagrancy "fines" owed to local courts became unwilling workers, corralled to toil in mines, factories, and on railroad track crews. In view of the profits, Northern partners like US Steel kept a low profile and looked the other way.[22] In that respect, not much changed after the Civil War. Recent court cases filed by the Southern Poverty Law Center indicate that a number of Southern debtors' prisons and work schemes *still* operate to this day with poor blacks as the primary victims.[23]

Meanwhile, large-scale manufacturing everywhere aggressively pursued new types of automation, both to intimidate and eliminate skilled labor. Hourly wages declined again, and average workweeks lengthened. By the late 1880s that meant seventy-two to eighty-four hours per six-day workweek on the job. In large steel operations, many men worked eighty to ninety hours a week, equivalent to two full-time, body-breaking jobs at *half* the daily wages of 1861 to 1865.

Young, healthy men who entered the workforce in their teens were often worn down by the increasing physical demands in mining, iron, steel, glass, and other heavy manufacturing during the 1880s, when shifts averaged 10.8 to 12 hours. Many men worked six or seven days a week. Normal teen growth spurts were blunted by those who went to work young. Exhausted and unskilled, more workers made mistakes, and work accidents skyrocketed.[24]

While we do not have height tables for them, the legions of women who worked in the glass industry and in the Eastern Seaboard textile mills, North and South, suffered similarly. At work in cotton or wool mills, suspended dust was their immediate enemy, and their wages were much lower than the men's. The young widows among them who supported several children must have lived in near constant fear of, "What if?"

In heavy industry, the male death rate due to accidents in 1880 was nearly four times that of females in Pittsburgh.[25] This is indirect but clear evidence of workplace risks, given Pittsburgh's unusually male-dominated workforce. Many work accidents were never reported, and businesses, especially the large works, accepted no responsibility for them at all. The realities of punishing eighty-hour weeks meant that highly skilled workers with the most experience were wearing out or aging prematurely under their increasingly intense 1880s workloads. Worse yet, they were exposed to increasing risks as the ratio of low-paid, unskilled workers rose around them on the mill floors.[26] It also meant that the cost of meat and eggs to fuel those work shifts absorbed an ever greater share of each diminished pay envelope.

The aging-out phenomenon struck surprisingly young men. Boys who had begun work at ages twelve to fifteen as mill helpers and apprentices in 1860 were often worn out and in poor health by the 1880s. The ordinary work span of a healthy iron or steel man was twenty to twenty-five years. Some men bettered that by more than a decade, but they were exceptions. F. H. O. "Ollie" Densmore was one of them. Addicted to the emotional comfort of his work, mind-numbing noise, heat, and the muscle-fatigued flow of endorphins, Ollie bore up surprisingly well in his long career. His inherited male or Y genes may have played a role—like later DNA-tested Densmore men, he carried about 4 percent Neanderthal genes. Those genes, we now know, favored both upper body muscle development and a robust immune system. Many other workers of his era crumbled both physically and psychologically.

CHAPTER 16

Ollie Densmore, the Machine:
Costs and Calories in an Iron Worker's Career

As mentioned, research into Anchor Nail and Tack, census data, Pittsburgh city directories, old deeds, plus nineteenth-century business realities, shop fires, depressions, and riots all collude to tell us that the historical sketch of Ollie and H. T. published in 1912, which claimed "38 full-time, consecutive years at Chess, Cooke and Company," cannot be confirmed. In fact, Ollie's total career was much longer than thirty-eight years.[27] At best we can determine that, from the winter of 1860 to 1861 until 1896, Ollie worked every shift that the Chess brothers allowed him. When Anchor was down, Ollie, like others in his family, probably worked at McKnight's Birmingham Iron and Nail works, or at Wharton's Rolling Mill nearer his residences. But his full-time years of iron work actually began in Fairchance when Ollie went to work at Oliphant's in 1855 at age fourteen.

His full-time work at Oliphant's (as opposed to after-school short shifts of five hours as a helper/apprentice or nailer) almost certainly began when Old Robert died in the spring of 1855. Prior to that time Ollie likely worked short shifts during his last two school years, plus full shifts each summer. His public education ended early. Still, he was well beyond nominally literate, for he kept meticulous rolling log and account books. Just as important, he was an avid newspaper reader. Moreover, his working career did not end when he retired from Anchor and returned to Fairchance with Elizabeth in the winter of 1895 to 1896.

The caloric costs of Ollie's work career can be estimated, as can the hours worked over the years from his first employ as a lad until he retired from Old Smokey in 1896.[28] His basal metabolic caloric needs are not computed, for they depend on his height, weight, and age. These factors changed significantly over the span of his working life that began, assuming the custom of the times, at age twelve. His full-time iron work began in 1855 and ended in 1896. Thus, his "full-time" iron career spanned forty-one years. Altogether he made iron for a remarkable forty-three years. Ollie "retired" in good health and returned to Fairchance at age fifty-six or fifty-seven as one of Pittsburgh's legendary veteran rollers. He had worked at charcoal furnaces, both soft and hard coal furnaces, coke furnaces, and, by the 1890s, gas-fired ones. It's no surprise that his sense of technological history had become rare. His work and experience had cost a mountain of time, calories, and food money.

Ollie's career can be understood in hours worked, the level of work intensity, and calories expended. The winter of 1852 had been cold and miserable, and the economy was running headlong into another nasty, cash-scarce downturn. Those conditions probably triggered Ollie's decision to begin working part-time at Oliphant's as a schoolboy in the late spring of 1853. As the Georges Township tax records indicate, Ollie's father, Old Robert, almost seventy-one, was no longer able to do heavy work. Ollie's older brother Robert Jr. likely brought him on at Oliphant's as a helper. By the time his father died in April of 1855, Ollie already would have put in over three thousand hours assisting a catcher or a puddler. That work cost about 350–400 calories an hour above basal metabolism, and it may have somewhat limited his normal early-teen growth spurt. Those two years also required Ollie's family to purchase food that allowed him to expend more than a million extra calories to meet his body's work needs. Ollie wasn't just an average modern kid with a growing kid's appetite—his body was also a manufacturing machine that required extra fuel for each hour worked.

In 1855, when Old Robert died, Ollie went full-time at Oliphant's. He would have worked about forty-six weeks a year, nine and a half hours a day, six days a week, for a total of fifty-seven-hour weeks. This equals out to a work year of 2,700 hours tending furnace, shoveling coal, or hammering slag from iron pigs at a cost of 442 calories an hour in excess of basal metabolism and body maintenance.[29] These years are summarized in table 9a.

From mid-1857 to November 1860, he had worked no less than 6,740 hours (forty-eight weeks for twenty-nine months, at nine and a half hours a day) as a nail cutter and a roller's apprentice, probably to Robert Jr. or Nehemiah Warman. That labor required 476 calories an hour in excess of basal metabolism. A conservative estimate of the calorie cost of labor at Oliphant's for these twenty-nine months totals 3,208,000 calories of food fuel.

By the time of Ollie's marriage to Elizabeth in 1860 at age nineteen, he had already graduated to the rarified and coveted title of "roller," for he already had 15,310 hours of work experience. That is equivalent to a modern era's seven years on the job, at a family-borne food cost of over 6.8 million calories (see table 9a). As a result of this intense work, Ollie's body mass consisted of a high ratio of muscle to fat. Muscle tissue metabolizes/burns more calories per pound than body fat. Like a highly conditioned athlete, even at rest he burned more calories an hour than an average modern male teenager of the same weight.

Between January 1861 and 1873 in Birmingham, Ollie became even more heavily muscled. His work at Anchor averaged 2,800 hours per year from 1861 to 1872.[30] From January 1873 to December 1878, we estimate the same, but for only forty weeks per year due to the Long Depression. That sums to 2,530 hours plus four of Ollie's long shifts a month, or 2,550 paid hours per year, as noted in table 9b. From January 1879 to December 1896, his own logbooks and other published accounts indicate an average workload of seventy-two hours a week, including his long shifts. The 1880s and 1890s were strong decades for the nation's iron and steel production and consumption, even though several episodic market dips intervened due to general economic downturns. One can assume 46 weeks of work a year[31] and 3,000 work hours yearly for eighteen years, which totals 54,000 hours, as noted in table 9b.

An unadjusted estimate of Ollie's iron-work hours, from part-time work in 1853, then full-time work at age fourteen through to December 1896 in Birmingham, totals 120,610 hours invested in making and rolling iron. In table 9c, that has been adjusted downward by 15 percent to account for work "spells" (rests) and by another 10 percent for unrecorded shutdowns—overall, a conservative estimate.

As author Malcolm Gladwell has observed, mastery of a skill requires an investment of 10,000 hours.[32] Ollie already had 15,000 hours of experience when he married Elizabeth in 1860 at age nineteen, *before* he went to Birmingham. His total iron career was equivalent to fifty-five current US standard work years of 2,120 hours each (see table 9c). His actual iron career of forty-three and a quarter years logged at least 102,520 adjusted hours of high-intensity work inputs, costing an adjusted, rounded-down minimum of 51 million work calories in excess of basal metabolism and body maintenance.[33]

TABLE 9A. Ollie Densmore's Apprenticeship in Iron work at Oliphant's in Fairchance, 1853–1860

Year	Note	Hours Worked	Work Intensity, Calories/Hour	Total Work Calories
1853	Age 12, part-time	1,585	400	634,000
1854	Part-time	1,585	400	634,000
1855	Age 14, full-time	2,508	442	1,108536
1856	Full-time	2,508	442	1,108536
1857	Full-time	2,508	442	1,108536
1858	Full-time	2,508	442	1,108536
1859	Full-time, nailer	2,508	442	1,108536
1860*	Full-time, 9 months, roller	2,000	442	884,000
	Grand Total:	17,710 hours		7,694,680 cal.

*Married Elizabeth Goldsboro on November 1, 1860

TABLE 9B. Ollie Densmore's Roller Years at Anchor Works in Birmingham, 1861–1896

Year(s)	Note	Hours Worked per Year	Work Intensity, Calories/Hour	Total Work Calories per Year
1861 through December 1872	Civil War Era	2,800	476	1,332,800
	Twelve-Year Total:	33,600		15,993,600
1873 through December 1878	The Long Depression	2,550	476	1,213,800
	Six-Year Total:	15,300		7,282,800
1879 through December 1896	Growth in Iron/Steel	3,000	476	1,428,000
	Eighteen-Year Total:	54,000		25,704,000
	Grand Total:	102,900 hours		48,980,400 cal.

TABLE 9C. Ollie Densmore's Iron Career, 1853–1896 (Summary of Tables 9A and 9B)

City	Work Years	Hours Worked	Work Calories Expended
Fairchance	7¼	17,710	7,694,680
Birmingham	36	102,900	48,980,400
Raw Totals:	43¼ years	120,610 hours	56,675,080 calories
Adjusted Totals:		102,520 hours *(Adjusting 15 percent to account for spells [rests/breaks] and shutdowns)*	51,007,572 calories *(Adjusting 10 percent for spells and shutdowns)*

Notes on Tables 9A, 9B, and 9C

Table A. Work years assume forty-four six-day weeks and long turns, except for forty-six weeks from 1879–1896.

Table B. Lengths of workdays assume 9.5 hours from 1853 to November 1860 and 10–12 hours from 1861 to 1896.

Table C. Adjustments also compensate for Anchor fires of 1864 and 1866 and the months Ollie spent in Fairchance in 1870 when daughter Ellen died and Nehemiah Warman was in Birmingham. Adjustments are based on reasonable estimates. "Spells" are variously noted as fifteen- to twenty-minute breaks between each heat in sources from the 1880s to the 1890s.

Comparisons

A modern, skilled manufacturing employee working the same forty-three calendar years of standard, full-time work (2,050 hours) would accrue about 88,000 hours. With assembly-line machinery to assist, the caloric cost of that career work output,[34] averaging 180 calories per hour in excess of basal metabolism and body maintenance, would add up to about 16 million calories. That is less than a third of the work calories Ollie and other iron-steel men would have had to provide from their own paychecks.

The cost of fueling Ollie's 51 million career work calories absorbed a much larger share of the family food budget in the 1800s than an ordinary modern worker's would. In contrast, the modern, unskilled, low-paid shovel worker on the roadside still expends between 300 and 400 extra work calories per hour, and he or she must spend a higher proportion of wages on food than more sedentary workers. The larger their families are, the greater the impact on manual workers' household budgets and on their children's nutritional well-being.

Unskilled daily laborers in the nineteenth-century iron mills typically worked off about 380 calories an hour, 20 percent less than Ollie's 476. But they were paid about 70 percent less per hour. Whereas Ollie was able to amass some wealth in large part because he had few children to support, the average married worker of his era spent a much greater percentage of their lower incomes on the food necessary to fuel their work. That is still true for modern Americans engaged in heavy labor. The food costs required by heavy labor are a subsidy to their employers, just as many skilled auto mechanics' or cabinetmakers' tools are assets brought to the job.

Sam Densmore, Kittanning

In the 1870s Sam Densmore had done much of the same work as his younger brother Ollie, but he had moved around more. Sam was devoted to his wife, Jennie, who had deep family roots in Mercer County, northwest of Kittanning. The progenitors of her family—five brothers—were Irish-born Ulster Scots, originally Presbyterian. By 1800 to 1801 four[35] had settled about thirty-five miles northwest of Kittanning in the sparsely inhabited Coal Springs and Wolf Creek Townships of Mercer County.[36] By about 1802 Jennie's grandfather James had struck out and bought land near Kittanning. A second brother, William, also left the Wolf Creek district about the same time and is almost certainly Hannah Glenn's father, who lived in Connellsville/Bullskin per the tax rolls of 1802 to 1803. Thus the geography of Sam's work sites reflected his family orbit as focused not just on Fairchance and the Densmores but also on the Glenn family of northwestern Pennsylvania.

In his teen years Sam had also first worked at Oliphant's, but in his adult life his wage world formed a flattened geometric diamond: Connellsville, Pittsburgh, and Kittanning, Pennsylvania; Jamestown/Celoron, New York; and Youngstown, Ohio. As a result of both his peripatetic work habits and other contemporary Samuel Densmores who lived in the same area, Sam's movements are difficult to pinpoint until after 1870, when he and Jennie regularly appear in Kittanning's St. Paul's Church, which kept excellent congregant records.[37]

According to a St. Paul's confirmation record dated May 1, 1883, Sam and Jennie already had eight children: Robert, age seventeen; Harry Parks A., age fifteen; "Fidelah"[38] H. O., age thirteen; Samuel, age eleven; Mary Ann, age nine; Elizabeth D., age six; and Edward, age four. Beginning in 1865 to 1866, Jennie, then about eighteen, bore children every two years until the birth of infant William Walter Densmore on September 11, 1881, who must have remained at home on confirmation day.

Apparently the couple lost no children as infants, and all but Robert and Fidelah were born in Armstrong County. The boys carried names that clearly identified their family roots. Robert, William, and Samuel could have been named for either Densmores or Glenns, convenient "two-fers" in the important family name honors of that era. On the other hand, Harry was clearly the Densmore Harry/Henry, and Fidelah H. O. was named in honor of none other than Sam's brother Ollie.

Their children's ages at death may reflect the early nation's biological advantage in length of life and—even more likely—reflect the advantage of being raised in a more rural environment than in Ollie's Pittsburgh. Sam and Jennie's oldest son Robert lived a long life of eighty-four years in Alaska, but Harry (an iron worker) died at age forty-five. Fidelah (an iron worker) died at age sixty-three, Samuel D. (a policeman) lived to age eighty-one, Mary Ann lived to age seventy-three, Elizabeth died young in childbirth at age twenty-one, Edward (a metal worker) died at age twenty-six, and William Walter (a farmer) lived to eighty-three. The three metal workers' lives averaged only 44.5 years. The other three sons lived an average of nearly 83 years.

Sam and Jennie's eight children form far too small a sample to be meaningful statistically, but their average age at death was 59.5 years. That, combined with no child deaths as of 1883, strongly implies good early nutrition and effective family care. The national average life expectancy for children attaining *age ten* had improved to sixty years for those born between 1871 and 1880. In contrast, children born a decade earlier in the 1860s who reached age ten could only expect to live to age fifty-four.[39] But *at birth*, American children born in 1860 could expect to live to about age forty-two. In contrast, those born in 1880 could only expect to live to age thirty-nine. Disease- and nutrition-wise, childhood became much riskier between 1870 and 1880 when wages declined but meat, milk, and bean prices stayed stubbornly steep.[40]

Environment and Ecology

The environment around Kittanning in the 1860s to mid-1880s was kinder to children than Birmingham's. The settlement at Slabtown, about five miles from Kittanning, was situated in a mosaic of lovely wooded hills and creek bottom interspersed with farms. A variety of farm produce was available: corn, barley, rye, buckwheat, chickens, pigs, cattle, and wild game. The region's game included grouse, wild turkey, deer, an occasional bear, rabbit, squirrel, and seasonal migratory wild fowl.

Despite this bounty it wasn't the Garden of Eden, for mining operations[41] were even then transforming swaths of Armstrong County. Sulfur had infiltrated some streams and reduced native fish populations. But the Allegheny River still ran fast and fairly clean. Pike, large trout, catfish, and carp were all still fairly abundant in the 1860s and 1870s.

Nearby Slabtown was named for a settlement of houses weather boarded with rough-cut exterior slabs, a cheap by-product of local sawmills, and it was distinctly dominated by Scots-Irish settlers. It was not a socially upscale community in the way that the blocks of housing surrounding Kittanning's town square and its Allegheny riverfront had become. A close-knit community where face-to-face networks, local barter, and peer pressure shaped behaviors, Slabtown worked just fine for raising children. Most any resident of Birmingham or South Side Pittsburgh would have envied its environment for their kids. Slabtown in the early 1870s would have seemed totally ordinary to the 1820 inhabitants of Old Robert's former home in Bullskin Township.

Six or seven of Sam and Jennie's eight children had been born in Slabtown or Kittanning. Fidelah was born in Pittsburgh on November 13, 1869, when Jennie, Robert, and Harry lived with Sam at Fox Alley, East Birmingham, a block or so from Ollie, who bunked that fall at Grimm's boardinghouse, 2114

Sidney.[42] Naming their son for Ollie is consistent with the value system of that era. The naming would have also encouraged Ollie to look out for his namesake later in life.

Though Samuel's family had moved for good to the Slabtown and Kittanning area, the best-paying industrial work was not there. At some point, we assume between 1883 and 1884, Sam parted ways with his high-profile job as repair-shop foreman at the Connellsville Coke Works. This meant he needed to seek out new employment in iron-making Birmingham. Even though Sam is not listed in Thurston's *Directory of Pittsburgh and Allegheny City*, we know from Ollie's own handwritten roller's log that Sam worked on his crew at Anchor in the spring of 1884. This is significant, as 1883 and 1884 were the years when Henry C. Frick was fighting for control of the Connellsville Coke district, including the Leisenring Coke operation where Sam had worked. District strikes resulted and were answered by management-forced shutdowns and violence-prone hired corporate "gun thugs." Frick had likely ruined Sam's best-ever job at the coke works. Sam disappears for a few months that summer, then he is listed on Ollie's Anchor crew in September 1885. Sam had likely made the rounds of his family and work orbit between the summer of 1884 and the early fall of 1885. Railroad expansion diminished sharply in 1882, a large factor in creating the 1882 to 1885 recession. Thus, demand for steel track declined, and big track producers were laying off thousands. That put even more downward pressure on iron workers' wages.

The Roller's Logbook of "H. O. Densmore," 1882 to 1888

Sam's return to the Pittsburgh area and the Anchor works[43] would not be known were it not for a compact, faded leatherette "Pay Roll and Account Book" found tucked into the lidded "Valuables" box built into a handmade 1820s-era[44] "Pennsylvania Red" stained blanket chest. Labeled as above, it was signed in Ollie's own hand, "H. O. Densmore." This formal roller's log is hand-dated as beginning January 17, 1882, and ends October 13, 1888.[45]

Recall that 1869 was an economically depressed postwar year. In the fall of 1867, and again from 1869 to 1870, Sam worked with Ollie as a second roller at Anchor and would have earned about $4.90 a day. Federal records suggest that rollers' wages had increased by 1867 to 1868 to about $5.60 per day, then suddenly dropped 20 percent in 1869 to $4.50 a day.[46] It is obvious from Pittsburgh city directories that Ollie had first placed Sam on his rolling crew in the winter of 1867 to 1868. As lead roller, Ollie could do that. By 1871 records of Sam in Old Smokey dried up again. Sam was apparently moving around, working mills and machine shops in Youngstown, southwestern New York, or along the Allegheny.

The 1880 US Census of Pittsburgh indicates that both Sam, age forty-one, and Robert Jr., age fifty-two, had been out of work four months that year. Sam's Pittsburgh occupation is given as "laborer," by then a two-dollar-a-day mill hand at Anchor. Just months later he would be advertised by Trotter's Coke Works near Connellsville and "on salary." Robert Jr.'s children, several already grown, had started families of their own.[47]

In 1880 or 1881 Ollie and Elizabeth had been joined at the new house on 2101 Sidney Street by Robert Jr. and Elizabeth. Henry C. Frick's managers had again lowered wages and increased hours for Oliphant's legacy workers in Fairchance. Robert Jr.'s wages declined rapidly under Frick management, and his work rights deteriorated notably from the "we are one big family" ethos of the Oliphant era. Worse yet, Robert Jr. was a puddler—one of the too-powerful, skilled "thems" targeted by big-box iron and steel combines as marked for extinction. The means of that extinction became reality as open-hearth furnaces—which poured the molten iron rather than hand-creating balls of it—transformed steel production and made many puddlers superfluous. Sources tell us that Oliphant's doubled its output between 1870 and 1880. Thus an aging Robert Jr. headed to Birmingham. This was Ollie's chance to give his older brother a much-deserved payback for his teenage work opportunities during his teen apprentice years at Oliphant's.

Ollie's oldest son, H. T., almost eighteen, also appears in the log entries going back to 1882. It is obvious from Ollie's log that H. T. worked primarily on other crews during the recession years of 1883 to 1884. Ollie had already trained him and, by 1884 to 1885, was focusing on his younger son Will's apprenticeship to a master roller. Working with Ollie and veteran roller Henry Rudolph was a huge asset for Will. Between them, the two veterans training him had already logged nearly fifty years of experience as rollers.

H. T. appears in Thurston's Pittsburgh City Directory of 1885 to 1886[48] with his own listing as "Densmore, H. T., mill hand, Fox Alley and S. 21st." This confirms H. T. as a resident of Ollie's Fox Alley bunkhouse. In 1883 he had married his sweetheart Sophia Vandergrift, three years his elder, and they had moved into the bunkhouse, where their first child, a son, was born in 1885. H. T. deferred to Sophia, who named their son Benjamin Vandergrift Densmore in honor of her steamboat captain father who had once held her, then died just three days later.

1885 also brought the Densmores a significant loss. At his home on the outskirts of Fairchance, oldest brother Nat, the teamster, died at age sixty-five. Details of his funeral and burial have not turned up. Sam and Ollie would have made the trip to Fairchance, consoled Nat's widow, Susan, and his youngest daughter, Mary, then taken up shovels to fill Nat's grave. The Densmore family's closest connection to the glory days of the National Road and its way of life had passed.

Ollie's roller log documents family connections and the creation of the third generation of skilled Densmore iron-forge and mill workers. The log entries are a rarity in published information, for in them we see direct reflections of an erratic national economy, pressures that fueled later labor movements, and the influence of an increasingly abusive corporate model of producing iron and steel. That business model was radically different from the forge-shop culture of America's first 150 years of forge and furnace operations. Those logs also reveal that average iron workers' wages as published by the federal government for that era significantly *overstated* payday realities.

In broader context the log also clarifies pay rates, piece work, and fixed daily wages. It was an era in which work shifts and pay oscillated dramatically from day to day, month to month, and year to year. "Piece work" refers to the age-old, standard practice of pay tied directly to the number of items produced, such as candles, chair spindles, rifle barrels, or aprons. On Ollie's rolling line at Anchor in the 1880s, it meant tons of thin-rolled iron, which became sheets or, at times, ingots, slabs, or iron construction beams of specified dimension.

In the 1880s iron workers' pay fluctuated dramatically as national market conditions oscillated due to unpredictable factors of product demand, recession, and increasing flows of cheap immigrant labor—as well as from both banking shenanigans and corporate manipulation. An iron worker's pay envelope in the 1880s was supposed to reflect a one- to two-year cycle of negotiated "industry wage scales." But temporary market conditions and the status of an unstable national economy frequently intruded. Furnaces and forges closed on short notice in response to sudden declines in orders, when fires destroyed part or all of the works, during frequent management changes, or merely to squelch demand for raises. "We'll close down and starve them a while" was becoming a standard corporate response from the new breed of large-scale iron producers when facing worker demands for better wages, shorter shifts, or effective safety measures.

One mitigating factor as wages deteriorated in the mid-1880s was the declining consumer-price index. This federal government index has compiled basic family costs for about a century and a half. It includes housing, food, energy costs, and so on for ordinary households. Estimated household costs were only about 5 to 10 percent higher in the mid-1880s than in 1860. The mid-1860s to 1870s had seen brutal wartime food cost increases.[49] Those increases declined during the 1870s and 1880s, but they never returned to their pre-1865 level. As the era's wages declined, so did property values. But due to demand, food costs remained elevated compared to wages.

By 1880 highly skilled iron rollers or puddlers were typically paid a per-ton rate of pay while the rest of the crew earned a fixed daily wage. As a consequence, factory "labor," like the rest of America, was being divided into more distinct "classes." The workday was nominally ten hours, but Ollie's log shows us that, in practice, it averaged out to about 10.8 hours daily for each shift, or "single turn." It is important to note that these log pages apply to Anchor, a medium-sized, benign work environment when compared to the big-box works employing thousands.

Log Entries, Pay, and Crew

Given its extraordinary rarity, every detail in Ollie's logbook merits publication, but here we focus on a few entries offering insights into well-being, social factors, and self-sufficiency.

On the payroll of January 17, 1882, the piece rate was 63¢ per ton of rolled iron (likely specialty sheet-iron). Anchor had just reopened after infusions of New York investment money. The shifts were single turns of about ten hours, and Sam Densmore's pay rate was $1.80 a day—only one-third that of the mid-1860s. Ollie led the shift. The assistant shift roller was veteran Henry Rudolph, earning $2.50 per day. And Ollie's sixteen-year-old son Will was a "hand," earning $1.25 a day.

The log entry lists the following workers:

1. J. Hays [catcher] and Henry Rudolph[50] [roller]—36¢ per ton, rolling output of sixteen puddling furnaces

2. Peter Grim[51] [furnace man, attending sixteen puddling furnaces]—$2.25 per day
3. Jon Weaver [roll turner]—$2.50 per day
4. Hankempf[52]—$1.75 per day
5. Bloom Boy—$1.25 per day[53]
6. Rougher—$2.00 per day

All of these named men save "Hankempf" are identifiable from historical records, as shown in table 10.

TABLE 10. F. H. O. Densmore's Identifiable Crew Members as Listed in Diffenbacher's 1883–1884 and 1884–1885 Directories*

Rudolph, Henry, Laborer, Larkins Alley (Birmingham)†

Hays, Jos., Catcher, 76 S. 19th (Birmingham)

Weaver, John—either "Weaver, J., Flattener, #1917 Mary (Birmingham)," or "Weaver, John, Roll Turner, Kerr Ave." They could be the same person.

Grim, Peter, Laborer, 107 20th (Birmingham)

* Diffenbacher, J.F. Diffenbacher's Directory of Pittsburgh and Allegheny Cities, 1883/1884 and 1884/1885.
† Henry Rudolph's family-owned saloon at Sarah and 18th Street, Birmingham.

All of the crew listed above are of Scots-Irish, English, or old German/Prussian heritage,[54] with established Pennsylvania roots. In the mid-1880s, Anchor's labor roster contained few recent immigrants. That was in dramatic contrast to industrial Philadelphia and Baltimore. The above men all lived in the same neighborhood, and several of their children intermarried. What is most notable is that Ollie chose his crew, so he had the power to rescue skilled family members from unemployment—the nineteenth-century working man's equivalent to a rich man bringing his youngest son into the family firm. It was one of an iron roller's most precious assets.

This power to grant work was a huge part of what made the rollers legendary among the over-four-hundred-work-calories-per-hour stratum of skilled American labor. It is also a primary reason why big-box metal producers would fight bitterly—even violently—in the late 1800s to take that power away. In the

1860s mill owners went to Ollie Densmore if they wanted changes in production. *He* consulted the puddlers, readjusted the roll train's specification (known as "sets"), then sorted the details so that, like magic, new products and specifications would become work-floor reality. But by 1890 some titan's well-placed nephew, with neither the labor experience nor the concern for safety, often gave the orders. This change extinguished extended family work units and vastly trimmed the possibility that a roller and his extended family unit could generate financial independence. In the 1870s and 1880s corporate models were specifically designed to destroy such self-sufficiency. A frightened, financially isolated iron man was a far more malleable one.

October 7, 1882 Payroll: A Short, Sweet Spot for Pay and Efficiency

The pace of orders at Anchor had picked up. The tonnage rate had risen to 68¢, but it was a larger crew of eleven instead of the seven men above. The larger crew allowed Ollie's team to maximize tonnage. With two puddlers, time between heats was shortened. The roller's larger crew could handle the output of two puddling furnaces because rested alternates allowed the metal thinning process to speed up. The cycle of heating iron ore and limestone to make the "melt" also sped up as men took turns puddling, resting, and eating to compensate for the extraordinary exertion. "Heats" defined each turn's overall pace and intensity.

More heats meant refilling the puddling furnaces more frequently—more 150- to 200-pound puddled iron balls were formed, then pushed through the squeezer press, and more hot iron ran through the roll trains.[55] This meant more money, more workers benefitting, and a bigger take for the roller and puddler. It also meant more human caloric costs per hour and increased food intake to put that iron in the loading yard. Full shifts and high iron output at Anchor also meant well-fed kids and biweekly deposits in the local savings banks of one or two dollars. Those deposits awaited the inevitable shutdowns and half turns of three heats, which would come in just months as the recession of 1882 to 1885 deepened.

This increased output also represents a Power Phase in miniature: pump it up, speed it up, and strategize the timing of every tiny production step to reintroduce efficiency. Frequent snack breaks maintain its peak output, then it dissipates as the turn ends and the complex, interconnected web of human-production behaviors breaks down into eleven exhausted men. They separate and walk to their boardinghouses amid the smoke and smog of Birmingham. There is now no complex structure, and their bodies cool down and burn about 150 calories an hour—not the 475 calories per hour of the work floor. The men eat. Then sleep. Then arise, eat, meet, and recombine again. Acting as a machine of eleven, they create another shift's Power Phase, cycle upon cycle. The physical coordination, timing, and extraordinary muscle development of those eleven *were* the production machine, backed up by the infrastructure of the furnace, the mechanical squeezer, and the roll trains.

The intricate coordination of the best crews saved their employers the high cost of more elaborate machinery, but they could not be scaled up rapidly. Within twenty years intricate movements of a crew like Ollie's would be replicated by machines as we now think of them. The rhythm, timing, and motion of manufacturing no longer belonged to the men. New machines set the rhythm and left yet another generation of skilled men behind, just as the packhorse captains had been unseated and replaced in the 1790s.

On the November 4 payroll of 1882, the nation in deep recession, all but one member on the crew had worked either nine or ten full single-turn days. Yet Ollie earned 36¢ per ton rolled, a dramatic decline from the October rate of 68¢. Henry Rudolph earned only 22¢ per ton for 234 tons, with a pay envelope of $51.48. Peter Grim earned 14¢ per ton for his piece work, or $32.76 for his ten days. Day workers J. Hayes, H. Densmore (H. T.), and J. Weaver each earned a fixed $22.50 for their ten days of work. J. Roop earned $25 for his ten days. J. Simmons and D. Woods, at $1.75 per day, earned, respectively, $15.75 for nine days and $14 for eight days. The helpers/apprentices J. Metzgar and W. Carothers each earned $1.25 per day for nine and ten days, respectively, at $11.25 and $12.50. The total ten-day payroll was just over $230. The fellows making over $20 for the ten days could support their families if they were careful. Those earning less lived on the edge, especially if they were married.

The December 2 payroll of 1882 records an increase in tonnage output, but the tonnage rate had again dropped from 36¢ to 22¢ a ton—a decline of nearly 70 percent in one year. The only way iron workers could compensate for a lower tonnage rate was to increase tonnage output and work harder and longer hours (and more heats). That sent mixed signals to the owners, as it suggested they could squeeze more work from their men during unstable wage cycles.

Samuel Shanabarger, an extended in-law family member from Fairchance, was on Ollie's crew. Samuel's father had worked with Robert Jr. at Oliphant's. This reciprocity meant that down the line, H. T. or Will might get onto

Oliphant's roster if Anchor closed down for an extended period or even went out of business. These personal networks maintained work options, moderated market instability, and contributed to self-sufficiency in the fragile post–Civil War era's uncertain labor environment.

By the late spring of 1883, the tonnage and fixed wage rates had not changed, but young H. T. had moved up to the position of rougher. By June 1883 a number of the men had worked the equivalent of twelve days, or about 130 hours in ten calendar days. Piece rates were steady, but then Anchor closed for several weeks as orders declined. The big-box iron and steel outfits continued to squeeze out smaller operators by dumping iron and steel on the market at a loss to destabilize them, all as a prelude to ridiculous buyout offers. Sure enough, new and even lower iron-industry wage scales were soon negotiated and announced for the entire region.

By the June 15, 1883, payroll Anchor had reopened, but with fixed daily wages—no tonnage pay. The results were dramatic all along Birmingham's riverfront. In just seven months veteran roller Henry Rudolph's pay for eleven days declined from the $60.28 of December 1882 noted above to $22, a wage rate of $2 per day! For a man of Rudolph's experience, that was shocking. H. T. remained on the crew, which now numbered only seven. Anchor closed again for three weeks between July 14 and August 6, 1883. The August 16 payroll indicates that Ollie's crew only got six days of work in that ten-day period. From July 1 to August 25, H. T. earned a total of $31.20. Compare this to his May/June pay of about $150 for the same number of elapsed workdays.

These were not living wages, and Anchor lost several of its most experienced rollers and puddlers. In September and October Ollie's crew took the long turns, and for twelve full days of work, they took home pay envelopes of $24 each—$2 a day. The core crew had been reduced to five regular members, and the wage spread between skill levels was disappearing. Food costs skyrocketed for the work calories needed to fuel increasingly grueling and longer work shifts, creating trying circumstances for those supporting large families. American-born girls and boys of this era had a life expectancy at birth of about forty years, sixteen fewer years than their counterparts born between 1800 and 1820.

By October of 1883 Ollie's payroll log had begun to calculate hours marked to the tenth of a day—a new level of recording apparently designed to gain every possible dime from management. Ollie made loans to others on the crew; loans as small as 38¢ are recorded.

On the payroll of November 2, 1883, Anchor reinstated the reduced piece rate of a stingy 22¢ a ton. Rudolph's pay envelope for 271 tons of rolled iron shot back up to $59.62. The crew again grew to eleven members. All but one worked either ten or eleven days. H. T.'s daily fixed wage increased to $3. His pay envelope contained $33 for eleven days of work. There are no fractional hours recorded in this log entry. Had "nickel and diming" Anchor's management played a role in Anchor's return to a tonnage rate? It appears so. It is also likely that Ollie's crew of eleven was designed to generate work for extended family and colleagues. Since he and his veteran crew of seven could have rolled the same amount of iron at their maximum physical output, extending access to wage work for those among Ollie's family network must have played a role.

On the payroll of November 17, 1883, 269 tons were rolled. But there are no payroll entries in Ollie's log between November 17, 1883, and March 30, 1884. Either Anchor closed down, or, more likely, Ollie temporarily stepped down as lead roller to deal with family matters in Fairchance. In either case, the logs for any paydays between those entries would have been kept by another roller.

Nehemiah Warman

During the interlude noted above, Fairchance's veteran iron roller and Ollie and Sam's brother-in-law Nehemiah Warman, about age sixty-three, fell ill and died on February 10, 1884. He had been living alone since 1880—another clue to a family rift. Nonetheless, the impact on Ollie and Sam must have been substantial. Nehemiah and their elder sister Elizabeth had taken both the boys into their home, where Elizabeth finished raising them after Old Robert died in April 1855. Sam, sixteen at the time of his father's death, and Ollie, fourteen, would have been guided into full-time apprenticeships at Oliphant's by Nehemiah and Robert Jr., both of whom lived just a few doors away. Nehemiah was buried in Maple Grove Cemetery on a lovely hillside above Fairchance. Burial traditions had changed somewhat since the 1850s, but it is safe to assume that Sam, Ollie, and Nehemiah's older sons George (thirty years old) and Samuel (twenty-seven years old) would have taken up shovels and filled in his grave. His grandson, Robert Densmore Warman, would later obscure the facts of his parentage, earn a degree at West Virginia University in 1900, and become an attorney and mayor of Uniontown. The parental denial also suggests a family rift of some sort.

Nehemiah's father, Francis, had died in 1838 in Cheat Neck, West Virginia, leaving a sixteen-year-old Nehemiah and his brothers to see to their mother and siblings. As a result, Nehemiah, like his brother-in-law Nat, never learned to read and write, but he had come up through Oliphant's ranks from mill hand to roller, and he, too, had rolled sheet iron in Old Smokey. Unsophisticated but reliable, generous, skilled, and a hard worker as a young man, Nehemiah was worn out by his sixties. Like many others of his era, he may have soured with age and taken to drink—especially after Henry Clay Frick's exploitative combine took over Oliphant's in 1870. But for Sam and Ollie he had once been another surrogate father figure. Only two remained—their much-older brothers Robert Jr. and Nat, who would die in just another year.

However angry or despondent Nehemiah may have become in the age of Frick, the data from Ollie's work log suggests that between 1842 and 1880, he produced a conservative lifetime output of well over a million tons of rolled iron. In that respect he had done the Warmans of Cheat Neck, West Virginia, proud.

A Look at Iron Work Dynamics, 1882 to 1884

The takeaway from Ollie Densmore's log entries of the 1880s is important to an understanding of the era. If owners of forges and mills kept labor on a roller coaster, first lowering wages and piecework rates per ton, many crews would respond by working more hours subsidized by their own cost of increased food intake to compensate for the increased exertion. When labor tensions became dangerous, wage rates would rise again temporarily, and there would be a feeding frenzy among the workers to raise output and get that sweet, temporary tonnage pay. These short bursts of better pay gave shop owners slightly increased profits on both the up and down cycles. It also began to more starkly differentiate the production and labor dynamics that separated big-box iron and steel operators from traditional iron shops.

The big-box iron and steel operators depended on maximum use of their sprawling plants at lower wages for long, high-speed production cycles—usually four to six months at a time. When they had stockpiled excess inventory, they merely shut down in the next soft market phase, laid off nearly everyone, and trimmed carrying costs to a minimum. Many sold their finished iron and steel at or below actual production costs—we now call it "dumping." That put enormous economic pressure on small, traditional shops like Anchor. The large combines then reopened weeks or months later to fanfare and desperate workers lined up, begging to get back on their rosters, often at a lower wage.

Meanwhile, as noted above, the small operators were bullied into also trimming wage rates by the industry "market makers" who had trapped them in a vicious up-and-down cycle that would never let them grow enough to compete with the corporate titans. If charted, as we do today, the small shops' monthly account/order histories would look like the teeth of a saw: all sharp ups and downs. The result was increasing specialization and separation in the scale of operations. Big-box operators supplied steel railroad track and big structural steel items like bridges and steel plate for warships, while the small shops increasingly produced sheet iron and specialty products in smaller, more confined economic niches. While economists provide quite refined models of such dynamics, the broad pattern is clear from Ollie's roller logs, industry reported wages, and piece rates.

The small operators obtained higher levels of output and profit efficiencies in short-duration production bursts through the intricately timed symphonic harmony of highly experienced crews working with fewer, simpler machines. That kept capital costs down. The big operations made much larger investments in machinery, but most of their profit and efficiencies were made by controlling and gaming the market in highly illegal ways, as well as from their protracted, decades-long downward pressure on wages and skill levels. High-level skills were crucial in the small shops but rejected or phased out in the big ones. By the mid-1880s, skill as a commodity was rapidly declining in value.

In the long haul, the large operators were to the small shops of two hundred men or fewer as the eight-gauge shotguns of the era's market hunters had been to the carrier pigeon. The only long-term big winners were a few hundred rich owners whose spending habits did not broadly support the national economy and the late nineteenth century's desperately needed upgrades in work safety, wages, and quality of life.

Log Entries from 1884 to 1887: Harsh Realities on Payday

Nehemiah buried, Sam Densmore appears again in Ollie's log on the February 23, 1884, payroll. He works two days, earning $2 a day. An identical entry for Sam appears on the next payroll, dated March 8, 1884. Sam then worked ten days on the March 22 payroll at $2.25 per day. By the February 7, 1885, payroll, both of Ollie's sons, H. T. and Will, are on his crew. Will, as an apprentice mill hand, earned $11.75 for eight days—a wage of about $1.45 per day. H. T., as a rougher, earned $20, or $2.50 per day. On the September 19, 1885, payroll, Sam Densmore returned, earning $21.60, or $1.80 per day for twelve days of work.

Pennsylvania iron manufacturers, perhaps disingenuously, appear not to have reported wages and hours to the US Bureau of Labor Statistics in 1882, 1883, and 1884. In 1885 they did report an average wage of $3.52 a day for roughers and other mid-level skilled iron jobs—but Ollie's son, H. T., earned only $2.50 a day at Anchor. No one on Ollie's crew earning fixed daily wages was paid anything near the government's reported wages. In fact, they were paid about 30 percent less. The value of skill and experience in iron and steel manufacturing was entering free fall, and those federally reported, and often cited, average wages were simply a fantasy along Birmingham's waterfront.

By the payroll of late October 1885, roller Henry Rudolph's two-week take-home was $10. Sam Densmore's was $7.20. Young Will Densmore earned $5.60, at $1.40 a day; his actual wage had declined to more than 50 percent below the federally published data. November and December 1885 payrolls were similar. Anchor then shut down until around February 9, 1886.

The next payroll was March 6, 1886, and Ollie again records the emergency loans he made to crew members. Fixed daily wages prevailed. In the summer and fall of 1885, Ollie's crews were taking home the "dollar a day" wages typical of the 1820s.

The tonnage/piece rates for a ton of rolled iron in Ollie's log had begun to oscillate dramatically in 1882; they began at a rate of 36¢, then rose to 68¢ in mid-summer, and ended the year at 22¢. The 22¢ rate prevailed in 1884 and 1885, then fell to 19½¢ in early 1886—a staggering decline in return on highly skilled labor in just four years.

Wages and Iron Production: The Payroll Entries of October 1886 to April 1887

Despite the dramatic wage fluctuations, the actual ten-day iron production on Ollie's crew at Anchor was surprisingly stable, varying from a high of 268 tons per ten-day payroll to a low of 249 tons. Total production and pay appear in table 11. Crew size varied from five to eleven workers. Take-home pay increased a bit. Grunting exertion, longer hours, and more heats were deployed to make the best of a terrible situation. During most of this period, Ollie's crew consisted of eight men. Four of the eight were Densmores: Sam, H. T., Will, and Ollie himself. Veterans Rudolph, Hays, and Weaver filled out the rest. The circle of wage access had shrunk to Ollie's closest family.

The pay handed out by Ollie to his crew between October 16, 1886, and the payroll of April 16, 1887, totals $2,800.24. Tonnage rates per pay period are also summarized in table 11, as dictated by Ollie and logged by H. T.

TABLE 11. H. O. Densmore's Crew: Tonnage of Rolled Specialty Iron per Pay Period, 1886–1887*

Payroll Date	Tonnage Rolled
16 October, 1886	258
30 October, 1886	264
27 November, 1886	262
11 December, 1886	264
22 January, 1887	268
5 February, 1887	254
19 February, 1887	259
5 March, 1887	252
19 March, 1887	251
2 April, 1887	256
16 April, 1887	249
Average Rolling Labor Cost/Ton:	98½¢
Average Tonnage/10 days:	258
Total Rolled Tons:	2,837
Total Labor Cost:	$2,800.24

* Fidelio Hughes Oliphant Densmore and H. T. Densmore, "Pay Roll and Account Book" (handwritten iron roller's log in possession of author, 1882–1887).

By September 17, 1887, the recession lifting, tonnage rates equal to those in 1884 were again reset to 68¢ per rolled ton of iron. If one looks at this one aspect of rolled-iron production as an equation made up of wage, work calories, and product output, several apparent trends emerge. The dramatic oscillations, industry-negotiated tonnage, pay rates, and work schedules generated far greater variation in an individual worker's take-home pay than Anchor's actual costs of iron production. The direct labor costs for puddling, squeezing, roughing, and rolling 2,837 tons of semi-finished iron summarized in table 11 cost an averaged 98½¢ per ton. On the largest payroll of October 30, 1886, labor cost for the 264 tons of rolled iron was $261.08, or 98.6¢ a ton, including all piece-work rates.

Ollie's payroll of April 16, 1887, paid out the lowest daily output (249 tons) of rolled iron, and the owners produced a high of $1.04 labor per ton. But on the following week's payroll, Ollie's crew produced 181 tons in five paid shifts of twelve hours each by a crew of twelve. The labor cost was $128.96, which averaged only 71¢ per ton! This sent the self-defeating signal to owners that short, intense work periods with larger, low-paid crews favored profit margins. The problem for Ollie's crew, of course, was that their take-home pay shrunk, depending on the month, by about 30 to 50 percent as the owners' average profit per ton temporarily rose in concert. Yet the higher a crew's work intensity, the greater the share of their pay that went to purchase their own food calories and the smaller the portion of food dollars left over for others at their household tables.

These short bursts of labor-cheap iron produced by large crews working five days boomeranged when they became scaled up by the big iron producers. The nation's iron and steel industry moved to six and seven-day workweeks, and weekly hours rose to between seventy-two and eighty-four, but effective work output per iron-worker hour degraded. As every National Hockey League coach knows, there is a reason why optimal "on ice" shifts are forty-five to ninety *seconds*. Highly tuned athletes can work short-term miracles again and again if peak performance is of short duration and rests follow. A brilliant manager/owner among the small 1880s iron manufacturers would have analyzed these patterns and made changes that split the production cost savings of nearly 30 percent (98.6¢ a ton versus 71¢) between the house and his best crews' wages and alternated between the best short-term, high-output work crews. Though big-box operators' dumping episodes would have temporarily dented this formula, it would have provided small shops a bit more payroll stability.

Working actively against the most sustainable solutions were the large iron and steel manufacturers, obsessed with maximizing both the hours and the speed at which their plants operated. Greed reigned supreme. Missing from their equations were the harsh effects of the nearly impossible sustained work inputs demanded from their most skilled workers. Sadly, they did not need to care—the short-term profits made from forcing their workers into endless seventy- and eighty-hour body-breaking workweeks actually allowed them to invest in the new machinery that would eventually render those same highly skilled workers as antiquated relics.

In stark contrast, the small- and medium-sized specialty iron works, like Anchor, depended on the skills of men like Ollie, Sam, and Robert Jr. Those skills and crew coordination lessened their need to rapidly invest the scarce capital needed to continually modernize their machinery.

Pride of Work

Of course, the Densmore men preferred to work at Anchor, where the culture of skill still reigned. But that culture was anathema to the Carnegies and Fricks of the era. They did everything possible to destroy that culture in both their own works and in the small, traditional shops like Anchor. The work culture of skills, respect, and reciprocity that had prevailed in America since the time of the Founders was under siege—a skilled, respected, self-sufficient worker was to be both feared and destroyed at all costs. Any hint of those values or requests for saner working conditions were met with reflexive pushback from the rapacious big-box operators, some of whom responded by demanding work schedules of 364 days a year and daily shifts of a full twelve hours! Big operators simply did not care about the biological stress they were forcing on workers. And why should they? They were not held legally accountable for either physical burnout or work-related injuries. America's growing love affair with big capital was generating an increasingly abusive marriage.

In the 1880s work practices imposed by large-scale manufacturers destroyed the health of many of the nation's most experienced iron workers as their middle-aged bodies failed. And few seem to have apprehended the caloric and nutritional dilemma that pushed higher food-fueled production costs onto workers *and* left many of their children undernourished. But modern data now tell us that height and longevity among American-born girls and boys continued to deteriorate during this period. Those children of "working stiffs" were not eating very well. Worse yet, childhood diseases increasingly wrought havoc in densely packed urban mill-town housing. What the Robber Barons stole included profits, lives, and the nation's founding cultural values. Their corporate practices consistently created both industrial cripples and improperly nourished children. Yet a nation of laws turned its head, refusing to confront big industry's increasingly amoral and illegal demands for unquestioned control. Given no concerted federal regulatory oversight, a new and aggressively cancerous breed of elite tyrants had sprung up and taken control in a way that redefined late nineteenth-century

"America"—a phenomenon the Declaration had explicitly intended to extirpate from American culture.

The Log in Cultural Context

Ollie's log also suggests a grander economic and technological context for these dramatic changes in wages, tonnage rates, and market conditions for the iron and early steel industries. In 1836 the iron industry in Allegheny County consisted of nine mills and a total of three hundred hands, who produced 28,000 total tons of pig iron. By 1856 the number of mills had increased to about eighteen in Allegheny County. By 1864, according to pioneer iron producer Charles A. McKnight,[56] there were nineteen rolling mills in Pittsburgh producing 98,850 tons of rolled iron. Workers numbered 2,720 hands.

Just twenty years later in 1885 to 1887, as table 11 illustrates, Ollie's crew of seven to eleven men rolled 2,837 tons of iron in twenty-one weeks. Had they been able to work fifty full weeks, three hundred days, in either 1886 or 1887 at table 11's average rate of 26 tons per day, they would have produced 7,800 tons of rolled iron. It would have taken only thirteen crews of nine like Ollie's in 1885 to *exceed* Pittsburgh's entire iron output in 1864! In traditional shops, 117 veteran iron workers in 1886 to 1887 could easily match the output of 2,720 workers twenty-two years before. That represented a huge gain in production efficiency. In fact, just four crews identical to Ollie's team of nine veterans could have rolled more iron in 1886 than three hundred workers could produce in 1836.

This explosive growth in iron and steel production was created by a combination of factors: the situational production demands of the Civil War; the shift to steel railroad track in the late 1860s; changes in the technology and automation of iron and steel manufacture; a large wave of foreign immigration; the fevered push to settle the American West; the rapidly growing scale of the industry; and the consolidation of economic power and management of it into ever fewer and richer hands. In general economic perspective, the iron and steel industry suffered from the classic problem discussed in most every Economics 101 textbook: far too rapid expansion of production followed by brutal competition. The workers and their families paid a disproportionate share of that competition.

The full scope of these changes was simply beyond the grasp of most individual iron and steel workers. The most experienced of them could easily grasp changes in real-world production techniques. They knew in a general way that the growing steel giants in the late 1870s and 1880s were mechanizing, gaming the market, sometimes flooding it, then choking it by closing down for weeks or months at a time. But the dynamics of the larger national, political, and economic mechanizations were beyond the ken of their world of furnace-floor reality.

They could not have predicted that when the transcontinental railroad's "Golden Spike" was driven, it would trigger yet another era of massive track laying, and that most of the track would be made of steel, not iron. Between 1865 and the Long Depression that began in 1873, the nation laid more than thirty-five thousand miles of track—classic Power Phase behavior that doubled the nation's rail-track mileage in just eight years.

When that process slowed down, the nation went into recession. Iron workers could not have foreseen that between 1865 and 1873, three million more immigrants would arrive, willing to work cheap to get a start in America. How could they have known from the street-level depression of the late 1860s that industrial production had actually increased by about 75 percent in America, even as they suffered short shifts? How could they have known that new operations like the Homestead Works, which opened with modern Bessemer furnaces in 1881 just a few miles up the Monongahela from Birmingham, would suddenly fall into the hands of Andrew Carnegie in 1883 and 1884? And how could they have known that Henry C. Frick, who had bought Oliphant's, was simultaneously cornering the region's coking-coal deposits along with the Connellsville Coke Works, which had given Sam Densmore the best salaried job of his life?

And who would have thought that while Frick collected coalfields and coke ovens, Carnegie was collecting men like Frick? If Carnegie, Frick, and others pursued business in the 1980s as they did in the 1880s, they would have ended up doing hard prison time under RICO[57] laws, for both price fixing and worker abuse. The big operators like Carnegie Steel, Jones & Laughlin, and even, at times, US Steel cared as much about *control* over the workers as they did about the bottom line. In direct opposition to Main Street America's cultural norms, control and domination were key values in their corporate culture.

The darkest, ugliest side of that control instinct would explode again in 1892.[58] For some of the Robber Barons of the 1880s and 1890s, their mantra seems not to have been, "Thy will be done," but rather, "*My* will be done." We still see this ugly phenomenon today in both American politics and in corporate enclaves.

Workers in the 1860 to 1900 era had far fewer legal avenues of redress than prevail now. And to make it even clearer, Ollie's log records wages for some of the best-paid and most elite skilled workers in America. The primary advantage a roller had from the mid-1840s to the 1880s was the right to pick his crew. From the perspective of a small- to medium-sized works owned by three or four partners, or of a family operation like Oliphant's, this system virtually guaranteed that fathers would bring in sons, nephews, and sons-in-law, teach them the trade while those apprentices worked for a low daily wage, then supply the next generation of highly skilled workers to replace their aging fathers.

As a roller, Ollie took full advantage. Over his years at Anchor, he trained two sons, brought on his brother Robert Jr. in the slump of the late 1860s, hired Densmore nephews and sons-in-law from Fairchaince and two generations of Warmans in the 1870s, and, of course, worked with Sam, his brother and friend, off and on from the 1860s to the late 1880s. In 1864 and 1866, when Anchor was "almost entirely destroyed by fire,"[59] reciprocity for Ollie meant day labor at Oliphant's in Fairchance, country ham, and garden produce when disaster struck in Pittsburgh.

In the 1880s to the mid-1890s, Old Robert's descendant Densmore clan and sons-in-law had no less than eleven men and boys simultaneously making iron and steel. Some were in Fairchance working for the new owner, Henry C. Frick, at Oliphant's, whose agents took working conditions down two full notches. Others worked in Kittanning or in Birmingham at Anchor, Wharton's, the National Tube Works, or even in Homestead where Frick himself was in charge of daily operations.

As skilled workers were replaced by machines operated by less-skilled labor, and as small- to medium-sized works like Oliphant's were gobbled up by the big box crowd, skilled workers' traditional rights took a deep hit, accompanied by lower pay rates. The loyalty that had once helped both the owners and the rollers through tough times was quickly ground down like rusty iron on a polishing wheel. The Oliphants' practice of paying crews in farm produce or local bartered goods when there was no cash had become, like the Civil War's five- or six-dollar work days, a quaint historical footnote. That polishing wheel also ground down self-sufficiency and well-being. Most of the next generation of Old Robert's male descendants would be shorter and die younger than Sam, Ollie, Robert Jr., and Nat.

On September 17, 1887, Ollie's son H. T. took over his father's logbook. Written in striking red ink with an elegant, flowing hand, the entries presage H. T.'s future and give us even more detail than Ollie had included. They allow us to see changes in the rhythm of iron making.

The Cadence of Iron

The iron makers' rhythm required the puddling furnaces at Anchor to bring a batch, or a "melt," to the correct heat for puddling. That triggered the puddler. His work triggered the bloom boy, the catcher, and the rougher, then the advanced rolling and the roll turner. It was rather like a symphony, where new sections of the orchestra are triggered by preludes, the rise and fall of tempo, then the crescendo. Iron making at its best created industrial music, and the lead roller was the conductor. His first violinist was the puddler. Just as in a symphony, the music only worked when coordinated.[60] In the seven-year span of H. T.'s log entries, this rhythm fades away, replaced by the discordant tones of music America's young folk would now call "Industrial."

While these log entries make for tedious, detailed reading, they make it clear that the erratic ups and downs in take-home pay forced most workers, even the rollers and the puddlers, the princes of American labor, to live *below* their means, ever fearful of the next pay-envelope disaster. How impactful was high-calorie work, coupled with wage instability and increased childhood diseases? If the princes were under siege, what about the rest of working America? American-born boys between 1880 and 1890 were, as adults, the shortest men in American history at 5'6.7" (1880) and 5'6.6" (1890). Their American-born great-grandfathers had averaged *over* 5'8.2" and had lived *much* longer.[61]

Chapter 17

The 1890s
Both the Gay and the Dour

By the US Census of 1890, cities like New York, Boston, Philadelphia, and Chicago were bursting at the seams. Urban housing was in short supply; tenements were packed, and communicable diseases flourished. Wave after wave of cheap, Eastern-European immigrant labor lowered wages and increased competition for jobs. Social stratification and economic inequality amplified. Just as the 1840s and 1850s had been especially hard for the Catholic Irish fleeing famine, the 1880s and 1890s were tough on Poles, Slavs, and Italians—it was Ellis Island's early heyday of activity. Community adaptations to new languages, religions, diets, skin tones, and family cultures were slow and often tense—but nowhere tenser than in the workplace.

Business titans regularly played the card of these differences to quell labor movements. Race and immigrant tensions of the 1870s and 1880s also operated as a fracture point in those Unions championed by American-born organizers.[1] More arriving immigrants who would work cheaply were many Union bosses' recurring nightmare. Just how could they get safer working conditions, an eight-hour day, and a five-day workweek and also slow the mechanization so blatantly designed to erase skilled job categories when hordes of new workers were willing to accept almost any terms in order to feed their children?

Traditional, tong-wielding puddlers were already at risk. Even the rollers no longer had uncontested rights to pick their crews as a new breed of shop and floor managers called "foremen" emerged in the big-box operations. They were chosen by upper management, too often with only limited experience in the hands-on production processes they managed. Senior managers often brought *their* kin into the works, skilled or not. Both safety and quality suffered. The traditional basis of skilled workers' status, role, and pay rates no longer depended on apprenticeship, experience, and years of hands-on skills and reliability. Instead it gave way to increasingly extraneous factors that made no sense in the American work culture that had evolved east of the Mississippi during the prior 150 years.

Pressuring a veteran roller, die cutter, metal finisher, or skilled glass worker through payroll tricks was trouble enough, but messing with precious work identities and statuses was intolerable. America's industrialists had been so busy getting rich, gaining power, creating their own rarified social class, and surrounding themselves with obsequious "Yes Men" that they were blind to the reality that America's shop-floor ethos was based on both wages and pride. Respect had always been a major part of the return-on-work equation among America's skilled workers. "Respect" is the most crucial cultural lubricant to the gears of any large, diverse society.

The early nation's rifle makers in Kutztown, Lancaster, Pennsylvania's Sugar Valley, Vincennes, Indiana, and Mason County, Kentucky—those that, for a time, defined an American industry—signed their rifles. When Eliphalet Remington first began hand forging rifle barrels in rural, 1800 New York, he stamped "E. Remington" into every barrel. Wagon makers in the Conestoga Valley typically signed or marked undercarriages. Master cabinetmakers in Philadelphia and Boston marked or signed their best work. And Oliphant's banner-painted, mule-driven wagons carrying his nails from Fairchance on the National Road in the 1840s weren't just any nails—they were Oliphant's nails, recognizable to tradesmen from Philadelphia to St. Louis as the best made in America during that era.

Separating workers' identity from the product of their work or the legacy of their skills was nothing less than an all-out cultural assault on nineteenth-century America as skilled workers knew it. Pride of work counted. Identity counted. Sweat and years of learning counted. Skill counted. Or did they? That was a question faced as the assistant marshals of the US Census of 1890 spread out across the East to visit millions of households and put America's twelfth census on paper. That year's native-born baby boys would grow up to be the shortest in all of American history. Declining wages, environment, working conditions, and public health issues had conjoined to claim their biological costs from both wage workers *and* their children. Life expectancy at birth for workers' American-born daughters and sons had declined from 44 years in 1870 to 39.4 years in 1880. Rising infant mortality played a role.[2] The Founders would have been shocked.

CHAPTER 17

The Densmores in the 1890s

On census day, 1890, Robert Jr. still worked at Oliphant's in Fairchance, but we have few details for him, or for most of the other Densmores, Harts, and Vandergrifts. In 1921 a massive fire consumed nearly the entire Census of 1890, creating yet another documentary enigma. What can be reconstructed is primarily derived from city directories, local tax records, and sources like St. Paul's Church in Kittanning. A special census of 1891 was created from pension records for Civil War veterans—it included Robert Jr. but not Sam.

From Diffenbacher's Pittsburgh directories, we know that in 1890, Ollie, listed as "Densmore, Oliver, Roller," lived at 2101 Sidney and was still rolling iron at Anchor.[3] In both 1888 and again in 1891, H. T. is listed as a roller, living at #51 South Twenty-first Street—the bunkhouse. Between 1887 and 1888, H. T. had graduated from rougher to roller status. Ollie's tutelage and that of H. T.'s uncles Sam and Robert Jr. had paid off, and just in time, for in 1887 a vibrant twenty-six-year-old Sophia Irene (Vandergrift) Densmore bore his second child, a daughter, Elsie Elizabeth Densmore. Sophia was ecstatic. H. T. named Elsie for a Densmore aunt who had died in Fairchance in 1881.

Sophia feared that she and H. T. might lose their children, as had Ollie and his wife Elizabeth.[4] But Benjamin and Elsie remained healthy. As joy radiated from their second-story home above the bunkhouse, other ethers swirled around H. T. and Ollie in Birmingham. The huge Homestead and Edgar Thompson Works of Carnegie Steel were squeezing their workers like a tuxedo-suited boa constrictor. The heats, mechanical production lines, and roll trains sped up nearly everywhere. Faster, faster, faster, and the shifts became successively longer. More heats, more rounds, more melts, more calories, more exhaustion, and more accidents. The coveted corporate yields were in both rising profits and declining worker self-sufficiency.

Union movements challenged the new class of corporate managers. The titans ordered a pushback and imposed even more brutal work schedules, followed by surprise shutdowns on a few hours' notice. Workweeks lengthened to seventy-two hours on average; a few ordered eighty-four hours. In a number of mills, six-day weeks turned into seven. As noted, the practices in those huge operations—ever faster, more mechanized, and number driven—rather perfectly mimic what one expects in a complex society's Power Phase: huge scale, fast paced, output obsessed, and aggressive to less powerful competitors. During Power Phases empires are created, wars are fought, individualism is tamped down, and those in the way are consumed.

A growing America had already brutally pushed the Native American world out of its way, sold and resold most of their lands, ignored treaty obligations, and reduced them to largely powerless, surviving enclaves with stereotypical identities. In this era of a missing census, steel and railroad magnates pushed down on smaller shops with predatory pricing. They bought up coal lands to control coke production and bought vast lands in the upper Midwest, among them the Mesabi deposits,[5] to control access to iron ore. Anchor's coal-coke acreages in Fayette County's Dunbar Township, where Henry Dunsmore had once distilled in the 1790s, was bought up by Frick and Associates. The small operators had little choice but to constrict crew size again or gouge down into the pay envelopes of those on their work rosters to seek relief. Work tensions thickened during the summer of 1891, just like the inescapable ash-laden haze that swirled around Birmingham's damp August streets, stripping every living thing of its summer color.

A workplace powder keg was filling rapidly, and in 1892 yet another twisted soul tossed the glowing match that set it off.

Homestead: 1892

One old iron/steel worker's song begins,

> Now the trouble down at Homestead was brought about this way: when a grasping corporation had the audacity to say, "You must all renounce your union and forswear your liberty. And we'll give you a chance to live and die in slavery."

"The Fort at Frick" is another tune, and "Father was Killed by a Pinkerton Man" is a third. In fact, an entire songbook of the period was published by a union organization after the unrest at Carnegie Steel's massive Homestead Works.[6]

The Homestead Strikes have been written about by many excellent scholars. Along with accounts of the Great Railroad Strike of 1877, the coal wars in southern West Virginia's Matewan district, and the massacre of union miners at Ludlow, Colorado, in the 1920s, the Homestead Strikes should be reading that American high schools and colleges emphasize. They illustrate the tensions that inhere and the abuses of power and behavior that are evident when "Main Street" and "Power Street" lose touch with one another. In a large, complex society, these differences form one of the primary fracture lines that threaten a society's integrity. Tensions over race, religion, and education are close behind. These tensions replay cyclically and endlessly in large, complex societies.

For our narrative, it is enough to know that Ollie's son, H. T. Densmore, the rougher and roller, worked at Homestead from the 1890s until 1912. H. T., as you know, started work at age fourteen.[7] If his daughter Elsie got it right, he had finished ninth grade, and he liked to draw the machines he worked on as a rougher. A rougher also rough-rolls iron to a basic shape for its final rolling. In the process there are big presses to adjust for depth or "draft" of the metal rolls. There are measurements to take and adjustments to be made with huge wrenches after order specifications have been read in order to set machine dimensions. A lead roller like Ollie made even more of these complicated and precise sets in order to roll a final, smooth, and uniform sheet or bar of iron/steel—hence part of the roller's pay differential.[8]

The Homestead Strikes followed strikes in western Pennsylvania's coalfields in 1884 and 1887. As already noted, Sam Densmore apparently left his job at the coke works in the midst of the 1883 to 1884 Frick-induced strike. But Goldsboros, Densmores, Carrs, Warmans, Prices, Shanabargers, and other descendants, direct and affines,[9] were also affected again in Fayette County, where Henry C. Frick's work-floor labor practices played a negative role in their lives, as did his use of Pinkerton agents and hired strike breakers during the 1887 strikes in Connellsville and Fairchance. He apparently liked the results.

We've Been "Fricked"

The structure of a Frick pushback was like a three-act play: shut down the plant to starve out the majority; bring in the Pinkertons to break heads; then bring in Italians, blacks, or Slavs to take away the "hand" and "helper" jobs and rehire the most-skilled labor at about 60¢ on the dollar of their prior pay. Carnegie had put Frick in charge of the massive Homestead Works on the Monongahela a few miles south of Pittsburgh's Point. When the existing union contract of 1889 expired on June 30, 1892, Carnegie and Frick did not renew it.[10] Instead, in April 1892 they summarily declared Homestead "non-union." Frick then played cat and mouse, rejecting, rejecting, and rejecting successive union requests to keep the same hours and pay. Once the union accepted a slightly lower scale, that, too, was rejected, and a new, even lower scale was demanded. This happened for the final time on July 1, 1892. Having stated his ultimatum, Frick walked out, "determined to close the Homestead Works and reopen July 6 with a non-union workforce."[11]

Shocked and angry, some 3,800 workers organized and took control of the area surrounding the Homestead campus on July 4. They invited the sheriff and his deputies to tour the works to witness that they had done no damage to company property. On the afternoon of July 6, two armed barges towed by the tug Little Bill,[12] carrying about three hundred heavily armed Pinkertons, pulled up to the wharves in front of the works itself. The tug's steam whistle triggered the first large wave of trespassers into the works. Consisting mostly of workers and a sprinkling of wives and children, their object was to defend the works so that strikebreakers could not come in. The strikers did not yet know that the barges were filled with Pinkertons. An immediate volley of rifle fire from the barges instantaneously clarified the situation. Rifles, pistols, hawksbill axes, clubs, and broomsticks in hand, it quickly turned into a short, pitched battle—thousands of rounds were fired on both sides. Memories of 1877 in mind, most of the children were quickly withdrawn. Initially, no one believed the Pinkertons would again shoot into a mixed crowd, as they had on Pittsburgh's Liberty Avenue in 1877. They were wrong. A number were killed, women among them. On vacation in his native Scotland, Andrew Carnegie telegraphed Frick and ordered the plant closed indefinitely.

However, the workers were still in possession of the works, which they had "invested." On July 11 seven regiments of Pennsylvania militia arrived, armed with cannon, Gatling guns, and .45-70 caliber "trapdoor" Springfields. Even then the strike and occupation went on, muddied by an attempted assassination of Frick in Pittsburgh. Broke, hungry, and weary, the strikers gave in and left the works on November 22. Several were tried in federal court for treason, a blatantly unconstitutional legal tactic[13] used again in the West Virginia "coal wars" of the 1920s. By 1893 the destitute families of blacklisted strikers began to drift away from Homestead. Company profits rose, as did the ratio of unskilled workers. The world of fast-paced, non-union, open-furnace steel production now reigned, and a roller's wage for sixty-hour weeks declined to an unbelievably low $1.85 a day by 1895.[14] These were the wages of the 1840s and 1850s! The Carnegie/Frick wage victory filtered down to the small shops in Birmingham. Less than a year later, Ollie retired from Anchor and returned to Fairchance.

Meanwhile, Carnegie rapidly became richer, but he and Frick lost much of their prestige, as the armed attack on 3,800 Homestead strikers and their families had shaken both the region's largest industry and Carnegie's social standing.

As an obsessed Frick and his Pinkertons continued their hunt for key strikers, the Commonwealth of Pennsylvania once again failed to record most of the reported iron and steel industry wage figures for 1893 and 1894, just as they had during the iron and coke/coalfield strikes of 1883 and 1884.

Harry Thomas Densmore

H. T. must have been especially frustrated in the late 1880s and early 1890s as shift lengths grew from 10.8 to 14 hours, six days a week. He was an excellent roller and made decent money, paying a preferential rent to his father. But his brain and his heart's desire carried him beyond the making of iron. H. T. was a cerebral guy. In photographs showing him in his parlor at 2101 Sidney in the mid-1890s, he is usually reading and smoking his pipe, dressed not in work blues but in a tweed jacket and often a tie. He bought books for his children and liked to talk to both his father and his uncle Sam about machinery.

We do not know the exact date on which he left Anchor, but sometime between 1891 and 1892 he began working at Homestead as a roller, then he graduated from roller to head shipping clerk in 1897. If his daughter Elsie, then age ten, had her facts right, he handled the orders, timing, paperwork, and sets for a number of rolling lines. He allegedly gauged and adjusted multiple roll trains[15] on a sequenced schedule. This generated logistical efficiencies. She also noted that the "Pinkertons came for him" in Birmingham when she was six or seven.[16] She recounted her father leaning out of the second-floor window at 2101 Sidney, 32-caliber revolver in hand, drawing a bead and bellowing, "Stand and deliver!" It sounds rather theatric in hindsight, but that is as she remembered it in the summer of 1961.

While it is not known whether young roller H. T. Densmore was an occupier of the works in the Homestead Strike itself, he worked there and was clearly caught up in its ripples. After the strikes he joined men's organizations and became involved in ad hoc committees about street-level infrastructure in the South Side. He was focused on water, sewer, health, and the vote.[17]

The Densmore Family Network, 1860 to 1905

As H. T.'s work world and social circle expanded, his father's life was narrowing into retirement. Ollie's world had focused on work, pay, saving, and the right to control the fruit of his strong arms. He remembered the color of the molten iron's sparks that made the best quality nails he had cut at Oliphant's as a young man and, later, the distinct batches of Anchor's sheet, billet, and bar he had rolled. He had also dreamed, indeed prayed, about the children he and Elizabeth had lost, and he had hoped to own his own house and garden. He first bought land in Fairchance during the 1860s to realize that dream.

But on July 6, 1877, Ollie and his wife sold a one-acre lot with two houses and a stable to support his older sister, the dark-haired Elizabeth, and Nehemiah Warman for the token sum of five dollars, yet another clue that Nehemiah was no longer able to work at Oliphant's. Clearly all was not well in the Warman couple's world. Ollie had bought that lot near Oliphant's Works from Henry Ward of Fairchance on February 3, 1868,[18] with his earnings at Anchor. The original deed had been presented to his petite but intrepid Elizabeth Goldsboro two days following, on February 5, as her twenty-sixth birthday present. On that birthday Elizabeth's two living children were H. T., age three and a half, and Jane, age two months. That lot, when sold in 1877, signaled both the reality of nineteenth-century family obligations[19] and a personal dream deferred.

His veteran's status on Anchor's roster allowed him to recoup from the generosity of that sale. By the 1880s he owned and occupied 2101 Sidney, the expanded bunkhouse on Fox Alley at Twenty-first Street, the homestead in Fairchance, and two acres near the homestead, bought and deeded July 24, 1881.[20] Business pertaining to building the house at 2101 Sidney had consumed late 1879, much of 1880, and part of 1881. But just one year later, the two-acre plot in Fairchance was purchased by Ollie and his brother Nat. After Nat died in 1884, the lot was sold to Peter Fisher in 1888 by Ollie and Nat's widow, Susan. She received the full two hundred dollar sale price, a family annuity, it seems. Nat, though deceased, was listed as the co-seller. This was likely done to avoid taxes and costs of resurvey, appraisal, and new deed.

Then on June 20, 1887, Ollie sold another property in consortium with his wife Elizabeth and his in-laws as referenced in the Fayette County deed book:

> George and Mary Goldsboro; Ephraim Price and his wife Mary Jane; John Rodgers and wife Margaret; Robert Goldsboro and his wife, M. J.; John Goldsboro and wife Jennie; and Robert Goldsboro, guardian of Robert Shanabarger,[21] widow and heir of Thomas Goldsboro deceased to James W. McFadden of Georges Township for the sum of $550.00, "a tract in Fairchance.... it being the same premises Thomas Goldsboro purchased.... March 4th 1882."[22]

Then on November 15, 1887, in-laws including the Prices, Abels, surviving Goldsboros, the Wilsons, and Rogers, along with Ollie and Elizabeth, quit claimed to "Mary Jane Goldsboro of Fairchance for $10, all their rights to a 9,000 square foot lot adjoining the Southwestern Pennsylvania Railroad." An extended family combine again conferred benefits on a descendant. The record of this last "co-op" sale punctuates the loss of Tom Goldsboro, born in 1809 in "East Virginia,"[23] who more than half a century prior had walked behind a beribboned horse to make peace with his father-in-law, John Ryland, of the Youghiogheny Valley. It was the succession of forges that Tom and his brothers had worked that Ollie committed to memory and passed to his granddaughter Elsie: Bear Creek, Muddy Creek, Valley Furnace, and Oliphant's. Tom Goldsboro ended his career as a coal digger/broker. Ollie had to have felt that death—they had been close, and Tom was a connection to the kind of forges his father Old Robert had worked in the 1820s.

By the time Thomas Goldsboro died, much of the Youghiogheny Valley timber had been clear-cut. It had become a world of railroad track crews, lumber camps, and a transient transportation corridor. Gone were the panthers, the forested Shades of Death, and the wagoners with their bull-hide whips, buckskins, and Bowie knives.

The land transactions noted above indicate that Ollie was the primary glue among the various branches of his large, extended kin network. Neither Sam nor Robert Jr. were co-owners of these lots. Sam's kin network was in Armstrong and Mercer Counties, while Robert Jr.'s was focused on Fairchance and the increasing number of Densmore descendants in Uniontown. That Ollie also played a primary economic role in a network of at least a hundred children, cousins, and in-laws is not surprising—he had the fewest children and had been able to save the most. His influence and resources softened disasters and held the extended family together. He had bought wisely with the savings from his grueling long turns. His largest property purchases, as noted in the Fayette and Allegheny County deed books, came in 1867 to 1868 and in 1879 to 1880. These were recession years, when the price of land and housing tanked. Ollie saved when markets were strong and wages peaked, then invested in hard assets when economic depression eroded prices.

Ollie's skills and brutal long turns in Birmingham had bought shared land, houses, stables, and tools—the stuff of both nineteenth-century dreams and homespun insurance policies actuated when death or disaster trespassed into the domain of the extended family network. The loss of three children, especially little Ellen in 1881, had left Elizabeth bereft and dashed Ollie's earlier dreams of house, garden, and a "passel" of happy, healthy children. Almost forty-one when Ellen died, middle age had hit Ollie like a sledgehammer. Ollie could not bring back the six named children he and Elizabeth had already buried, but he could do more to look out for others. Thus the 1880s saw him step in again and again to mitigate disaster and soften the harsh realities besetting others in his circle.

Ollie Densmore's generosity was based on a concept of "I have enough" common among nineteenth-century working men. The Densmore anthem hammered into me as a child was, "Happiness is not having what you want; it is wanting what you have." This concept was utterly alien to men like Frick and Carnegie. It remains alien to our current version of an economic aristocracy.

New Dreams, New Worlds

In the emerging industrial world of the late nineteenth century, H. T. Densmore's dreams differed from those of his parents. He and Sophia had only two children, and that was it.[24] They were demographically structured like a modern family, and they had the ideas and freedoms to go with it. H. T.'s most prized personal possession was a huge barrel-top desk with bookcases jutting above it to nearly nine feet tall. It was furniture one would expect an up-and-coming lawyer to have, not a rougher at Anchor. And it was full of books—catalogs of gears, a treatise on business efficiency, reports of the Iron and Steel Institute, and some of the classics.[25]

At home, H. T. liked to relax at his desk and bask in tranquility after ten hours on the rolling line amid the heat, steam clouds, and glowing "blooms" that coughed and spat out infectious oxides, slag, and crusty impurities like dying "lungers" as they passed through the mechanical squeezer. It was good money. There was a certain prestige. But H. T. was cerebral. Instead of finished tonnage dancing in his head at night, he dreamt of machines, diagrams, logbooks, and processes.

He liked the idea of what one could do with iron and steel once it passed from the high, partially open tin-roofed expanse of Anchor's work floor to the loading yard along the river. Where did it go? What would it become? Where might he see *his* iron again so that he could carry little Benjamin on his shoulders, point to it, and say, "Sonny, that's *my* iron there in the façade of that shoe store. See there? I made the pillars between those big windows."

And indeed he had, as the log he maintained for his father after 1884 lists a "bloom boy," who process large billets of iron, on virtually every crew. At Anchor, that suggests Ollie's crews were rolling structural iron. That iron was high quality, puddler forged, squeezed, roughed, fine-rolled, and finished to shape before it hit the loading yard where he and Ollie took their breaks. In iron directories it would be listed as "specialty iron." That iron, unlike cheaper and more brittle cast iron, was nearly shatterproof. Winds, side pressure, and cycles of extreme heat and cold might make it groan or shrink and expand in subtle fractions of an inch, but it would not shatter or collapse. It lived and breathed, and as H. T. became a lead roller around 1886 or 1887, it was he and his crew that had given it life.

His father's life, especially in those cycles of grief over the loss of yet another child, had always focused on retreat *into* the mill's dominating symphony. The sound, fury, heat, and noise discouraged delicate conversation, swallowed his pain, and hid it from the outside world. H. T. had not suffered in the same way. For him the meaning of the heat and roar was the creation of a product and its life *beyond* the mill. The symphony of fire and steam was merely a prelude.

Flowers, Funerals, and Family Capital

In another world across the Monongahela, a different kind of music played—somber and funereal—in 1895. J. J. Vandergrift's mother, born Sophia Irene Sarver on July 5, 1804, and wife of William Knowles Vandergrift, died at the age of ninety-one. The last female of her Vandergrift generation, Sophia's name lived on in Sophia Irene Vandergrift Densmore. As the matriarch, Sophia was given a funeral by the flashy and immensely rich J. J. that might well have supported a half dozen working families for a year. The farmer's daughter from Perrysville, about five miles north of old Pittsburgh, is unlikely to have approved of money spent on a lavish funeral. But, like a botanist in possession of a rare butterfly, J. J. displayed her. Then a long procession of black caparisoned horses, a hearse, wagons, and carriages conveyed her and the funeral party to her anointed place in the Allegheny Cemetery near the foot of an imposing obelisk that marked the center of J. J.'s growing eternal family. Young Sophia had often visited her father's grave across the river from Birmingham as age, time, accidents, and a militia officer's bullets shrank her paternal family circle. But the loss of her namesake and only living grandmother was both poignant and painful.

Despite the Vandergrift prosperity that surrounded her as an old lady, Sophia Sarver Vandergrift remained deeply rooted in the frontier, farm-country values of her upbringing. According to her granddaughter, Sophia Vandergrift Densmore, she was possessed of a sunny disposition, loved flowers, widely gifted her small, handmade presents of doilies and scarves, and shared the root stock of the deep, blood-red peonies from her father's farm with virtually every Vandergrift home. Even in-laws were included. That root stock's progeny still survives in the backyards of the last Vandergrift-Densmore house near Philadelphia, in a home in Frederick, Maryland, in a home in Charlottesville, Virginia, and in another in Morgantown, West Virginia. These plant cuttings and their genes were transmitted female to female as symbolic cultural property spanning five generations. They not only represented a "home place" but cemented the multi-generational network of spirited women who would stick together as time, layoffs, deaths, or derelict husbands triggered "make-do" responses to compensate.

The legacy of the Vandergrift, Hart, and Densmore men focused on property, cash in hand, tangible iron and steel, wagons, forges, tools, furniture, riverboats, land, and business assets. In contrast, the legacy of the women focused on cultural capital and family connections, traditions, customs, and, above all, relationships that transcended material success. The Harts' prominence had already begun to fade from the Ohio Valley as Jesse, Aaron, and Scudder Hart's descendants spread across the nation. The last, true East Coast stronghold of the Harts would remain in Randolph County, West Virginia, where they had produced succeeding generations of sheriffs, schoolmasters, carpenters, farmers, and local officials.

By the fall of 1896, as the aftershocks of the Homestead Strike faded, H. T., age thirty, was living in the main house at 2101 Sidney with Sophia and their two children. Out back, the bunkhouse's first floor had become a rip-snorting bar, presided over by Will, age twenty-six. Like his father, Ollie, Will had also left Anchor by then and taken work at the National Tube Works in Birmingham, where he would later become a shop foreman. Will was much more like his father in outlook and attitude. He was a working stiff's working stiff non pareil. Work blues, beer, baseball, pickled eggs, and his gal Margaret defined his ethos. A man of far fewer words, fewer years of formal schooling, and a more localized worldview, he and H. T. could not have been more different. H. T. wrote beautifully and expressively; Will, clumsily and painfully. But, as a boy, Will had made and painted some lovely pottery—and he was straight-arrow honest. Will and H. T. were close in a family way, but far apart in their ideas and chosen social networks.

H. T. got around, but Will *did* his rounds. By the late 1890s H. T. was actively working at community affairs. He lobbied the local health board for better sewers,[26] cleaner water, and a clinic for iron and steel workers. Later, he would become president of the Carrick Health Board. At night, while Will managed the bar out back, H. T. worked on his projects, one of which was an innovative railroad-track fastener that could withstand far more torsional stresses than current ones. He was also interested in electricity, and he had taken his son, nine-year-old Benjamin, to the World's Fair in Chicago in 1893, bringing back souvenirs and anything he could obtain on the applied use of electricity.

As Ollie's two sons pushed to earn a living in Pittsburgh and make their way in the world, Ollie and Elizabeth retreated to Fairchance, taking up residence in the two-story homestead a few blocks away from the Fairchance Works.[27] Ollie was simply no good at retirement. But market troubles and the consequent iron slump of 1895, when even a roller's earnings were cut by nearly 60 percent[28] and a new industry standard workweek of sixty-nine hours was announced, convinced Ollie to leave Pittsburgh. In 1896 he rented his property to his sons.

Ollie's retirement involved a partnership in the Fairchance brickyard that he managed. At age fifty-six Ollie still left the house for the brickyard around 6:40 each morning. He worked short days of seven hours, shoveling, filling molds, and tending the brick oven. He employed several yard boys and one experienced "hand." Most would have been extended family members.[29] He also managed the Fairchance Town Waterworks, owned by Henry C. Frick. That consumed more of his time daily. His two-job "retirement" consumed about fifty to fifty-five hours weekly. Yet he also found time to relax, wandering the hills around Fairchance with the prized model 1885 Winchester single-shot .22 rifle he owned.[30] He and his male relatives shot quite a number of squirrels in the wooded chestnut groves above the valley before widespread blight thinned out the trees. Surviving in a cedar chest of Sophia Vandergrift Densmore, one of his daughters-in-law, is an unfinished skin coat exquisitely sewn of large, gray squirrel pelts. Not a single hide is marred by a repaired body hole from a .22 caliber bullet.

I envision Ollie at the homestead in Fairchance on a bright October afternoon in 1898. He is relaxing over coffee at the kitchen table[31] with one of the twenty-something Goldsboro boys, Robert, perhaps, and one or another of the Carrs, Prices, or Warmans. Elizabeth puts the finishing touches on a platter of fried squirrel. The smell of cornbread radiates from her coal cook stove. Ollie leans forward, nodding, "Boys, have I ever told you about the time Sam and me went squirrel hunting with our father Robert and our brother Nat down at Cheat Neck in '49? Was squirrel heaven in the rocks above the Cheat. Pop used a flintlock, and Nat had a good percussion musket bought from Rossel's store up in Connellsville. Nat paid thirteen dollars for that rifle in '47, the year he made big money hauling Mexican war troops for Oliphant. We all went down in Oliphant's wagon with a load of his best nails for the store at Bruceton's Mill and stopped to hunt on the way back. Nat's rifle was a dandy . . . tiger maple stock, .36 caliber . . . and damn, did it shoot."[32]

I imagine Elizabeth reacting at the stove. "Oliver, no cussin' in my kitchen!" Chuckles likely followed.

"So, how did Old Robert manage to hit them with that flintlock? Thought he was blind."

"No, only half blind, and he loaded it with bird shot. When that didn't work, he just cussed 'em out so's Nat could shoot 'em." As the laughter dies down, a tray of the buttermilk-fried squirrel comes to the table.

On March 13, 1898, Ollie sold part of their Fairchance homestead to his son Will. The Fayette County *Deed Book* recorded it as, "William Densmore of Pittsburgh for $1,200 all that certain lot of land in Fairchance Borough containing 1 3/4 acre along a public road known as Marie Street. It being the same lot conveyed to Hugh O. Densmore by Jonathan Jordan and wife by deed of November 23, 1867."[33]

Ollie may have hoped that one day his son Will and his family would join him in Fairchance. The land was sold to Will below its market value, another insurance policy for his son and grandchildren as Fairchance had blossomed in size and output of iron, brick, coke, coal, and blasting powder. But Will never did leave Pittsburgh, as he died there in 1928 at age fifty-nine.

In 1900 Ollie went back to Pittsburgh for a while and stayed with Will above the saloon. The front house at 2101 Sidney had been rented to German brew master William Würster and his family. Will was engaged to Margaret Elizabeth Nelson, born 1872. Her father had been a crew member listed in Ollie's log. On August 16, 1898, page five of the *Pittsburgh Post-Gazette* listed the marriage license issued to "William E. Densmore and Margaret E. Nelson" as executed on August 15. Will married Margaret soon after; as of 1900, when Ollie stayed with them, no child was recorded in the US Census taken of their upstairs residence at "51S, 21st Street."[34]

Though retired to Fairchance, Ollie continued to list his occupation as "Roller,"[35] and he listed Will as a "Roll-turner." In that census, H. T. lived with his wife, Sophia; Benjamin; and his daughter Elsie in a rented house in Knoxville, just south of Birmingham.[36] H. T. and Will had sold 2101 Sidney and were already building a house in a new subdivision on the Brownsville Road south of Birmingham. Their lot lay in a hilly area that had been farm, wood lots, and dairy lands since the early 1800s. H. T. and his family attended the recently built Presbyterian Church in Knoxville, about a mile north of the house they had commissioned.

Listed in Birmingham on the US Census of 1900, it seemed plausible that Ollie had returned to work at Anchor. But a letter Will later penciled to Ollie in Fairchance comments on his father's "fretting while cooped up" in the residence above the saloon. He also cautions Ollie not to push himself too hard at the brickyard.

At age sixty Ollie was still pumping out those excess work calories, about three hundred per hour to be exact, for seven-hour days on his "retirement" schedule of five-day weeks. Ollie's other job at the town water plant owned by Frick mostly involved maintenance and equipment repairs. Why would he work for Frick, you ask? Simply because by the 1890s Frick and his associates owned virtually all the infrastructure in southwestern Pennsylvania.

Ollie's anvils and forging tools, later inherited by his grandson Benjamin, tell us that, like many men born in the 1840s, he also had blacksmithing and machinist skills—rollers set up and gauged huge complicated presses day after day. They looked for worn parts and filed off burrs or big dings as groaning machines beat themselves up during long, vibrating production runs. A few water pumps and valves, pipe fittings, a gas-fed boiler to drive the pump shafts in the water works? Nothing to it. Like his brother Sam, Ollie could service, repair, or fabricate small parts for most common machinery.

An Era of Miseries, 1880 to 1900

Not long after the 1890 census was taken, Sam Densmore's wife Jennie was coughing again. She was suffering from "consumption," or tuberculosis. As her infant child was baptized at St. Paul's Episcopal Church in Kittanning, the baptismal record notes, "Mother at home, dying." She died on February 26, 1890, at age forty-three and was buried in the new Kittanning Cemetery on February 28.[37] Sam's world had collapsed.

He soon left Kittanning for Pittsburgh to work at Anchor with Ollie. Thurston's Pittsburgh Directory of 1890–1891 lists him as "Densmore, Samuel, Roller, 2114 Carey Alley." That address was at the rear of Grim's[38] old boardinghouse, just a half block from Ollie at 2101 Sidney Street. Sam's family remained in Kittanning, and his two eldest sons took over family affairs. Sam, like Ollie, sought solace and privacy amid the din and steam at Anchor. Then, on June 22, 1891, Sam bought a lot southeast of Pittsburgh in rural East Liberty Township for $150 in cash. That deed lists Sam as "of Vanderbilt, Fayette County."

The new Vanderbilt address suggests that Sam left Anchor before June, returning to the village and furnaces at the Falls of the Youghiogheny where, seventy years before, his father Old Robert had worked for Fidelio Hughes Oliphant, then a young ironmaster. Sam may have hoped to move his surviving family and start fresh, but that never happened. Restless and grieving, he again moved around: Pittsburgh, Mckeesport, Vanderbilt, Uniontown, Youngstown, Jamestown, and Celoron, New York—and iron works in between. Roller, heater, rougher, mechanic, and engineer are all possible jobs he could take on. With the exception of several baptisms of grandchildren, records at St. Paul's Episcopal Church in Kittanning started to run thin on Sam Densmore's presence. In 1892 about 110 acres of farmland Jennie had inherited on the Allegheny was divided into equal parcels among her children. Sam did not keep his share.[39]

Meanwhile, tuberculosis was not the only disease to devastate the Glenns and Densmores in Kittanning. Waves of epidemics again raged along the Allegheny in the 1880s as increased river and rail traffic enhanced disease vectors emanating from Pittsburgh and the rough-and-tumble upriver oil fields. Diphtheria struck the Kittanning area in March 1882. St. Paul's records document its cyclic return in 1883, 1884, and 1885. Cholera followed the diphtheria. On March 29, 1884, Robert Allen Glenn, age one, died of diphtheria. On Tuesday, April 17, 1884, James Howard Glenn of Slabtown, age six months, also died of it. In September of 1885, David Ritner Glenn, age eleven, and John Oswald Glenn, age four, both died of diphtheria. On September 17, 1885, James Glenn, age twenty-one, of East Franklin, "died of blood poisoning from Diphtheria," and was buried in the "old graveyard."[40] On December 16, 1886, James Glenn,[41] the local family patriarch, age eighty-six—and first cousin to Old Robert's wife Hannah—died of "old age" and was buried in the old cemetery. On June 21, 1888, Sarah Glenn of Manor Township, age twenty-nine, died of "consumption," and her baby, Richard Glenn, eight months, died of "inherited consumption" on August 2.

Sorrow upon sorrow piled up in the once relatively healthy outlying communities as the effects of "progress" in transportation and industrial expansion eroded public health and well-being. Communicable diseases were no longer just a city problem. And as health declined, regional social and work tensions rose. Meanwhile, Sam Densmore was everywhere and nowhere, "attending to business affairs." Who could blame him? The staggering losses in his family, both Glenns and Densmores, had been unrelenting throughout the late 1870s and 1880s.

The 1890s were also miserable for less-skilled workers throughout the East and industrial Midwest. Manufacturing-industry accident rates rose, and the use of toxic and corrosive chemicals like sulfur, mercury, and cyanide skyrocketed. A large, furtive industry of strike breaking services had formed: gangs of heavily armed "special police" materialized out of the night, sometimes in armored rail cars fitted with heavy-caliber machine guns. All of this would follow in a day or two with rail cars jammed full of strike breakers, often blacks or non-English-speaking immigrants desperate for $1.20 to $1.60 a day in wages. The respected and decently paid skilled workers of the 1850s and 1860s were to industrial titans as the buffalo, and those once impressively tall, healthy Native Americans who had subsisted on them[42] were to the western plains, merely just scorned species in the way of industrial "progress."

In the eyes of the era's corporate titans, skilled men whose wages were high and whose traditions favored quality and pride of manufacture occupied a costly energetic niche. That niche was an impediment to untrammeled speed of output and the last percent or two of profit. Unlike iron, steel profits depended on massive open-hearth furnaces and rapid, semi-automated heats—many more a day than in small shops. The veteran heaters and rollers were careful and deliberate. That drove the steel bosses crazy, so even more skilled roles were automated. As this is written, another generation of male and female American industrial workers is centered in the crosshairs of corporations that favor robotic automation or overseas production in places where both wages and human rights are trifling. The pursuit of raw, nineteenth-century Robber Baron labor practices overseas is easily hidden from the country's consumers.

The nineteenth-century American battle was for control of industrial process itself. This struggle can be viewed simply as who *owned* skills and knowledge. Was it the fellows with forty year's experience, like Ollie Densmore and Henry Rudolph, whose many small innovations made them and their crews the most profitable princes of a local rolling line? Or was it the corporation that owned both work output *and* the intellectual output of its most skilled? According to the corporations, those fellows simply could not learn their trade without the infrastructure that the owners and shareholders had so generously "provided" them.

It was no contest. As a result of these tensions, American industry continued to automate and dumb down manufacturing by design. A "skilled" machine owned no property rights, could join no guild or union, and never went on strike. But who conceived of these machines? Who built prototypes, serviced them, and reengineered them to higher efficiencies over time? And just who owned the intellectual output of those mysterious few innovators? This would matter to at least three branches of America's Densmores and span four generations.

Brainwork

Brothers James and Amos Densmore were just two of the Densmore men who contributed to the body of American patents between 1860 and 1940. Before patenting typewriters, they greatly modified and perfected the concept of bulk boats around 1860.[43] Recall that their first commercial use was on the Allegheny River in shipping J. J. Vandergrift's oil from the oil industry's founding oil field[44] to Pittsburgh. They created, in succession, the world's first three versions of railroad tank cars, which entered commercial service shipping oil to New York City in 1866. When you are stuck at an interminable suburban railroad crossing as a two-engine freight train groans past, count those tank cars and think, "the Densmore brothers."

James Densmore, educated at Allegheny College in Meadville, Pennsylvania, was also the co-inventor, with Christopher Sholes, of the prototype Sholes and Glidden typewriter.[45] The two had a falling out in 1869 or 1870, and James walked. He later returned and bought out the other designer. His typewriter did reach the market in 1874, but the Sholes and Glidden model's carriage[46] simply did not hold up to intense use. Still, the often-brittle James was not satisfied, and more changes were made, mostly by Sholes. The third version of this typewriter, patented in 1871, was the one that was assigned to gun makers E. Remington and Sons. We know it as the original "Remington" typewriter.

Later, together with his older brother Moses Densmore in Pittsburgh and other partners, James opened a branch of his own Densmore Typewriter Company, which brought an even better typewriter to market in 1893. They never achieved the huge market reach that Remington's famous brand name attracted, but the Densmore typewriter had the most efficient keyboard and the most durable carriage arrangement. In fact, its keyboard was *the* keyboard eventually adopted throughout the western world. When you look down at your computer keyboard and notice the QWERTY arrangement, think "Densmore/Scholes typewriter."

At about the same time that the third-version typewriter was patented, Byron Densmore, a descendant of the 1715 New Hampshire family, then residing in New York City, was issued patent #108,333 for his Sectional Steam Boiler on October 18, 1870. This boiler was more compact than earlier ones; its interior sections/baffles were much more energetically efficient in heating water, and interior pressures were far better controlled. "Smaller, more efficient, and safer" would become his formula for success. The extra bonus was that the rapid movement of water through its compact tube sections also largely prevented the scaling that plagued all kinds of boilers in that era, especially those on steamboats.

In 1875 Byron Densmore conjured up an even more efficient "Sectional Steam Generator," US Patent #117,223, granted December 15, 1875. On March 31, 1876, he filed letters of patent again for a much more fuel-efficient natural-gas burner to power his furnaces and steam generators, US Patent #117,121. In an expanding world of industry and multistory heating needs, these improvements got much more heat and steam generated than the same amount of fuel had once produced. It was rather like putting a two-horse wagon on Braddock's deteriorated road in 1800, which had allowed the same amount of farmland to produce enough food and fodder to dramatically increase the speed and load capacity of travel transport. Byron Densmore's sons in Brooklyn went on to patent many other devices, leaving us an important but little-noted family empire of practical inventions.

Other Densmores logged patents in the late 1800s as well. Edwin Densmore of Ohio, later Michigan, patented a number of industrial machines under US patent numbers 347,329, 347,331, 446,585, 472,014, and 485,372. Samuel Densmore of Richmond, Missouri, patented a flat-iron heater, #189,198. Lyman Densmore of St. Joseph, Missouri, patented a truss bridge, #188,107. Robert Dinsmore of Weston, West Virginia, a second or third cousin to the Fayette County Densmores, filed patents for magazine rifles and industrial pipe couplings in the 1890s. These include US patent numbers 444,666, 462,894A, 492,864, 517,448, and 560,348.[47]

We have no records of Sam Densmore's innovations at the Connellsville Coke Works in the 1880s, but we do know that after his wife's death, while living in Vanderbilt, Pennsylvania, near the Little Falls forge in the 1890s, Sam filed patents both in Canada (#57,254) and in the US (#576,558) for an innovative window-sash fastener that eliminated sash weights and pulleys. He paid an assistant, James Dolan, with a share in the rights. The majority rights were then assigned to John P. Kane, a well-known regional builder. Sam and Dolan also patented an innovative, easily cleaned spittoon (US #576,589) for taprooms and men's bathrooms. Prosaic, but practical in its era. These patents generated income.

In contrast, Ollie's inventions at the Frick Water Works in Fairchance are unknown, as are the mechanical details of how he and his crew maintained their high output of rolled tonnage at Anchor. We do, however, have a record for Ollie's son, the cerebral H. T. About the time Ollie was cooped up with Will in 1900, and H. T.'s new house was under commission, H. T. was working through his love of iron and steel. The result was the innovative railroad-track joint mentioned above. It was stronger, used fewer parts, and required much less time or skill to install than those in use at the time. He filed his patent application on March 19, 1901, in the same month he moved his family into their new brick house at 1035 Brownsville Road, Carrick Borough. US Patent #693,788 was issued to him on February 18, 1902.[48]

This patent did not likely earn H. T. much money, as no assignment to a major manufacturer has been identified. But it gave him a ton of cultural and social capital. H. T. quickly became a major figure in the Knoxville Presbyterian Church, responsible for fundraising, according to his surviving account books. He was also promoted to president of the Carrick Board of Health.

It is also remarkable that the Densmore/Sholes typewriter patent of 1870, numbered 108,333, had exploded to another Densmore patent number—693,788—by 1901. America had logged nearly a sevenfold increase in inventions in just thirty years! This represented an explosion in American innovation. More important to a culture of innovation was that ordinary individuals like H. T. could still patent *in their own name*. Over time that, too, would become harder to accomplish as corporate America sought ever-greater strangleholds on the products of inventive minds.

Part 3

The 1900s

In the early 1900s rural and urban populations in America lived in increasingly different economic and environmental worlds. Those differences enhanced diverging value systems. Ruthless labor markets and massive immigration separated families, both geographically and in wealth. Large corporations, north and south, adopted legal strategies that flew in the face of main-street definitions of "fair." As height, infant mortality, and longevity data indicate, 1900 did not begin as a bright, new century. Life expectancy at birth for all America-born children was 47.8 years—more than 8 years shorter than when the Constitution was adopted.

The twentieth century began in mild recession, followed by the Panic of 1907, which reduced industrial and business activity about 30 percent and led to the creation of the Federal Reserve Bank as an economic safety valve. Next came the Panic of 1910–1911, followed by a deep recession from 1913 to 1914. World War I followed, improving work opportunities for those who stayed behind. When the Great War ended in 1918, recession struck again, just as it had after the War of 1812, the Mexican War, the Civil War, and the Spanish-American War. Then came the short, deep depression of 1920 to 1921, followed by a crazy run-up in national markets during the late 1920s. Then came the Great Depression of 1929 to 1933, followed by hard times up until 1938, when Adolph Hitler began to reshape Europe's map. Most of us would not have preferred to be born to working families in the first three decades of the 1900s. However, nutrition, pasteurized milk, more effective pregnancy care, and vaccines did enhance American-born children's life expectancy, which rose to 54.1 years by 1920. Children's heights also rose, but males did not exceed Old Robert's height of 5'7" until 1910, and they did not surpass the Founders' 5'8.2" average until the mid-1920s.

During this era, the richest Vandergrifts lived well, while working-class ones struggled. The Harts continued to scatter, and they became hard to track, as more families changed the German "Hardt" to Hart, as did Dutch immigrants. The Harts of Randolph County, West Virginia, stuck together, and more Densmores struggled even as several branches, mainly inventors, made it to middle-class status.

Chapter 18
Middle-Class Dreams

The year 1900 did not merely mark the passage of another century—it signaled a world where farmers were becoming a minority, steel track starkly divided towns by race, religion, and wealth, and rapid technological advances transformed daily life. The fascination with electricity brought it into fashionable homes. Pull-chain, wall-mounted toilet tanks a la Englishmen Harrington and Crapper began to morph into Americanized toilets as we now think of them. Electricity and indoor plumbing began to define the middle class. Home ice chests became larger and more numerous as electricity made commercial ice production possible year round. And early automobiles began to appear as stimulating eccentricities among scattered elites.

Horses and mules still provided a huge percentage of the nation's rural farm power and short-haul motive power in cities. But coal, natural gas, and petroleum dominated industry and urban life. Electricity was still primarily an urban feature, replacing gaslights. Evolution in the nation's mix of energy sources was contested as change again upended jobs and entire industries. These changes were most potent in city and large-town life. The countryside, however, where an energy-scape of horses, mules, water, and windmills still dominated, became ever more detached from the urban pace of change. Many families began to diverge into more separate rural and urban branches.

That divergence was at once energetic, economic, cultural, and ecological. Raised in relatively open spaces and dependent on sustainable farms, the *natural* world, driven by weather and season, generated and reinforced a very different worldview[1] than did the industrial cities and large regional towns. Urban life, in contrast, was driven by *human*-created cycles of production, markets, transportation, and the magic of commodities that appeared by train from faraway sources. Urban life was also driven by crowding, diversity, and nuanced rank in wealth. This led to increasingly different value systems. Urban America quite simply believed more in the power of human action than did rural America, which favored divine agency as the great driving force. Rural areas became increasingly suspicious of change, and urban ones increasingly addicted to it.

As holiday conversations at family tables highlighted these differences, many families struggled to adapt to the widening gap. That gap is still a singular factor in American society and politics. These two worlds need one another, but harnessing both into one cohesive, functional mega-community takes constant work, for they are evolutionarily as different as wild wolves and family lap dogs. Same genus; but different species. These differences in belief systems based on perceptions of daily reality as actually lived in quite different settings are still with us. We play them out daily, as rural Americans are quite overrepresented by US Senators when compared to the more urban states that produce the lion's share of America's tax dollars. That reality, and its tensions, is abundantly clear in every presidential election, just as it was in the election of 1900.

For a time, Old Robert's descendants bucked this trend toward widening cultural divides more than most. True, the Densmore men and their sons, with the exception of Nat, had all divided their worlds between higher urban wages and rural subsistence. But even Ollie's sons, raised in East Birmingham's crush, stuck together. When H. T. moved to his new brick house on the Brownsville Road, his brother Will followed suit. By 1908 Will had become a foreman and product inspector at the Tube Works. The house, bunkhouse, and saloon complex on Sidney Street had been sold, and Will's bartending days were over. Will was living at No. 35 Calhoun Street in Carrick with his wife, Margaret, and his family. His house backed onto a lane, later paved, which passed behind H. T.'s house on the Brownsville Road. They both kept gardens.

But the era of 1900 to 1940 unleashed powerful divisive forces among Old Robert's descendants. Robert Jr. had died in Fairchance on July 31, 1903, and was buried in White Rock Cemetery. There would be no more Christmases accompanied by real candles on the tree, nor his big Civil War Colt revolver's annual celebratory thump-boom of acrid black powder. Times and burial customs had changed. His sons in Uniontown did not wash his body, nor did they make his coffin. Rather, the funeral was arranged by his daughter, and Robert Jr.'s body was prepared for burial by the William's Funeral Home in Fairchance.[2] The intimacy of death itself had diminished. We can suppose that his living children threw dirt onto his coffin, but we cannot be certain. As his great-grandson H. Thomas Densmore of Chadds Ford notes, only the record at the funeral home still exists. America had begun to distance itself from death. A funeral had become more of a commercial service and less an act of personal devotion. Death was becoming a business rather than a family sacrament.

With Robert Jr. gone, so was his narrative of Oliphant's in the early 1840s, his firsthand tales of the Civil War, and the stories he could tell on his brothers Ollie and Sam, who were born when he was already in his teens and working. After his passing, his children would have a tough time both spiritually and economically. The consequences of diminished demand and respect for skills, surges of new immigrants competing in the workplace, and declining wages would extract easily measurable physiological tolls on them.

In contrast, by 1905 H. T. and Will were living middle-class lives on Carrick's Brownsville Road. Their childhood memories of tiny alley apartments and Birmingham's tough 1880s had begun to fade. H. T.'s daughter Elsie was already in her late teens, and she attended the private Pittsburgh Academy across the Monongahela, where she graduated in 1905. Her education level was equivalent to attending a modern public high school plus a year or two at a good college.[3] Elsie was well-read, well-dressed, and generally associated with a decently well-off group of peers. She threw costume parties and loved history and art. Her older brother Ben, in contrast, was expected to work. By the time of Elsie's preparatory school graduation, he was already working at Mesta Machine Works, south of Carrick, as an engineering draftsman. He had finished high school before he went to work. Both were clearly immersed in the growing urban middle class.

Meanwhile, the family that moved in several blocks south of them at 1141 Brownsville Road would directly connect Elsie and her brother Benjamin to their mother's past. Sophia's stepfather, Samuel Wheaton, master riverboat repairman, and his wife, Sarah Ann,[4] had returned to Pittsburgh when Samuel retired from the Kanawha Docking Co. and its repair shop[5] in Point Pleasant, West Virginia.[6] He turned seventy in 1906 and, worn down, had given in to Sarah Ann's pleas to retire and move back to her native Pittsburgh, where they had met and married. Samuel and Sarah Ann had raised four children: oldest son John F., Joseph, Samuel, and daughter Grace (also spelled *Grayce*). The oldest two were born in Pittsburgh, and the two younger ones were born on Water St. in Wheeling. Sophia was ecstatic at their arrival. For her, having her mother nearby was a blessing. H. T. was, as his daughter Elsie later stated, "Good about it."[7] Elsie was fascinated with her grandmother and the Wheatons. The Wheaton rivermen, not city slickers, struck her as romantic figures. For her, they represented a fabled era in American history.

Samuel and his three sons knew as much about riverboats as anyone. Samuel's occupation at the time of the US Census of 1900 was listed as "River Dock Foreman," and Joseph and John were only too happy to tell all their stories. John liked to be addressed as "Captain," though he had never been one in fact—only a pilot and a hull caulker. Joseph was a bit more solemn, but he made up for it in tales of adventure. He loved to talk of faraway places like Cincinnati, Vincennes, Louisville, and St. Louis. At one time or another, he had been sent to all those places by his father to patch up hulls on riverboats, and he was only too delighted to go—the farther the better.

But the idyllic period of this reunion did not long endure. On August 6, 1908, Samuel, at age seventy-two, died of a stroke.[8] Sarah Ann died just nine months later on May 5, 1909.[9] They were buried in the South Side Cemetery on the Brownsville Road near their final residence.[10] Daughter/stepdaughter Sophia assisted with the funeral arrangements. Samuel's skills would still be respected and memorialized nearly a century later by legendary riverman Charles P. Stone, who stated in a Charleston, West Virginia, newspaper retrospective, "One of the best of Point Pleasant's [paddle] wheelwrights was a man named Wheaton, whose home was right at the top of the Kanawha Docking Company."[11]

A downturn in economics also played a role in the pall that settled in. The years from 1907 to 1909 were economic roadblocks for millions of ordinary folks. As Europe destabilized, immigration rates remained high, depressing American wages. And once again the consequences of foolish banking and investment practices took a toll. In October 1907 the New York Stock Exchange lost 50 percent of its value in several weeks when Knickerbocker Trust Company's attempts to illegally corner the market on United Copper Company stock backfired.[12]

Known variously as the Knickerbocker Affair or the Panic of 1907, the situation stabilized only when John D. Rockefeller infused his own cash into failing New York banks. Undaunted by the experience of this national economic near-death episode, another Wall Street brokerage house pulled a similar stunt just several months later as it attempted to seize control of the Tennessee Railroad and Coal Company combine.[13] The stock market tanked again, threatening a complete American economic collapse.

President Teddy Roosevelt stepped in, ordered hearings, and empaneled a group to find a solution to the unstable banking sector. A year later the Federal Reserve Bank was created to protect the national banking system from recurring bank failures due to ruinous investment shenanigans. But deep systemic damage had already been done to the general economy. Small-business operators were unable to get loans and were forced to scale back. Consequently, America's ordinary workforce took a hit in both available jobs and wage levels. This economic climate severely limited possibilities for millions of ordinary families.

Sam and Sarah Wheaton's survivors struggled. Most of the Densmores in Fairchance, Uniontown, and Kittanning also struggled. And a second generation of more ordinary, working-class descendants among the Pittsburgh and Allegheny City Vandergrifts also struggled, even as J. J.'s younger children and grandchildren scattered to places like Manhattan, Boston, or Paris.

Flashy J. J. had died on December 26, 1899. That day, feeling unwell, he went home at noon from his office in Pittsburgh's Conestoga building,[14] and he was found dead that evening, presumably from a coronary, at his home near 5th Street and Shady Avenue. His funeral service was held in that house at noon on December 29, 1899. It was attended by an impressive crowd of Pittsburgh, Philadelphia, and New York notables. An equally impressive entourage followed the elaborate, horse-drawn hearse to Allegheny Cemetery.[15] Oddly, among the many pallbearers, both actual and honorary, not a single male Vandergrift has been publicly identified.

J. J. had left a large fortune, which before his death had sheltered about one third of the Ohio Valley Vandergrift descendants from ever having to do ordinary work. Even more impressive, however, was the magnitude of the fortune disbursed at his death. The lengthy will was parsed in detail on the pages of the *Pittsburgh Press*.[16] Amounts twenty-five thousand dollars to one hundred thousand dollars were bequeathed to several of the children of his brothers Lewis, James M., and Benjamin B. These were the kin who had most often invested with him in the riverboat and oil trades. Several cousins received smaller bequests. His niece Sophia was not a legatee. Still, she was not forgotten entirely. From the peony-growing wife of J. J.'s oil-broker son William, who lived in Jamestown, New York, came two small Victorian-aged boxes of gold jewelry that had once belonged to J. J.'s deceased wife, for whom Sophia had been named. The female peony-growing network lived on.

J. J. left most of his assets to be divided among his own children. Each of their shares was more than a million dollars, a staggering sum for 1900. In spite of their good fortune, they wrangled. The will was not fully settled for more than sixty years, as final arguments were made before the Pennsylvania Supreme Court on October 5, 1961. The court's decisions were entered on January 2, 1962, two full generations—and countless well-compensated lawyers—after J. J.'s death.

The Vandergrift combine that had build riverboats costing $75,000 to $150,000 each in the 1840s through the 1870s had effectively ended in the late 1870s when J. J. and his branch of the family moved to Oil City. Still, the higher-ranking Vandergrifts made it to the Allegheny Cemetery right up until J. J.'s death. The waiters, clerks, laborers, and salesmen did not. By 1907 the Vandergrift waiters, laborers, and clerks were still in Pittsburgh, but a number of J. J.'s legatees had decamped to "smarter" places, as the parlance of the day described midtown Manhattan and an emerging Greenwich Village.

The US Census of 1910

By 1910 there are census data, letters, postcards, family ledgers, and more public records available to follow the Densmores and Vandergrifts. The documents signal more family fragmentation as entire branches slip away to new, faraway American places. Among the Densmores of western Pennsylvania, the economic slippage of the early 1900s was especially stark. The conditions in the 1860s through the 1890s that allowed iron rollers Ollie and Sam to act as a backstop in family emergencies was hard to repeat. Instead we see a dramatically widening gap in well-being emerge among the different branches of the Densmores descended from Old Robert. Both an unstable economy and increasingly scattered family units played a role. In the case of the Vandergrifts, great wealth had first divided the descendants of Jacob Vandergrift and Mary Hart. In contrast, it was deepening poverty between 1875 and 1915 that had begun to separate the less fortunate Densmores from the more fortunate.

The US Census of 1910 also tells us that the surviving Wheaton family just a few blocks from both the graveyard and the Densmore brothers H. T. and Will were caught in a serious economic squeeze. Their household at 1141 Brownsville Road was headed by Samuel and Sarah Wheaton's eldest son, forty-three-year-old John.[17] Listed as single, occupation, "riverboat caulker," he was unemployed during the first twenty-six weeks before census day in July 1910. Next listed is his younger brother Samuel Jr., age thirty-four, same occupation, and he was also out of work for twenty-six weeks. Sam's wife, Margaret, twenty-nine, born in England, does not work. John's brother Joseph, age thirty-six, riverboat caulker, was also out of work for twenty-six weeks.

Next listed are his sister Grace (Wheaton) Stone, twenty-seven, her one-month-old baby, Grace Virginia, and her husband, Fred Stone. Fred, a bookkeeper at a construction company, had been unemployed *all* of 1909, and he began studying to become an attorney.[18] A descendant of the 1820s to 1840s Ohio riverboat Captain Charles Stone, he was an unemployed scion of one of the region's most famous pioneering riverboat families. By Fred's generation, the grandeur of the steamboat era had waned. Trains had ended the wagoner's glory days in the 1850s. By 1910 trains and bridges had done the same to the Stones and other family dynasties of Ohio River steamboat captains. Efficiency of land transport had begun to leave the last robust generation of rivermen behind. Last on the census list is Jay (James) Stone, age two, son of Fred and Grace.

In their household of eight, six wage earners had been out of work for more than half of the year before. Both John and Samuel Jr. would later die essentially broke. John died alone on November 12, 1938, and is described in his Pennsylvania death certificate as "abt age 70." Cause of death, an "abscess." He was not interred until December 26, 1938, suggesting the high cost of funeral or scattered family as factors. Samuel Wheaton Jr., retired steel worker, just like several of his iron-worker Densmore cousins by marriage in Kittanning, died of cancer of the stomach on Thanksgiving Day, November 25, 1947. He was also buried in South Side Cemetery near his brother John. His final address had been a house at 228 Brownsville Road.

By 1910 the first generation of Old Robert's children had thinned down. Ash-gray and plagued by rheumatism, the once "dark-haired, steady" Elizabeth Densmore Warman, at age seventy-six, had already died in Fairchance in 1902, followed in 1903 by her brother Robert Jr., age seventy-five. Ollie, Samuel, and Elizabeth's elder sons saw to her funeral. Her body, according to her granddaughter Elsie, was attended in a traditional sitting up, then committed to Sharp's funeral parlor in Fairchance. Family rift or not, she was buried with Nehemiah in Maple Grove Cemetery. Robert Jr.'s wife, Elizabeth Carr Densmore, died in 1901, two years before Robert Jr. Old Robert's daughter Jane Densmore Pastorius was long dead, as was Rachel, about whom little is known from available documents.

The widowed Sam Densmore continued to move about, restless and likely depressed. By about 1911 he was living in the Youngstown, Ohio, suburb of Girard with his son William W. and William's wife, Harriet. William W. was in steel work at the time, and he and his family rented their house. Sam's health had already deteriorated by the time the Densmore genealogical narrative prepared by his sister-in-law Sophia and grandniece Elsie[19] appeared in print, listing him as "retired from business affairs."[20] Those business affairs may have involved several of the US and Canadian patents he and James Dolan had filed in the late 1890s.

On March 20, 1915, Sam died of a stroke at the age of seventy-six after lingering for a week. His attending physician in Ohio was W. D. Cunningham, whose descendant Mary Haun asserts that he was a fine doctor and that Sam was well attended at the end.[21] Sam's Ohio death certificate indicates his age as seventy-six years, nine months. His occupation is listed as "retired." The certificate's informant was his son William W., who mistakenly filled in *his* parents' names rather than his father's parents, creating no end of confusion in online records about Sam's origins.

The Ohio death certificate indicates that Sam's body was removed for burial in the Kittanning Cemetery.[22] Sam's newspaper obituary[23] further confirms his identity as the husband of Amanda Jennie Glenn. That photocopied obituary, provided by Sam's great-grandson Paul Densmore (of California), maintains the standard of enigma, if not irony, that suffuses this narrative. To whit: "Samuel Densmore, a Civil War Veteran . . . was captured by Mosby's Cavalry . . . and his reminisces of Mosby's raids have been much quoted."

Had Sam deserted, or had he merely "straggled" and been embarrassingly captured in the summer of 1864? If so, a later desertion hearing might have led to him being discharged without pension rights. In essence, "no money, no foul, and no endless paperwork."

William W. and his family moved soon after Sam's death to Asheville, Chautauqua County, New York, north of Jamestown. There William bought and managed a fine dairy farm. Living a far healthier life as a farmer than several of his brothers who continued in industrial employ, he died in 1964, age eighty-three, and left a number of descendants in western New York and in California. Sam's other seven children, most still in the Kittanning area, left many early 1900s descendants in western Pennsylvania. Sam and Jennie's eldest son, Robert, made it to Alaska during the 1899 rush for gold. He stayed in touch, sending a photo of himself at his cabin in Fairbanks.[24] The Densmore diaspora had expanded.

The Coal Patch, Uniontown

Meanwhile, several of Robert Jr.'s children in Fairchance had already moved to Uniontown, about ten miles away. Son John Robert Densmore, born February 18, 1850, in Fairchance, had married Virginia O'Sullivan.[25] At age nineteen in 1870, he had already attained the rare status of a roller at Oliphant's, a role he would soon lose after Frick's agents took over. He never fully recovered from the disappointment. By the early 1900s they were living in the Beeson Work's "coal patch" miner's village of company housing on the outskirts of Uniontown. It was not an upscale way of life. Hours were long, wages were very skimpy, and the work was very dangerous. The first decade of the 1900s was an era in America in which life expectancy fluctuated between forty-five and forty-seven years—better than in 1860 or the child-risky decades of the late nineteenth century,[26] but still much shorter than the fifty-six years in the 1790s era of the Founders. John Robert consoled himself by home brewing beer in their basement and inviting his mine buddies in on Saturday nights.[27] These soirees occasionally approached the revelry at Tomlinson's Wagon Stand where his grandfather, Old Robert, had splurged after crossing the Alleghenies in 1800.

His wife, Virginia, did not rejoice at this strategy. Virginia O'Sullivan was a midwife, with a largish practice in the area's coal patches. She delivered quite a few babies in those drafty company houses, and "later she went to court for several of them to swear as to their time and place of birth."[28] When John Robert died in 1914 in his fifties,[29] Virginia and their children, including sons Robert and Charles Percival, regrouped. Charles P. Densmore, born November 3, 1885, was already married at age twenty-seven when his coal miner and beer-brewing father died. His wife, Ethel Cramer Densmore, was twenty-three, and they already had three children: Marguerite, born 1907; Helen, born 1911; and Albert M., born July 29, 1913.

The year of 1913 was not a salutary one for working-class America. The first hints of the great influenza epidemic had hit. Miners and coal patches were plagued by "Miner's Cough." We now know it as black lung disease. Tuberculosis, measles, whooping cough, typhus, diphtheria, and other diseases endemic to crowded areas where clean water, clean air, and ample health facilities were lacking took their toll. Most coal-patch housing was nothing to crow about—the cheap, uninsulated wooden houses on raised foundations leaked winter winds like a sieve. In the summer the heat factor was unbearable. Wages were paid partly, sometimes mostly, in company scrip or tokens, usable only at the company store. In the words of Cousin Tom, who descends from Charles Percival,

"[Charles] worked in coal mines with horses and pulled loaded wagons out of the mines and empties back into the mine. He was a hard worker and hard liver. ... The combination killed him [age forty-six] in 1931 when my Dad [Albert M.] was starting his senior year in High School."[30]

Charlie, as Charles Percival was known in the Uniontown area, stands in for hundreds of thousands of men working in company towns—coal, lumber, coke, or iron-ore mining—throughout Pennsylvania, northern Ohio, and West Virginia. Note that his great-grandfather Old Robert had lived to age seventy-three, his grandfather, Robert Jr., had lived to his mid-seventies, his father had lived into his fifties, but he died at age forty-six. For more than half of American-born males born and trapped in the late nineteenth-century growing underclass, these men are testaments to the late nineteenth century's downward trajectory of well-being.

Like the Densmore forgemen, iron rollers, puddlers, and roughers of the 1820s through the 1890s, their company town life was based on equally hard work, but without the soul-saving respect or the sweeter wage scales once enjoyed by the princes of America's skilled labor. Coal dust, methane gas, mine floor "bumps," slate falls, volatile charges of black powder, or the dreadful flash fires from suspended coal dust saturated with methane[31] simply did not lift up the soul like the symphony of a steel mill. Instead of light, heat, and steam in glorious concert, working in a mine was rather like being accidentally locked in the symphony hall's damp stone cellar: no light, dripping water, lung-choking air, and the uncertainty of whether you will be found. It is quite simply unearthly. All human senses are muted, stifled—not energized or uplifted.

And Charlie was definitely among those not uplifted. Too much home brew in the tradition of his father was among the factors that weighed him down. About the time his last child was born in 1921, angry and disappointed with life, Charlie bailed out on his family. It was a breach of responsibility commented on as a cautionary tale to this day among his line of Fayette County Densmore descendants. The norms of that era violated, Charlie wound up in Pittsburgh's Work House, where his pay—what little there was of it—was sent to his wife in Uniontown courtesy of the regional judicial system. Meanwhile, Ethel took in washing to feed her seven children.

Several years later Ethel caught a break and got a regular job as a cleaning lady at the Fayette County Courthouse.[32] Walking those courthouse halls on my own search for documentary records, I envision Ethel scrubbing the base of General LaFayette's statue, installed to commemorate his visit to Uniontown in the 1820s. She pays no attention as I pass, but I salute her anyway. She fed those kids. True, their nutrition might not have been optimal, but no one can fault Ethel—the wage and corporate pressures of the 1880s through the 1920s had not only eroded the wages of skilled workers but had forever eliminated a significant portion of those skilled jobs through automation. A world war had also sent many regional workingmen overseas, and the inevitable economic postwar slump had followed in the new century's late teens. That slump hit the nation's coal patches like a sledgehammer. Then Wall Street cupidity, in concert with another wave of heavy-handed, military-supported strikebreaking in the 1920s, contrived to further reduce incomes, career opportunities, and hopes for a very large segment of blue-collar American society.

The fragile circumstances in Charlie's line of the family during that era are echoed in the shorter height of his male children, found on their World War II enlistment papers. Charlie himself was between 5'4" and 5'5" tall. His son Albert M. was 5'7.5".[33] Albert's brothers Kenneth and Harold measured 5'6" and 5'5", respectively.[34] Albert's other brother Frank T. Densmore also served in World War II, but his enlistment papers do not note his height. From family photographs, Frank's height is similar to Albert's. This male generation of Old Robert's descendants born between the 1880s and 1913 was even shorter than the average American male born between 1900 and 1920 (1900 = 5'6.9"; 1910 = 5'7.8"; 1920 = 5'8.1").

A starch-rich, protein-and-vitamin-scarce childhood diet does not maximize physical development. Bread of that era was not yet enriched with B complex vitamins. Milk was not yet fortified with vitamin D. In crowded coal-patch settlements, childhood diseases, inadequate housing, and degraded environment also played a major role in deteriorating well-being. Thus we have information on a cohort of young men descended from Robert Jr. who were born in the 1820s and were about 5'4". His sons had averaged 5'6" to 5'7" in height, and his grandsons, noted above, a tad less than the same.

But the sons born in the late 1930s and 1940s of the same Densmore World War II veterans listed above averaged at least two to three inches taller! Two inches in height doesn't seem like much, but in large population samples, being two inches shorter than average correlates with a shorter life-span of ten to thirteen years.[35] Three of Charlie's sons beat those odds, probably because they were, just like their grandfather Robert Jr., blockier than average. Kenneth S. Densmore weighed 153 pounds at a height of 5'6" at his enlistment. Photographs show him as stocky. His brother, H. Thomas Densmore's father, Albert M., who lived to ninety, was quite stocky, and so were Frank and Harold. Just like height, one's body mass factor is statistically important in shaping one's life expectancy.[36]

In World War II veteran Harold's case, his stockiness likely saved him. He was in service at Hickam Air Force Base, Hawaii, on December 7, 1941. Later taken prisoner by the Japanese on Corregidor, he was enslaved and tortured for forty-one months, yet he survived to complete a full military career. Had he weighed 110 to 120 pounds when captured instead of his 153, he may not have survived. He later testified that he was fed only a handful or two of rice daily.

While still a prisoner his name was given to his nephew, H. T. Densmore (cousin Tom), when he was born in 1943. Tom grew to nearly six feet in height and had better healthcare,[37] courtesy of his hardworking parents, Albert M. and Lenora. That height differential between Harold and Tom was not due primarily to Lenora's genetics. How do we know? Albert's brother Frank T. had a son about 5'9"; his brother Kenneth (5'6") had a son about 5'8"; and Harold's (5'5") two sons were about 5'11" and 6'2".[38] Raised partly on military bases, they all clearly benefitted from consistently better nutrition and healthcare than could be afforded by work in the bleak coal patches and company towns of the early to mid-1900s. It's not merely about the number of calories; it's also about the kinds of foods eaten and access to childhood healthcare. In the Densmore's world, the cornmeal mush had begun to fade as a widespread working-family staple by the 1940s.

Marguerite Densmore Avera's Coal-Patch Testament

Charles P.'s abandoned wife, Ethel Densmore, a struggling mother and cleaning lady, was not alone in her era. Thousands upon thousands of women in western Pennsylvania, northern West Virginia, and Ohio were also washing, scrubbing floors, or taking in boarders by putting two or three children in one bed in order to rent a spare room. The poignant reality of this era's coal-patch existence comes alive in the handwritten narrative left by Ethel's daughter, Marguerite Densmore Avera. Dated Sunday, February 19, 1978,[39] it begins, "My name is Marguerite Densmore Avera and I was born in House #30, Beeson Works . . . near Uniontown, PA. My birthdate is May 9, 1907."

Her maternal ancestors included her grandfather Henry Cramer, born in Prussia/Germany, who immigrated in the 1800s. He was a "fire boss" in the Beeson Mines. Her other kin include Carrs, McKibbons, and Campbells. Both of these branches had large houses, big gardens, or small farms. She and her siblings would often walk a few miles to one house or another and stay several days. Her smallpox vaccination in 1917 was received at the Campbell family's homestead. Marguerite and her siblings' world ranged from Fairchance to Hopwood to Hollydaysburg and Uniontown, a rough circle of five to six miles in diameter.

Too often, accidental mine and railway workplace deaths intruded on Marguerite's extended family, aborting dreams and leaving both sorrow and orphaned cousins in their place. Among those intrusions was the horrific death of her cousin James McGregor.[40] In 1923 James was decapitated by machinery at the Homestead Works.[41]

The winters were the toughest time for her family. There was no water in the Beeson houses. Hand pumps were spaced every four or five houses apart. As Marguerite explains, "First one out in the winter took a tea kettle of hot water to thaw the pump out. . . . It was very cold in winter. Scrub rags froze to the wooden floor as you scrubbed. During the night, the kettle would freeze on the banked stove." She goes on to explain, "We had boardwalks, if we had *any* walks and we used to have to scrub them to outhouse and then scrub [the] outhouse. We had no toilet paper, only catalogs or newspaper."[42]

At one point her grandmother and three aunts *all* simultaneously lived nearby at Beeson's Works. Marguerite and her family lived during what many historians call the "Roaring Twenties." But it was in 1921 that Charlie caved in and walked away. At Beeson's coal camp, and thousands like it, there simply was no "roar" to the 1920s—just the silent smoke and coal ash that smothered the surfaces of their leaky clapboard houses.

Fortunately, a wider kin network provided support for Ethel and her kids. When the kids were out visiting, Ethel got a little more rest and the kids got meals with meat and farm-fresh eggs. Most everyone had outside privies, but not everyone could afford pork and eggs—standard assets among the farm-holding relatives.

Marguerite notes that her mother's solution to hunger or illness was "to eat more mush." That meant cornmeal mush. Nutritionally, cornmeal mush is a mixed blessing. If too much of it is consumed with too little meat and vegetables, it can easily lead to pellagra or pre-pellagra, a very dangerous metabolic disease due to a paucity of thiamine.[43] A diet high in cornmeal in proportion to all food intake weakens the immune system, sometimes causing telltale seasonal rashes. The "cure" for initial pellagra-like symptoms is fresh vegetables, eggs, beans, and meat—especially turkey or chicken.[44]

So the risk for Ethel's children was not a lack of calories but the balance of daily diet and her era's ignorance in the matter. That none of her kids succumbed to pellagra[45] during her washing-woman days was quite likely due to a combination of those generous but occasional country meals, day visits, and gifts of farm produce courtesy of those extended family gardens. Also helping to balance the diet was the fact that House #30 had several peach trees, a raspberry patch, and a large vegetable pit that the kids maintained. They prepared that pit by lining it with grass, and they fully stocked it each late fall—potatoes, turnips, parsnips, and carrots. Canning and pickling added to the winter larder, as Marguerite mentions: "There was also a farm cooperative at the local High School [North Union]. You Could go and can fruits and vegetables."[46]

Obviously Ethel's kids also pursued this option, harvesting both extended-family food gifts and their own modest garden plot at Beeson's. Other foods in their own garden included strawberries, rhubarb, and grapes.

Marguerite describes the Hungarians, Slavs, Germans, and Italians living nearby in the patch. She often visited such families and enjoyed "seeing their customs and traditional dress, as well as their holidays and celebrations." She also speaks well of the "colored folks" with whom she came in contact. Yes, Marguerite's Densmores were poor. But economically hard-pressed haters of immigrants and the outside world, they were definitely not.

Marguerite graduated from North Union High School in the class of 1925. The only other sibling to graduate was Albert M., who graduated in the class of 1932. Trapped in the maw of the Great Depression, Bert, as he was universally known, entered the Army at the age of nineteen on December 16, 1933. He served in the 6th Artillery until 1936.[47] Familiar with gunpowder, upon discharge he landed a job at the Liberty Powder Mill in Mt. Braddock, about seven miles from Uniontown.[48] Dynamite was made there for blasting in the surrounding coalfields.

Depression and World War II ration cards notwithstanding, Bert did not follow in his father's beer-brewing trajectory. He and his wife Lenora worked hard. In the first two and a half years of their marriage, they built a three-room house in Uniontown and paid it off. According to the US Census of 1940, Bert earned $1,400 at the powder mill in 1939 to 1940.[49] He worked forty-five weeks that year. In that era, powder manufacture was particularly dangerous. Deadly fires and explosions were common. There were several big explosions at the Liberty Mill while Bert worked there. Their son H. Thomas Densmore was born to them in their three-room house at No. 68 Wilmac Street shortly after another explosion in 1942.

A worried Lenora convinced Bert to take up another line of work. Bert did make a change, to the "best job I ever had," his son Tom recalls him saying. Bert became a motorman on the West Penn Power Company's[50] trolley line. He didn't make a big salary, and he often worked long hours. But he loved it because he got to meet people and talk to them: kids, old ladies, boys with their cane fishing rods, farm boys with boxes of vegetables, and veterans—any veteran.

A long trolley ride cost a nickel. One could make it to Pittsburgh for fifteen cents in the 1940s. One did not need a car to "go to town" for a ballgame. The simple luxury—and energy efficiency—of this kind of transportation is now long gone.

Bert's trolley cars were shut down in 1952,[51] just about the time my own paternal grandfather, John Moody Stuart of Philadelphia, was commissioned to take part in a staged municipal salvage project to recycle trolley engines and electric parts. That is when Philadelphia scrubbed its exotically managed electric transportation infrastructure as inefficient and old-fashioned. The tragedy for my grandfather was that he and his older brothers had hand-wound the copper armatures of those same motors in the early 1900s. They often found their own maker's mark on motor housings as they dismantled them for scrap.[52] Just like the packhorse captains, they had outlived their skills and technology. In contrast, the tragedy for Bert, a warm, gregarious man, was the loss of the people contact that fed his very essence. Perhaps to partially compensate, Bert's hobby became baking. He made bread for his immediate family—nut rolls, cookies, and so on. He loved to treat the clan's kids.

Both men lost aspects of their own identities in the service of declining profit margins for what was once a far more efficient form of transportation than the autos most of us rely on today. In mourning those losses they probably never realized that the emerging science of transportation efficiency was on their side. As a nation where the general efficiency levels of public infrastructure—transportation, heat, light, water—are a major factor in the nation's capacity for global or regional competitiveness, the pullback from trolleys and trains plays an inhibiting role to this day.

With the trolleys gone, Bert went back to the Dynamite Works. By the 1950s it was owned by Olin-Matthieson, the same folks who still make powder for shotgun shells. The Dynamite Works near Mt. Braddock shut down in 1961, a victim of declining demand as massive coal-digging machines replaced both blasting powder and thousands of mine workers' jobs in Pennsylvania, Ohio, and West Virginia. Bert was out of work for about two years during the period when his son Tom was a freshman in college and on his way to becoming the first of Old Robert's lineal male descendants to earn a four-year college degree.

Meanwhile Tom's mother, Lenora, who had graduated from the Uniontown Hospital School of Nursing in 1937, "went to work [full time] and kept the family fed."[53] Bert worked as a laborer, a handyman—anything he could get—but it did not turn into a regular salary until a bit later, when he managed to get full-time work as a manager at Uniontown's Ferguson Funeral Home. Bert retired from this job at the funeral home on his eighty-seventh birthday. His retirement lasted but three years. On January 20, 2004, he got up, started breakfast at his modest home on Uniontown's Carnation Avenue, went to the bathroom to brush his teeth while the coffee brewed, and fell dead on the bathroom floor. Lenora followed Bert on June 2, 2006. They are buried at Church Hill Cemetery in Uniontown. Bert's stunning work ethic says much about the values and tough economic realities of his era. So do stalwart women like Ethel and Lenora.

South Side Pittsburgh

In Pittsburgh, Old Robert's descendants were living in better circumstances. Both his sons Ollie and Sam were still alive when Bert was born in Uniontown. William Densmore, his wife, Margaret, and their children were doing well at their home in Carrick. Their lifestyle can be characterized as "solid, top-end blue collar" given Will's job as supervisor at the National Tube Works and his 1910 annual income of about $1,400, according to the US Census. That put him on the cusp of middle class.

Will's elder brother H. T. had done even better. In 1910 he made nearly $2,700 in annual wages as Chief Shipping Clerk at the huge Homestead Works southeast of Carrick. His upward trajectory was generated in no small part by the attention to detail that had begun with organizing and keeping his father's roller log in the 1880s. By 1910 he kept a log at the Homestead Works, where entire freight trains were filled with everything from huge machine forgings to armored steel plate used in Navy battleships. The engraved, rolled-steel bar his crew presented him in 1897 had officially marked H. T.'s passage from a blue-collar world on an iron-making crew, like his brother Will's, to a white-collar one. His role on the Board of Health further confirmed his move up, as had his patent of 1901–1902.

His wife, Sophia, maintained contact with her Vandergrift clan, especially with several married aunts[54] in Pittsburgh as well as J. J.'s oil-dealer son William, who had moved to Jamestown, New York, to specialize in oil shipped to New York City. Patriarch J. J. had already died, but she had his signed letter that designated the burial plots assigned her in the South Side Cemetery. J. J. was, of course, a co-founder and co-owner of that cemetery, in which several Vandergrift clerks are buried. Sophia paid for her plots, but not at prevailing market rates. Her family connections undoubtedly helped H. T. in both his social ranking and job opportunities, but it was their educational investments in their two children that would most shape their future.

As noted, by 1903 H. T.'s son Benjamin V. Densmore was already a high school graduate working as a draftsman at the huge Mesta Machine Works. Mesta Machine produced a wide variety of industrial machinery. Among its wonders were huge forging presses weighing twenty tons or more and casting equipment of a scale that produced the massive electric turbine rotors and battleship propellers made at the Homestead Works less than two miles away.

As a young draftsman of age sixteen or seventeen, Ben had likely drawn his father's 1901 track-joint plans for patent submission.[55] Mesta was successful in part because it was both forward thinking and invested in its employees' development. By late 1903, shortly after Andrew Carnegie and others founded the Carnegie Institute, now Carnegie-Mellon University, Mesta began sending some of its most promising employees to the Institute for further training in engineering, drafting, and industrial design. Ben was among them in the Night School. According to his notes, classes ran about fifteen hours a week. His specialty was drafting and applied engineering. In 1907 he graduated with the Institution's first class.

At Mesta Ben worked primarily on drafting scale plans for turbines: industrial, electrical, and ship propulsion. Armed with his engineering certificate from Carnegie Tech, he began to experiment with the configuration of turbine blades—the angles, edge grinding, hardening, and other nuances. He consulted with Sam Wheaton about paddle-wheel efficiency and with both his father and grandfather Ollie about hardening metal. By 1910 he moved to the George Westinghouse Manufacturing's Drafting Department, where he worked under master draftsman Alan Ray, one of George's early employees. There Ben drafted ship's turbines and experimented on the Westinghouse Development section's "modeling" work floor. He moved up rapidly, worked hard, and made enough money to treat himself to what became his signature dress: a nice suit, a rakish straw hat, and the rolled umbrella he carried all winter.

Still living as a bachelor[56] in H. T. and Sophia's house on the Brownsville Road, twenty-seven-year-old Ben had his own darkroom in the basement to support his passion for photography.[57] Like his father and grandfather Ollie, Ben also saved a share of his salary and kept copious records. The savings proved crucial when, on August 4, 1912, his forty-nine-year-old father suffered a massive stroke out of the blue and died a few hours later.[58] Poor Sophia was thunderstruck—first she had lost her father too soon, and now her husband, nearly three years her junior, was also gone.

Sophia, accompanied by Ben, took J. J. Vandergrift's old letter to the South Side Cemetery down the Brownsville Road and selected in which of their eight plots they would bury H. T. He was interred on August 7, 1912. Ben stepped in, handling most of the messier issues: probate, redeeding the house in his mother's name, and comforting his mom and sister, Elsie.

Elsie, twenty-five and single, had graduated near the top of her class at the Pittsburgh Academy. She could read French and some classical Spanish. After graduating she had immersed herself in attending concerts, the theater, and, above all, the opera. Among her memorabilia are hundreds of opera tickets, playbills, and art-exhibition catalogues. She was the first of Old Robert's descendants to experience a comfortable middle-class existence, relatively free of troublesome housework or financial worries.

Her grandfather Ollie, perhaps seeing in her the shadow of his beloved daughter Ellen, who died so young, had also indulged her. All she would have to do was pout, and he'd give in. Her father had often sent letters during her summers in Fairchance, scolding her for being thoughtless, but to no avail. On more than one occasion Elsie failed to be on the train for her scheduled return home, leaving Ben or Sophia frantic as they waited in vain for her at the Mount Oliver station. Meanwhile, Ollie doted on her, slipping her money for theater tickets.

The painful loss of a father combined with the sudden specter of a change in lifestyle, for which she was unprepared and which she was unwilling to accept, put Elsie in a profound shock. Instead of backing off on her social and cultural pursuits as a "modern woman," she stepped them up. But her frenzied exuberance could not overcome the reality that the family now had only one wage earner—young Benjamin.

With H. T.'s death a number of Elsie's modern expectations had been shattered. In denial, she continued to compensate through her social life, creating a whirl of glamorous, late-night parties and revelry.[59] She had begun to see a young fellow named Marion[60] who played in the horn section of the Pittsburgh Symphony

Orchestra. In 1915 she married him in a quiet ceremony at the Knoxville Presbyterian Church. Her new husband was of recent immigrant stock, and he was Catholic. Ollie and Elizabeth in Fairchance, already old, were not included in the ceremony, and they were apparently lied to about his identity. Her grandmother Elizabeth's will clearly identifies her granddaughter as "Elsie Moyer," which was not Elsie's married name. Moyer was an old name in Connellsville—of Pennsylvania German extraction. Something of a Pittsburgh family conspiracy had evolved to hide cultural details from Ollie and Elizabeth in Fairchance.

Social realities of that marriage notwithstanding, Ben and his aging uncle John Wheaton signed the horn player's petition for naturalization prior to their marriage. At Elsie's wedding, her uncle Will gave her a ten dollar gold piece, her uncle Joe Wheaton gave her a ten dollar gold piece, John Wheaton gave her a five dollar gold piece, and Ben gave her a twenty-five dollar gold piece. Two years later Elsie bore her strong-headed daughter, Natalie. In Natalie's first few years life was tumultuous. Violence was involved. This became very complicated, as Sophia had also taken in her son-in-law's recently immigrated mother and two adult sisters. For a time, life at the house on Brownsville Road was tense.

And Then There Were None

As Elsie's marriage deteriorated, the Densmores faced yet another loss in 1920, when patriarch Ollie, age seventy-nine, gave up his ghost and joined the rest of Old Robert's children.[61] His work at the brickyard had pushed his body too far. More than sixty years of hard physical labor had left him gaunt and arthritic. That arthritis began to impede his work on Fairchance's town council as early as 1909. His joints had taken stunning abuse. About four or five years before his death, he became somewhat housebound. His wife, Elizabeth, and one or another of their grandnephews[62] in Fairchance would steady him on his trips to church and help him onto the rocker on their front porch. By 1920 Elizabeth, a gaunt wisp of a woman, was with him constantly until the end. His obituary appeared in multiple newspapers in Uniontown, Connellsville, and Pittsburgh, where he was labeled everything from "a veteran iron roller" to "legendary."[63]

His grandson Ben and daughter-in-law Sophia went to Fairchance for his funeral, as did his son, Will. He was buried in Tent Presbyterian Church's cemetery about 150 feet above his father on the hill overlooking the Georges Valley. Times had changed in the sixty-five years since Old Robert's burial. Tent Church's bell did not toll seventy-nine times for him, there was no "sitting up," and his male survivors did not personally wash and dress his body. But one poignant detail was the same: Will did symbolically place quarters to close his father's penetrating gray eyes. Then, "Dust to dust. Ashes to ashes," intoned Reverend Carlile, and the last eyewitness to Old Robert's lived America was no more.

What died on May 3, 1920, was not just a man, but an era in the lived experience of Old Robert's line of Densmores—experience of a time when the most skilled and most experienced artisans widely controlled crucial aspects in the processes of industrial production. The princes of American labor were a dying breed in a world based increasingly on status, wealth, political influence, connections, and cunning. That left an uneasy and often unrequited yearning to fulfill America's idealized Colonial values of fair play, reward for hard, honest work, and the pride and identity that was due those who faithfully lived those values. That yearning still burns brightly in vast swaths of contemporary America. When a modern politician offers to "restore" America, the message is heard in much of America as the restoration of this fundamental value system. The idea of it remains both powerful and volatile.

The Trail of Male DNA

True, after his death in 1855, Old Robert's "Y" genes[64] still survived in his male descendants, in Robert Jr.'s and Sam's sons and grandsons. In Ollie's line, those Y-DNA genes were carried by Will and his son, Nelson Oliver, and by H. T.'s son, Ben. Old Robert's line of Y-DNA stretched back in history from early Pennsylvania to the Ulster Plantation, thence to the Scottish/English borderlands. From there it stretched back even farther in time and space to western Europe, thence to the plains of Hungary about seven thousand years ago, and in unbroken upward ascent into the far reaches of known antiquity, from father to son into the "fertile crescent" of the Middle East and the dawn of agriculture there about 10,000 BC. From there, at fabled places like Mohenjo Daro and other bastions of village agriculture, a succession of great-great-great-great-great-grandsons had eventually migrated westward into eastern Europe as growing population and limited farmlands in the fertile crescent forced youngest sons to leave the family fold and seek new farmable lands. On these migrations those sons took local wives from ancient nomadic tribal populations unrelated to their male ancestors, leaving Europe with its commonest genetic signature of male Y-DNA—R1B1b2—and the far more varied genetic signatures of ancient female mtDNA.[65]

In each of those moves, from the dawn of agriculture toward the day of Ollie's death, land has been settled and population has grown, even if at times, as in the plagues of Black Death in Europe, it was temporarily trimmed. In each sustained growth cycle the land eventually fills up. Some are impoverished, and others move on. The Densmores' arrival in Pennsylvania and the subsequent branches that moved west toward the Ohio, then the Mississippi, and eventually to the shores of Alaska and California was just one more ripple in the cyclic processes of ebb and flow first unleashed by growing crops and storing them. For the arriving Pennsylvania Densmores of the middle to late 1700s, it was likely the thirtieth or fortieth such move since the dawn of agriculture. All were unleashed by investing more work calories per hour in farm labor than were required by foragers in order to increase output of domesticated food calories. The details were new in Pennsylvania, but not the process. Agriculture set a successive series of Power Phases into motion. Some were aborted by famine, some by war, others by disease—just like spreading ripples on a pond, when the perfect concentricity is interrupted by a rock. Now, in the twenty-first century, there are no more viable empty places to fill. Thus the ancient dynamics *will* change . . . and humanity will be inexorably changed in the process.

In the months after Ollie's death, Elsie separated from her husband. He had broken little Natalie's nose and battered her—that was it. The errant husband's mother and sisters exited the scene. Will, along with John and Joe Wheaton, closed ranks, as did Ben and Alan Ray.[66] Shamed and angry, Elsie withdrew from her modern lifestyle. Meanwhile, the Westinghouse Corporation had already expanded its ship turbine operations in Essington, Pennsylvania, to accommodate the military needs of what would become World War I. After the war their plant on the Delaware River, about five miles west of the Philadelphia city line, was again expanded to meet commercial shipping needs. Company housing was available, centered on Saude Avenue in the village of Essington, then known as Westinghouse Village.

Alan Ray was detailed to the transfer along with Ben and two other young engineers. The men arrived late in the summer of 1920. Elsie, Natalie, and Sophia remained in Pittsburgh at the Brownsville Road house as they cleaned and packed, waiting for a sale and visiting with Elizabeth, who was failing in the aftermath of Ollie's death. She had been with him for sixty of her seventy-eight years. Months later, ailing, her son Will took her to the South Side hospital in Birmingham. She died there on November 22, 1920.[67]

With her died the tales of her mother's 1829 elopement with Tom Goldsboro, the beribboned horse, her father John Ryland on the porch, cradling his flintlock Pennsylvania rifle, and memories of her ancestor Thomas Goldsberry, a mile from Harper's Ferry, who had entertained George Washington in the 1700s. She was the last in the family to have witnessed the long-gone "Great Railroad Strike" of 1877 and the last to have visited her great uncle Sylvester Ryland's grave on Ryland's Hill near Friendsville, Maryland. Also lost was her version of the recipe for buttermilk-fried squirrel. Her mtDNA wound back through her mother to 1730s Pennsylvania, thence to Holland and Prussia, then back to Eastern Europe, thence into the trackless mists of time. Like most living women, her mtDNA derives from the statistical "Seven Daughters of Eve" in East Africa, an original fountain of our species.[68]

Elizabeth lies to the left of Ollie[69] in Tent Cemetery. A large headstone spans both graves. It was Elizabeth's will[70] that was probated in Fayette County.[71] Her son Will and grandson Ben were the executors.[72] Ben shipped his share of belongings along with the furniture from 1035 Brownsville Road by rail to Essington, where they went into storage for some months as they house hunted. Will handled most of the executor duties, dividing up Ollie and Elizabeth's estate, valued at $3,628.44. That included the homestead when it sold for $2,500.

After burial and hospital expenses, just over $1,500 remained to distribute among the heirs. Ben took the mirror that had been designated by Elizabeth for her son Will.[73] The mirror was, perhaps, the last straw in a festering dispute that had begun about 1901 between Will and H. T. over division of the proceeds from the sale of the house at 2101 Sidney in the early 1900s. In a handwritten letter to H. T. in 1906, Will states, "I have always tried to act square and honest with you. You think I have treated you badly. I do not see where it is."[74]

Contact between Will and his family in Carrick and the Densmores in Ridley Park withered after Elizabeth and Ollie's deaths in the deep depression years of 1920 and 1921. It was Will, not Ben, who arranged for the large double tombstone for them in the Tent Church cemetery.[75]

The Main Line, 1920 to 2015

Ben's October 1918 draft card lists his height at "Tall," in the category for men 5'10" or taller.[76] His height was due, in part, to good nutritional and living conditions—a legacy from his recently deceased, white-collar father, H. T. He carried that legacy in early 1921, when he, Elsie, Sophia, and Natalie settled into a composite household in Ridley Park after moving out of cramped company housing in Essington. Their house at 110 Chester Pike, bought at a depression price, would become "home" until 2015 and would be owned by four generations of family. Sophia hung the beveled mirror above the fireplace when they moved in. It still hangs there to this day.

That home, a three-story, stone, half-timbered house with a slate roof built around 1910, had cost exactly fifteen thousand dollars. The cancelled check for full payment, as written by Sophia, survives.[77] Those were the proceeds from the sale of 1035 Brownsville Road in Carrick. Sophia's savings account, opened at a nearby bank in 1921, had a balance of $3,002. She had funded the house. Ben funded the weekly budget from his wages. At that time he was earning an impressive wage of about $280 a month at Westinghouse. He had not served in World War I, as his skills in battleship-engine design had been declared crucial to the nation's interest. Those skills were being put to good use at the Westinghouse Ship Turbine division, which had spread along the Delaware to Eddystone.

Ben's sister Elsie rued the loss of many social connections in Pittsburgh and felt isolated in Ridley Park. Some ugly details of her disastrous marriage had leaked out. In Pittsburgh the response was mixed. Several loyal girlfriends, like teacher Irene Feirst, sent letters expressing sorrow at the "tragedy and horror" of the situation. Other social friends positioned a bit higher up in Pittsburgh's social scale quickly and quietly became ex-girlfriends.

Some sort of attempt at a marital reconciliation between Elsie and Marion took place in late 1921. The details are unknown, but the outcome was tangible: a second daughter was born on May 30, 1922, named Avis Elsie Densmore. The marriage reconciliation came to nothing, and Elsie's marriage was legally nullified in 1924. She kept her maiden name.

Life in the household was frequently strained by Elsie's moods and troubles, but her brother Ben loved playing father to Elsie's two girls, and he soon became their formal guardian. As a family they developed passions for stamp collecting and coin collecting. Ben had bought a used automobile, and they all enjoyed weekend driving trips. By the late 1920s they engaged in driving tours to collect "first day of issue" postal-stamp cards. One such trip began at 4:45 a.m., and in one frenzied day they drove to Scranton, Reading, Harrisburg, York, West Chester, Downington, and Philadelphia.

Apart from his family life, Ben had an active social life at work, including poker games and a billiard table and bar for himself and his male friends on the third floor. He spent summer weeks at Atlantic City, the stylish regional vacation spot of that era.

The late 1920s also marked a new high point in Ben's Westinghouse career. On May 28, 1921, he filed his own letters of patent through Westinghouse attorneys, serial number 366,618, for a major advance in turbine-blade technology. This technology dramatically improved the stability of complex, multiblade assemblies and the forces they could withstand. The amended patent was issued February 24, 1931, as #1,793,468A. Westinghouse owned the patent, but Ben was awarded a cash bonus large enough to put $2,000 in his savings account.

A second patent application, which had actually been first filed a few months before the one above, was awarded patent #1,828,409A in October 1931. A seminal innovation,[78] that brought a company bonus large enough for Ben to buy two things: a farm in upstate Pennsylvania's rolling hills, and a 1932 Packard town car, with crystal bud vases at each rear window and the initials B. V. D. on the two front doors.

Years after Ben died that Packard remained spotless, ritually washed and polished by his spinster niece Natalie each year on Ben's birthday. It was still parked in the old carriage garage across the side street from the house on Chester Pike in the 1960s.[79]

By then Ben had already ascended to family sainthood, and the Packard stood in as a family altar. Ben, like signer John Hart, was the subject of many household conversations. It was as if either fellow had temporarily stepped out of the dining room to do whatever men do on the long side porch while the women cleared dishes for dessert, and they would be stepping back in at any moment. Oddly, what Ben actually did at work was not a main feature of those conversations. Yes, he was an engineer at Westinghouse—but never once were his patents mentioned, nor the ways in which the nation used his services. Instead the conversations focused on his parenting, his tastes in music, his kindness, and most of all the sense of security he provided the women.

Ben's engineering days at Westinghouse began in late 1909 and ended the summer of 1936, when he suffered a sudden series of strokes. The first stroke, in May of 1936, incapacitated him. He made a bit of a comeback that summer, then had another stroke. He died at Taylor Hospital in Ridley Park on August 14, 1936, at 12:05 a.m.[80] He was fifty-one years old, and he had died from the very same cause that had taken his father, H. T., at almost the same age.

Ben's co-workers paid tribute—Westinghouse sent four of them by train to Pittsburgh as honorary pallbearers. Warm, loving Sophia was once again crushed. Her father, her husband, and now her son were gone. Elsie once more faced lifestyle issues after the brother who had both acted as father to her girls and brought home his pay was buried beside their father, H. T., in J. J. Vandergrift's selected burial plots at the South Side Cemetery.

In his experiments and constant tweaking of turbine blades, materials, designs, and assembly, Ben had made large turbines far more efficient and far, far more durable. In his era those two major patents in his name had first made American warships faster, more energy-efficient, and more reliable. But later, commercial transport also benefitted. Ben's inventions became crucial to the turbine technology used to create prop-jet[81] engines. His patent numbers are cited in dozens of later technological innovations.

Before Ben's death he had spent part of the 1930s as a technological emissary for Westinghouse in its role as a defense contractor, spreading his technology to other countries. Among them were Cuba, Peru, and Argentina, as documented by the postcards he sent home to Sophia, Elsie, and her girls. Ben's notebooks, correspondence, original patent drawings, and pitch-angle studies for those turbines were found in a box on the third floor of the Ridley Park house in 2008. They revealed the accomplished Benjamin Vandergrift Densmore of the engineering world. His keen eye for innovation isn't surprising, considering his roots.

Childless, Ben's death terminated his unbroken chain of male Y-DNA that went back to Old Robert, to the Dunsmores of the 1630s in Ulster, to Scotland in the late 1000s, to western Europe. Instead, what survived of him were industrial drawings, files, and glass photographic plates. Recently the Heinz History Center in Pittsburgh accepted all of Ben's original logs, patterns, drawings, and correspondence relating to these patents. As "technological DNA," they make a far more useful shrine than his Packard.

Because of a chain of events stretching back three generations—Ben to his father H. T., H. T. to his father Ollie, Ollie to his father Old Robert—and due to his access to both their industrial knowledge and a formal education, Benjamin Vandergrift Densmore prospered during the Great Depression—an amazing outcome. That he died during that Depression in 1936 also had drastic social and economic consequences for the women he left behind.

At Ben's death the household economy went into emergency mode. Sophia drove the move to economize, pushing Elsie to improve her sewing skills—no more store-bought clothes for her or the granddaughters. They scaled up the canning of fall produce from Ben's farm. They had spent summers there through the 1930s, but in 1936 most of its open fields were leased for hay and grazing. Meanwhile they canned huge quantities of snap beans, peaches, strawberries, onions, pickles, grapes, succotash fixings, and sweet corn. They traded excess for local flour, barley, and buckwheat. Sophia, then in her mid-seventies, did the baking. Old clothes were patched. Many of Ben's silk ties became dress bodices and women's scarves. "Waste not, want not" drove every aspect of life—except for Elsie's addiction to the theater, lectures, and art exhibitions. She craved connections to "polite society." Thus the sacrifices and thrift were, for her, acts of shame to be carefully hidden from the outside world.

Two very different worldviews co-existed uneasily in their household. Sophia raised her granddaughter Avis in Ben's second- and third-floor rooms,[82] while Elsie and Natalie lived in the rest of the second floor and dominated the large downstairs parlor. Everyone gathered for dinner. Natalie's worldview as absorbed from Elsie was based on wariness and cocooning from the outside world—aftershocks, one supposes, from the dreadful marriage Natalie was old enough to have witnessed. In contrast, her younger sister Avis's world was instilled by Sophia. It was based on warmth, love, hope, and connections to others "out there."

In late 1937 a grieving Sophia confided to fifteen-year-old Avis, who shared a room with her, that she was tired and that her belly hurt all the time. She also lamented that Elsie was unable to count her blessings: her daughters, a farm, a house owned free and clear, and some savings still in the bank. The following year, Sophia died in agony from cancer of the colon. She had refused extensive hospital treatment so that Natalie could dip into those $3,002 of savings to earn a teaching degree "in town."[83] Instead, she managed her own pain by using a teacher's bell to ring Avis when she needed morphine to reduce the unbearable pain. That bell rang more frequently as 1937 came to an end, and the second Christmas without Ben passed somberly.

On January 21, 1938, Sophia died in Ridley Park.[84] There was no "sitting up," and no men left to fill her grave. Her body was prepared by a funeral home for transport by train to Pittsburgh, accompanied by Elsie and Ben's senior colleague, Alan Ray. She was buried in Southside Cemetery next to H. T., her gravestone identical to his. Initially Elsie withdrew into herself. It became Natalie and Avis's turn to be heartbroken. Avis kept the teacher's bell. Both Sophia's prized art-glass lamp and that bell were at Avis's bedside until her death nearly seventy years later.

Natalie finished her degree in 1939 and got a job teaching at Ridley High

School. Each summer, when the teaching year ended, she took on summer secretarial work for Robert O. Anderson, a rising big shot in Corporate Oil. The farm was sold outright in 1940, replenishing the savings account, and Avis began her first year at a teacher's college in nearby West Chester. These were lean years for most Americans, for whom prewar, Depression-era habits lingered well into the 1950s. But the Densmore women persevered, as they had done for generations.

Natalie never left home. She worked both her teaching and summer secretarial jobs most of her life. Later she earned two MAs at night school, the first at Temple University and the second at the University of Pennsylvania, just as her uncle Ben had done at Carnegie Tech in the first decade of the 1900s. When mother Elsie died—on the Ides of March in 1968[85]—Natalie saw to it that she was buried in South Side Cemetery with Ben and their parents. Still, Natalie stayed on. The house was her safe haven until a fall put her in a nursing home at age eighty-seven. Natalie never married, but she had cared for Elsie as she failed, then cared lovingly for Alan Ray, who was by then a widower, when he failed. She died at age ninety in 2007, having outlived her younger sister by six months. Toward the end of her life, her neighbors looked in on her—among them Fanuccis, Bernardis, Pacé, and D'Agostinos.

With Natalie's death the chain of unbroken female mtDNA she received from Elsie, who received it from Sophia, who had received it from her mother Sarah Ann Hoffman Vandergrift, later Wheaton, who had received it from Catharine Page Hoffman, born in Pittsburgh, was ended. What still live on are the progeny of those rootstock peonies from the Sarver farm in 1804. And in several trunks, stacks of boxes, and chests of drawers, hundreds of letters and old documents reveal the lives they lived and fragments of the stories they told.

The other thing that lived on is not as tangible—the power of Natalie's influence on a number of her suburban Philadelphia high school students. Among them were several members of the Ridley Park Police Department. As I searched through bags of her newspaper clippings one night before her death, trying to find her power of attorney, the silent alarm went off, bringing two patrolmen to the back door. I answered their shouts of, "Who are you? No hands in pockets!" They were professional, but clear. I answered, "Natalie's nephew. I lived here as a boy."

"Okay," came the response. "But are you *sure* you should be going through her things? Miss Densmore would *not* like that." Frugal, iron-willed, smart, exasperatingly stubborn, high strung, and a workaholic, Miss Densmore had left her mark on the community of memory created among her former students. Others in the village remembered her only as the gaunt old lady who walked long blocks alone to the small grocery store near the mainline railroad station to buy leftover bread and overripe bananas on discount. In the winters she wrapped up in Ben's seventy-year-old overcoat and fedora. The specter of a bygone era, she reveled in that image.

Chapter 19

Paths to Well-Being

Despite World War I, the deadly flu epidemics of 1918 to 1920, and the Great Depression that began in 1929, American-born males in 1940 grew up to average 5'9" as adults. Medical advances and expanded quarantine laws, a legacy of the World War I era, led to lower mortality and fewer childhood diseases. The majority of American babies were now born in hospitals and could expect to live 59.7 years. Finally, the Founders' legacy had been bested.

By the early 1950s America had undergone transformations in multiple dimensions. The Long Depression, two world wars, the Great Depression, and police actions in Korea had again changed the nation. The population in 1950 stood at over 152 million—*forty* times larger than when it was first censused in 1790. Town and city dwellers outnumbered country folk. High school had become nearly universal, and scientists at Wyeth laboratories working with the mushroom growers of Pennsylvania had given the world penicillin.

Unlike America's earlier wars—the Revolution, the War of 1812, the Mexican War, the Spanish-American War, and even World War I—most men returning from World War II did not want to remember as they once had. Densmores, Harts, and Vandergrifts all served in substantial numbers. World War II had been too big, too brutal, and too frightening a commentary on the depths of outright human depravity for the average soldier to resolve. Those soldiers had also seen places and people very different from themselves. Most veterans returned grateful to be alive. Having seen too much death and chaos, they were anxious to marry and have children, build a little house with a white-picket fence, or work a modest farm and woodlot with a stream running through it. Seventy or eighty bucks a week in a job making something useful would suffice, and they craved raising children who would never have to see what they had seen.

Most of the children of that generation never heard war stories. It was the cash-poor, buttoned-down, early 1950s. Church, Little League, Sunday dinners, Easter sunrise services, and forgetting were high on the nation's to-do list. The forgetting and the deaths that left holes in families were agents of transformation. So were the millions of hunts for jobs, which often as not separated family branches into different places endowed with distinct regional cultures. Blacks moved north. Whites moved south or west. And troubled vets wandered everywhere.

Yet it may have been a piece of war-era legislation that became the nation's most profound agent for change. Signed on June 22, 1944, by President Franklin D. Roosevelt, the GI Bill had several parts.[1] It gave veterans twenty dollars a week in readjustment bonuses. Even more significant, the bill sent veterans to college and trade schools. By the time it expired on July 25, 1956, 7.8 million veterans had used the educational benefits, and 2.4 million had taken out its VA mortgages and owned their own houses. There was no thirty-year wait for benefits, as many men of Old Robert's era had experienced. America was focused on *now*, as powerful societies tend to do.

Suddenly, half-empty colleges and vocational-technical schools filled up,[2] and higher education filtered down to "working-class" and "farm" families on a scale previously unimaginable. The first "land grant" colleges and universities—the legislative legacy of the Civil War era when Southern politicians were *not* present in Congress to block Yankee Senator Justin Morrill's Land Grant Act—had initiated important advances in access to higher education. But those advances had not penetrated deeply enough to create rapid, widespread change. After all, many families still could not afford even modest tuition, meals, and books. There simply was too little "discretionary income" in millions of American households, or among barter-prone farm families, to send kids to college in the tough years of the late 1880s and 1890s or during the Great Depression. Even a full tuition scholarship meant little to the thousands of families who could not support so much as books, room, and board for a son or daughter. That was Avis Densmore's dilemma. She had won a full tuition scholarship to New York's prestigious Barnard College, but there was no money for expensive Manhattan room and board in their female-based household.

The GI Bill finally helped to reverse that reality and save the nation from a bad case of too many veterans and too few postwar jobs to offer them. Many who went to college on the GI Bill remained in the armed forces' Reserves for a few dollars a month and worked feverishly to graduate quickly. Police actions in Korea soon soaked up some of them and their younger brothers. The cascade of changes generated by the GI Bill operated at many levels: freshly minted engineers, agronomists, foresters, teachers, skilled tradesmen and women, business majors, accountants, and young research scientists all drove the American economy forward. By the early 1950s the second wave of education saw hundreds of thousands graduate with professional degrees in medicine, law, chemistry, geology, and new specialties like nuclear energy and information systems.

For the first time in America's history, a large portion of a generation did not follow the life ways of the families that had raised them. Grandfathers lamented a grandson who would not join the brotherhood of their skilled trade nor recognize and enjoy union rights that they, their fathers, and their grandfathers had fought and even died for. A grandson determined to become a ... what? A Cytologist? What *is* that? Can you make a living off of it?

Grandfathers and fathers who had worked open furnaces, manned semi-automated manufacturing equipment, or worked as electricians and plumbers had generally perceived themselves as bearers of the early twentieth century's new technologies and as founders of a hopeful twentieth-century industrial America. Now they were in their fifties and sixties, facing a rate of change that had already made them technological relics in their own time. The majority of their sons and grandsons were going off to college and university—worlds they simply could not fathom. Even the language spoken in those places was foreign. So were the rules of etiquette. "If they bring their college friends here, what will we *say* to them?"

In French sociological terms, those working men's cultural capital was devalued. A place in "the brotherhood" in 1955 was *not* as valuable as it had been in 1920. From a cultural perspective, America, while solving an immediate problem, was again underestimating the value of a work DNA. It is nearly as important an identity legacy as plain old genetic DNA. Devaluing someone's work identity has consequences: anxiety, sorrow, depression, and diminished self-worth. Legions of female nurses and teachers were constantly reminded of their de facto second-class economic status at every pay period—a status that negatively impacted their children's well-being and their own sense of self-worth. It could also make a man sick, angry, or depressed, given the male role that eighteenth- through mid-twentieth-century American society enforced.

The GI Bill and the exodus from fathers' and grandfathers' life ways and work cultures was massively significant. Economically it was genius. In terms of new knowledge and advances in science, medicine, agriculture, and industry, it was wondrous. Like J. J. Vandergrift's wealth, however, it separated countless American families into a future-focused, fast-paced college generation and a tradition focused rather defiantly on "working-class" America.

The disappointment and tumult among an older generation of workingmen who mourned the cultural loss of unity in work culture and identity with their sons and grandsons still bounces off the increasingly brittle social and ideological walls that separate contemporary America: rural versus urban, college educated versus high school, working class versus middle class, and politically "conservative" versus "liberal." As with the Civil War, the echoes of this disjunction over work culture, knowledge, and value systems is destined for a long shelf life, since the communities of memory on each side of it are huge and vibrant. The harder that highly educated America pushes for even higher levels of education, the heavier the pushback by those on the other end of the spectrum.

Tragically, this education chasm has been increasingly identified as one about "credentials" as well as an arrogance that too often attaches itself to the idea that one person is better than another based primarily on those credentials: "I'll see your Penn State, and raise you a Princeton." That attitude, all too common in contemporary education, downplays individual behavior, experience, and talent. For Pennsylvania iron and steel workers, it was always about identity, the definitions of cultural capital, and the assignment of self-worth. It also leaves this nation with an ongoing, ambiguous cultural divide. This unclaimed vacuum between diverging value systems is dangerously unwise—it leaves open and unguarded cultural spaces in which eccentric behaviors flourish uncontested. It was precisely this type of ambiguous cultural space—defined in the "All men are created equal" declaration as a generous middle ground—that America's Founders wished to promote and protect. They discussed equality at great length. While their original definition of it falls far short of a full-throated shout-out for racial and gender equality, it was stunningly bold in its own time.

Looking Back on Family Trajectories
The Harts

The vista backward from early twenty-first-century America allows us a long view of three families who stand in for many others. The Harts, literate, came to the Connecticut River colonies in the late 1630s. They farmed, built houses as carpenters, and made fine cabinetry. One branch moved southwest to Long Island and produced the Flushing Remonstrance in the 1650s. That document may have contributed a piece[3] of its philosophical DNA to our Constitution by bolstering the case for religious freedom. One hundred twenty years later, John Hart, a great-great-grandson of the Flushing signer, also signed the Declaration of Independence.

In his private life John Hart was a farmer, politician, and co-owner of a mill complex in New Jersey that his brother Daniel staffed largely with black slaves. Daniel was actually murdered by one of those slaves, a household servant at odds with his master. Later the signer's youngest son, John Jr., was a slave owner in Pointe Coupee, Louisiana, in the 1780s, and he was unable—or unwilling—to care for his youngest daughter, Mary, who became the wife of Jacob Vandergrift in Frankford, Philadelphia, in 1791, the year after her father died. Signer John Hart and his sons left many, many descendants. Like others, his descendants migrated west or south at the end of the eighteenth century, to western Pennsylvania, Maryland, Delaware, western Virginia, and Kentucky. His oldest son, Jesse, who was among the founders of Beaver, Pennsylvania, was both an innkeeper and a riverman. By the 1870s they were spread out most everywhere in the United States.

By European standards the early Harts lived long lives, and most of their children survived infancy, as did their children's children. They benefitted from the nation's original biological advantage. Most had 200- to 350-calorie-per-hour occupations, like carpenter, farmer, and miller. Evolutionarily successful and historically significant, they worked hard at the standard occupations in early America but were not the untainted saints that several websites and historical biographies fantasize. They owned slaves. The European world had rejected slavery by the first decade of the nineteenth century. Did signer John Hart of New Jersey himself own slaves? Yes. In his will he bequeathed a slave girl named Hannah to his teenaged daughter Deborah.[4] We also know that the original line of American Harts was still interacting with the Vandergrifts—Deborah scratched her initials into the handmade glass pane of a Vandergrift house on the Delaware in the 1770s. Later, the two families would team up again to build riverboats on the Ohio.

Some of the signers' descendants fought for the Union in the Civil War, while others enlisted in the Confederate Army. But today most of their living descendants likely do not know much about their own roots. Losing track of roots is one consequence of a nation that operates on a scale and fevered pace that confounds ancient community and family traditions.

The Vandergrifts

Before Jacob Vandergrift married Mary Hart in 1791, both the Vandergrifts and the Harts of New Amsterdam had moved successively from Manhattan,

Newtown, and Flushing, Long Island, to the South River (the Delaware), taking on farming and milling. By 1791 the deep cultural rifts between the Dutch and British had waned, softened by time, familiarity, and experience.

Like John Hart's sons, Jesse and Scudder, some Vandergrifts moved west to the Ohio Valley. The Harts left the Eastern Seaboard roughly between 1790 and 1795. The Vandergrifts left between 1810 and 1816. The original Dutch Vandergrift brothers, especially Paulus, had been powerful in the Old Dutch colony of the 1600s, but the flamboyant, swashbuckler Paulus returned to Holland, and most of his descendants stem from there. Ironically, his return to Holland in the 1670s was to a world that eschewed slavery and demanded far more moderate behavior than he had indulged in on Manhattan Island.

His younger brother, Jacob, and his descendants both retained more cultural freedom and benefitted from America's biological advantage. They had a large farm and "riverman" families on the Delaware, and they left many descendants. Most of the men were farmers, carpenters, boat builders, millers, or stonemasons, 200- to 350-calorie-an-hour occupations. Most made their own hours, worked their own land, and managed their own farms and flour mills. Few engaged in wage-based public work until the 1800s. When Jacob and Mary Vandergrift moved west in the early 1800s, they left behind a large, multi-branched extended family in New Jersey, Pennsylvania, Maryland, and Delaware. If any owned slaves, no explicit records of it have turned up. They were a self-sufficient lot, and they were not prone to Paulus's flamboyances.

In the Ohio Valley Jacob and his sons had shifted away from running the established family mills[5] near Philadelphia as depression set in following the War of 1812. They turned to bridge building, boat building, and related work. Most of them managed business operations suffused with their own hands-on experience. They jobbed out boat hulls but controlled the expensive finishing work. They commissioned steam engines and added their own twists to methods of propulsion. Their riverboat activities were clearly intertwined with those of their Hart cousins. The brothers invested in concert, spreading risks among them. Flashy J. J. aside, they were prominent in their trades, but they were subdued spenders. They produced large families and lived secure but rather ordinary lives in and around those who worked for them. As the 1800s wore on and younger generations arrived, those generations enjoyed a fair measure of America's economic advantages. But as the 1800s bore on, the progeny of less wealthy Vandergrift branches took on public work and enjoyed fewer benefits of early America's biological well-being.

And what legacy did the Vandergrifts stimulate or create? Pushing coal barges instead of pulling them, funding the development of bulk oil boats, tank cars,[6] pipelines for gas and oil, faster and more efficient steamboats, and corporations aplenty.

The early nineteenth-century Ohio Valley and its industry was simply more dangerous and the environment more toxic than Long Island, New Jersey, or thinly populated northern Pennsylvania. So was the steamboat era. Boiler explosions, snags, shipboard fires, and drownings all took their toll. By 1870 the family was separating into a case study of America's emerging class system. By the 1880s the wealthy descendants focused around J. J. of Standard Oil. The last of the riverboat captains, James and Lewis, stood in for the comfortable middle class. The waiters, clerks, carpenters, and iron workers found in city directories increasingly represented ordinary working-class America. Some among them were as deeply challenged by limited household budgets in the 1870s through the 1890s as were the Densmores.

J. J, his son William, and his other children were either engaged in management at work inputs of about 100 to 150 calories an hour or were well-married daughters keeping house, one Elsie-like rogue among them. By 1880 the biological Advantage of J. J.'s branch was far more pronounced than that among the clerks and waiters. The Vandergrift tradesman—carpenter, glass blower, iron-mill hand—invested 250 to 450 calories per hour on the job and enjoyed, like most workers, rapidly diminishing control over their own working conditions.

Between 1830 and 1880, Vandergrift divergence in wealth, health, longevity, and cost of work calories is striking. The divergence in value systems is even more striking. First there is J. J. Vandergrift, captain of industry, on the board of directors of Standard Oil, the pinnacle of a corporate monopoly. Then there is his Uncle George's son, his close blood kinsman, William Vandergriff,[7] shot down in West Virginia by a militia captain while defending laborers' rights to strike and buried in a local cemetery without a whisper of approbation from the family's Captain of Industry. By 1877 corporate power and wealth had apparently trumped family and DNA in the "upper chamber" of the House of Vandergrift.

The Densmores

In culture and worldview, the Ulster Scots Densmores of eighteenth-century Pennsylvania were a breed apart as late guests to the party called America. They pioneered western trans-Appalachian territory, even as Atlantic Seaboard cities like Boston, New York, and Philadelphia had already begun to gentrify and celebrate their centennials.

In an ambiguous world caught in a tug-of-war between political entities (Virginia and Pennsylvania) and cultural entities (Native American, German, Scots-Irish, and slick, city-bred hustlers like those in Philadelphia) they fashioned lives and gravitated to occupations where they could make some of the rules: farmer (Samuel, 1751); wagoner (Old Robert); distiller (Henry of German and Dunbar townships); traveling clothier/fuller (William). Their occupations depended on skill, initiative, and risk-taking. They created a Pennsylvania family network that linked Cumberland County / Carlisle on the east to Beaver and Lawrence Counties and Ohio on the northwest, with Fayette, Westmoreland, Washington, Venango, and Allegheny counties hanging like pendants on a chain.

This was their Densmore line's primary world from about 1751 to the 1870s. Compared to previous generations living in Ulster, a higher percentage of their children survived and grew taller. Some of them owned their own land. A number owned their own houses. These were American miracles. Even better they all still owned their own skills. Those skills—forge, furnace, farm, wagoner, coal digger, and coal broker—all meant hard physical labor. Most of the men pursued 250- to 460-calorie-an-hour jobs. Most of the women gardened, sewed, washed clothes by hand, made some of their own fabrics, cut wood, fed chickens, and tended more kids than most modern parents can fathom. Those women's work was utterly essential—an inseparable part of family economy. By the 1870s public wage work narrowed their ability to make rules as corporate power systematically transformed craftsmen into wage-based servants and pushed their wives into side occupations[8] to compensate for the declining wages offered.

And what legacy did the Densmores leave America? Contemporary Californian Paul Densmore, a great-great-grandson of Sam Densmore of Kittanning, captured it well. "We were hard-working and a tick or two smarter than average."[9] His understatement is pure Densmore. This work ethic's legacy can best be described in modern context as lying somewhere on a scale between admirable and terrifying. In two and a half centuries, only a handful of the males failed the full Densmore standard. Cousin Tom put it similarly to me in 2012 at his kitchen table in Pennsylvania. "I would say our family worked very hard, pretty well stuck together, and were not prone to stupidity . . . well, there was an exception or two along the way."

As for the "tick or two" smarter than average, I let the case rest on the body of US patents made by Densmores: improved farm equipment,[10] and the precursors to tank cars, bulk boats, typewriters, spittoons, magazine rifles, sash fasteners, efficient steam boilers,[11] rail joints, industrial fans, ship turbines, prop jets, and bridge patterns. Nearly everything that the Densmores had created generated efficiencies in transport, in information systems, and in machines that simply worked better and consumed fewer calories/BTUs from natural gas or oil.

Their technologies created wealth, but only relatively modest portions of it stuck to most of them in the late nineteenth-century era when the bulk of American wealth migrated upward as never before. And yes, their innovations and efficiencies combined with those of thousands of other inventors to move America forward technologically. Nothing fuels growth in a massive economic system more predictably than efficiency gains to balance out the enormous resources consumed by growth processes. And nothing steamrolls traditions—and those who live them daily—so dramatically as those very same efficiencies. Some Densmore efficiencies would both transform the world they most cherished and eventually deeply erode some of their own descendants' self-sufficiency. Technological efficiencies nearly always act as a double-edged sword on the societies that embrace them.

Chapter 20

The Great Emptiness

One photograph of Ollie Densmore, taken in Fairchance about 1890, captures a way of life that would fade away by the 1960s. Its black-and-white scene of a hog slaughter next to a house or shed has gradually given way to softer sepia tones, but the power of its central figures is undiminished.

Ollie, about age forty-five to fifty, stares over his shoulder toward the photographer, his hands gripping the ropes that suspend a hog over the huge iron tub in which it will be boiled to soften the bristles. His stare is intense, as if to say, "Hello—I'm busy here!" He is thick and powerful. In iron workers' parlance of the time, he was built "like an elephant." There are other men in the photo. Most appear younger and less powerful. They wear canvas jeans and work jackets. Even though it is late fall, Ollie and several others do not bother with sleeves. Cut-off jackets were once the signature of men who made their own heat as they worked.

There is utterly no pretense in this photograph. He and the boys are simply "pulling together" and preparing for a long Pennsylvania winter. Someone's back pocket hints at a tin of snuff. A subtly distended cheek suggests a twist of chew. All the shoes in view are ankle-high leather work boots. The nails fastening thick leather soles to the uppers could easily be Anchor's famous brand, cut from thin plates rolled by either the photo's central figure or his son, H. T. Two large hawksbill axes likely forged at Oliphant's in the 1840s or 1850s lean against the nearest weatherboard wall.

Once that hog is butchered, its hams will be hung in someone's smokehouse. Some parts will be pickled in brine, and others will be salt-packed or smoked. The hide will go to the small tannery near Fairchance to become other items, perhaps even baseball gloves for the Pittsburgh "Alleghenies" team in Old Smokey fifty-one miles away.

I spent several years quietly mourning the loss of that photograph's world.

By the time the photo came to light, I was the lone survivor of my immediate family, and I missed the experience we used to have of "pulling together." I also missed going to West Virginia's fall apple harvests and taking turns stirring apple butter in the massive copper kettles my mother had inherited. "Made in Fairchance," she claimed. They were more than a century old, even then. And most of all, I missed the idea of a more self-sufficient era.

In late March 2011 my wife and I took the nosedive that passes for a "normal" landing at the Pittsburgh airport, picked up a rental car, and headed to Uniontown and the nearest hotels to Fairchance. It was unseasonably cold. We awoke to frost on the ground, quite like the harsh spring of 1806 when Old Robert was hauling wagon freight out of Bullskin. After breakfast, a short drive took us to Fairchance. I wanted to find the homestead. The road through the village curves in a broad circle that sweeps southwest. We passed orange-red slag piles from the old forge, following the Western Pennsylvania Railroad's abandoned tracks to the skeletal remains of an old iron work's open-walled shed. There, rolled iron had once been loaded onto freight cars.

Seeing no life except for several crows, we moved on toward the first cluster of nearby houses, each two stories tall and weatherboarded. They were narrow, front-to-back, as most old log houses are, and likely built in the 1840s. From each, perfectly straight plumes of smoke rose from tall, brick chimney stacks. We heard rhythmic banging ahead but saw no one, so we entered a dirt lane and drove toward the sound.

There, in a tangle of open lot, barbed wire, and metal-roofed sheds, a group of men were chopping scrap wood and breaking old furniture into firewood for the row of houses we had just passed. Winter woodpiles depleted, they improvised, swinging huge hawksbill axes forged about 150 years ago, yards away from where they were standing. They wore work blues and brogans.

One of the men, tattooed on his upper arm, was sleeveless. He looked up, stared for a moment, ejected a stream of tobacco juice, then turned back to the business at hand. "Hello—I'm busy here! And what are you staring at?" I imagined his eyes saying. I stared back through the car window, touched the brim of my hat, and continued down the lane, oblivious to the fact that this row of houses and the open lot south of the tracks was one of the lots Ollie had bought from the Jordans in the 1860s. When purchased, his family was small, the money at Anchor in Birmingham was good,[1] and the long turns were nearly unlimited. That row of houses and the tracks are visible on the 1872 atlas map of Fayette County.[2]

We drove around looking for the homestead—up one lane then down the next, but we could not find anything that looked like the early 1900s photo Benjamin V. Densmore had taken of his grandfather Ollie and the homestead. That morning, Fairchance's Main Street was darned near moribund: a saloon with three patrons on the left, a small pharmacy and convenience store on the right. Several churches, two funeral parlors, several small shops, and Fire House / Town Hall rounded out the scene.

At noon we met a college-aged woman and her parents. I'd met her online at Ancestry.com. She was a descendant of one Warman's branch, and she wanted to know more about the Densmores. I was still in the learning phase, but I had information on Nehemiah and his wife, Elizabeth. They escorted us to the Maple Grove Cemetery on the ridge above town where the two are buried. We parted ways. Before leaving the cemetery I scanned the Georges Valley below, wondering what had happened to all the furnaces, machine shops, brickyards, general stores, railway sheds, and powder and grist mills.

I could see five or six square miles spread out below. Except for a few tarmac lanes and the somnolent main street, there was simply no more new infrastructure. I struggled to process the surrounding emptiness. It was as if a giant hand had descended from the heavens and ripped the beating industrial heart from the body that had cast cannonballs for the War of 1812, made the New World's best nails in the 1830s, and sent Oliphant's premium bar iron on flat boats to Pittsburgh—which then transformed into the bridges, train tracks, rifle barrels, and ship's hulls that had formed America's envied backbone of infrastructure and its rise to world power.

The area I could see had also produced the New World's most prodigious output of premium-quality coke to make steel. That coke had ushered in a wave of industrial efficiency that both enriched American corporations and squeezed out the autonomy of the era's most skilled workers. No Fairchance and Connellsville coke fields, no legion of men like Samuel Densmore to invent the efficiencies needed to produce it. That, in turn, would have meant no Pittsburgh, no "Steel City," no Carnegie, Frick, Captain Jones, or partner Laughlin ... and no "American Century," as the twentieth century came to be called.

The hills around me were studded with large graveyards. Those graveyards are full of men who had been glad to work fifty to sixty hours a week of 400-calorie-per-hour jobs—musicians of the industrial symphony that is now silent. And the cemeteries are filled with the women, wives, and daughters who worked hard raising kids, and even harder when fortune frowned. They are the ones who could always "make do" and who held families together—even if it meant scrubbing floors, as Ethel Densmore had done.

The graveyards, slag piles, and abandoned railroad tracks nagged at me that evening, until it hit me. Of course! I'd seen this before in my early days of archaeological fieldwork: small, fading communities eking out a living in sight of abandoned cities and infrastructures that once shouted "Empire!" I saw it in the small village of San Juan de Teotihuacan north of Mexico City, just two hundred yards from the great stone room blocks of the huge city of a quarter million that had once dominated trade in Central America's obsidian tool sources. Then there was the humble village of Ingapirca,[3] Ecuador, next to the Inka's great, walled citadel on their main road, which had once stretched from Ecuador to southern Peru. All these were spaces and "works" emptied by the process of dying empire. Those great ruins, so many of which had graced the cover of *National Geographic*, were to human society as are the pale, empty exoskeletons of locusts attached to the bark of late-summer sycamores. The shell was left, but the life it had once contained was gone.

In turn, the empty spaces in the Georges Creek Valley surrounding Fairchance were also the signature of a waning growth phase in the industrial world that had defined America's nineteenth and early twentieth centuries. Beyond the emptiness, the value system of that era had changed. In the mid-1800s the Densmore men who had worked those skilled, 460-calorie-an-hour jobs of roller, catcher, heater, and puddler were paid the most, and they played the "keystone" species role in the wage-earning manufacturing pyramid. After 1870 their place in the wage/power industrial food chain declined precipitously as corporations rose in power and Robber Barons replaced them as the industrial keystone species. Worse yet, Densmore men like Charlie in the 1920s, whose hourly work input in the mines was about 400 calories an hour, were paid near the bottom of the American wage scale. This signals a major shift in the values placed on hard work and skill, as mechanization and its efficiencies generated—as intended—both unprecedented profit margins and unprecedented control over worker's autonomy and their family well-being.

The long-term consequences of that value shift are still with us today. Modern America imports thousands of skilled engineers and computer-programming experts annually on special visas instead of investing in its own skilled workers. And when we need repairs to failing infrastructure created eighty years ago, we often rip it out and start over for lack of the time, care, and know-how to repair the original. In the process iron is often replaced with plastic. But the worst of it may be the sociological failure to pay both respect and decent wages to the workers who make and restore things. Need a repair to a 120-year-old shotgun inherited from your great-grandfather? There are only a few dozen reliable places to get that done in a nation of over three hundred million.

In the late 1900s the "hot money" in American industry first relocated to low-wage states then increasingly moved offshore. This is evolutionarily risky. If a society needs something to function—energy, steel, shoes, medicines, or smart, flexible craftsmanship—it must maintain both the resources and the workforce's ability to make it here at home. I did not sleep well that night.

The next day was better. After spending a day tidying up my parents' graves on a hill above Morgantown, my wife and I returned to Fairchance to continue our search for the homestead. We stopped at Goldsboro's Funeral Home, hoping to find one or another of Tom Goldsboro's descendants.[4] Unfortunately, they had retired to Florida several years before.

I explained to the new owners that we were looking for an unnumbered house on Morgantown Street that had once stood between numbers 34 and 36, possibly near neighbors Coughenhour or Rhitenour. The torn-off corner of an old note in Sophia's spidery hand found marking the 23rd Psalm in her bible was a clue. We were told, "Look for the white metal siding . . . that *might* be the house. The houses were all renumbered when the zip codes came." Three minutes later we pulled up to a house that might have been the one Ollie and Elizabeth retired to; luckily, there were half a dozen men in the yard.

I stepped out and crossed the street. "Hello!" I said with a smile. A crisp-looking fellow stepped forward and looked me over. His gaze alternated between my tie and my gray fedora. "What do you want, *Boss*?" He must have noticed my surprise at being called this, and he softened a little. "You looking for something?" Several of the other men turned and stared.

"Yes, looking for my great-great-grandfather's house."

"Oh, well there was a death here early this morning. The folks here have only lived in it about thirty years. Gotta go now."

He turned to walk away, then looked over his shoulder again. "Your great-great-grandpa got a name?"

"Yes, Oliver Densmore. His wife was Elizabeth Goldsboro." Mr. Crisp stopped dead and turned, gaping. "Ollie Densmore, the *iron roller*?" I nodded.

"Whooo, my granddad told me about him. Whooo! Really, though, sorry, gotta go!"

I thanked him. He cast one more baffled glance at my tie and trotted off.

I thought long about the effect of wearing a hat—one that had not come from a feed store—and a tie in a place where those simple accoutrements create social distances as wide as the Ohio River and as deep as an old shaft mine. But the reality is that all the surviving branches descending from Old Robert's sons have been shaped by a nation now quite different than the one that shaped Nat, Robert Jr., Sam, Ollie, and their sisters, Elizabeth, Jane, and Rachel.

Chapter 21

How Many Americas?

As a nation, the United States is more than one hundred times more populous than it was in 1751, when Samuel Densmore patented land in what was then Lancaster County, Pennsylvania. The geographic expanse of the nation has also grown more than fourfold. Only a few cities existed in Samuel's time: Boston, New York, Philadelphia, Baltimore, and Charleston. Even in the 1800 of Old Robert's wagon trip, there were no cities of Chicago, Cincinnati, St. Louis, Atlanta, Houston, or Denver.

In 1800 the urban world ended well before one reached the banks of the Ohio River. The vast majority of Americans lived in rural or village settings. Expected life-span was remarkably longer than in Europe or the British Isles. The percentage of mothers and newborns who survived was also much higher than in the more crowded countries from which so many immigrants reached American shores. There were unfathomable tracts of timber for fuel and building fences and cabins. There were rich, extensive bottomlands along the creeks and rivers from which native peoples had been displaced—first by pandemic diseases, then aggression. Food was plentiful and cheap when compared to ancestral countries across the Atlantic. American-born children, male and female, lived far longer lives than their old-world counterparts, and American-born men were the tallest and longest lived by a measure that ordinary folks could see and apprehend. Labor demands exceeded supply, so wages were higher than in Europe. This was the Colonial advantage that the Declaration most sought to protect.

Yet by the time Old Robert Dunsmore's younger sons Sam and Ollie began their work lives in the early 1850s, American-born men were already more than a half-inch shorter than the Founders' sons. By 1860 American-born boys were a full inch shorter than those born in 1830, and the life expectancy at birth for both boys and girls had declined from fifty-six years in the period from 1790 to 1800 to about forty—a loss of sixteen years. Grandfathers' farms had already been divided two or three times among sons and grandsons, and the American daily-wage-to-cost-of-living advantage had begun to erode in the face of massive immigration. Economic life *was* tougher in the American West during that era. Per capita income was twice as high in New England as in the north-central states like Pennsylvania and Ohio.[1] That gave us two distinct Americas. The South was a third, in which the majority of ordinary white males had increasingly been excluded from wage work by a rapidly growing slave population. The new trans-Mississippi west became the fourth. By 1860 the circumstances among blacks and surviving Native Americans varied enormously according to their location.

Growing regional differences in wealth, income, class, race, religion, and industry combined with cultural traditions to reinforce those distinctive regional cultures. In New England, wealth and class were core assets; in north-central states like Pennsylvania and Ohio, skills, work ethic, and family networks were key—self-sufficiency still ruled, as did the Declaration's vision of life, liberty, and the pursuit of happiness (well-being). Respect in New England generally translated to wealth and class status. In the north-central states, respect was closely tied to skills and work ethic. These regions came to see the world differently because those differences were lived daily in response to different biological, ecological, and economic realities.

The plantation South was another cultural and demographic animal altogether. Politically and legally structured from the outset to benefit a small, aristocratic, land-owning, labor-owning (indenture or slavery) caste, in 1840 to 1850 it still embraced the transplanted—and long abandoned—culture and worldview of a late seventeenth-century European landed gentry. As author Keri Leigh Merritt incisively lays out in her book *Masterless Men*, the South's planter gentry utterly reviled its own large underclass of poor, white males who were chronically unemployed or underemployed. Those white males became both shorter and died younger than did those planters' valuable black slaves between the 1820s and the 1850s.[2]

In a broad sense, the facts and fortunes of birth in plantation society, coupled with a cultural and legal devotion to the idea of eldest male son as heir apparent, simply did not mesh with any narrative about what most contemporary Americans think of as an "American Dream." As culturally important, the plantation world's scions utterly disdained hands-on work. The South's middle and elite classes scorn for it likely played a much larger cultural role in the regional cultural and economic tensions that triggered the Civil War than many historians have realized. Pennsylvania and the Ohio Valley's definition of "skilled" or "honest" work viscerally disgusted them.

Those regional differences[3] all became magnified as native-born American male height sunk to an unprecedented low of 5'7.2" by 1860. As average height declined, so did American-born life expectancy, male and female, which sank to only 38.3 years in 1850. These known losses in well-being form a biological backdrop to the Civil War. No, these statistical declines in height and longevity did not *cause* the war, but they did raise public anxieties and work stress and gave life to a sense of things drifting out of control. Those things all focused acutely on the "How will our kids fare?" "Who am I?" "Who is in control?" and "How are we doing?" questions. These very same questions still drive the American nation's trends in public opinion, political views, and reactions to external events. The contemporary American nation still frets daily about the issues surrounding well-being: access to healthcare, take-home wages, the security of a pension, the cost of a child's education, and the quest for enough fundamental family self-sufficiency to sleep well at night. Desperation, fear, uncertainty, and anger generate very powerful and often unstable social dynamics.

Workingmen in the public wage-work sector during the later nineteenth century—like the West Virginia Harts and Pennsylvania Densmores—were, in real, measurable, *biological* terms, losing "their America." It was slow and confusing, but it was there nonetheless. Losses to their definition of American well-being, therefore true "Americanness," were inescapable. Rough estimates of infant mortality hovered between 15 and 20 percent in their region. Many felt left behind because they *were* left behind. The mid-1840s for Old Robert and his family were, as we already know, quite awful. He was in his mid-sixties and failing in vigor, but he had to keep working. His pension arrears provided a partial rescue, but hundreds of thousands of other men rather like him died in utter poverty. Even the Vandergrifts of Pennsylvania, Delaware, and Maryland were unable to build great wealth in the 1830s and 1840s.

Later, the wealthy Vandergrifts in Pittsburgh and Oil City pursued a more New England style of American culture based on class, commerce, and ownership. For them the Civil War both limited economic opportunities and opened up new ones. In the period from 1860 to 1880, they sold boats, built new ones, and moved into oil, gas, and transport. So pronounced and increasingly expensive was their definition of American success that it contributed directly to the fragmentation of their family into ever more loosely connected branches. Winners like the flashy J. J. took for granted the biological advantage of the Founder's era without having to think about it or struggle for it. Thus he and others of his economic class simply did not fully apprehend its power. But between 1870 and the late 1890s, the ordinary wage-working Vandergrifts, spread from New Jersey to Michigan, had begun to understand it all too well.

The Hart family, having lost their patriarchs—signer John and his eldest son, Jesse—blended in ever more with ordinary western Pennsylvania, Ohio Valley, Kentucky, and northern West Virginia regional cultures. Most of their descendants who took public work also experienced erosion of height and longevity (see tables A2, A4, and A8) and rising infant mortality in the late nineteenth century. Those who pursued the family tradition of becoming public officials fared better. While they began their American sojourn in the 1640s with a "new England" version of American culture, they, as did most families, scattered and absorbed new settings. Their early need to protect their religion, language, and culture from an overweening Peter Stuyvesant and, later, from England's King George III had largely evaporated in the dry air of passing time. Thus, for many, their ancestral cultures had become blended with Appalachian. Situated on the border between North and South, several fought for the Confederacy. Our nation's regionalism was complicated.

In contrast, the children and grandchildren of Old Robert Dunsmore kept the faith with the Founder's version of American happiness and well-being—no longer an automatic benefit, they needed to fight for it. Every day was a workplace struggle to bring in wages, keep up food calories, and improve skills in several of the world's toughest, most important, and most demanding industries—iron, steel, and coal. As compared to their immigrant, wagoner father, they gained a bit of ground in height and longevity during the war economy of the 1840s through the 1860s through long work schedules and body-breaking exertion. Then Old Robert's grandchildren and great-grandchildren lost ground to the post–Civil War depression, and the subsequent depressions generated by crooked bankers in 1873, the massive strikes of 1877, the decline of wages amid the rise of cold, grasping, uncontrolled industrial and banking Robber Barons in the 1880s, and the fallout of events like the Homestead Strike in 1892. Those Robber Barons had become the very kind of predatory aristocracy that had denied access to well-being among Britain's ordinary citizens during Colonial times. It would take most of Old Robert's descendant great- and great-great-grandchildren until the 1930s to regain the height and longevity lost between 1860 and 1910. Two generations of hopeful wives looked on in frustration as more of their children died in childbirth or grew up to be shorter than their own generation.

For the well-off, America had become a vision of titillating dreams and new heights to yearn for, which might be attained with enough wealth, education, and influence. From those visions derive the cultural habit of incessantly redefining and relitigating the American dream. But Nat, Robert Jr., Sam, and Ollie Densmore—and the millions of skilled workers like them who worked furnace, forge, and shop—understood and hungered for the original promise of America as no prosperous upper-middle- or upper-class stratum ever has. For these working citizens, the Founders had got it right: enough food, work, wages, or land so that a working family's kids might survive, grow strong and tall, and might endure long enough to hold their grandchildren or great-grandchildren in their arms. The goal, of course, was that those grandchildren would live an even better life than they had. That was their originalist vision of America as a "Promised Land." Legions of others, including desperate nineteenth-century immigrants, embraced this view. In the early twentieth-century words of Welsh-born American labor leader James J. Davis, "America was the land of children, and that's why parents broke their old-home ties and made the hard pilgrimage to America; it was for the benefit of their children."[4]

The problem for late nineteenth-century America was that those children were not doing well by Benjamin Franklin's standards. They were doing so poorly, in fact, that chapter six of the landmark book *The Changing Body* focused specifically on the period between 1870 and 1900:

> Beginning at the 1870 cohort, diet and height of American-born males divert from the positive trend until 1940. In particular, the 1880–1900 cohort seems to have been well fed, but their heights were among the shortest since 1800. This is not clearly explained solely by diet and food consumption. There must be another factor on the side of claims on food intake that substantially reduced the positive impact of diet on height in the second half of the nineteenth . . . and early twentieth century."[5]

This is a crucial observation! Might that "other factor" be due to the *combined* effects of eroding environmental conditions, changes in the era's food production, processing, packaging, and distribution, and work conditions? During that era there was a dramatic increase in industrial work intensity, dramatically lengthening shifts, declining wages (as evidenced by Ollie Densmore's roller log), and physiologically expensive stresses. Might factors like higher levels of muscle development and long, overnight shifts that altered circadian rhythms have created a continually elevated metabolic rate that demanded more calories and protein than the norm for a worker's body mass? If so, the declining wages that led to the Great Strike of 1877, and later ones, might well have prematurely pushed several generations of ten- to twelve-year-olds out of school to work ten-hour shifts as helpers, water boys, or loom girls to supplement their parents' incomes during the critical developmental periods of their early-teen growth spurts. We already know that many male breadwinners were physically breaking down under oppressive work schedules and the notorious sweatshop conditions of the late 1800s. Could young mothers working ten- to twelve-hour shifts in a textile mill or glass-finishing room of the 1880s produce enough breast milk to optimize a child's first eighteen months of development? What nourishment did such infants receive while mom worked a loom, sewing machine, or glass-polishing drum for ten to twelve hours a day in a hot, dirty, and crowded environment? We also know that wage scales of that era were over-reported in several major national industries and that workplace safety and sanitation were dreadful.

Who Stepped on the Declaration?

By the 1890s American industry from the upper Midwest to the East Coast, in both the North and the South, was handily winning its struggle to simultaneously increase productivity and reduce wages. The cost of this bitter, sometimes violent strategy, coupled with unprecedented waves of new immigration, extracted a biological cost from most of the Densmores, the working-class Harts and Vandergrifts, and millions of others like them. In the statistical goalposts created by the census years of 1880 and 1890, native-born American male heights and longevity hit rock bottom. Male height for those born in 1880 had declined to 5'6.7", nearly an inch shorter than for Colonial American males born in 1710. By 1890 height tanked at 5'6.6", a loss of more than an inch and a half since the last of the surviving Founders departed to celestial realms. Life expectancy tables for American newborns, as variously published by Fogel and Steckel for 1880 and 1890, bobble between 45.2 and 39.4 years. That represents a ten- to fifteen-year loss in life expectancy among a generation of American-born children when compared to the envied early-American advantage of fifty-six-year average life-spans from 1790 to 1800.

Economists and the multidisciplinary researchers of height, longevity, and standard of living do wrangle over methodology—and the methodologies are quite complicated. But what is clear is that explanations based on any single causative factor are downright silly given the multiple shifting forces in play: genetics, which play a 60 to 70 percent role in shaping adult height; the body effects of epidemic and childhood diseases; changing diets; the intensity of manual work in late childhood and again in early teen years; public water and sewer systems; environmental hazards; and access to medical care. The episodic timing of events that most impact a child's biological well-being are crucial to understand: birth to age one; disease to age five; nutrition and work at roughly ages ten to thirteen; and, looming largest, the mid- to late-teen growth spurts. If we look again at Old Robert's second son, Robert Jr., born 1827 and 5'4" tall, we would most want to know what his family circumstances were in his first year of life in 1828 to 1829, then during his first growth spurt at ages ten to thirteen in 1837 to 1840, and finally his last growth spurt in 1844 to 1847. We know that both the late 1820s and the late 1830s were depression years (remember those "hard times" tokens) and that the economic roller coaster of the 1840s was terrible for Old Robert's family. If Robert Jr. began heavy work at Oliphant's in the late 1830s when he was eleven or twelve and continued that hard work into his teen growth spurt between age fifteen (1842) and twenty (1847), that work could easily have robbed his adult height of several inches—as could an early childhood disease or his mother Hannah's inability to nurse him normally after four or five pregnancies between 1821 and 1828.

But what did those same factors mean to Old Robert Densmore's grandsons and great-grandsons in the workforce during the late 1800s? It meant that Robert Jr.'s sons, like John Robert, and John Robert's sons, such as Charles Percival, were shorter and died much younger—and much poorer—than their grandfathers. It also meant that his grandsons' wives had also begun to take on public work as washerwomen, piece-work seamstresses, midwives, and cleaning ladies. These and millions like them became the "company-town" and "coal-patch" folks who struggled through the 1870s to the 1920s in ways that utterly defied the Founders' definition of American happiness and well-being. The stress levels of "our family is living on the precipice of disaster" could have been stratospheric . . . and they were certainly corrosive.

Between 1890 and 1930 the majority of American wage workers simply were not living anything approaching a common vision of the Declaration's manifesto. Unacceptable living and working conditions *did* play a large role in deaths due to work accidents, cancer, black lung, drink, poor diet, poor housing, suicide, and other stress-related factors. The daily struggle and hard work in mines and forges, or scrubbing floors, laying railroad tracks, or selling newspapers in the cold of a snowy winter for a half-penny profit (as described in Marguerite Densmore Avera's handwritten memoir) make it utterly clear that no matter how hard they worked, they, their cousins, and neighbors in communities like the coal-patch village at Beeson's Works were somehow just another wave of the "left behind."

Glimmers of Hope

By 1940 native-born male heights finally surpassed the Founder's era of 5'8.2". Despite the Great Depression, President Roosevelt's proactive response to it was sufficient to keep the nation's biological statistics on an upward track. Thus life expectancy in 1940 had risen to about 62.9 years. It had taken the nation 140 years—five generations—to match, then to surpass, the height and longevity advantages enjoyed by the Founders and their neighbors' children.

Medical advances like penicillin, vaccines, quarantine laws, and better hospitals all played significant roles in those longevity gains. So did Roosevelt's Works Progress Administration, school lunches, and better water, sewer, and food processing. Bread became vitamin B fortified in the 1930s, reducing pellagra and pre-pellagra metabolic syndromes. Milk became vitamin D fortified. Even urban America's daily pasteurized milk deliveries both dramatically reduced scrofula and bovine tuberculosis and employed hundreds of thousands of milkmen and milk ladies, whose deliveries improved child health. But the debate over paying for things like public health and public education still rages on. A healthy, secure, and educated workforce requires good public schools—both academic and trade. Both public health and education are crucial efficiency and productivity investments. Untaxed profits illegally hidden in a Caribbean bank are not.

Twentieth-century Densmores and working-class Harts and Vandergrifts all began to win more battles as the age of Robber Barons faded. Those who did best invented or created. Brainwork began to trump high-calorie work. Ollie's son H. T. was the first in his family to make it to white-collar status, as commemorated by that iron presentation bar of 1897. By 1900 he lived a middle-class lifestyle and educated his children. But it was a brief ride, as he died at age forty-nine in 1912. His son, Benjamin, invented even more things and lived well until he was felled at age fifty. His female survivors struggled. Cousin Tom's parents scratched out high school and a nursing degree. They did not quite make it to undisputed middle-class statistics, but they came close, and their son Tom earned two university degrees and educated his sons, securing full-fledged "I worked my butt off" membership in the solid middle-class realm. The same is true of Sam's descendants now living in California:[6] higher education, strong work ethic, high-tech work, and highly educated children.

Among Old Robert's descendants we now have two full generations who have neither gone hungry for a medically significant period nor worked under stark nineteenth-century conditions. So, as an anthropologist, I was surprised at how often "hard" work and "smart" work came up in Densmore family conversations. I was equally surprised by the consistent focus on fundamental well-being, both their own and others'. These conversations, combined with letters and memoirs, revealed just how deeply that value system reflected the Founders' ideas that an American nation could lock in its status as "the best country for a poor man." That reality played an unheralded role in the Founders' drawn-out and highly improbable victory over England. The lived reality of the American Advantage—height, longevity, survival of children, food, decently paid work, and family self-sufficiency—was the Founders' winning formula. It continues to be the essence of our national heritage. That original formula was real and measurable. It is also in deep trouble as this is written.

The Twenty-First Century

If Benjamin Franklin and his close colleagues could travel among us today, they would tell us that we face the same fundamental problem they did when they put together the modest core of our nation—just how does one combine five or six different regional cultures, diverse language speakers, and distinct religions into a coherent, procedural whole, while bridging harsh, stubborn divides between rural and urban life and different races, into one functioning society? To answer that challenge, Franklin himself, then one of the western world's four of five most famed scientists, would undoubtedly tell us that we first need to reassess our realities, then address any failures.

Among "first-world" nations our rate of infant mortality currently puts us in twenty-seventh place,[7] even as competing nations continue to improve. In literacy we currently rank thirty-eighth.[8] Several small European nations have made significant educational outcome gains by awarding formal community roles and respect to their teachers. While those teachers' pay was enhanced a bit, the formal "respect" bonus was a winning factor in better outcomes.[9]

Do we still own the biological and quality-of-life advantages that launched us as a nation? No. In records published in 2016 and 2017,[10] a host of other developed nations—twenty-five of them—surpassed us in adult male height (see table 12). In that same year all but one European nation from which we once drew Colonial immigrants has bested our male average height of 5'9.2" by one to two and a half inches.[11] Worse yet, the heights of American-born children, static for several decades, have begun, ever so slightly, to decline since 2010. In recent decades Americans have gained no height, but they have gained about forty pounds of body weight. As a nation we are eating much more highly processed food than we did in earlier generations.

TABLE 12. All American Male Heights Compared to All European Males, 2016–2017[*]

Country	Height	Trend
United States	5'9.2"	declining slowly
UK/Scotland	5'10"	increasing
Wales	5'9.""	increasing
Switzerland	5'10"	rapidly increasing
Sweden	5'10"	increasing
Poland	5'10.5"	
Norway	5'10.5" to 5'11"	younger generations taller
Netherlands	5'11"	increasing
Italy	5'9.5"	stable
Ireland	5'10.5"	increasing
Germany	5'9" to 5'10.5"	younger generations taller
France	5'9"	increasing
Denmark	5'11.5"	increasing

[*] "Height Chart of Men and Women in Different Countries," https://www.disabled-world.com/calculators-charts/height-chart.php.

By 2015 our once-envied longevity advantage had also been erased, and it is now in decline. For three years in a row (from 2016 to 2018), American life expectancy at birth has declined—a brightly flashing danger sign of even more national problems to come. Suicide, an epidemic of opioid abuse centered on the Ohio River Valley, and increased stress over access to healthcare all play a role in this decline. In Franklin's post-revolution era, we reigned supreme with a life expectancy (for both sexes) at birth of fifty-six years, besting the United Kingdom by nearly twenty years and France by twenty-three. As this is written, our life expectancy (male and female combined) is about 78.7 years. But *every* European nation now offers a life expectancy of 81 to 83 years. How did we go from decades ahead in 1800 to three and four years behind two hundred years later?

Amazingly, our nation spends about 18 percent of our Gross Domestic Product—that is more than ten thousand dollars a year for each of us—on healthcare. This is about 40 percent more than our peer nations. Yet we are sicker, die younger, and are far more stressed out than our European peers. The lash of comparative information cuts deepest when one reviews international surveys to determine the "happiest" national populations: the winners are always countries like Denmark, Switzerland, Sweden, or Norway. We are not currently a "happy" nation. We die sooner, sicker, lonelier, more stressed out, and sadder than those in other "first world" nations that generate less per-capita wealth than we do—and we spend *twice* as much on healthcare as those countries. That is a harsh reality.

A recent series of contentious presidential and midterm elections make it clear that we are still as culturally conflicted and diverse as the Colonies our Founders wrestled when it comes to finding a compromise upon which a nation could move forward. The fundamental dynamics are different only in terms of scale—and technology—but well-being remains at the core of it. How do we know that? Despite wide pockets of rural and industrial collapse, a resurgence in white nationalism, and an even greater disparity in wealth than in Emperor Nero's Rome, there is surprising consensus. Recent opinion surveys tell us that access to healthcare, one that includes pre-existing conditions, is the current number-one priority among 62 percent of ordinary Americans. Analysis of voting patterns in the contentious presidential election of 2016, when a populist president was seated, also tells us clearly that American counties where "despair" deaths (drugs, alcohol, suicide, stress) contributed to county-wide death rates of 8 to 15 percent above the national average all voted *most* heavily for the perceived populist.[12] They apparently hoped to be rescued from their lived reality of contemporary America.

American Reality

As this is written, we need to acknowledge that the Robber Barons have returned. No, we don't award them noble titles—instead, we know them as CEOs, hedge-fund managers, bankers, and cabinet members to a current president. One percent of Americans own 51 percent of the nation's total wealth. The 1 percent pays a smaller percentage of their income as taxes than do everyday workers making twenty to fifty thousand dollars a year. These financial aristocrats are powerful. For them, the law is gently applied. They have become the predatory aristocracy that the Founders hoped to prevent. In the oft-repeated words of indicted New York landlord Leona Helmsley, "Only the little people pay taxes." She was, by the way, fairly honest about it. Currently, 40 percent of American households cannot cover a four-hundred- to five-hundred-dollar emergency. They are as much on the edge as were the iron and railroad workers of the 1870s and 1880s. And just where do middle-aged factory workers go when their assembly lines shut down forever?

These are the rhythms of America: well-being increases, as it did from the 1780s to the 1820s; then it ebbs as technology, population, and competition all increase. That brings us to the Civil War, when great, temporary profits and technological change nurtured both increased well-being and the founding of a predatory business class that would take the former away in short order. In that environment, both well-being and efficacy of the federal government took a hit.

Teddy Roosevelt, a populist favorite, yet a scion of great wealth, took office as president in 1901 after President McKinley's death. Inequality in wealth again rose rapidly until new federal income taxes in the 1920s slowed the widening gap. War, disease, immigration, and a Great Depression reset the nation into a more productive twentieth century. For much of that century, most workers left behind by technological changes found new and productive roles. But by the 1980s change overwhelmed new opportunity and left a large portion of America in the same circumstances as the once-legendary packhorse captains of the Allegheny Mountains. And here we are again—another populist president, the scion of wealth, and declining statistics of height and longevity.

The View from Chestnut Ridge

The sky, a deep, forbidding gray, rumbles uneasily as Old Robert's great-great-great- and great-great-great-great-grandchildren, cousins, and spouses gather at the forested ridgetop homestead, which was lovingly hand-built and crafted by James Klink and his wife, Connie (Densmore). The property lies about a thousand yards (as the crow flies) above the rock outcrop where George Washington and his party shot the French nobleman, Sieur de Jumonville, and triggered the French and Indian War.

Among those gathered are Klinks, Carrs, Frazees, Densmores, and others. Most everyone present has ancestors who appeared on the US Census of 1790 or 1800. Their ancestors, and millions like them, built nineteenth-century America. They are of this place: people without pretense but rich in skills. Sadly, they have become poor in hope.

As the wind rises, the rain comes in sheets, and I usher a fragile, old gentleman under the tent where the food is served. He is short, about 5'6", and pale. His oxygen tank is at hand. I guess him to be in his late seventies. He tells me of his son, who was an accountant—employed, but barely making it.

"He lost hope . . . I tried so hard to lift him up, but . . ." He averts his eyes. "Suicide. I prayed for more hope." He sighs. "In my generation, many of us remember going hungry, but we thought it would get better. It did in some ways . . . but not enough to last."

He was absolutely correct in his assessment, as recent publications make clear: in the statistical population district where we are standing near Uniontown, median annual income is about forty-two thousand dollars a year—about fifteen thousand dollars below the national median—and life expectancy is currently about seventy-two years—six years less than the national average.

It is eerie to look at the statistics. In Fayette County, population tract 2625—just miles away—annual median income is $45,724 and life expectancy is 78.2 years. In tract number 2628 near Fairchance, median income is $40,824 and life expectancy is only 72.5 years. But in tract number 2627.01, a dozen miles to the southeast, median income is $49,119 and life expectancy is over 80 years. It is sobering to realize that a combination of high school diplomas and $10,000 more or less in annual income can so dramatically shape the length and quality of an American citizen's life.

Virtually everyone at the family gathering, except H. Thomas Densmore and myself, live in this statistical shadow. Tom lives in Chadds Ford, Pennsylvania, an 82-year district where median annual income is about $129,000. I live in a population tract in Albuquerque, New Mexico, where life expectancy is about 79.8 years and median income is about $70,000.[13]

Atop historic Chestnut Ridge, three statistical well-beings meet in a lovely clearing beside Klink's Road: Tom Densmore's, mine, and that of our gathered kin. All that separates us are zip codes, education, and income. The things we have in common are DNA, value systems, and the fact that all of us support the aristocratic class now casting a rapidly lengthening shadow over the American vision of a "level playing field." The loss of that vision has already dramatically reduced the respect that skills and hard, smart work once received, which defined self-identity among the majority of ordinary Americans.

In spite of its substantial flaws, the American nation was forged in the *reality* of a taller, stronger, longer-lived, better-fed, and better-paid citizenry, as compared to Europe's home nations. As that reality faded between 1850 and 1900,[14] the idea of its restoration morphed into a powerful cultural ideal. Simply being "American" meant enjoying the nation's early biological and economic advantage. Thus, since 1780, in every era when both height and longevity declined and infant mortality rose, the nation became trapped in the politics of anger, hatred, and despair. No single factor ruled—it was the *combination* of biological and economic factors that created a toxic playing field. Beware the return of "despair deaths," "loss of hope," and the currently declining statistics of well-being . . . These factors **continue to** determine the nation's course.

APPENDIX

Methodology

The tables below display height data at the time of military enlistment, primarily during the War of 1812, among the Densmore, Hart, and Vandergrift families. Because of the inconsistency in recording height at the time of enlistment, several individuals were included in the tables who enlisted shortly after the War of 1812. The vast difference in age of enlistment for men who did fight in the War of 1812 means that the data above reflects the heights of several generations of Densmore, Hart, and Vandergrift men. The Densmores (also spelled *Dinsmore, Dunsmore,* and *Dunsman*) lived primarily in Pennsylvania and western New York; however, individuals from Massachusetts, Maine, and Vermont were included in this data set due to the lack of height data available from this period. Pennsylvania Densmores do appear in the enlistment rolls from the War of 1812, but none of their heights were recorded. The Harts had spread south into Pennsylvania and New Jersey by the time of the War of 1812, and these later locations are reflected in the corresponding data set. The Vandergrift family inhabited areas of Pennsylvania and northern Virginia at the time of the war—reflected in that data set as well.

TABLE A1. Male Heights

	Vandergrift	Hart	Densmore
Before 1830	5'9.6"	5'7.6"	5'7"–5'7.5"
Civil War	5'8.2" (b. 1826–1846)	5'6.53" (b. 1827–1847)	5'9.22" (b. 1827–1847)
World War I	5'8.71" (b. 1873–1891)	5'7.08" (b. 1880–1893)	5'9.1" (b. 1877–1888)

TABLE A2. Enlistment Heights of Densmore Men Before 1832

Name	Estimated Year of Birth	Height (inches)	Town/County (if available), State
William Dinsmore	1783	69	Augusta, ME
John Densmore	1789	68	Lunenberg, MA
John Densmore	1789	71	Hereshill, MA
Joel Dunsman	1795	69	Vermont
Camell Dinsmore*	1799	71	Homer, NY
Amos P Densmore*	1812	68.5	Conway, ME

Mean: 69.42
Median: 69
Mode: 69, 71
Range: 68–71 (3 inches)
Birth Year Range: 1783–1812
Standard Deviation: 1.28

TABLE A3. Enlistment Heights of Hart Men in the War of 1812

Name	Estimated Year of Birth	Height (Inches)	Town/County (if available), State
Joseph Hart	1777	69	PA
Daniel Hart	1778	66.5	Cumberland, PA
Theodorus Hart	1778	65.5	Dutchess Co., NY
Sawtell Hart	1779	69.5	Pittstown, NJ
James Hart	1784	68	Farmington Co., PA
Jacob Hart	1785	71	Monmouth, NJ?PA
Phillip Hart	1785	66	Butcher, PA
John Hart	1785	64	Nine Partners, NJ
Joseph Hart	1790	67	PA
Thomas Hart	1791	68	Blount Co., PA
William Hart	1792	69	Lewis, PA

Mean: 67.59
Median: 68
Mode: 68, 69
Range: 64–71 (7 inches)
Birth Year Range: 1777–1792
Standard Deviation: 2.02

TABLE A4. Enlistment Heights of Vandergrift Men Before 1820

Name	Estimated Year of Birth	Height (inches)	Town/County (if available), State
Aaron Andrew Vandergrift	1774	70	PA
Jacob Vandergrift	1785	73.25	Bucks Co., PA
Thomas Vandergrift	1789	71.5	PA
Abraham Vandergrift	1790	69.75	Botecourt Co., VA
Frederick Vandergrift	1791	68	PA
Jeremiah Vandergrift*	1792	67	Philadelphia, PA

Mean: 69.62
Median: 69.88
Mode: n/a
Range: 67–73.25 (6.25 inches)
Birth Year Range: 1774–1792
Standard Deviation: 2.27

* These men enlisted in the US Army between 1816 and 1832, following the Peace Establishment of May 17, 1815, that ended the War of 1812.

References

Maine State Archives, St. Augusta, Maine. *1435.* "Maine War of 1812 Records."
ancestry.com. *U.S. Army, Register of Enlistments, 1798–1914.* Online database. Provo, UT, 2007.

Methodology

The tables below display height data at the time of military enlistment during the Civil War among the Densmore, Hart, and Vandergrift families. While the pertinent Densmore/Dinsmore/Dunsmore families lived primarily in Pennsylvania and western New York in the decades preceding the Civil War, individuals from Ohio were also included due to the lack of height data available from this period.

TABLE A5. Enlistment Heights of Hart Men in the Civil War

Name	Estimated Year of Birth	Height (inches)	Town/County (if available), State
Charles Hart	1827	63	Montgomery Co., PA
William F. Hart	1834	67.5	Tioga Co., PA
John O. Hart	1841	71	Springfield, NJ
Henry Hart	1842	68	PA
John Hart	1844	66	Harrisburg, PA
Henry Hart	1845	66.75	Fayette Co., PA
Oliver L. Hart	1845	66	Pittsburgh, PA
Henry C. Hart	1846	63	Philadelphia, PA
Henry Hart	1847	67.5	Lancaster Co., PA

Mean: 66.53
Median: 67.5
Mode: 63, 67.5
Range: 63–71
Birth Year Range: 1827–1847
Standard Deviation: 2.49

TABLE A6. Enlistment Heights of Densmore Men in the Civil War

Name	Estimated Year of Birth	Height (inches)	Town/County (if available), State
Robert Densmore	1827	64	PA
Martin Densmore	1827	67	PA
Samuel S. Densmore	1832	70.25	NY
Jacob Densmore	1832	74	Northumberland Co., PA
Joseph Densmore	1834	69	NY/PA
Robert Dinsmore	1836	70.25	Philadelphia, PA
Robert G Dinsmore	1838	69.5	OH
Samuel Densmore	1839	68.5	PA
Andrew Dinsmore	1839	69	Phildelphia, PA
William Densmore	1840	71	NY
Harvey Dunsmore	1847	69	OH

Mean: 69.22
Median: 69
Mode: 69
Range: 64–74
Birth Year Range: 1827–1847
Standard Deviation: 2.47

TABLE A7. Enlistment Heights of Vandergrift Men in the Civil War

Name	Estimated Year of Birth	Height (inches)	Town/County (if available), State
Strecklin Vandegrift	1826	66	Philadelphia, PA
James C. Vandegrift	1827	69.75	Bucks Co., PA
Harrison Vandergrift	1840	70	Delaware
William Vandergrift	1842	70	Newcastle, DE
James Vandegrift	1842	64.5	Harrison Co., WV
James Vandegrift	1844	71	Delaware Co., PA
Henry S. Vandegrift	1845	67.5	Bucks Co., PA
Jesse Vandegrift	1846	71.25	Laurel Mountain, PA

Mean: 68.75
Median: 69.88
Mode: 70
Range: 64.5–71.25 (6.75 inches)
Birth Year Range: 1826–1846
Standard Deviation: 2.47

References

ancestry.com. *U.S. Army, Register of Enlistments, 1798–1914.* Online database. Provo, UT, 2007.

fold3.com. *Compiled Military Service Records of Volunteer Union Soldiers Belonging to Units Organized for Service from the State of West Virginia.* Online database. 2010.

Methodology

The tables above display height data at the time of military enlistment during World War I among the Densmore, Hart, and Vandergrift families. Because World War I draft cards merely characterize enlisted men's height as "short," "medium," or "tall," only heights for Hart and Vandergrift men who enlisted in the military either prior to or after World War I could be utilized in this sample. These disparities in military experience mean that the data above may come from different generations of each family, but the oldest and youngest Hart above are only separated by thirteen years, while the oldest and youngest Vandergrifts were born eighteen years apart.

TABLE A8. Enlistment Heights of Densmore Men in World War I

Name	Estimated Year of Birth	Height (inches)	Town/County (if available), State
Clarence Carey Dinsmore	1877	70	Parnassus, PA
John H. Densmore	1878	68	Fayette, PA
Owen O. Densmore	1878	65	Oswayo, PA
Archie Anson Densmore	1880	67	Oswayo, PA
George Elmer Densmore	1880	68	Spring Creek, PA
William W. Densmore	1881	68	Kittaning Armstrong, PA
Ray Densmore	1882	69	Erie, PA
Alex F. Dunsmore	1883	73	Morris Run, PA
John Morris Dunsmore	1886	72	Arnot, PA
Thurman Addison Dinsmore	1888	71	Greene, PA

Mean: 69.1
Median: 68.5
Mode: 68
Range: 65–73 (8 inches)
Birth Year Range: 1877–1888
Standard Deviation: 2.42

TABLE A9. Enlistment Heights of Hart Men in World War I

Name	Estimated Year of Birth	Height (inches)	Town/County (if available), State
William A. Hart	1880	67	NJ
Elwood J. Hart	1884	65.75	Adamstown, PA
John P. Hart	1884	65.75	Trenton, NJ
Martin A. Hart	1885	69	Scranton, PA
John L. Hart	1886	68.5	Pittsburgh, PA
Frank Hart	1889	65.75	Philadelphia, PA
George Hart	1889	64.25	Waterford, PA
Miles A. Hart	1889	68.5	Pittston, PA
John J. Hart	1891	68.5	PA
James S. Hart	1893	67.75	Harrisburg, PA

Mean: 67.08
Median: 67.38
Mode: 65.75
Range: 64.25–69 (4.75 inches)
Birth Year Range: 1880–1893
Standard Deviation: 1.62

TABLE A10. Enlistment Heights of Vandergrift Men in World War I

Name	Estimated Year of Birth	Height (inches)	Town/County (if available), State
Frederick B. Vande Grift	1873	70.25	Parry, NJ
William K. Vandergrift	1874	67	Oil City, PA
Howard F. Vande Grift	1876	69.25	Parry, NJ
Harry G. Vandegrift	1879	67	Wilmington, DE
Russell Green Vandergrift	1889	70	Philadelphia, PA
Walter Vandergrift	1890	71	Philadelphia, PA
Charles D. Vandergrift	1891	66.5	Jefferson, PA

Mean: 68.71
Median: 69.25
Mode: 67
Range: 66.5–71 (4.5 inches)
Birth Year Range: 1873–1891
Standard Deviation: 1.84

References

ancestry.com. *U.S., World War I Draft Registration Cards, 1917–1918*. Online database. Provo, UT, 2005.

ancestry.com. *U.S. Army, Register of Enlistments, 1798–1914*. Online database. Provo, UT, 2007.

The National Archives at St. Louis, St. Louis, Missouri. *World War II Draft Cards (Fourth Registration) for the State of New Jersey*. "Records of the Selective Service System, 1926–1975." Record Group Number 147. Series Number M1986.

NOTES

Preface

1. Fogel, *Escape from Hunger*.
2. See Floud et al., *Changing Body*.
3. Stuart, *Anasazi America*.

Chapter 1

1. Fogel, *Escape from Hunger*, 2, table 1.1 and 13, table 1.4.
2. The data published by scholars Michael R. Haines and Richard Steckel assert that the life expectancy of American-born women paralleled that of the men. See also Steckel, *History of the Standard of Living*, table 3.
3. Deming, *Science and Technology in World History*, vol. 4, *The Origin of Chemistry*, 23. See also Hitchcock et al., *Caring in Action*, vol. 1, *Community Health Nursing*.
4. Steckel, "Nutritional Status," 31–32.

Chapter 2

1. Now approximated by old US Route 40.
2. Many wagoners received about fifteen cents a day from their employers for board costs.
3. A one-half-gill cup is two ounces. Most locally distilled Pennsylvania rye whiskey of the period varied between 90 and 110 proof.
4. Richardson and Wilson, "Hannas Town and Charles Foreman," 157.
5. Early wagoners often wore their hair long, especially in winter, as protection from the cold.
6. "Pennsylvania Weather Records, 1644–1835."
7. "Work calories" in this work are in addition to basal metabolism / body maintenance of about sixty calories per hour for a man of Old Robert's height and body mass.
8. Searight, *Old Pike*, 206.
9. The traditional packhorse enterprises that emerged in the 1740s had long lobbied against road improvements. They could negotiate paths and shortcuts as narrow as three feet wide through the mountains, so they had long monopolized freight hauling west to the Ohio River. See Dunbar, *History of Travel in America*.
10. See Dietle and McKenzie, *In Search of the Turkey Foot Road*.
11. Innkeepers acted as bankers and receivers of notes of credit and bills of lading in that era.

12. *Peach leather* is peach puree pressed and dried to a leathery consistency—an instant carbohydrate-loaded energy boost when eaten. *Jerk* is jerky, usually either dried bear meat or venison. See Olsen, *Indian Blood*, 135.
13. Searight, *Old Pike*, 206; and Bruce, *National Road*, fig. 4.
14. In the later days of the National Road, 1815–1855, this became known as the "Long Stretch," the straightest part of the National Road in the Alleghenies.
15. The name of which has since been lost.
16. America's first "Continental Divide."
17. Schecter, *George Washington's America*, 23–24, 29, 36, 38–39, 45, 55.
18. Now Grantsville, Maryland.
19. Williams, "Samuel Vaughn's Journal."
20. This settlement would later grow and become Smithfield, Pennsylvania. Even later, in the heyday of the National Road, it would be renamed Somerfield. Its remains are now hidden under the lake created by damming the Youghiogheny in the 1900s.
21. Ellis, *History of Fayette County*, 609.
22. See Bailey, *Thomas Cresap*; and Gibson, *History of York County*, 602–4.
23. More about William and Henry follows.
24. "History of Trevor's General Store, Founded 1795," 18.

Chapter 3

1. They departed from the Arsenal at Harper's Ferry, Virginia, where the Shenandoah River empties into the Potomac, in late 1803.
2. Also in old records spelled *Dinsmore, Dunsmore,* and occasionally *Dunmore*.
3. In fair fall weather.
4. Seymour, *History of Travel in America*, 981.
5. This speed-up is a signature of the "Power Phase."
6. His tombstone indicates this birthdate, but he may have been older, as working men were not typically taxed until age twenty-one.
7. This portion of Lancaster County would later become Cumberland County.
8. England's King George III had issued a decree forbidding English settlement west of the first ridge of the Appalachian mountains to reduce tensions between settlers and Native Americans.
9. Federal court. His papers do not state his exact age or place of birth in Ireland.
10. German Township 1785–1834, vol. 1, 1785–1815; Fayette County Tax Rolls of 1797–1799; DGS film #1449309, digitized and available on Family Search online.
11. Fulling was an essential step in the manufacture of finished wool cloth.
12. DGS film #1449305, Dunbar Township 1799–1843, vol. 1, 1799–1815.
13. DGS film #1149303, Tax Roll, Bullskin Township, 1801–1849.
14. Ellis, *History of Fayette County*, 371.
15. Some sources claim the 1200s, but surnames were not yet common among ordinary folk.
16. The Borderland Scots spoke a Celtic-laced dialect of English, and their family structure was a bit more egalitarian than among the Highland clans.

17. Loyal to the English monarchy.
18. Bardon, *Plantation of Ulster*; and Baren, "Plantation of Ulster."
19. Leyburn, *Scotch-Irish*, 173.
20. This group might have included the Samuel Dinsmore who patented land in Lancaster County in 1751.
21. Kelly, *Graves are Walking*.
22. Longer in New England; shorter on the western frontier.
23. Fogel, *Escape from Hunger*, 2, Table 1.1.
24. The Portuguese may have come to Newfoundland on annual cod fishing forays even earlier. And, of course, there are the Viking promoters.
25. "Brief History of New Sweden."
26. Koot, "The WIC," 16.
27. Martin, *Treasure of the Land of Darkness*, 92–109.
28. Now the capital of the Dominican Republic.
29. Dunn, *Sugar and Slaves*, index and "Vital Statistics."
30. Some of the immigrants were British slaveholders from Bermuda.
31. "History: South Carolina's Connection to Barbados."
32. Bissell, *Monongahela*, 51.
33. Sipe, *Indian Wars of Pennsylvania*.
34. Fulling mills produced woolen cloth.
35. Nowadays, young urban families expect that infrastructure and are seeking safe, "walking" neighborhoods, coffee shops, cafes, cultural venues, and good public transportation.
36. Stewart and Bowen, "History of Wages in the United States."
37. Egle, "Virginia Claims to Land in Western Pennsylvania."

Chapter 4

1. See the listed tax rolls in Nixon, "Descendants of Robert Densmore."
2. Now Pennsylvania Route 30.
3. In contrast, Braddock's southern route required many bridges, which were often swept away by the region's recurring floods.
4. Atop the second huge hill, my great-great-great-grandmother, Elizabeth (Ryland) Goldsboro, was born in the spring of 1815.
5. Pronounced "Yock."
6. Smith, *Grant*, 23–24.
7. Miller and Maxwell, *History of West Virginia*, 42–43.
8. Miller and Maxwell, *History of West Virginia*, 232.
9. Miller and Maxwell, *History of West Virginia*, 43.
10. Darlington, "Pennsylvania Weather Records," 118–19.
11. I capitalize the Point, as it was one of the most fabled and strategically important places in Colonial America. Many died merely to possess it: Native American, French, British, Colonial military men, and Virginians. The Point *was* America's first icon of a fabled "West."

12. Ohio became a state in late spring of 1803. In anticipation of statehood, a rush of new migrants headed west to squat and claim the best farmland. A number of these settlers were the sons and daughters of those who settled western Pennsylvania in the 1780s and 1790s. They, in turn, were often the sons and daughters of those who had settled central Pennsylvania from 1750 through the 1770s.
13. Lebergott, "Wage Trends," 457, 462, 471–72, 482.
14. The area around Kutztown to the northeast was another.
15. "Close up" meant able to land neck or base of ear shots at thirty to forty yards with the .44 caliber.
16. The last breeding group of eastern woodland bison were hunted out in what is now Greenbrier County, West Virginia, by a party of aristocratic Virginia sports hunters in 1816 (https://wildwill.net/blog/2015/07/12/the-history-of-bison-in-southeastern-north-america/-2; and Belue, *Long Hunt*). A sole surviving male straggler was killed at Valley Head / Randolph County, West Virginia, in 1825.
17. Schecter, *George Washington's America*.
18. "Colonial and Early National Transportation, 1700–1800," www.roads.maryland.gov/OPPEN/II-Colon.pdf.
19. Scharf, *History of Western Maryland*, 995–98; and Searight, *Old Pike*.
20. Now West Virginia, as of 1862–1863.
21. The role of Virginia's meddling and mayhem in western Pennsylvania is superbly documented in the 1983 doctoral dissertation by James Patrick McClure entitled, "The Ends of the American Earth: Pittsburgh and the Upper Ohio Valley to 1795." It is eye-opening research.
22. Evans, "Blast from the Past."
23. See the Pennsylvania State University's Jstor.com for online records of Colonial Pennsylvania weather.
24. Post, *Last Great Subsistence Crisis*.
25. Tryon, *Household Manufactures in the United States*, 250–52.

Chapter 5

1. Woodard, *American Nations*.
2. Egle, "Virginia Claims to Land," 488–95.
3. His agent/agitator in chief in western Pennsylvania was the brash and brutal John Connolly.
4. McClure, "Ends of the American Earth," 246–301.
5. Such climactic variability often leads to "over cropping" to generate a surplus that is stored for the times when weather prevents a harvest. The net effect is to farm more acreage and try to get shorter season crops into the mix. One of these crops is buckwheat, a seed crop high in protein that was, until the 1950s, a food staple in the region where Old Robert once lived.
6. Nixon, "Descendants of Robert Densmore."
7. Nixon, "Descendants of Robert Densmore."
8. US Census 1810 Fayette County, Pennsylvania; and Morgan, "1810 United States Census of Fayette County, Pennsylvania."

9. In the 1840s and 1850s several waves of cholera were "on the rivers," terrorizing Pittsburgh and other Ohio River cities, killing thousands.

10. 1850 US Census of North Huntingdon Township, Westmoreland County, Pennsylvania, US Bureau of Census, Washington, DC, 75, line 36.

11. *Registration of Deaths*, Westmoreland County, Pennsylvania, August 24, Roll of 1854, 6, #199.

12. Nixon, "Descendants of Robert Densmore," 1.

13. Sage, " Sheetz Rifle."

14. Tryon, *Household Manufactures in the United States*, 239.

15. The first nail-cutting machine, invented by Joseph Perkins in 1790, signaled the end of home manufacture of crude, hand-forged nails on the frontier.

16. Now in West Virginia.

17. By the roughest eyeball review of local tax rolls, the average acreage fell into broad categories: house and garden lands of 2–20 acres, or farms of 60–160 acres.

18. My use of male-gendered terminology is not a resistance to modern political correctness; it is used because, legally and culturally, America was a male-focused world at that time.

19. Fogel, *Escape from Hunger*, 17, Fig. 1.2.

20. Fogel, *Escape from Hunger*, 2, Fig. 1.1.

21. Fogel, *Escape from Hunger*, 2,Table 1.1.

22. Fogel, *Escape from Hunger*, 2, Table 1.1; and 13, Table 1.4.

23. Fogel, *Escape from Hunger*, 17.

24. Stuart, *Anasazi America*.

25. Fogel, *Escape from Hunger*, 11, Table 1.3.

26. Fogel, *Escape from Hunger*, 11, Table 1.3.

27. That is, cost relative to wages.

28. The long haul from Philadelphia to Pittsburgh on an 1805 wagon route (along Forbes Road) ran about five dollars per hundred weight, or about a week's wages on the frontier; this was a discount to shorter routes, but it was still costly enough to encourage local manufacturing.

29. Feedyourhorse.com, accessed 6/22/2016.

30. Richardson and Wilson, "Hannas Town and Charles Foreman," 156–57.

Chapter 6

1. If one is Native American, the label "infamy" is more accurate.

2. Others enlisted at Carlisle, Pennsylvania.

3. Now known as Fort Covington.

4. US Censuses of 1800 and 1810 (Washington, DC: US Bureau of Census).

5. Ellis, *History of Fayette County*, 366–68.

6. Ellis, *History of Fayette County*, 399.

7. Also spelled *Mountz*.

8. Also known as Mud Island.

9. Tragically, John Gibson's son Joshua drowned on February 24, 1808, in the river next to the forge.

10. Ellis, *History of Fayette County*, 239–40.
11. Ellis, *History of Fayette County*, 400.
12. Ellis, *History of Fayette County*, 371; and 1819–1820 Tax Rolls, Bullskin Township, Fayette County, Pennsylvania.
13. Ellis, *History of Fayette County*, 399.
14. Ellis, *History of Fayette County*, 399.
15. It is possible Hannah and Nathaniel were twins.
16. Densmore, "Historical Sketch of Robert Dunsmore."
17. The US Census was taken mid-summer in 1820.
18. Ellis, *History of Fayette County*, 399.
19. 400-calorie-an-hour jobs.
20. Nixon, "Descendants of Robert Densmore."
21. Ellis, *History of Fayette County*, 399.
22. A 400- to 450-calorie- an- hour job.
23. Nixon, "Descendants of Robert Densmore."
24. Later Confluence, Pennsylvania, mapped by George Washington in the 1750s.
25. Ellis, *History of Fayette County*, 371–77.
26. Ellis, *History of Fayette County*, 384.
27. Ellis, *History of Fayette County*, 385–87.
28. A Spanish silver "bit" was cut from the pillar coin into eight twelve-and-a-half-cent wedges. "Two bits" was a quarter, "four bits" was fifty cents, and so on. Seaboard bankers possessed American minted dimes, quarters, and half dollars. Western small businessmen, however, had barter and bits.
29. Richardson and Wilson, "Hannas Town and Charles Foreman," 179–80, and plate 14.
30. Ten-hour workdays were the norm, as were six-day workweeks.
31. Stewart and Bowen, "History of Wages in the United States," 21.
32. Officers often received twice that amount.
33. Ellis, *History of Fayette County*, 368.
34. The cash pensions of that time were trifling.
35. The large families guaranteed both rapid natural population increase and an increasing supply of local labor.

Chapter 7

1. Elsie may have confused William with a younger son or nephew. That Timothy Glenn was a cabinetmaker and lay preacher born in 1820, whose shop was in Pittsburgh in the 1850s. He was buried in Connellsville.
2. Ellis, *History of Fayette County*, 582–83.
3. The hunt for a deed has been meticulous but unsuccessful.
4. A manufactured Virginia adventure with ugly consequences.
5. See Egle, "Virginia Claims to Land," 494–95.
6. Recall it was the *French* and Indian Wars, then later the southern Cherokee, Creek, and Seminole Wars in Spanish-held lands.
7. The University of Pennsylvania's Wharton School of Finance is named for descendants of this Wharton family.

NOTES TO PAGES 61–74   355

8. McClure, "Ends of the American Earth," chapters 4 and 5.
9. That is why most wills of the era designate who inherited a set of bedclothes.
10. Iron stoves were long advocated by Benjamin Franklin.
11. This is in contrast to the legal value of surviving adult sons to protect a widowed mother and their father's estates among the Virginia and Maryland plantation owners.
12. The Appalachian core includes a piece of southern New York, big chunks of Pennsylvania, a piece of western Maryland, West Virginia, eastern Kentucky, and east Tennessee.
13. Wagoners were the truckers of their day, and they are the reason modern truckers are represented by the Teamsters Union.
14. As opposed to farmers, cabinetmakers, blacksmiths, saddlers, and so on, whose shops were often their living quarters.
15. Western Pennsylvania, western Maryland, West Virginia, and the west bank of the Ohio River settlements.
16. Built in 1818, the arched stone bridge across the Youghiogheny at Smithfield/Somerfield, aka "The Great Crossing," was a true wonder (see illustration).
17. Lemon, "Household Consumption in eighteenth century America," 68.
18. Native Americans were the least likely to be counted or censused.
19. Those who reached age five could expect to live into their late sixties or seventies.
20. Maine, Vermont, Connecticut, New Hampshire, Massachusetts, and northern New York.
21. Cold winters often blunted disease cycles.
22. Demographers focus on female/male sex ratios as a computational factor in assessing a community's reproductive potential.
23. Rutman and Rutman, "Now-Wives and Sons-in-Law."
24. Main, *Tobacco Colony*, 91–92.
25. Walsh, "Till Death Do Us Part," 127–28.
26. Husbands often bequeathed specific plots of land, as well as tools or furnishings, to one child or another.
27. Hardening meant a pick head was successively heated and quenched in water to harden its surface.
28. Hand-digging surface coal in the middle of a Pennsylvania winter was virtually impossible. The coal would freeze solid, and snow was a recurring impediment.
29. Fayette County Tax Lists for Robert Dunsmore, 1807 and 1821, Bullskin Township. Archives of Fayette County, Pennsylvania, Courthouse, Uniontown, Pennsylvania.
30. Ellis, *History of Fayette County*.
31. The "Sixteen Tons a Day" of song and legend applied to coal miners shoveling coal blasted out by black powder.
32. Wright, *Historical Review*.
33. Now West Virginia.

Chapter 8

1. The presidential elections of 1824 and 1828 broke the Virginia and Massachusetts hold on the presidency, and Hamilton's Federalism was contested by a wave of gritty Jacksonian populism.

2. Elizabeth's gravestone in Maple Grove Cemetery, Fairchance, states her birth as "11-19-1826." Other sources indicate 1827. She may have been born in what is now West Virginia.
3. In 1823 Bullskin Township was separated from Connellsville proper.
4. Jordan, *Genealogical and Personal History*, 582–87.
5. The cemeteries there are censused, and many early iron men and barge carpenters' graves are represented.
6. The southern bank, at that location.
7. Ellis, *History of Fayette County*, 584.
8. Margo, "Wages and Prices," 193.
9. Coin collectors know this era through the "Hard Times" tokens privately minted as a surrogate for scarce federal coinage.
10. In general, girls got a bit more schooling than boys in that era, as most boys went to work at age twelve or thirteen.
11. Sixth Census of the United States, Fayette County, Pennsylvania, Georges Township rolls. US Census Bureau.
12. The household cow was not listed or taxed on tax rolls after 1840 in Fairchance.
13. Stuart, *Anasazi America*.
14. Gillman and Gillman, *Perspectives in Human Malnutrition*, 20, 440–42.
15. Ellis, *History of Fayette County*, 585.
16. Along Old Robert's 1800 route.
17. We know it now as Fort Necessity National Historic site, well worth the visit.
18. Steckel, *History of the Standard of Living*, table 3.
19. "Goldsberrys" is actually Goldsboro, whose family will come into play later in the family saga.
20. Andrew's mother was an Oliphant.
21. Journal of the 19th US Congress, Session 2, 1827; and Journal of the 19th US Congress, Session 1, p. 160, National Archives.
22. Pennsylvania's counties gradually emerged from a geographic food chain of sorts. Western Chester County became both York and Lancaster Counties; parts of Lancaster became Cumberland County; and part of Cumberland County later became Franklin County.
23. In the Gettysburg region.
24. US Revolutionary War Pensions (for Robert Densmore), 1801–1815 and 1818–1872, table 718 ("1801 to 1815" and "1818 to 1872"); and 11 ("Invalid Pensions 1843 to 1856") (Harrisburg, PA: Pennsylvania State Archives).
25. There is indirect evidence that Old Robert or his older children also purchased a lot or two in Fairchance near the iron works.
26. Searight, *Old Pike*, 247–48.
27. Nehemiah was born on January 11, 1822, according to his tombstone in Cheat Neck, Monongalia County, West Virginia.
28. Also spelled *Raeger*, of Pennsylvania German stock.
29. "Linsey-woolsey" fabric; the bottom fringe decoration had become less common.
30. Cumberland to Wheeling on the National Pike/Road.
31. Oliphant only used mules on his company wagons. Matched replacement teams

were stationed about every fifteen or twenty miles. The mules could haul greater weight per pound of body weight, were surer-footed, and cost a bit less to feed—more efficient than horses.

32. Fogel, *Escape from Hunger*.
33. Steckel, *History of the Standard of Living*, table 2.
34. Twelve years later, western Virginia will become West Virginia, as its citizens refuse to follow eastern Virginia slave society into secession.
35. Elizabeth Densmore Warman listed her birthplace as Virginia or West Virginia on every census through 1900. Her birthplace is a likely clue to Old Robert's whereabouts during part of the mid-1820s.
36. Shadrack was actually seventy-one.
37. Fanshaw, "Twelfth Annual Report of the American Tract Society," 42–43.
38. Ellis, *History of Fayette County*, 399.
39. Locally pronounced "Galla Police."
40. Both in their twenties, Nehemiah and Robert Jr. were already working their way up to their later coveted Roller and Puddler statuses.
41. There are two burials that cannot currently be explained. First is a William R. Dunsmore gravestone with no date. William was the name of the Densmore fuller/clothier in Connellsville about 1813 associated with the Mary Densmore who was widowed about that time. His middle initial "R" probably stands for "Robert." Next to William's grave lies Thomas Joseph Dunsmore. His gravestone reads, "10-21-1831, 11 years." This could mean he was bn in 1820 and lived eleven years, or that he was born in 1831 and died eleven years later in 1842. The *Dunsmore* spelling is a strong indication that these two males are related to Old Robert. Was William R. Old Robert's father? Uncle? Elder brother? And who was the eleven-year-old? A son of Old Robert's and Hannah's born in the birth gap between Robert Jr. (1828) and Rachel (1835)? Ah, that tangle of enigma and uncertainty yet again.
42. Miller, *Some Fayette County Pennsylvania Cemeteries*, 25, 36, 127.
43. John Kennedy Oliphant, born 1826.

Chapter 9

1. Kelly, *Graves are Walking*.
2. Nixon, "Descendants of Robert Densmore," 3–7.
3. twelve thousand pounds of freight are sometimes claimed, but these were extraordinary and required six huge draft horses.
4. Brushed out for the packhorse captains.
5. Data on those defunct stagelines' total costs are simply not available.
6. Forrest, "The National Pike."
7. The Devil, in Nat's world, was also known as "Old Scratch." Alleged sightings of his popping up out of the earth unexpectedly were a theme in regional folklore and superstition.
8. Well-documented examples of this phenomenon occurred with numbing regularity during the Great Railroad Strikes in 1877, as discussed later.

9. Fogel, *Time on the Cross*.
10. Merritt, *Masterless Men*.
11. A term coined in 1912 by *The Russian* in reference to a prosperous but classless society.
12. Sources vary on height. At his death (age sixty-seven), when measured for his coffin, he was 6'3.5". Still others list him as 6'2".
13. Fogel, *Escape from Hunger*, 17, fig. 1.2.
14. Steckel, *History of the Standard of Living*, table 3.
15. Steckel, *History of the Standard of Living*, table 2.
16. Fogel, *Escape from Hunger*, tables 1.1 and 2.
17. In addition to daily basal metabolism and body maintenance.
18. Fogel, *Escape from Hunger*, fig. 1.2, tables 1.3 and 1.5.
19. Wells, *United States Report of Special Commissioner of Revenue*, 118–24.
20. Fogel,*Escape from Hunger*, tables 1.1 and 2.
21. One can lose height, however, during advanced years as gravity and tissue or bone loss robs one of an inch or so.
22. "History of Wages from Colonial Times to 1928: Bulletin of the US Bureau of Labor Statistics" (Washington, DC: 1929), no. 604, table D-1, 225–26.
23. Gallman and Wallis, *American Economic Growth*, 12–18; and Margo, "Wages and Prices," 173–216.
24. Walsh, "Consumer Behavior," 224–26, 251.
25. Steckel, *History of the Standard of Living*, table 3.
26. Haines, "Vital Statistics."
27. Steckel, *History of the Standard of Living in the United States*, tables 2 and 3.

Chapter 10

1. Hannah was named for her grandmother, Hannah Glenn Dunsmore, who died about a year before she was conceived. Mary was almost certainly named for the widow Mary Dunsmore of Connellsville, who died about the same time.
2. Elizabeth was named for Nathaniel's sister, and Hannah for her grandmother. Mary was named for Susan (Rager)'s mother.
3. The original lot, acquired from Mr. Jordan, was 2.75 acres.
4. See listed tax rolls in Nixon, "Descendants of Robert Densmore."
5. Could be "Anc." Either way, a fistula is somewhat disabling, especially an anal one.
6. *Pennsylvania, War of 1812 Pensions, 1866–1879*. Archives, Harrisburg, Pennsylvania.
7. The Pension IDs are W029351 and WC 22796.
8. From Shadrack's headstone in Tent Presbyterian Cemetery.
9. "Connellstown" is actually Connellsville.
10. Born about 1839, George W. O'Brien died at age fifty-nine—much younger than his father, just like others of his generation—near Fairchance in 1897.
11. Ancestry.com cites November 22, 1865. Another online source cites November 10, 1866. We may have some sympathetically backdated papers here to support an annuity for Eliza.

12. The area surrounds modern Clarksburg, West Virginia.
13. Moreover, the newspaper article spells Shadrack's surname as *O'Brian*.
14. In 1862 he would also be found in George H. Thurston's Pittsburgh city directory, compiled in late 1861.
15. It is now known as Southside, or the Southside Flats.
16. Lincoln, *Political Debates*; and Lincoln and Douglas, *Political Debates*.
17. The five years' birth spacing between daughter Elizabeth and her two younger siblings suggests the possibility of a failed pregnancy or infant death. This makes me wonder if the cholera epidemics of the 1850s in Pittsburgh and "on the rivers" played a role.
18. Before his puddling days, he was a catcher.
19. Info provided by my cousin Tom H. T. Densmore, from Robert Jr.'s Civil War enlistment papers.
20. Dew, *Apostles of Disunion*.
21. Steckel, *Standard of Living in the United States*, tables 2 and 3.
22. Floud et al., *Changing Body*, 335; and Fogel et al, "Secular Changes."

Chapter 11

1. *Journal of the Senate of Indiana During the Thirty-Ninth Session of the General Assembly* (Indianapolis, IN: J. Bingham: 1857), 473; originally published in *The South Carolina Gazette*, 1856, as entered in the Senate's records.
2. *Journal of the Senate of Indiana During the Thirty-Ninth Session of the General Assembly*, 472.
3. The legacy of those enduring political tactics of minority rule became crystal clear again the night President Obama took the Oath of Office in 2009, when Senator McConnell gathered his minions to plan an obstructive political response.
4. Defeated Confederate General Nathan Bedford Forrest helped to found what became the Ku Klux Klan.
5. Young, "From North to Natchez."
6. Turner, "The Abolition of Slavery in Pennsylvania," 135, 137–38.
7. Prigg vs. Pennsylvania, 41, US 539, United States Supreme Court, Washington, DC, March 1, 1842.
8. They could not sit on juries.
9. Smith, "End of Black Voting Rights," 279–99.
10. There was a large number of free black voters in southern York County adjacent to the Maryland border, and a large black vote in Philadelphia by the 1830s.
11. Trotter and Smith, *African Americans in Pennsylvania*; and *The Constitution of the Commonwealth of Pennsylvania, as Amended by the Convention of One Thousand Eight-Hundred and Thirty Seven-Thirty Eight*, Article III, Section I, Harrisburg, PA, 1838.
12. See historical marker HM2A in Baker Alley, Uniontown, Pennsylvania.
13. "The African-American Experience in Southwestern Pennsylvania" (For Necessity National Battlefield: National Park Service, 2009).
14. Old Robert's wagon trip of 1800 followed the main route of this branch of the Underground Railroad. Humanitarians along the National Road maintained safe havens

in Cumberland, Uniontown, Brownsville, and Washington, Pennsylvania. Many black runaways made it safely to New England and Canada.

15. Records for Union and Confederate soldiers include all spelling variations of the name: *Densmore, Dinsmore, Dunsmore,* and *Dunsmire.*
16. Military records accessed from www.ancestry.com.
17. Records accessed conflict in places. This is an estimate.
18. See appendix tables.
19. Robert E. Lee, born 1807, was 5'10½" tall, more than two inches above the national average for his era of birth. The iconic "Stonewall Jackson," born 1824 near what is now Clarksburg, West Virginia, was 6'0" tall. Jefferson Davis was over 6'0" tall.
20. Warren, *Legacy of the Civil War.*
21. Anchor Nail and Tack was in East Birmingham.
22. There are multiple sources on the 82nd Pennsylvania's history. A simple one to access is www.pacivilwar.com/regiment/82nd.html. For Samuel, the years 1863–1864 apply.
23. Dyer, *Compendium of the War of Rebellion.*
24. www.ancestry.com.
25. For which Ollie's granddaughter Elsie E. Densmore was an important informant.
26. *Genealogical and Personal History of Western Pennsylvania*, vol. 2, 1915.
27. Death Certificate 18066, Weatherfield Township, Trumbull County, Ohio, March 20, 1915, Ohio Bureau of Vital Statistics.
28. Since entries in Thurston's Directory of Pittsburgh were prepared months prior to publication, Sam was likely in Pittsburgh in the spring of 1864.
29. Spelled *Goldsborough* or *Goldsberry* up to the 1860s, and mainly spelled *Goldsboro* thereafter, possibly to distance themselves from the powerful slave-owning Goldsborough family of Maryland's Eastern Shore.
30. Thomas Goldsboro had been an iron worker and forgeman at furnaces in Maryland, West Virginia, and other parts of Pennsylvania prior to moving to Fairchance in the 1840s.
31. Ryland, *Sylvester Ryland Handbook.*
32. According to notes written by H. Thomas Densmore that were given to the author.
33. All of Elsie Densmore's mistaken names and assumptions are overshadowed by this taking of dictation from her grandparents. Since Pennsylvania did not systematically keep marriage, birth, or death records until 1906, this handwritten scrap is factually precious.
34. 1863 Muster Roll, Col. James B. Fry, Washington, signed by M. Foster, Pittsburgh. Accessed on www.ancestry.com.
35. Ellis, *History of Fayette County*, 221.
36. My cousin Tom recounts that, in the years after the war, Robert Jr. would load his model 1861 Colt percussion pistol with black powder and cardboard wads to celebrate Christmas morning. Banging away, barrel toward the skies, spitting sparks and hooting from the front of his modest house in Fairchance, he would signal his children to descend to the parlor, where they would find their gifts waiting by a pine tree festooned with homemade decorations and real candles.

37. Grand Army of the Republic.
38. Thurston, *Directory of Pittsburgh and Allegheny Cities*, 73.
39. According to the recollection of Elsie Densmore in the summer of 1961.
40. Some online sources claim 1850 as her birth year, based on a US Census record. It is unlikely she bore little Robert just five weeks after her fourteenth birthday. In that era very few females of that age had reached menarche. Age at first birth was typically between age seventeen and eighteen.
41. St. Paul's Episcopal church registry of baptisms, p. 124, accessed through ancestry.com. Kittanning is straight up the Allegheny River, another right turn at the Point, just across the Monongahela from where Ollie and Sam were living on Perry near Carson.

Chapter 12

1. Kussart, *Allegheny River*, 175, 178.
2. Including Heinz.
3. Also variously spelled *Vander Grist*, *Van de Grist*, or *Griff* in early records of the 1500s and 1600s.
4. Translates as "Paul, Leonard's son."
5. Schmidt, *Innocence Abroad*, 250–51.
6. Deglar, *Neither Black nor White*, 226.
7. Van der Zee and Van der Zee, *Sweet and Alien Land*, 111.
8. Old Dutch for "captain."
9. Wilson, *Memorial History of New York*, 211.
10. Wilson, *Memorial History of New York*, 211.
11. Curaçao simply could not feed more people. It had been in a famine situation since 1643.
12. Van der Zee and Van der Zee, *Sweet and Alien Land*, 153–54.
13. Van der Zee and Van der Zee, *Sweet and Alien Land*, 163.
14. Van der Zee and Van der Zee, *Sweet and Alien Land*, 172.
15. Jameson, *Narratives of New Netherland*.
16. The "spotted cow."
17. Think Blackwater security force "contractors" in Afghanistan and Iraq during the early twenty-first century.
18. Or *Zwöll*, the "swallow."
19. *Calendar of History of Dutch Manuscripts* (Albany: New York State Archive), archive.org/stream/calendarofhistyoonewy#page/328.
20. Other Council members also signed.
21. James Stuart, soon to become King James II.
22. Van der Zee and Van der Zee, *Sweet and Alien Land*, 475.
23. Multiple authors, "Paulus Leendertz Vandergrift (c. 1613–1670)," www.geni.com/people/Paulus6000000004206729763.
24. Rink, *Holland on the Hudson*, 190.
25. Rink, *Holland on the Hudson*, 200.
26. The Dutch briefly recaptured New York in 1667.

27. Haifeli, *New Netherland*, 222.
28. About eight miles north of downtown Philadelphia.
29. Recall that Scots immigration was spurred by their lost battle with the English at Culloden, 1746.
30. Isaac Monsanto was an early relative of the later Monsanto agribusiness and chemical combine.
31. Hammond, *John Hart*.
32. An online search of its membership records and its occasional membership booklets easily confirms this.
33. Beer bottling, according to New Amsterdam records in Albany, New York.
34. Vandergrift, Jacob, 1810 US Census of Pike Run Division, Washington County, Pennsylvania, 82, line 2, reel M252-57, censused by G&W Baird, © US Gen Web, 2001.
35. Daughters of the American Revolution; Sons of the American Revolution; Descendants of the Signers of the Declaration of Independence.
36. http://www.findagrave.com/cgi-bin/fg.cgi?page=gr&GSln=Vandergrift.
37. Nearly all early American maritime law focused on the Ohio River. Wheeling and Pittsburgh were home to those practicing, writing, and adjudicating that growing body of law.
38. Bissell, *Monongahela*.
39. Dixon and Eberly, *Index to Seamen's Protection Certificate Applications*, 139.
40. Variously spelled *Nole, Nolls, Knows, Knowls*, and *Knowles*, the name is a legacy of an old Dutch family matriarch from New Amsterdam, later Neshaminy Creek.
41. Gould, *Fifty Years on the Mississippi*, 648.
42. The *Beaver* was probably built in Beaver, Pennsylvania, its super structure supervised by Scudder Hart, Jesse the Innkeeper's son, cousin of Mary Hart Vandergrift.
43. Batchelor, *Incidents of My Life*, 46.
44. Way, *Way's Packet Directory*, 616.
45. Early on captains handled most of the onboard and dockside transactions.
46. There were also many shifting shoals and sandbars out there "on the rivers."
47. Kussart, *Allegheny River*, 240.
48. Batchelor, *Incidents of My Life*, 46.
49. Kussart, *Allegheny River*, 260.
50. "B" means "below."
51. Harris, *Harris's General Business Directory*, 53.
52. In Old Birmingham, as opposed to newer East Birmingham. "Water" means Water Street, fronting the west bank of the Monongahela.
53. Way, *Way's Packet Directory*.
54. Way and Rutter, *Way's Steam Towboat Directory*.
55. These were located by a local archivist, Amy Arner of Arner Research.
56. The *Red Fox* was co-owned by uncle John and elder brother Jacob Jay Vandergrift.
57. Kussart, *Allegheny River*, 238.
58. Benjamin Franklin Vandergrift, born July 29, 1833, in Pittsburgh, died November 5, 1862.
59. Examples are trade tariffs and sanctions, federal tax policy sanctions against

singles versus married couples, regressive tax schemes, special tax benefits to large businesses that small competitors cannot claim, and so on.

60. Though the *Red Fox* only had a hold capacity of a modest seventy-eight tons, it was built for pushing or pulling, with a powerful engine.

61. Way, *Way's Guide to Towboats & Tugboats*, entry #2526.

62. Bissell, *Monongahela*.

63. A phenomenal sum at that time when a very highly skilled worker made about $1,400 a year and an average worker made $700–800 a year.

64. Most likely at Pringle's Yard.

65. *Harper's Weekly, A Journal of Civilization*, June 20, 1863.

66. Its first president was Captain John Vandergrift's son-in-law, C. W. Batchelor.

67. The Densmore brothers had family roots in Rochester, New York.

68. "Biographies: Crawford County," http://rootsweb.com/pacrawfo/Biographies/amos, accessed 5/31/2010.

69. Small lake boats had sometimes used waterproof bins below the waterline to transport grain or whiskey. It was likely that one of J. J.'s partners, Daniel Bushnell, had contributed to the concept of an entire "tank boat."

70. "Oil 150's Pioneering Petroleum Series," www.oil150.com/densmore.htm.

71. It is likely that Old Robert's son Sam was also involved in the mechanics of the bulk boats and/or the first railroad tank cars, as he was also a mechanical genius. One note in Derrick's oil reports mentions the Densmore group as working on these projects. It is also possible Sam worked at times in William Knowles's engine shop in East Birmingham.

72. Van der Zee and Van der Zee, *Sweet and Alien Land*, 337.

73. Thurston, *Directory of Pittsburgh and Allegheny Cities*, 135.

74. The name Scudder is striking evidence of a deep connection to Jesse Hart, eldest son of Signer John Hart, and his brother, Scudder, whose son Scudder was a coach builder. Scudder Vandergrift would have been the go-to guy in the family combine when it came to complex woodwork for boat cabins and the like.

75. This address is just a block and a half from Ollie Densmore's in the same directory.

76. In 1863 or 1864 William Knowles Vandergrift listed himself as an "Engineer" in Thurston's Directory of Pittsburgh. In that time and place, that meant engine build and repair. Diffenbacher, *J. F. Diffenbacher's Directory of Pittsburgh and Allegheny Cities, 1864/1865*.

77. Samuel was born September 15, 1836, in East Port, Maine, according to his Pennsylvania Death Certificate, #74672, dated August 2, 1908.

78. By 1865 and 1866 Ollie was listed as "Densmore" or "Dinsmore" in Pittsburgh and Birmingham city directories, as was his brother Sam. In that era *Dinsmore* was the most common spelling of their surname.

79. Henry Thomas Densmore, universally identified as "Harry Thomas," was named for Ollie's father-in-law coal digger Thomas Goldsboro. H. T. would become Elsie's father.

80. Still locatable today by following the old Brownsville Road that runs to the countryside south-by-southeast of Birmingham's core.

81. Like those at McKeesport up the Monongahela, Lawrenceville up the Allegheny, and Homestead.

82. Kleinberg, *In the Shadow of the Mills*.
83. Its population in 1850 was 46,601; in 1870 it was 139,500.
84. www.wqed.org/education/units/wpahist/pop_growth.html, accessed 10/15/2016.
85. It was later changed to Birmingham; even later, between 1885 and 1890, it was changed again simply to South Side.
86. Demographic History of the United States, https://en.wikipedia.org/wiki/Demographic_history_of_the_United_States, accessed 6/25/16.
87. Knowles, *Mastering Iron*, 73–74.

Chapter 13

1. Kleinberg, *In the Shadow of the Mills*, 45.
2. Kleinberg, *In the Shadow of the Mills*, 28–29, 94–97.
3. If you have ancestors who worked in these mills, this book is worth a reading.
4. Kleinberg, *In the Shadow of the Mills*, 51.
5. For their service, they received wages averaging forty to fifty cents a day. Among them numbered many orphans of iron worker fathers. Few of the boys were in school.
6. Steckel, *History of the Standard of Living*, table 3.
7. Winter ice packs on the rivers or dramatic spring or mid-fall floods remained facts of life, just as in Old Robert's time.
8. See directories of the National Iron and Steel Institute, published in Philadelphia.
9. Ingham, *Making Iron and Steel*, 146.
10. Ingham, *Making Iron and Steel*, 193–95.
11. His exact first work date is unknown. It is estimated from the birth of his second child, per Elsie Densmore's list made around 1905.
12. He could easily have been running a nailing machine or sorting stacks of unused plate or helping reline a furnace with firebrick.
13. William Knowles Vandergrift lived at Joseph Street, one block west and one block south.
14. The list dates from about 1905 when Elsie was about seventeen years old.
15. American Iron and Steel Association, "Directory to the Iron and Steel Works," 247.
16. Ingham, *Making Iron and Steel*, 205–7.
17. All these borders between the three states were subject to legal battles in the late 1700s.
18. The Turkeyfoot settlement of earlier chapters.
19. Most of Selbysport, an early iron-manufacturing village, is now under water from the dammed-up Youghiogheny River.
20. Olsen, *Indian Blood*, 36–42, 113, 116.
21. On the outskirts of what is now Harper's Ferry National Monument.
22. Tuberculosis.
23. Often called "swamp fever" in that era.
24. From low blood sugar.
25. Her father's brother, Robert, was the proprietor.
26. See sutler tax records, 1862–1865 and 1867–1868, Fayette County.

27. Diffenbacher, *J. F. Diffenbacher's Directory of Pittsburgh and Allegheny Cities, 1869/1870*.

28. Jennie had inherited some of that farmland.

29. This estimate assumes a few weeks of layoff, when Anchor closed for refitting and repairs.

30. By my estimate this is enough to buy a house and lot in Fairchance, or a lot only in East Birmingham.

31. Grandmother Elsie spoke of it as the source of her father H. T.'s weekly family budget logs.

32. William was the mysterious "Uncle Will" of the stories from my childhood. He was probably named for the William Densmore who disappeared from Connellsville records in 1812 or 1813.

33. The house was on the large lot previously acquired from Mr. Jordan and was likely enhanced by Ollie between 1870 and 1872.

34. Ninth Census of the United States, Pennsylvania, Allegheny County (US Census Bureau, Washington, DC, 1870). Available at census.gov.

35. These are cousin Tom's paternal great, great-grandparents.

36. US Census of 1870, Fayette County, Pennsylvania, Georges Township.

37. Ancestry.com caught the error after I first found this entry in 2010, correcting the listing in two stages: (1) Nicolas Warman; then (2) Nehemiah Warman.

38. Ninth Census of the United States, Pennsylvania, Allegheny County (US Census Bureau, Washington, DC, 1870).

39. Thurston, *Directory of Pittsburgh and Allegheny Cities, 1869–1870*.

40. Jordan, *Genealogical and Personal History*.

41. Later renamed Chess, Cooke & Co.

42. 1864 is the year Ollie bought some land from Mr. Jordan in Fairchance.

43. Thurston, *Allegheny County's Hundred Years*, 20.

44. Ellis, *History of Fayette County*, 521.

45. Ellis, *History of Fayette County*, 238.

46. Sons Samuel and Ethebert were said to be present.

47. A cheap cigar, formally a Conestoga cigar, had risen from two cents to two for a nickel. Millions had been made in the early days of the 1820s and 1830s and were transported from Philadelphia, Baltimore, or, later, Pittsburgh in Conestoga wagons on the National Road.

48. Fairchance Centennial History Committee, *Fairchance Through the Years*.

49. Hoover, "Retail Prices After 1850," 150, 153, 164, 172.

50. ExplorePAhistory.com/hmarker. Text with historic marker labeled "Densmore Tank Cars" in Venango County, Highway US-8, south of Titusville.

51. Kussart, *Allegheny River*, 249.

52. *Derrick's Handbook of Petroleum*, 320–24, 327–31.

53. US Census of Venango County, Pennsylvania, Venango Township, p. 31, censused August 29, 1870, family numbers 285 and 286.

54. Born July 5, 1804, she had actually celebrated her sixty-sixth birthday the month before. Her husband, William, born in 1805, is actually sixty-five.

55. As spelled on the census. Various censuses spelled the surname *Vandergrift*, *Van de Grift*, or *Vandergriff*.
56. He later moved to Jamestown, New York.
57. Thurston, *Directory of Pittsburgh and Allegheny Cities, 1869–1870*.
58. The one universally known as Captain John Vandergrift.
59. Lewis often captained or clerked on one or another steamboat where family shares were owned.
60. Thurston, *Directory of Pittsburgh and Allegheny Cities, 1869–1870*.
61. West of the Mississippi.
62. The hangers from which pans and Dutch ovens were suspended over the fireplace.
63. Hogeland, *Whiskey Rebellion*, 97–103.
64. Faust, *Mothers of Invention*.
65. Faust, *Mothers of Invention*.
66. The Red Cross formed from these efforts.
67. "North Carolina's Voting Restrictions Struck Down as Racist," *The New York Times*, July 29, 2016.
68. Many Northern POW camps were not much better than the average Southern ones with regard to disease and diet. But the outright barbarism of places like Andersonville stood out.
69. Hoover, "Retail Prices After 1850," table 2, 143.
70. Mitchell's Index, appendix E, 186.
71. There were breaks for the fires in 1864 and 1866.
72. Ollie's wages include two long turns a month.
73. Wells, *United States Report of Special Commissioner of Revenue*, 118–24.
74. Given conflicting census records mentioned earlier, she likely lived longer. Granddaughter Elsie Densmore might have listed 1867 instead of 1869.
75. Also known as a puddler.
76. Wells, *United States Report of Special Commissioner of Revenue*, 118–24.
77. Robert's full name was Robert Densmore Warman.
78. Sometimes the US Census transcriptions are wondrously inaccurate.
79. Wells, *United States Report of Special Commissioner of Revenue*.
80. The Ninth Census of the United States, Pennsylvania, Fayette County, Georges Township (US Census Bureau, Washington, DC, 1870).

Chapter 14

1. The Texas Education Agency's textbook commission has recently edited school history textbooks to downplay Jefferson and elevate Madison. Their edits also downplay the Civil War as generated primarily by slavery. So egregious and dishonest are the recent revisions of history that one textbook publisher, McGraw Hill, publicly apologized in 2015.
2. Blackmon, *Slavery by Another Name*.
3. This counting trick also left generations of Americans erroneously believing that blacks were formally declared as three-fifths of a person. It was much more complicated than that.

4. The residual effect of that compromise still expresses itself in every national election's real-world results. The long-term effects of this Constitutional bartering have been dramatically compounded by 240 years of migration, immigration, and population increase.

5. https://www.statistica.com/statistics/184968/US-health-expenditure-as-percent-ofgdp-since1960/.

6. Fogel, *Without Consent or Contract*.

7. Import of slaves from overseas was federally outlawed in 1808. Thus ownership of slave-born children became an increasingly important factor in the Southern plantation economy.

8. Most Pittsburgh boats accepted all paying passengers.

9. See descriptions in Batchelor, *Incidents of my Life*.

10. Way, *Way's Packet Directory*; and Way, *Way's Steam Towboat Directory*.

11. Dried beans were sold in units of one-quart measures. The 1860–1861 price was six and a half cents. The 1866–1867 price was thirteen cents.

12. Wells, *United States Report of Special Commissioner of Revenue*, 118–24.

13. Fogel, *Escape from Hunger*, 11, table 1.3.

14. Steckel, *History of the Standard of Living*, tables 2 and 3.

15. Steckel, *History of the Standard of Living*, table 3.

16. Steckel, *History of the Standard of Living*, table 4.

17. Fogel, *Escape from Hunger*, 11, table 1.3.

18. Steckel, *History of the Standard of Living*, table 4.

19. "The Great Chicago Fire and Web of Memory," https://www.greatchicagofire.org/, n.d.

20. *The Great Fires of 1871*, www.glenallenweather.com/historylinks/1871/ChicagoFire.pdf, n.d.

21. As noted, the KKK Act was enacted in response.

22. For those who lost a job or a house in the US economic meltdown of 2008, the word "derivative" will ring a bell.

23. Kussart, *Allegheny River*, 214.

24. "Jacob J. Vandergrift (1827–1899)," Pennsylvania Historical and Museum Marker, Oil City, Pennsylvania.

25. Kussart, *Allegheny River*, 217–18.

26. Recall that in the 1650s, Paulus had warehouse, beer, bottling, farmland, and coastal freighting among his New Amsterdam enterprises.

27. He is identified as occupying a Mr. Murphy's farm, which was noted as his residence in Kittanning's St. Paul's Church records.

28. Some boilers also formed the molten ball, a puddler's job.

29. As opposed to cast iron.

30. Ninth Census of the US, June 1870, Armstrong County, Manor Township, Pennsylvania.

31. Political correctness in naming did not figure in much during that era. Sam was the treasurer called "Keeper of Wampum" for the Wichacoma Tribe, No. 242, Improved Order of Red Men, in 1881.

32. Ellis, *History of Fayette County*, 38.
33. Ellis, *History of Fayette County*, 520–21.
34. His modest gravestone stills lies to the right of his parents in Tent Cemetery.
35. The prevailing party in the South and contested border states like Missouri. The Republicans, party of Lincoln, dominated the populous in the Northeast and upper Midwest.
36. Remember, our democracy is mediated by the representative Electoral College. Our direct votes guide the process but do not fully control its outcome.
37. Steckel and Prince, "Tallest in the World."
38. Bellesiles, *1877*, 43–44.
39. Bellesiles, *1877*, 45.
40. Of South Carolina, Louisiana, and Florida.
41. Michael Bellesiles's discussion of all these dynamics in *1877: America's Year of Living Violently*, as well as his supporting sources, are worth reading, especially pages 23–51.
42. Bellesiles, *1877*, 113.
43. Thurston, *Directory of Pittsburgh and Allegheny Cities, 1876–1877*, 601.
44. Special US Civil War tax rolls from 1863 to 1865.
45. Kleinberg, *In the Shadow of the Mills*.
46. This most often fell to state law—much of it legislated a century or more before America had only three million citizens.
47. Kleinberg, *In the Shadow of the Mills*, 30, table 5.
48. Kleinberg, *In the Shadow of the Mills*.
49. Bellesiles, *1877*, 144–46.
50. And unreported perjured testimony at those trials.
51. Bellesiles, *1877*, 142.
52. Dividends.
53. The fireman was a 4,500- to 5,000-calorie-a-day job.
54. Bellesiles, *1877*, 146.
55. Steckel, *History of the Standard of Living*, table 3.
56. Some historical sources give July 14, but the telegrams' warnings of labor unrest are all dated the July 16 or later.
57. Author Bellesiles notes that on the day before July 15, B&O President Garrett's board of directors signed off on a 10 percent dividend for shareholders as business was good.
58. It is unfathomable that this businessman thought he had judicial powers. These "deputies" were legally nothing more than hired muscle.
59. Ironically, in that Berkeley militia were several of signer John Hart's other descendants.
60. He had three sisters; his father, George, was a son of Jacob Vandergrift and Mary Hart Vandergrift.
61. Poisal was, in fact, the commander of the militia company, previously an officer in the Confederate army.
62. "B&O Railroad Strike of 1877," *Statesman*, July 24, 1877, Martinsburg, Pennsylvania. www.wvculture.org/history/labor/bandostrike01.html.

63. Ida was born in 1856 near Harrisburg, Cumberland County, Pennsylvania. She would never remarry after William's death. She lived with her parents until they died. Ida died in Harrisburg at the age of sixty-nine on May 19, 1926. Her address was 2216 Green Street. Two blocks from the Susquehanna, that house is still a private residence. Her son, William George Vandergrift, died near Harrisburg in 1941.

64. West Virginia death index for William Vandergriff, July 28, 1877, FHL film #831271.

Chapter 15

1. Telegram sent by Pennsylvania Adjutant General James Latta to Major General, James Beaver, National Guard of Pennsylvania, July 20, 1877 (Pennsylvania historical marker, 1D: 1-A-1C1).

2. Armed with Gatling guns and Springfield rifles, these troops were called out by US President Rutherford B. Hayes, who owed political debts to Thomas Scott, president of the Pennsylvania Railroad.

3. Kleinfield, *Savage Order*, 364.

4. As told by Ollie to his granddaughter Elsie in the summer of 1905. Retold to me in the summer of 1960.

5. Online historical notes, http://explorepahistory.com/hmarker.php?marker-id=1-A-1C1.

6. This .38 caliber rim fire ammunition has not been available for nearly a century.

7. Especially in the smaller, less socially stratified cities and industrial towns.

8. Many are believed to have hidden their wounds to avoid repercussions.

9. The Great Western Gun Company was founded in 1866 by J. H. Johnston, a native of Franklin County, Pennsylvania.

10. The long business cycles, sometimes called Kondratieff's waves, run roughly every forty to fifty years. The shorter cycles more frequently referred to run about nine to twelve years apart. Economies tend to expand and contract rhythmically.

11. Fogel, *Escape from Hunger*, 17–19.

12. Fogel, *Escape from Hunger*, 2, table 1.1; and Steckel, *History of the Standard of Living*, table 2.

13. Steckel, *History of the Standard of Living*, table 2.

14. See figure XX. Founded in 1865 in Allegheny County across the Allegheny River, north of downtown Pittsburgh.

Chapter 16

1. Thurston, *Directory of Pittsburgh and Allegheny Cities, 1876–1877*, 173.

2. SS = South Side.

3. Thurston, *Directory of Pittsburgh and Allegheny County, 1876–1877*, 170.

4. The Anchor works changed names a number of times as partners came and went. In iron and steel magazines, it is identified as "Anchor," since it was a brand name. On period maps and legal documents, however, it is most often found as "Chess, Smythe & Co." or "Chess, Cooke & Co." for the owners and partners.

5. Thurston, *Directory of Pittsburgh and Allegheny County, 1879*, 188.
6. Listed on the map as Grum instead of Grimm, 2114 Sidney is now gone, replaced by the concrete complex called Sidney Square.
7. Tenth Census of the United States, Pittsburgh, Allegheny County, Pennsylvania (Washington, DC: Bureau of the Census, 1880).
8. Both maps are available from the Historic Pittsburgh Collection online.
9. This is known from my personal conversation with H. T.'s daughter, Elsie Densmore, approximately July 15, 1961.
10. In the 1860s that railway ended on the bank of the Monongahela at a large coal tipple. In the 1860s and 1870s barges loaded there and carried coal to Cincinnati, St. Louis, and New Orleans.
11. Now designated "Fox Way."
12. The Large brand of Monongahela rye whiskey dates to between 1820 and 1830, when Jonathan Large of Fayette County increased production to brand and sell it regionally. Gone were the days of Hamilton's whiskey tax, which had been imposed on small distillers like Henry "He Distills" Densmore of the 1798 Census in Dunbar Township, Fayette County.
13. Elsie's lists contain a minor discrepancy. An old transcription on the back of an envelope from Ellen's tombstone, now gone from Tent Cemetery, emerged from her trunks full of papers. Her death was October 21, 1881. In 1905 Elsie had listed her death as October 24. That was likely her burial date.
14. By 1880 Joseph had moved north of Pittsburgh to Pine Township with his second wife, the widow of a Captain Fetzpatrick, and his younger children. However, he came to town often and stayed with his son at #70 Joseph Street.
15. That company was first incorporated in Oil City, Pennsylvania, as Vandergrift and Sowers Co. Andrew Sowers had been a large grocer in Birmingham.
16. Diffenbacher, *Diffenbacher's Directory of Pittsburgh and Allegheny Cities, 1883/1884*, 791 and 979.
17. A = Allegheny City.
18. S. H. is Scudder Hart Vandergrift mentioned in earlier chapters.
19. Two of the younger Vandergrift rivermen had moved down the Ohio to Cincinnati and Vincennes, Indiana.
20. Steckel, *History of the Standard of Living*, table 3.
21. Steckel, *History of the Standard of Living*.
22. Blackmon, *Slavery by Another Name*.
23. "Alabama Town Agrees in Settlement to Stop Operating Debtors Prison," Southern Poverty Law Center, March 14, 2017, www.splcenter.org/.../alabam-town; and Bryce Covert (ed.), "Debtors' Prisons Are Back. This Is the Fight to Get Rid of Them," Think Progress, September 23, 2015, www.thinkprogress.org/debtors-prisons-are-back.
24. Kleinberg, *In the Shadow of the Mills*, 27–40.
25. Kleinberg, *In the Shadow of the Mills*, 27–40.
26. Kleinberg, *In the Shadow of the Mills*, 27–40.
27. Jordan, *Genealogical and Personal History*, 620–22.
28. By late 1895 or early 1896, Ollie had "rented" 2101 to his oldest son, H. T. His

younger son William "rented" the bunkhouse and tap room. Details of what went on there are unknown.

29. www.calorielab.com/burned/?mo=se&year=11&ti=occupational&wt.
30. Twenty-four workdays at 10.8 hours per day and two long shifts at 12.5 hours each.
31. Fires, strikes, lockouts, and repairs all intruded.
32. Gladwell, *Outliers*.
33. Washing, eating, dressing, etc.
34. An average of three manufacturing jobs: sheet-metal working, machine tooler, and welder.
35. The four brothers were Robert, James, William, and Samuel.
36. *History of Mercer County*, 157.
37. Most of the Glenns were either Presbyterian or Methodist—the family produced several Methodist ministers—but Jennie, due to her mother's preference, was Episcopalian.
38. Fidelio became "Fidelah," written as it was spoken, in many Kittanning records.
39. www.jbending.org/uk/stats3.htm, accessed 12/28/2016.
40. Other references based on birth cohorts yield even lower expectations due to childhood disease and death.
41. Iron ore and coal.
42. Thurston, *Thurston's Directory of Pittsburgh and Allegheny Cities, 1869–1870*.
43. Anchor Nail and Tack had a long history. See Thurston, *Allegheny County's Hundred Years*.
44. H. Thomas Densmore, pers. comm., 2013.
45. Densmore, *Payroll and Account Book*.
46. Stewart and Bowen, "History of Wages in the United States," 241–43.
47. Tenth Census of the United States, Pennsylvania, Fayette County, Georges Township (US Census Bureau, Washington, DC, 1880).
48. Information for the directory was compiled in late 1884.
49. Hoover, "Retail Prices after 1850," 153.
50. Henry's surname is consistently spelled *Roudolph* in Ollie's logs, and it is alternatively spelled *Rudulph* or *Rudolph* in city directories.
51. Also spelled *Grimm*. Peter Grim is likely a member of the family who owned the boardinghouse where Ollie once bunked.
52. The log entry is hard to read here, as the pencil marks are fading. *Hankempf* is also rendered as *Hencamp* and various other spellings.
53. This is Will Densmore, unnamed in the log.
54. Older West Birmingham was originally known as "Germantown" due to its core population of German and Prussian tradesmen in the early 1800s.
55. Fitch, *Steel Workers*, 91–93.
56. Thurston, *Allegheny County's Hundred Years*, 148.
57. Racketeering in Interstate Commerce.
58. The Homestead Strikes.
59. Thurston, *Allegheny County's Hundred Years*, 146.
60. Davis, *Iron Puddler*.
61. Steckel, *History of the Standard of Living*, table 3.

Chapter 17

1. Immigrant proportion of union members grew quickly in the late 1880s to the early 1900s.
2. Steckel, *History of the Standard of Living*, table 2.
3. Diffenbacher, *Diffenbacher's Directory of Pittsburgh and Allegheny Cities, 1890/1891*.
4. Sophia largely raised my mother, Avis Elsie Densmore, until her mid-teens. Always a warm presence, Sophia often spoke of her memories and feelings to Avis.
5. Knowles, *Mastering Iron*, 40.
6. "The Homestead Strike," in Foner, *American Labor Songs*, 243.
7. US Census of 1880 for Sidney Street, Historic Pittsburgh.
8. The pay differential also acknowledged the roller's traditional responsibility to reliably bring a high-functioning crew onto the manufacturing floor. Rain, sub-zero Pittsburgh weather, train strikes, etc. were the roller's problem—not management's.
9. Anthropology term for "in-laws."
10. Wolff, *Lockout*.
11. Serrin, *Homestead*, 12–13, 73–82.
12. Stephanie Johnson, "Battle of the Monongahela: Homestead Steel, 1892," pabook2.libraries.psu.edu/palitmap/Homestead.html, accessed 2/15/2017.
13. Treason is when one aids a *foreign* power while engaged in declared conflict with one's own nation.
14. It had been nearly $6 in 1865.
15. There is no way to know if he attended two or three roll trains, or more. This is oral history, and I have no logbooks. The presentation roll-stamped steel bar given him by his crew when he became shipping clerk is dated 1897. It is as good as any other supporting "document."
16. 1893 or 1894.
17. Punitive work schedules of 364 days a year, with Christmas as a holiday, did not allow men to vote. Legal cases based on that reality grew in number.
18. Fayette County, Pennsylvania *Deed Book*, Vol. 29 (Fayette County Courthouse, Uniontown, Pennsylvania), 652.
19. Remember that Ollie was partly raised in Nehemiah and Elizabeth's home even before his enfeebled father died in 1855.
20. Fayette County, Pennsylvania *Deed Book*, Vol. 82, 249.
21. The same teenaged Robert Shanbarger who Ollie had put on his crew at Anchor.
22. Fayette County, Pennsylvania *Deed Book*, Vol. 47, 135.
23. Likely near Harper's Ferry, where an earlier Thomas Goldsberry, who had hosted George Washington, patented land in 1756.
24. Knowledge about family planning was both more sophisticated and available.
25. H. T.'s annotated, two-volume copy of Edward Gibbon's epic *Decline and Fall of the Roman Empire* provided my own initiation into Roman history and elegant prose sixty odd years after he penciled in his neat marginal notes.
26. Over at the Tube Works, Will likely updated H. T. about efficiencies of metal-tube manufacture and use for sewers, as opposed to fired clay pipe, which crushed easily under the weight of wagons and horse-drawn trolleys.

27. Once Oliphant's, and since had been much modified.
28. Stewart and Bowen, "History of Wages in the United States," 238–51.
29. Carr, Wilson, Price, Goldsboro, Artis, Warman, Sullivan, Shanabarger, and Pastorius are among the extended family surnames.
30. The cartridges it fired were either 22 short or 22 long. The long rifle had not yet been manufactured when the rifle was purchased.
31. The table restored by my cousin Tom.
32. Nat's rifle, purchased from Rossels in Connellsville, was almost certainly made by gunmaker John White, who worked in Fayette County between 1832 and 1842.
33. Fayette County, Pennsylvania *Deed Book*, Vol. 20, 173.
34. Above the saloon in the bunkhouse.
35. The "Roller" remained his prized work identity, his brickyard notwithstanding.
36. At 302 Miller Street.
37. Sixth US Census of 1850, Armstrong County, Manor Township, Pennsylvania, lists Jennie as age three. The Seventh US Census of 1860, Armstrong County, Manor Township, lists Amanda J. as age thirteen.
38. Also spelled *Grimm's*, an old family in both Fayette and Allegheny Counties.
39. Armstrong County Deed book images, supplied by Alice Densmore, 1892, Kittanning, Pennsylvania.
40. St. Paul's Episcopal Church records, Kittanning, "Burials" section, 312–16.
41. James Glenn was a son of one of the founding Glenn brothers, William Glenn of Connellsville, and Hannah Glenn Densmore's father was either a cousin or uncle of James. As noted earlier, he may have been Hannah's twin.
42. Steckel and Prince, "Tallest in the World."
43. Pees, "Early Bulk Boats."
44. Within sight of Drake's original well.
45. Godcharles, "Scholes, Inventor of First Common Typewriter," 7.
46. A number of interested inventors and industrial historians referred to it as the "Glidden and Densmore" typewriter, anyway.
47. Gazette of the US Patent Office, Washington, DC, editions of 1892, 1893, and 1894.
48. One can go online and view his drawings and descriptions at the US Patent Office by entering the patent number.

Chapter 18

1. And reproductive behaviors.
2. H. T. Densmore, pers. comm., as recorded from Williams Funeral Home (Uniontown, PA) records, January 10, 2017.
3. Urban high school standards were higher then, compared to now. Most high school teachers had a Master's degree, and in big cities like Pittsburgh and Philadelphia, a number held Doctorates.
4. Neé Hoffman.
5. In 1909 the Kanawha Dock Company where Sam worked was superseded by new management and a new corporate structure. This likely played a role in Sam's retirement,

as William F. Smith, the new manager, was not part of Kanawha's original management team.

6. Callahan, *History of West Virginia*, 332–33.
7. Another conversation with Grandmother Elsie in the summer I painted her house.
8. Pennsylvania Department of Vital Statistics, Samuel Wheaton, Death Certificate #74672, 1908.
9. Densmore, Benjamin V., Application to the SAR, 1912.
10. Findagrave #93129691, Sarah Ann Wheaton.
11. *Gazette-Mail*, Charleston, West Virginia, Sunday, October 24, 1974, 91.
12. Bruner and Carr, *Panic of 1907*.
13. Tucker, "Panic of 1907."
14. Named for his former steamboat, which, as the USS *Conestoga*, had famously run the Confederate cannonade at Vicksburg.
15. *Pittsburgh Post-Gazette*, December 30, 1899, 4.
16. *Pittsburgh Press*, January 2, 1900, 7.
17. Born in South Side Pittsburgh on October 31, 1866 or 1867. John married Mary Sturgeon in Point Pleasant on December 30, 1904. The marriage did not last.
18. From family letters.
19. H. T.'s sudden and shocking death in 1912 had triggered a deep urge on the part of bereaved Sophia and daughter Elsie to document H. T.'s vanishing family line. They researched their roots, applied for membership in the Daughters of the American Revolution (DAR) and the Descendants of the Signers of the Declaration of Independence (DSDI), and enrolled son Ben in the Sons of the American Revolution (SAR). It is as if they were trying to reestablish a family and commemorate it in order to soften their loss of the smart and affable H. T.
20. Jordan, *Genealogical and Personal History*, 260.
21. Mary Haun, pers. comm., August 26, 2016.
22. Death Certificate #18066, No. 27, State of Ohio Bureau of Vital Statistics, March 20, 1915.
23. The obituary is a photocopy of original newspaper text inherited by Paul H. Densmore, but it is not clear whether it was published in Kittanning, Pennsylvania. or in Jamestown, New York, where Sam was well-known. An important but imperfectly documented source.
24. Copy of photo owned by Paul Densmore.
25. Daughter of Civil War Veteran William T. O'Sullivan of Preston County, West Virginia. He served in the 6th West Virginia Cavalry (Union).
26. Preston and Haines, *Fatal Years*.
27. Letter from H. Thomas Densmore, 9/12/16, in possession of the author.
28. Excerpt of handwritten narrative authored by Bertha Densmore Dean, Robert Jr.'s granddaughter, who died in 1990 in Uniontown. Narrative in possession of cousin Tom Densmore.
29. John Robert Densmore, Death Certificate #70904, Reg. #453, Fayette, North Union.

30. Letter from H. T. Densmore, 9/12/16, in possession of the author.
31. The suspended coal dust acts like gunpowder, and the methane is the volatile accelerant. It takes just one spark and a mineshaft is transformed into a giant cannon barrel as a wall of flame and exploding gas flash-sears everything in its path.
32. "Twenty Fifth Annual Report of the Controller of Fayette, County, Pa," *The Connellsville Daily Courier*, January 11, 1936, 16.
33. H. T. Densmore, pers. comm., November 11, 2016.
34. Kenneth S. Densmore, US Army enlistment document, February 3, 1942; and Harold William Densmore, US Air Force enlistment document, March 3, 1939.
35. Fogel, *Escape from Hunger*, 60–61, 65.
36. Fogel, *Escape from Hunger*, 60–61, 114–15.
37. Mother Lenora was a nurse.
38. H. T. Densmore, pers. comm., December 3, 2016.
39. Marguerite Densmore Avera, handwritten narrative, 1978 (a photocopied and plastic bound edition is in possession of the author and H. T. Densmore).
40. James McGregor was the son of James K. McGregor and Elizabeth Densmore; he was one of Sam Densmore's grandsons.
41. James H. McGregor, Death Certificate #100676, Reg. #8066, 1923.
42. Marguerite Densmore Avera, handwritten narrative, 1978.
43. That is why commercial bread has been fortified with vitamin B since the 1940s.
44. Main, *Tobacco Colony*, 202.
45. Its causes were still not fully understood when Marguerite was a child. Many of the occupants of the Allegheny County Insane Asylum were not truly "insane" in the modern diagnostic scheme of things—they suffered from thiamine deficiency, which a month or two of meat, eggs, and fresh vegetables would have cured.
46. Quoted punctuation and spelling is as Marguerite rendered it. Things, even verbs, she capitalized conveyed *her* emphasis.
47. *The Morning Herald*, Uniontown, Pennsylvania, January 10, 1933, 11.
48. H. T. Densmore, letter to the author, September 12, 2016.
49. Sixteenth Census of the United States, Pennsylvania, Fayette County, Uniontown (US Census Bureau, Washington, DC, 1940).
50. J. J. Vandergrift was a shareholder in the original company in the 1890s.
51. H. T. Densmore, letter to the author, September 12, 2016.
52. As recounted to me by John Moody Stuart Sr.
53. H. T. Densmore, letter to the author, September 12, 2016.
54. Darraghs, Harts, and Vandergrifts.
55. Trial drawings of it were found in a file signed by Ben with folios of later industrial drawings.
56. Ben did have a lady friend at this time, and he had talked to his parents; he was confused about the idea of marriage, not certain that he was ready to be tied down.
57. He left hundreds of photographs to both of them, most dating to between 1900 and 1930. To this day, boxes of never-printed glass plates remain as he left them.
58. H. T. Densmore, Death Certificate, August 6, 1912, File #80397, Register # 5489, Bureau of Vital Statistics, Commonwealth of Pennsylvania.

59. Elsie's own words as she reminisced during my "summer of painting."
60. Legal reasons prevent his full name from being used in this book.
61. "Record of Deaths," *The Methodist Recorder*, Springfield, Ohio, May 22, 1920, 20.
62. Those included the Carr, Price, Artis, Warman, Shanabarger, and Goldsboro families.
63. *The Morning Herald*, Uniontown, Pennsylvania, May 7, 1920.
64. Y-DNA connects successive male generations, whose surnames are the standard in documentary evidence for much of American history. The exclusion of the females' genetic lines is a genuinely unfortunate side effect of historical obsession with male surnames.
65. Both males and females carry unbroken mitochondrial or mtDNA back to a statistical Eve, thus obscuring lineal family structure. Archaeological finds and DNA analysis in 2016 and 2017 strongly suggest that a modification of our understanding of early human subspecies will refine and complexify the story of our species' origins. Stay tuned!
66. The Rays never had their own children. They adored and protected Elsie and Natalie.
67. *The Morning Herald*, Uniontown, Pennsylvania, November 23, 1920, 6.
68. Sykes, *Seven Daughters of Eve*.
69. His left view.
70. Ollie left no will.
71. Elizabeth Goldsboro, Last Will and Testament, Fayette County, Index to Orphan's Court, Records A-D, 1783–1950, 12-1920.
72. *The Morning Herald*, Uniontown, Pennsylvania, November 12, 1921, 8.
73. Letter from William Densmore to Benjamin Densmore, March 23, 1921, in possession of the author.
74. April 19, 1906 letter from William Densmore to H.T. Densmore, in possession of author.
75. Letter from William Densmore to Benjamin Densmore, December 22, 1920, in possession of the author.
76. Draft card, Benjamin V. Densmore, Registrar's report #37-1-5C, Serial No. 295, Order #1986, Local Board No. 5, Carrick, Pennsylvania, Allegheny County, September 10, 1918.
77. Check signed by Sophia V. Densmore, in possession of the author.
78. The invention has been referenced by BorgWarner, General Electric Company, United Technologies Corp., Siemens, and others as late as January 2014.
79. As a first grader, my brother John once bragged to his classmates that our uncle was famous for his underpants, believing that the B. V. D. on the Packard's doors was iron-clad proof of the same.
80. Benjamin V. Densmore, Certificate of Death, File #77214, Reg. 114, Commonwealth of Pennsylvania, Department of Health and Vital Statistics, Harrisburg, Pennsylvania, August 16, 1936.
81. Also called "fan jets."
82. His third-floor billiard room became her parlor.
83. Downtown Philadelphia.

84. Sophia V. Densmore, Certificate of Death, File #6956, Reg. 15, Commonwealth of Pennsylvania, Department of Health and Vital Statistics, Harrisburg, Pennsylvania, January 22, 1938.

85. What classical irony.

Chapter 19

1. GI Bill, www.benefits.va.gv/gibill/history.asp, accessed 12/10/2106.

2. In 1947—the peak of college-bound soldiers—49 percent of the nation's admissions were GI Bill vets.

3. Other philosophical influences played a more prominent role in framing the Constitution.

4. Hon. John Hart, Last Will and Testament, April 16, 1779 (New Jersey State Archives, Trenton, NJ, www.laurellynn.com/genealogy/hart/John_hart_marriage_children.htm).

5. Batchelor, *Incidents of My Life*.

6. Bulk oil boats and tank cars created with the help of Densmores.

7. Seventh Census of the United States, Pittsburgh Ward 6, Allegheny County, Pennsylvania, 1850 National Archives Microfilm Publication M432, 1009 Rolls, Records of the Bureau of the Census Record, Roll M432.746, 248A.

8. Many of these occupations have been mentioned: boarding single workers, making up lunch buckets for a husband's crew, sewing and mending clothes for neighbors, taking in wash, etc.

9. Paul Densmore, pers. comm., December 4, 2016.

10. Improved Harvester by Byron Densmore of Sweden, New York, US Patent Model of 1852, and a Reciprocating Harrow by son Jay Densmore of Holky, New York, US Patent #66,684, July 16, 1867.

11. Includes the "Densmore Pipe Cleaner" by Leroy F. Densmore of Kenosha, Wisconsin, US patent #18311099A, January 8, 1930.

Chapter 20

1. By 1866 inflation had eaten up some of the wage advantage.

2. That map can now be purchased on disk at the Fayette County Historical Society website.

3. Translates as "Inka walls."

4. He is the one who ran off with fourteen-year-old Elizabeth Ryland in 1829.

Chapter 21

1. Steckel, *History of the Standard of Living*, 2.

2. Merritt, *Masterless Men*.

3. Differences were cultural, legal, and economic.

4. Davis, *Iron Puddler*, 75.

5. Floud et al., *Changing Body*, 332.

6. Paul D. and Alice H. Densmore.
7. Ingraham, "US Lags Behind in Infant Mortality."
8. 2017, PISA results online at www.pewresearch.org/fact-tank/2017/02/15/V-S-students-internationally-math-science.
9. The American nation supports West Point, the Naval Academy, the Army War College, and the Air Force Academy. Why not a "National Academy" for math and science teachers? This could be open to MAs and include the five-year degree awarded tuition free, and candidates could be granted entrance by exam only and required to give five initial years of public school teaching upon graduation.
10. From World Bank online database.
11. "Height Chart of Men and Women in Different Countries," https://www.disabled-world.com/calculators-charts/height-chart.php.
12. Fox, "Where 'Despair' Deaths Were Higher."
13. Kimelman and Chiwaya, "Map."
14. Editor James Ayers, PhD, helped crystalize this observation.

REFERENCES

American Iron and Steel Association. "Directory to the Iron and Steel Works of the United States." 16th ed. N.p.: Philadelphia, PA, 1904.
Bailey, Kenneth P. *Thomas Cresap, Maryland Frontiersman*. Boston, MA: Christopher Publishing House, 1944.
Bardon, Jonathan. *The Plantation of Ulster*. Dublin: Gill & McMillan, 2011.
———. "The Plantation of Ulster." September 18, 2014. www.bbc.co.uk/history/british/plantation.
Batchelor, C. W. *Incidents of My Life*. Pittsburgh, PA: Joseph Eichbaum & Co., 1887.
Bellesiles, Michael A. *1877: America's Year of Living Violently*. New York: The New Press, 2010.
Bellue, Ted Franklin. *The Long Hunt: Death of the Buffalo East of the Mississippi*. Mechanicsburg, PA: Stackpole Books, 1996.
Bissell, Richard. *The Monongahela*. New York: Rinehart and Co., 1952.
Blackmon, Douglas A. *Slavery by Another Name*. New York: Anchor Books, 2008.
"A Brief History of New Sweden in America." The Swedish Colonial Society, 2016. www.colonialswedes.net/history/History.html.
Bruce, Robert. *The National Road*. Berryville, VA: The Prince Maccus Publishers, 1983.
Bruner, Robert F., and Sean D. Carr. *The Panic of 1907: Lessons Learned from the Market's Perfect Storm*. New Jersey: John Wiley and Sons, 2007.
Callahan, James M. *The History of West Virginia, Old and New*. Vol. 3. New York and Chicago, IL: The American Historical Society, Inc., 1923.
Darlington, William M., comp. "Pennsylvania Weather Records, 1644–1835." *The Pennsylvania Magazine of History and Biography* 15, no. 1 (1891): 109–21.
Davis, James J., with C. L. Edson. *The Iron Puddler: My Life in the Rolling Mills and What Came of it*. New York: Grosset and Dunlap, 1922.
Deglar, Carl N. *Neither Black nor White: Slavery and Race Relations in Brazil and the United States*. Madison: University of Wisconsin Press, 1971.
Deming, David. *Science and Technology in World History*. Volume 4, *The Origin of Chemistry, the Principles of Progress, the Enlightenment, and the Industrial Revolution*. Jefferson, NC: McFarland & Co., 2016.
Densmore, H.O. *Payroll and Account Book, Time and Weight*. N.p: n.p., 1882–1888. In possession of the author.
Densmore, H. T. "Historical Sketch of Robert Dunsmore." Uniontown, PA: Uniontown Library, The Pennsylvania Room, n.d.

The Derrick's Handbook of Petroleum. Vol. 2. Oil City, PA: Derrick Publishing, 1900.

Dew, Charles B., ed. *Apostles of Disunion: Southern Secession Commissioners and the Causes of the Civil War*. Charlottesville: University of Virginia Press, 2016.

Dietle, Lannie, and Michael McKenzie. *In Search of the Turkey Foot Road: Unraveling the Mystery, Charting New History, Plotting the Route*. Edited by Nancy E. Thoerig. Fourth Edition. Mount Savage, MD: Mt. Savage Historical Society, 2014.

Diffenbacher, J. F. *J. F. Diffenbacher's Directory of Pittsburgh and Allegheny Cities, 1864/1865*. Pittsburgh, PA: Diffenbacher and Thurston, 1865.

———. *J. F. Diffenbacher's Directory of Pittsburgh and Allegheny Cities, 1869/1870*. Pittsburgh, PA: Diffenbacher and Thurston, 1870.

———. *J. F. Diffenbacher's Directory of Pittsburgh and Allegheny Cities, 1883/1884* Pittsburgh, PA: Diffenbacher and Thurston, 1884.

———. *Diffenbacher's Directory of Pittsburgh and Allegheny Cities, 1890/1891*. Pittsburgh, PA: Diffenbacher and Thurston, 1891.

Dixon, Ruth P., and Katherine G. Eberly, comps. *Index to Seamen's Protection Certificate Applications, Port of Philadelphia: 1796–1823*. Baltimore, MD: Clearfield Publishing Co., 1995.

Dunbar, Seymour. *A History of Travel in America*. Indianapolis, IN: Bobbs-Merril Co., 1915.

Dunn, Richard S. *Sugar and Slaves: The Rise of the Planter Class in the West Indies*. Chapel Hill: University of North Carolina Press, 1972.

Dyer, Frederick H. *A Compendium of the War of Rebellion*. Des Moines, IA: Dyer Publishing Company, 1908.

Egle, William Henry, Editor. "Virginia Claims to Land in Western Pennsylvania." In *Pennsylvania Archives, Third Series*, volume III, 483–771. Baltimore, MD: Genealogical Publishing Co., Inc., 1896.

Ellis, Franklin, ed. *History of Fayette County, Pennsylvania*. Philadelphia, PA: L. H. Everts & Co., 1882.

Evans, Robert. "Blast from the Past." *Smithsonian Magazine*, July 2002. smithsonianmag.com/history/blast-from-the-past-65102374/?.

Fairchance Centennial History Committee, comp. *Fairchance Through the Years*, 2nd Ed. Fairchance, PA: Fairchance Centennial History Committee, 1989.

Fanshaw, Mrs. Daniel. "Twelfth Annual Report of the American Tract Society." New York: American Tract Society, 1837.

Faust, Drew Gilpin. *Mothers of Invention: Women of the Slaveholding South in the American Civil War*. Chapel Hill: University of North Carolina Press, 1996.

Fitch, John A. *The Steel Workers*. Pittsburgh, PA: University of Pittsburgh Press, 1989.

Floud, Roderick, Robert W. Fogel, Bernard Harris, and Sok Chul Hong. *The Changing Body: Health, Nutrition, and Human Development in the Western World Since 1700*. Cambridge: Cambridge University Press, 2011.

Fogel, Robert. *The Escape from Hunger and Premature Death: 1700-2100*. Cambridge: Cambridge University Press, 2004.

———. *Time on the Cross: The Economics of American Negro Slavery*. New York: W. W. Norton and Company, 1974.

———. *Without Consent or Contract: the Rise and Fall of American Slavery*. New York: W. W. Norton & Co., 1994.

Fogel, Robert W., Stanley L. Engerman, Roderick Floud, Gerald Friedman, Robert A. Margo, Kenneth Sokoloff, Richard H. Steckel, T. James Trussell, Georgia Villaflor, and Kenneth W. Wachter. "Secular Changes in American and British Stature and Nutrition." *Journal of Interdisciplinary History* 14, no. 2 (1983): 445–81.

Foner, Philip S. *American Labor Songs of the Nineteenth Century*. Urbana: University of Illinois Press, 1975.

Forrest, Earle. "The National Pike—Road of History, Romance." *Washington Observer*, Monday, March 21, 1955.

Fox, Maggie. "Where 'Despair' Deaths Were Higher, Voters Chose Trump." *NBC News*, September 5, 2018. https://www.nbcnews.com/health-news/where-despair-deaths-were-higher-votes-chose-trump-n906631.

Gallman, Robert E., and John J. Wallis. *American Economic Growth and Standards of Living Before the Civil War*. Chicago, IL: University of Chicago Press, 1992.

Gibson, John. *History of York County, Pennsylvania*. Chicago, IL: F. A. Batley Publishing Company, 1886.

Gillman, Joseph, and Theodore Gillman. *Perspectives in Human Malnutrition*. New York: Grune & Stratton, 1951.

Gladwell, Malcolm. *Outliers: The Story of Success*. New York: Little, Brown, and Co., 2008.

Godcharles, Frederick A. "Scholes, Inventor of First Common Typewriter." *The Morning Herald*, February 14, 1923.

Gould, Emerson W. *Fifty Years on the Mississippi: Or, Gould's History of River Navigation*. St. Louis, MO: Nixon-Jones Printing Co., 1889.

Haifeli, Evan. *New Netherland and the Dutch Origins of American Religious Liberty*. Philadelphia: University of Pennsylvania Press, 2012.

Haines, Michael R. "Vital Statistics." In *Historical Statistics of the United States: Millennial Edition*, vol. 1, edited by Susan B. Carter et al., 381–90. New York: Cambridge University Press, 2002.

Hammond, Cleon. *John Hart: The Biography of a Signer of the Declaration of Independence*. St. Paul, MN: Pioneer Press, 1977.

Harris, Isaac. *Harris's General Business Directory of the Cities of Pittsburgh and Allegheny*. Pittsburgh, PA: A. A. Anderson, 1847.

"History: South Carolina's Connection to Barbados." Statehouse Report, 2015. http://www.statehousereport.com/2015/09/04/history-south-carolinas-connection-to-barbados/.

History of Mercer County, Pennsylvania, its Past and Present. Chicago: Brown, Runk, and Co., 1888.

"History of Trevor's General Store, Founded 1795." *The Daily Courier* (Connellsville, PA), September 24, 1965.

Hitchcock, Janice E., Phyllis E. Schubert, and Sue A. Thomas. *Caring in Action*. Volume 1, *Community Health Nursing*. Clifton Park, NY: Delmar/Thomson Learning, 2003.

Hogeland, William. *The Whiskey Rebellion*. New York: Simon and Schuster Paperbacks, 2015.

"The Homestead Strike." In *The Homestead Strike Songster*. Rpt. in Philip S. Foner, *American Labor Songs of the Nineteenth Century*, 243. Urbana: University of Illinois Press, 1975.

Hoover, Ethel D. "Retail Prices After 1850." In *Trends in the American Economy in the Nineteenth Century*, 141–90. Princeton, NJ: Princeton University Press, 1960.

Ingham, John N. *Making Iron and Steel: Independent Mills in Pittsburgh, 1820–1920*. Athens: University of Ohio Press, 1991.

Ingraham, Christopher. "US Lags Behind in Infant Mortality." *The Washington Post*, September 29, 2014.

Jameson, J. Franklin. *Narratives of New Netherland: 1609–1664*. New York: Harper and Row, 1909.

Jordan, John W., ed. *Genealogical and Personal History of Western Pennsylvania*. Vol. 2. New York: Lewis Historical Publishing Company, 1915.

Kelly, John. *The Graves are Walking: The Great Famine and the Saga of the Irish People*. New York: Henry Holt and Company, 2012.

Kimelman, Jeremiah, and Nigel Chiwaya. "Map: How Long People in Your City are Expected to Live: An Analysis of Government Data Shows How Race and Class Can Shape How Long You Live." April 14, 2019. https://www.nbcnews.com/news/us-news/map-neighborhood-life-expectancy-united-states-n979141.

Kleinberg, S. J. *In the Shadow of the Mills: Working Class Families in Pittsburgh, 1870–1907*. Pittsburgh, PA: Pittsburgh Press, 1989.

Kleinfield, Rachel. *A Savage Order: How the World's Deadliest Countries Can Forge a Path to Security*. New York: Pantheon Books, 2018.

Knowles, Anne Kelly. *Mastering Iron: The Struggle to Modernize an American Industry, 1800–1868*. Chicago, IL: University of Chicago Press, 2013.

Koot, Gerard. "The WIC, The Dutch West India Company." University of Massachusetts, 2015. www1.umassa.edu/euro/resources/imagesessays/thewic.pdf.

Kussart, Mrs. S. *The Allegheny River*. Pittsburgh, PA: Burgum Printing Co., 1938.

Lebergott, Stanley. "Wage Trends, 1800–1900." In *Trends in the American Economy in the Nineteenth Century*, 449–500. Princeton, NJ: Princeton University Press, 1960.

Lemon, James T. "Household Consumption in eighteenth century America." *Agricultural History*, Vol. 41. Winter Park: Agricultural Historical Society, 1967.

Leyburn, James G. *The Scotch-Irish: A Social History*. Chapel Hill: University of North Carolina Press, 1989.

Lincoln, Abraham. *The Political Debates Between Hon. Abraham Lincoln and Hon. Stephen A. Douglas*. Columbus, OH: Follett, Foster & Co., 1860.

Lincoln, Abraham, and Stephen A. Douglas, *The Political Debates Between Abraham Lincoln and Stephen A. Douglas in the Senatorial Campaign 1858 in Illinois, Plus Other Previous Speeches*. New York: G. P. Putnam & Sons, 1924.

Main, Gloria L. *Tobacco Colony: Life in Early Maryland, 1650–1720*. Princeton, NJ: University of Princeton Press, 1992.

Margo, Robert A. "Wages and Prices During the Antebellum Period." In *American Economic Growth and Standards of Living Before the Civil War*, edited by Robert E. Gallman and John Joseph Wallis, 172–216. Chicago: University of Chicago Press, 1992.

Martin, Janet. *Treasure of the Land of Darkness: The Fur Trade and its Significance for Medieval Russia*. Cambridge: Cambridge University Press, 1986.

McClure, James P. "The Ends of the American Earth: Pittsburgh and the Upper Ohio Valley to 1795." PhD Diss., University of Michigan, 1983.
Merritt, Keri Leigh. *Masterless Men: Poor Whites and Slavery in the Antebellum South*. Cambridge: Cambridge University Press, 2017.
Miller, Kathryn Cooley, comp. *Some Fayette County Pennsylvania Cemeteries*. Apollo, Pennsylvania: Closson Press, 1996.
Miller, Thomas Condit, and Hu Maxwell. *History of West Virginia*. Volumes 2–3, *Family and Personal History*. New York: Lewis Historical Publishing, 1913.
Morgan, James F., comp. "1810 United States Census of Fayette County, Pennsylvania." Unpublished manuscript. Pinellas Park, FL: James F. Morgan, 1974.
Nixon, Pamela. "Descendants of Robert Densmore." Westland, MI: Whispers from the Past Family History Research Service, 2011.
Olsen, Evelyn Guard. *Indian Blood*. 2nd edition. Friendsville, MD: The Friend Family Association of America, 2014.
Pees, Samuel T. "Early Bulk Boats." *The First Oil Barges* (2016), www.petroleumhistory.org/oilhistory/pages/"barges"/Barges.html.
"Pennsylvania Weather Records, 1644–1835." *Pennsylvania Magazine of History and Biography* 15 (1891): 109–21.
Post, John D. *The Last Great Subsistence Crisis in the Western World*. Baltimore, MD: Johns Hopkins University Press, 1977.
Preston, Samuel H., and Michael R. Haines. *Fatal Years: Child Mortality in Late Nineteenth-Century America*. Princeton, NJ: Princeton University Press, 1991.
Richardson, James B., III, and Kirke C. Wilson. "Hannas Town and Charles Foreman: The Historical and Archeological Record, 1770–1806." *Western Pennsylvania Historical Magazine* 59, no. 2 (1976): 153–84.
Rink, Oliver A. *Holland on the Hudson: An Economic and Social History of Dutch New York*. Ithaca, NY: Cornell University Press, 1989.
Rutman, Darrett, B., and Anita H. Rutman. "Now-Wives and Sons-in-Law: Parental Death in a Seventeenth-Century Virginia County." In *The Chesapeake in the Seventeenth Century: Essays on Anglo-American Society*, edited by Thad W. Tate and David L. Ammerman, 153–82. New York: W. W. Norton & Co., 1979.
Ryland, Henry Halleck. *The Sylvester Ryland Handbook*. Ligonier, PA: Life Line Printing Company, 1935.
Sage, Mark. "The Sheetz Rifle." *American Rifleman*, May 30, 2013. www.americanrifleman.org/articles/2013/5/30/the-sheetz-rifle/
Scharf, J. Thomas. *History of Western Maryland: Being a History of Frederick, Montgomery, Carroll, Washington, Allegany, and Garrett Counties from the Earliest Period to the Present Day; Including Biographical Sketches of Their Representative Men*. Pittsburgh: Pennsylvania Genealogical Society, 1983.
Schecter, Barnet. *George Washington's America: A Biography Through his Maps*. New York: Walker Publishing Company, 2010.
Schmidt, Benjamin. *Innocence Abroad: The Dutch Imagination and the New World, 1570–1670*. New York: Cambridge University Press, 2001.
Searight, Thomas B. *The Old Pike*. Berryville, VA: The Prince Maccus Publishers, 1983.

Serrin, William. *Homestead: The Glory and Tragedy of an American Steel Town.* New York: Random House, 1993.

Sipe, C. Hale. *The Indian Wars of Pennsylvania: An Account of the Indian Events, in Pennsylvania, of the French and Indian War, Pontiac's War, Lord Dunmore's War, the Revolutionary War, and the Indian Uprising from 1789 to 1795; Tragedies of the Pennsylvania Frontier Based Primarily on the Penna. Archives and Colonial Records.* Harrisburg: Telegraph Press, 1929.

Smith, Eric Ledell. "The End of Black Voting Rights in Pennsylvania: African Americans and the Pennsylvania Constitutional Convention of 1837–1838." *Pennsylvania History: A Journal of Mid-Atlantic Studies* 65, no. 3 (1998): 279–99.

Smith, Jean Edward. *Grant.* New York: Simon & Schuster, 2001.

Steckel, Richard H. *A History of the Standard of Living in the United States.* Edited by Robert Whaples. Economic History Association, 2002. eh.net/encyclopedia/a-history-of-the-standard-of-living-in-the-united-states/.

———. "Nutritional Status in the Colonial American Economy." *William and Mary Quarterly* 56, no. 1 (1999): 31–52.

Steckel, Richard H., and Joseph M. Prince. "Tallest in the World: Native Americans of the Great Plains in the Nineteenth Century." *American Economic Review* 91, no. 1 (2001): 287–94.

Stewart, Estelle, and J. C. Bowen, Preparers. "History of Wages in the United States from Colonial Times to 1928: Bulletin of the United States Bureau of Labor Statistics." No. 604. Washington, DC: United States Department of Labor, 1934.

Stuart, David E. *Anasazi America.* 2nd Edition. Albuquerque: University of New Mexico Press, 2000.

Sykes, Brian. *The Seven Daughters of Eve: The Science that Reveals our Genetic Ancestry.* New York: W. W. Norton & Co., 2001.

Thurston, George H. *Allegheny County's Hundred Years.* N.p.: G. H. Thurston and A. A. Anderson and Son, 1888.

———. *Directory of Pittsburgh and Allegheny Cities, 1864–1865.* Pittsburgh, PA: G. H. Thurston, 1864.

———. *Directory of Pittsburgh and Allegheny Cities, 1869–1870.* Pittsburgh, PA: G. H. Thurston, 1869.

———. *Directory of Pittsburgh and Allegheny Cities, 1876–1877.* Pittsburgh, PA: G. H. Thurston, 1876.

———. *Directory of Pittsburgh and Allegheny Cities, 1879–1880.* Pittsburgh, PA: G. H. Thurston, 1879.

Trotter, Joe William Jr., and Eric Ledell Smith, eds. *African Americans in Pennsylvania: Shifting Historical Perspectives.* University Park, PA: Penn State University Press, 1997.

Tryon, Rolla M. *Household Manufactures in the United States, 1640–1860: A Study in Industrial History.* Chicago, IL: University of Chicago Press, 1917.

Tucker, Abigail. "The Panic of 1907." Interview with Robert F. Bruner, October 9, 2008. smithsonian.com/history/the-financial-panic-of-1907-running-from-history-82173632/B.

Turner, Edward Raymond. "The Abolition of Slavery in Pennsylvania." *The Pennsylvania Magazine of History and Biography* 36, no. 2 (1912): 129–42.
Van der Zee, Henri, and Barbara Van der Zee. *A Sweet and Alien Land: The Story of Dutch New York*. New York: Viking Press, 1978.
Walsh, Lorena S. "Consumer Behavior, Diet, and the Standard of Living in Late Colonial and Early Antebellum America, 1770–1840." In *American Economic Growth and Standards of Living Before the Civil War*, edited by Robert E. Gallman and John Joseph Wallis, 217–64. Chicago, IL: University of Chicago Press, 1993.
———. "Till Death Do Us Part: Marriage and Family in Seventeenth-Century Maryland." In *The Chesapeake in the Seventeenth Century: Essays on Anglo-American Society*, edited by Thad W. Tate and David L. Ammerman, 126–52. New York: W. W. Norton & Co., 1979.
Warren, Robert Penn. *The Legacy of the Civil War: Meditations on the Centennial*. New York: Random House, 1961.
Way, Frederick Jr. *Way's Guide to Towboats & Tugboats*. Athens: Ohio University Press, 1990.
———, comp. *Way's Packet Directory 1848–1894*. Rev. ed. Athens: Ohio University Press, 1994.
Way, Frederick, Jr., and Joseph W. Rutter. *Way's Steam Towboat Directory*. Athens: Ohio University Press, 1990.
Wells, David Ames. *United States Report of Special Commissioner of Revenue for the Year 1868*. Washington, DC: US Government Printing Office, 1868.
Williams, Edward G., Ed. "Samuel Vaughn's Journal." *Western Pennsylvania Historical Magazine* 44, no. 3 (1961): 261–86.
Wilson, James Grant. *The Memorial History of New York: From its First Settlement to the Year 1892*. New York: New York History Company, 1892.
Wolff, Leon. *Lockout: The Story of the Homestead Strike of 1892: A Study of Violence, Unionism, and the Carnegie Steel Empire*. New York: Harper and Row, 1965.
Woodard, Colin. *American Nations: A History of the Eleven Rival Regional Cultures of North America*. New York: Penguin, 2011.
Wright, Carroll D. *Historical Review of Wages and Prices, 1752–1860*. Boston: Massachusetts Bureau of Statistics, 1889.
Young, Cory James. "From North to Natchez during the Age of Gradual Abolition." *Pennsylvania Magazine of History and Biography* 143, no. 2 (2019): 117–39.

INDEX

Acts of Clearance, 16
Adams, John Quincy, 104
Africans, 1–2. *See also* blacks; slavery
aging out, 233
American Dream, 104, 205, 330
American Exceptionalism, 99, 200, 205
Amish, 183
Amnesty Act (1872), 189
Anchor Nail and Tack, 153–58, 160–62, 168, 176–77, 226–27, 369n4
Anderson, Bill, 172
Anderson, Robert O., 309
animals, 349n9, 356n31; taxes for, 78–79; transportation and, 46–48, *47*, 58; for wagoners, 70
aristocratic class, 4, 36–37
Avera, Marguerite Densmore, *217*, 294–96, 375n45

banking, 329
Batchelor, C. W., 138, 171
Big Savage Mountain, 8, 10
biology: calories and, 349n7; census records for, 1, 280; culture and, 33, 339; of Densmore family, 293; environment and, 110, 146, 261, 331–33; of Europe, 44–45; Fogel on, 182; history of, 99, 117–18; medicine and, 333; of men, 302–3; of metabolism, 46, 69–70, *70*; mtDNA, 302, 304, 309, 376n65; in the North, 98; psychology and, 105, 224; self-sufficiency and, 117–18; of US, 4–5, *335*, 335–36; wages and, 328; work culture and, 313, 330–31; Y-DNA, 302–3, 307, 376n64
Birmingham, Pennsylvania: culture of, 125; iron and, 108–11, 153, 160–62; for Vandergrift family, 144, *145*, 146–47
blackmail, 140
blacks, 359n10, 366n3; after Civil War, 172–76, 195–96; Long Depression for, 195; the North for, 43, 114–15; the South for, 179; work life for, 276
blacksmiths, 8–9, 41–42
boilers, 192
B&O railroads, 199–203, 199–206, 368n57
Border Reivers, 15–16
bounty lands, 60
Braddock, Edward, 27
Braddock's Road, 8, *13*, 24, 26–28, 31, 32
Brazil, 126
British Isles, 4
Brown, John, 172
Bushnell, Daniel, 140, *141*, 142–43, 170
business, 369n10; acumen in, 129, 317, 329; efficiency phases for, 269; titans of, 260–61. *See also* corporations; Robber Barons

calories: calories per hour, 28, 41, 68–70, *70*, 101–2, 110, 238, 245–47, 303, 317, 349n7; Densmore, F. H. O., and, 234–36, *236–37*; direct caloric cost, 95, *96*; food calories, 72, 79, 238; labor and, 46–49, *47*, 318; longevity and, 248, 295–96; in US, 187–88;

388   INDEX

calories (continued)
    work culture and, 100–102, 192, 238, 245–47, 303
Carnegie, Andrew, 257, 264–66
Carr, Elizabeth, 86, 109. See also Densmore family
census records: for biology, 1, 280; before Civil War, 111–12; for demography, 71–72; Densmore, F. H. O., in, 166; for Densmore family, 105, 164–65; from 1840, 78–79, 81; from 1850, 85–87, 361n40, 373n37; from 1860, 113–23, 373n37; from 1870, 163–65, 178, 185–86; from 1880, 226–27, 232–36, 236–37, 242; from 1890, 260–61; history and, 25, 39–40; labor in, 43, 111, 177; from 1900, 274, 280, 286; from 1910, 288–90; from 1940, 296; for taxes, 15, 76
The Changing Body (textbook), 330
cigars, 149, 365n47
citizenship, 116, 137, 179–81, 189, 195
Civil War, 343, 344–45, 366n68; blacks after, 172–76, 195–96; census records before, 111–12; culture after, 179–80; culture during, 113–23; demography of, 117; for Europe, 188; food after, 150–51, 176–77; government and, 180–81; immigration after, 171–72; labor before, 138; legacy of, 171–75; *The Legacy of the Civil War* (Warren), 118; longevity and, 223; manufacturing during, 150, 155; in Maryland, 160; pension funds from, 262; politics of, 327–28, 368n35; puddlers and, 149, 154; for Vandergrift family, 139–42, *141*; wages after, 232–33; Washington, DC during, 119, 121; well-being before, 98–103
class: American Dream and, 330; aristocratic class, 4, 36–37; economics and, 181; education and, 313–14; farming and, 283; labor and, 327;

middle class, 200; in US, 221–23; for Vandergrift family, 204–5, 281; well-being and, 200–203, 223–25
clothing, 83–84, 173
coal, 147–49; self-sufficiency in, 69; wages and, 70; work culture of, 291–94
coke: Densmore, S., in, 279; labor with, 193–94; technology of, 186–87
Colonial America: culture of, 1–2, 107–8; history of, 18; infant mortality in, 3–4, 17–18; Jamestown Colony, 18–19. See also United States
Columbus, Bartolomeo, 19–20
communism, 200
community, 54–58
Conestoga (ship), *141*, 142
Connell, Zachariah, 29, 51, 55, 57–58
consumption, 274–76
corporations: greed and, 254–55, 276–77; labor and, 222–23; self-sufficiency for, 202, 224, 244–48, 262; unions and, 262
corruption: blackmail, 140; in culture, 97–98; environment for, 337; Robber Barons and, 232
Cousin Tom, 292–94, 296, 318, 361n36
coylers, 53; iron for, 69; self-sufficiency of, 70; taxes for, 59–60
Cramer, Henry, 294
Cresap, Thomas, 11
culture: of Amish, 183; biology and, 33, 339; of Birmingham, 125; of Border Reivers, 15–16; after Civil War, 179–80; during Civil War, 113–23; of Colonial America, 1–2, 107–8; corruption in, 97–98; cultural rigidity, 182–84; Declaration of Independence for, 331–33; efficiency phases for, 183, 319; environment and, 182, 280, 327–28, 331–33; of frontier, 58, 88–89; GI Bill for, 312–14; identity politics and, 180–81; of immigration, 36–37, 148; infrastructure and, 43, 351n35; of New Amsterdam,

127–28, 130–33; of Northern Ireland, 12; of Pennsylvania, 9; of Pittsburgh, 147–49, 219–21; Robber Barons for, 202, 255–57, 333–34, 337; self-sufficiency in, 12, 14–15, 198, 321; technology for, 283; of urban life, 283–84; of US, 22–23; after war, 184–85; well-being and, 65; Y-DNA in, 302–3, 307, 376n64. *See also* work culture

Cunningham, W. D., 290

Custer, George Armstrong, 189

Davis, Jefferson, 360n19
day laborers, 106
Declaration of Independence, 4, 45, 134, 331–33
decontenting, 17
demography: census records for, 71–72; of Civil War, 117; height and, 44–46; regional dynamics and, 65–68, *66*, 71–72; women in, 355n22
Densmore, Albert M., 293–94, 296–97
Densmore, Amos, 143, 169–70, 277
Densmore, Avis Elsie, 305
Densmore, Benjamin V., *215*, 269–70, 272, 299–300, 303–8
Densmore, Byron, 278
Densmore, Charles, 291–93
Densmore, Connie. *See* Klink, Connie
Densmore, Elizabeth (née Elizabeth Goldsboro), 74, 79–80, 120–21, 158–60, 161–62, *209*; death of, 303–4, 356n2; family of, 267–69, 358n1. *See also* Densmore, Fidelio Hughes Oliphant
Densmore, Elsie E., 59, 79–80, 134, *213–14*, 264, 266; family of, 285–86, 303, 305, 307–8, 374n19; psychology of, 300–301, 307
Densmore, Ethel Cramer, *216*, 291–93, 294–95
Densmore, Fidelah, 240–41
Densmore, Fidelio Hughes Oliphant ("Ollie"), 78, 106–8, 118–21, 146, 221, 320–25; calories burned by, 234–36, *236–37*; in census records, 166; death of, 301–2; Densmore, H. T., and, 271–74, 279; Densmore, S., and, 241–43, 251–52; family of, 153–58, 160–62, 226–30, 267–69. *See also* Densmore, Elizabeth; memorabilia of, *210–11*; at Oliphant Works, 167; work life for, *244*, 244–50, 252–55, *253*, 262, 330–31
Densmore, Freddie, *211*, 226
Densmore, Hannah. *See* Dunsmore, Hannah
Densmore, Harold, 293–94
Densmore, Harriet, 290
Densmore, Harry Thomas. *See* Densmore, Henry Thomas
Densmore, Henry, 11, 15, 31
Densmore, Henry Thomas ("H. T."), 52–53, 59, 146, 176–77, *212–13*, 252; childhood of, 227–30, 264; death of, 374n19; Densmore, F. H. O., and, 271–74, 279; Densmore, W., and, 284–85; logbooks by, 259; in Pittsburgh, 242–43, 262, 298–99; success for, 269–70, 333–34; work life for, 266
Densmore, H. O. *See* Densmore, Fidelio Hughes Oliphant
Densmore, H. Thomas. *See* Cousin Tom
Densmore, James, 25, 143, 277
Densmore, Jane, 74
Densmore, Jennie, 238–40, 275–76
Densmore, John Robert, 291
Densmore, John S., 60
Densmore, Kenneth S., 293–94
Densmore, Lenora Dulaney, *217*, 296–97
Densmore, Margaret (née Margaret Nelson), 271–74
Densmore, Mary, 15, 52
Densmore, Minnie, *211*, 226
Densmore, Moses, 278
Densmore, Natalie, *215*, 301, 306, 308–10

Densmore, Nathaniel, 40, 53, 74, 79–80, 83–84, 191–92; Dunsmore, R., Jr., and, 109; family of, 95–98, *96*
Densmore, Nelson Oliver, 302
Densmore, Ollie. *See* Densmore, Fidelio Hughes Oliphant
Densmore, Paul, 290
Densmore, Rachel, 76–77, *77*
Densmore, Robert (Samuel's son), *216*, 239
Densmore, Robert, Jr., 76–77, *77*, 109–12, 121–23, 175–76, *209*; death of, 284; employment for, 178, 332
Densmore, Samuel, 17, 24, 35, 78, 162, 244, 286, 318; in coke, 279; Densmore, F. H. O., and, 241–43, 251–52; family of, 274–75, 289–90; Frick and, 264; in Kittanning, 238–40; skills of, 166; success for, 192–94
Densmore, Sophia Vandergrift, *212–13*, 262, 270–71, 298–99, 307–8, 374n19
Densmore, Virginia (née Virginia O'Sullivan), 291
Densmore, William, 11, 15, 31, 50, 228, 244, 271–74; Densmore, H. T., and, 284–85; family of, 303–4
Densmore, William Walter, 239, 290
Densmore family, 118–23, *214*; biology of, 293; births in, 76–77, *77*; census records for, 105, 164–65; coke for, 186–87; in Colonial America, 2; Densmore map of, 20, *21*, 22; economics of, 28; in 1870s, 175–78; in 1890s, 262–70; family member tables for, *xviii–xix*; height of, 109–10, 341–42, 344, 346; history of, 5, 154–56, 322–25, 333–34; innovation by, 277–79; labor for, 146; migration of, 23–24; 1900s for, 284–88; Old Robert, 2, 7; in Pennsylvania, 14, 20, 71, 191; in Pittsburgh, 177–78, 298–301; property for, 273, 288, 304; self-sufficiency of, 74–81, *77*, 197, 319; Vandergrift family and, 139–40, 270–71, 288–90; war for, 184; well-being of, 317–19; work culture of, 255–59. *See also* Old Robert Dunsmore; *specific family members*
Densmore map, 20, *21*, 22
Densmore Samuel, 118–21
Densmore Tank Car, 169–70
Denzemore family, 122
Descendants of the Signers of the Declaration of Independence (the DSDI), 134, 135
diet, 187
Dillon, Moses, 52
Dinsmore, John Sutton, 39–40
Dinsmore, Samuel, 82
Dinsmore, Sutton, 39–40
Dinsmore, William, 39–40
Dinsmore family. *See* Densmore family
direct caloric cost, 95, *96*
disasters, 188–89
diseases: infant mortality and, 123, 185; military and, 188; miner's cough, 291–92; for Native Americans, 131–32; nutrition and, 240; in Pittsburgh, 100, 148; in rivers, 353n9; tuberculosis, 274–76; for work culture, 291–92
Dock, Jacob B., 205
Dolan, James, 279
Donegal, Marquess of, 17
the DSDI. *See* Descendants of the Signers of the Declaration of Independence
Dunsmore, Hannah, 358n1
Dunsmore, Hannah (née Hannah Glenn), 39, 52–53, 74–79, *77*, 81–82, 85, *207*, 332
Dunsmore, Henry (b. 1755), 25, 37
Dunsmore, Mary (widow), 25
Dunsmore, Robert, 14
Dunsmore, Robert "Old Robert," 2, 7, 24, 38–41, *96*, *207*; as Border Reivers, 15–16; death of, 87–89; economics for, 9–10; family of, 52–53, 59–60, 76–81, *77*, 82–83, 329–30; height of,

25, 46; military for, 50–51; Oliphant, F. H., and, 74–75; as pioneer, 8–9; self-sufficiency of, 11, 87–89; as wagoner, 57–58
Dunsmore, Susan (née Rager), 83, 86, 358n2
Dunsmore, Thomas Joseph, 357n41
Dunsmore, William (b. 1770), 25, 40, 357n41
Dunsmore family. *See* Densmore family
Dutch empire, 125–30, 128, 130
Dutch West India Company (WIC), 19, 125–29

Early, Jubal, 121
Eastlake, George, 201
ecology, 71–72, 240–41
economics: for aristocratic class, 4; of business, 369n10; class and, 181; of coyler taxes, 59–60; of Dunsmore family, 28; economies of scale, 91; efficiency phases for, 46–49, *47*; environment and, 110, 126, 280; of family, 88–89, 176–77; of farming, 327; of food, 28, 68–69, 101, 178, 244; of health, 181; of immigration, 37, 64–65; infant mortality and, 223–24, 334–35; of iron, 246–49; of legal action, 82–83; longevity and, 338; of military, 40–41, 155, 378n9; of National Road, 93–94; New York Stock Market, 189; for the North, 173; for Old Robert Dunsmore, 9–10; Panic (1907), 280, 286–87; of Pittsburgh, 65; of plantations, 34; of property, 268–69, 305; reports, 177–78; of schools, 55–56; of shipping, 33; of slavery, 35, 67, 112, 114–15; of steel, 167–68; of subscriptions, 54; of transportation, 29; in US, 45–46, 80–81; of wages, 103; after war, 122–23; for WIC, 19. *See also* Long Depression
education: class and, 313–14; for efficiency phases, 333; in Europe, 335; Free Public School Act (1834), 56; illiteracy and, 87; migration and, 56–57; public education, 174–75; religion for, 174; schools, 54–56, 78; slavery in, 366n1; technology and, 299; urban life and, 373n3
efficiency phases: for business, 269; for culture, 183, 319; for Dutch empire, 130; for economics, 46–49, *47*; education for, 333; industrial efficiency, 322; for manufacturing, 62–63, 222, 256; power phases and, 152; for technology, 319; for transportation, 33–34, 64, 94–99, *96*, 289, 297, 299; for US, 4–5, 35; wages and, 246–49
1840 census records, 78–79, 81
1850 census records, 85–87, 361n40, 373n37
1860 census records, 113–23, 373n37
1870 census records, 163–65, 178, 185–86
1880 census records, 226–27, 232–36, 236–37, 242
1890 census records, 260–61
Electoral College, 194–95
electricity, 283
Ellis, Franklin, 52, 86–87
England: aristocratic class in, 36–37; France and, 102, 188, 336; history of, 3–4; longevity in, 188; Native Americans and, 350n8; religion in, 16–18; taxes for, 129; tobacco for, 34; US and, 114. *See also* Europe; Great Britain
environment: biology and, 110, 146, 261, 331–33; for corruption, 337; culture and, 182, 280, 327–28, 331–33; ecology and, 71–72, 240–41; economics and, 110, 126, 280; for farming, 16; health and, 67–68, 317; hunting and, 19; infant mortality and, 194, 229, 239; labor and, 196, 232, 248; of manufacturing, 169; for military, 119–20; nutrition and, 117; pollution of, 147–48, 293, 330–31;

environment (*continued*)
  psychology of, 182; for resources, 54; self-sufficiency and, 30, 327; of slavery, 111; of work culture, 228, 244
ethics, 298
Europe: biology of, 44–45; Civil War for, 188; Dutch empire in, 128; education in, 335; Europeans, 18, 22, 36; farming in, 17; Great Britain and, 4; height in, 335; immigration from, 175–76, 286; infant mortality in, 43, 66; pioneers from, 31; US compared to, 3
exchanges, 189–90, 194

family: of Densmore, E., 267–69, 358n1; of Densmore, E. E., 285–86, 303, 305, 307–8, 374n19; of Densmore, F. H. O., 153–58, 160–62, 226–30, 267–69; of Densmore, Nathaniel, 95–98, 96; of Densmore, S., 274–75, 289–90; of Densmore, W., 303–4; of Dunsmore, N., 95–98, 96; of Dunsmore, R., Jr., 110; economics of, 88–89, 176–77; food and, 103; history of, 66–67; labor and, 57, 62–63; nutrition for, 187–88; for Old Robert Dunsmore, 52–53, 59–60, 76–81, 77, 82–83, 329–30; pension funds for, 110–11; psychology of, 45–46; religion and, 165–66; self-sufficiency and, 85–87, 328, 334; slavery and, 315; taxes for, 39; for Vandergrift, J. J., 270–71; for Vandergrift, P., 128–29; war for, 103–4; well-being and, 85–87. *See also specific families*
family member tables, *xvii–xviii*, *xx–xxi*
farming: calories per hour for, 303; class and, 283; economics of, 327; environment for, 16; in Europe, 17; food from, 352n5; hunting compared to, 23; labor of, 72; slavery and, 114; technology for, 35; wages compared to, 60–61, 101–2

Federal Reserve Bank, 280
Feirst, Irene, 305
Flannigan, Andrew, 11
floods, 30
Floud, Roderick, 330
Fogel, Robert, 182, 330
food: after Civil War, 150–51, 176–77; clothing and, 173; economics of, 28, 68–69, 101, 178, 244; family and, 103; from farming, 352n5; food calories, 72, 79, 238; infant mortality and, 201; livestock for, 28–29; longevity and, 110–11; in New Amsterdam, 131; peach leather, 350n12; wages and, 168–69, 189; for wagoners, 46–47, 47
Forbes, John, 26
forges: for blacksmiths, 41–42; Franklin Forge, 75; for iron, 52; labor at, 74; technology of, 53–54
Forrest, Nathan Bedford, 359n4
Foster, Stephen, 231
France: England and, 102, 188, 336; immigration from, 42–43; US compared to, 28. *See also* Europe
Franklin, Benjamin, 3, 54
Franklin Forge, 75
Free Public School Act (1834), 56
freight, 95, 139–41
Frick, Henry C., 167, 241, 242, 257, 264–66
frontier, 12, 14, 27–28; culture of, 58, 88–89; government for, 38; history of, 57; hunting at, 30–31; Kentucky as, 86–87; migration to, 73; technology for, 36; for wagoners, 95
fuel, 53–54, 68–70, 70
funerals, 88–89
furnaces, 53–54

Garrett, John, 203–5, 221
George III (King), 3, 22
Gerishmier, Oliver. *See* Densmore, Fidelio Hughes Oliphant
GI Bill, 312–14

Gibson, John, 14, 51
Gibson, Joshua, 52, 76
Gibson family, 51–52
Gladwell, Malcolm, 236
Glenn, Amanda Jennie, 122
Glenn, Hannah. *See* Dunsmore, Hannah
Glenn, James, 373n41
Glenn, Nathaniel, 52, 76, 86–87
Glenn, William, 52, 373n41
Glidden, Carlos S., 277
Golden Age, 182
Goldsboro, Elizabeth. *See* Densmore, Elizabeth
Goldsboro, Thomas, 69, 121, 158–60, 268, 324, 360nn29–30
Goldsborough, Robert, 67
government: Civil War and, 180–81; corruption in, 97; disasters and, 188–89; economic reports by, 177–78; for frontier, 38; for health, 174; history of, 45, 54–55; militias for, 204; for National Road, 41; in Pennsylvania, 56; for pension funds, 82; for schools, 54–55; for self-sufficiency, 58
Grant, Hiram Ulysses, 29, 189
Grant, U. S., 189
Great Britain, 4
Great Depression, 311, 333, 337
Greater Pittsburgh, 91
Great Philadelphia Wagon Road, 26
Great Railroad Strike (1877), 199–200, 203–6, 219–21, 223–24
Great War. *See* World War I
greed, 254–55, 276–77; in the North, 196. *See also* Robber Barons; strikes

Hamilton, Alexander, 37–38, 61, 189, 356n1
Harris, Bernard, 330
Hart, Aaron, *xvii*
Hart, Daniel, *xvii*, 315
Hart, Deborah (daughter), *xvii*, 315
Hart, Deborah (née Deborah Scudder), *xvii*

Hart, Edward (b. 1625), *xvii*, 131
Hart, Edward (grandson), *xvii*
Hart, Edward (great-grandson), *xvii*
Hart, Jesse, *xvii*, 136, 363n74
Hart, John (great-grandson), *xvii*, 131, 133, 314–15
Hart, John, Jr., *xvii*, 134, 314–15
Hart, John F., 220
Hart, Mary, *xvii*. *See also* Vandergrift, Mary
Hart, Nathaniel, *xvii*
Hart, Scudder, *xvii*, 136, 363n74
Hart family, 271, 281, 329; family member tables for, *xvii*; height of, 341–42, 344, 346; history of, 5, 133–34; Vandergrift family and, 315–17; well-being of, 314–15. *See also specific family members*
Haun, Mary, 290
Hayden, John, 64, 95, 96
Hayes, Rutherford B., 195, 219, 223, 369n2
health: economics of, 181; environment and, 67–68, 317; government for, 174; productivity and, 333; stress and, 183–84; unpasteurized milk and, 79; working conditions and, 199
height, 360n19; demography and, 44–46; of Dunsmore family, 109–10; infant mortality and, 329–30; longevity and, 99–100, 102, 104, 112, 326–28; of men, 5, 6, 7–8, 72, 81, 85, 151, 169, 187–88, 232, 280–81, 293, 335; methodology for, 341, *341–47*, 343, 345; nutrition and, 304–5; of Old Robert Dunsmore, 25, 46; in War of 1812, 124. *See also* biology
Helmsley, Leona, 337
high-level skills, 251, 333–34
history: of biology, 99, 117–18; census records and, 25, 39–40; of Colonial America, 18; of Densmore family, 5, 154–56, 322–25, 333–34; of England, 3–4; of family, 66–67; of frontier, 57;

history (*continued*)
of government, 45, 54–55; of Hart family, 5, 133–34; *History of Fayette County, Pennsylvania* (Ellis), 52, 86–87; of immigration, 5; of labor, 102; of Maryland, 73; of National Road, 34–35, 64–65; of Native Americans, 263; of Pennsylvania, 23, 26–27, 30–31, 52, 86–87, 317–18, 350n20, 356n22; of Pittsburgh, 26–30; of power phases, 33–34; of railroads, 199–206, 257; of slavery, 1–2, 182; of steamboats, 137; of taxes, 37, 94–95; of transportation, 12, 14, 31–32; of unions, 355n13; of urban life, 326; of US, 87–88; of Vandergrift family, 5, 125–30; of war, 280; of West Virginia, 29–31, 38, 142
Hitler, Adolph, 280
Hoffman, Joseph, 206, 229
Hoffman, Sarah Ann. *See* Wheaton, Sarah
Holland. *See* Dutch empire
Homestead Strikes, 263–66
van Hoornbeeck, Gillis, 129
horses. *See* animals
hunting, 19, 23, 30–31

identity politics, 180–81, 261, 339
illiteracy, 87
immigration: citizenship and, 180–81; after Civil War, 171–72; culture of, 36–37, 148; economics of, 37, 64–65; from Europe, 175–76, 286; from France, 42–43; history of, 5; from Ireland, 93; labor and, 68, 323–24; longevity and, 45, 198–99; male height and, 8; for Native Americans, 22–23; New Amsterdam for, 127; from Northern Ireland, 14, 17; pioneers after, 22; politics of, 296; population and, 62–63, 111; power phases and, 303; psychology of, 24; from Scotland, 18; self-sufficiency and, 16–24; from Spain, 18; taxes and, 32; for Ulster, 16–17; for unions, 372n1; to US, 12, 19; of Vandergrift family, 19–20; wages and, 260, 276
income, 102–4
The Indian Wars, 195
industrial efficiency, 322
infant mortality, 165, 239–40; in Colonial America, 3–4, 17–18; diseases and, 123, 185; economics and, 223–24, 334–35; environment and, 194, 229, 239; in Europe, 43, 66; food and, 201; height and, 329–30; psychology of, 226–27; in US, 99; war and, 311
inflation, 178
infrastructure: bridges for, 42; culture and, 43, 351n35; iron for, 147–48; of Pittsburgh, 41–42; rivers for, 91; of towns, 54–55; of US, 41; after war, 173
Ireland: immigration from, 93; longevity in, 25; Northern Ireland, 12, 14, 16–17; potato famine in, 17–18. *See also* Europe
iron, 42; Birmingham and, 108–11, 153, 160–62; boilers for, 192; for coylers, 69; economics of, 246–49; forges for, 52; heaters, 177; for infrastructure, 147–48; keelboats for, 74–75; Pittsburgh for, 106–8, 151–52; for the South, 162; steel and, 152–53, 256–59; unskilled labor in, 238; wages in, 243–44, 252–55, 253; for war, 105–12; work culture in, 236–37, 250–52

Jackson, Thomas ("Stonewall"), 360n19
James, Frank, 172, 189
James, Jesse, 172, 189
Jamestown Colony, 18–19
Jefferson, Thomas, 32, 33
Johnson, Andrew, 174

Jumonville, Sieur de, 338

Kane, John P., 279
keelboats, 74–75
Kentucky, 86–87
Kieft, Willem, 127
King, John, 203–4, 221
KKK. *See* Ku Klux Klan
KKK Act (1871), 172
Kleinberg, S. J., 151
Klink, Connie (née Connie Densmore), 337–38
Klink, James, 337–38
Knickerbocker Trust Company, 286
Ku Klux Klan (KKK), 38, 172, 359n4

labor: business titans and, 260–61; calories and, 46–49, *47*, 318; in census records, 43, 111, 177; before Civil War, 138; class and, 327; with coke, 193–94; corporations and, 222–23; day laborers, 106; for Densmore family, 146; environment and, 196, 232, 248; family and, 57, 62–63; of farming, 72; at forges, 74; high-level skills for, 251, 333–34; history of, 102; in identity politics, 261; immigration and, 68, 323–24; Oliphant, F. H., for, 94; politics and, 113–14; in power phases, 262; for Robber Barons, 276, 323; teamsters in, 80; unskilled labor, 198–99, 238; in West Virginia, 297–98; World War I and, 280, 305
Land Grant Act, 312
Lee, Robert E., 360n19
The Legacy of the Civil War (Warren), 118
legal action, 82–83
Lewis and Clark expedition, 12
Lincoln, Abraham, 111–12
Little Savage Mountain, 10
livestock, 28–29
Long Depression, 168–69, 190, 194; for blacks, 195; psychology of, 196–97; for railroads, 201–2; wages after, 224–25
longevity: calories and, 248, 295–96; Civil War and, 223; economics and, 338; in England, 188; food and, 110–11; height and, 99–100, 102, 104, 112, 326–28; immigration and, 45, 198–99; in Ireland, 25; for men, 18; metabolism and, 48–49; race and, 181; in US, 5, 6, 7, 44, 188, 280, 291, 336; of women, 349n2. *See also* biology
Louisiana Purchase, 40–41

Manhattan, 129. *See also* New Amsterdam
manufacturing, 151–52; during Civil War, 150, 155; efficiency phases for, 62–63, 222, 256; environment of, 169; in the North, 35; politics of, 256–59; power phases in, 152, 246–47; of rifles, 261; self-sufficiency and, 35; in US, 232–33; Westinghouse Manufacturing, 299, 303, 305–7; for widows, 184–85; work culture of, 276–77; for World War I, 303
marketing, 17
Marshall, George C., 175
Maryland: Civil War in, 160; history of, 73; public-private partnerships in, 32; for railroads, 97; "runaway slave" law in, 117; taxes in, 89; Virginia and, 32–33. *See also* frontier
Masterless Men (Merritt), 98–99, 327
McConnell, Zachariah, 51
McGregor, James, 295
McKinley, William, 337
McKnight, Charles A., 256
McNeill, John, 172
Meason, Isaac, 52
medicine, 311, 333
men: biology of, 302–3; height averages of, 5, 6, 7–8, 72, 81, 85, 151, 169, 187–88, 232, 280–81, 293, *335*; longevity for, 18

Merritt, Keri Leigh, 98–99, 327
metabolism, 46; biology of, 46, 69–70, *70*; longevity and, 48–49
methodology, for height, 341, *341–47*, 343, 345
middle class, 200
migration: of Dunsmore family, 23–24; education and, 56–57; to frontier, 73; to Pittsburgh, 91, 135–39; of Vandergrift family, 186; wagoners and, 28, 48–49, 84
military, 204, 219; diseases and, 188; economics of, 40–41, 155, 378n9; environment for, 119–20; National Guard, 220–23; networking with, 82; for Old Robert Dunsmore, 50–51; Pennsylvania for, 42; pension funds from, 106–7, 121–22, 174; during Reconstruction era, 173
militias, 204, 219–22
miner's cough, 291–92
money, 55, 354n28
Morrill, Justin, 312
Morris, Robert, 61
Moyer, Elsie. *See* Densmore, Elsie E.
mtDNA, 302, 304, 309, 376n65

National Guard, 220–23
National Road, 34, *207*; economics of, 93–94; freight on, 95; government for, 41; history of, 34–35, 64–65; for self-sufficiency, 62, 88
Native Americans: Americans and, 10–11; Braddock's Road for, 31; Colonial America for, 1; diseases for, 131–32; as documentary statistics, 1–2; England and, 350n8; Europeans and, 18, 22, 36; history of, 263; immigration for, 22–23; in Manhattan, 129; in Pennsylvania, 22; pioneers and, 23–24; war against, 189, 195
natural gas, 142–44
Nelson, Margaret Elizabeth. *See* Densmore, Margaret

networks, 81–84
New Amsterdam, 125–26, 367n26; culture of, 127–28, 130–33; food in, 131; for immigration, 127
New York City, 169–70
New York Stock Exchange, 189, 194
1900 census records, 274, 280, 286
1910 census records, 288–90
1940 census records, 296
non-union workers, 265
the North: biology in, 98; for blacks, 43, 114–15; culture of, 182; economics for, 173; greed in, 196; manufacturing in, 35; the South and, 112–13, 118, 173–74, 179–80, 331; Washington, DC and, 179. *See also* Civil War
Northern Ireland: culture of, 12; immigration from, 14, 17; Scotland and, 16. *See also* Europe; Ireland
nutrition: disease and, 240; environment and, 117; for family, 187–88; height and, 304–5

oats, 35
Obama, Barack, 359n3
O'Brien, George W., 358n10
O'Brien, Shadrack, 81–83, 85–86, 106–8
Ohio, 33, 91, 352n12
Ohio Company, 11
Ohio National Guard, 223
oil: natural gas and, 142–44; for New York City, 169–70; Oil Trader's Exchange, 189–90; shipping of, 142–43; Standard Oil, 190, 204; steamboats and, 124; technology for, 51–52
Oliphant, Andrew, 80
Oliphant, Fidelio Hughes, 52, 74–77, 86, 194; for labor, 94; mules for, 356n31; Oliphant Works, 167, 178
Oliphant, John, 75–76
Oliphant Works, 167, 178
O'Sullivan, Virginia. *See* Densmore, Virginia

Panic (1907), 280, 286–87
patents: by Densmore, B. V., 306; by Densmore family, 319; in US, 277–79
Pauwelse, Maritje, 125
pay. *See* wages
peach leather, 350n12
Penn, John, 22
Penn, William, 22
Pennsylvania, 12, 28; culture of, 9; Densmore family in, 14, 20, 71, 191; government in, 56; history of, 23, 26–27, 30–31, 52, 86–87, 317–18, 350n20, 356n22; maps of, 27; for military, 42; National Guard of, 220; Native Americans in, 22; populism in, 61–62; racial politics of, 115–17; schools in, 78; taxes in, 54; Vandergrift family in, 105, 197, 287–88, 328–29; Virginia and, 352n21; wagoners in, 353n28. *See also* Birmingham; frontier; Pittsburgh
Pennsylvania Railroad Company, 168–69, 199–203
pension funds: from Civil War, 262; for family, 110–11; government for, 82; from military, 106–7, 121–22, 174
Percival, Charles, 291–92, 332
Percival, Robert, 291
Pinkertons, 38, 219–20, 222, 263–66
pioneers: from Europe, 31; funerals for, 88–89; after immigration, 22; Native Americans and, 23–24; Ohio for, 33; wagoners as, 8–9, 12, 25–26; winter for, 29
Pittsburgh: culture of, 147–49, 219–21; Densmore, H. T., in, 242–43, 262, 298–99; Densmore family in, 177–78, 298–301; diseases in, 100, 148; economics of, 65; history of, 26–30; Homestead Strikes in, 263–66; infrastructure of, 41–42; for iron, 106–8, 151–52; migration to, 91, 135–39; Pittsburgh Petroleum Exchange, 189–90; riverboats in, 208; steamboats for, 170–71; steel for, 185; technology from, 322; unskilled labor in, 198–99; wages in, 166. *See also* Birmingham; Pennsylvania; *specific topics*
plantations, 34–35. *See also* slavery
politics: blackmail in, 140; of citizenship, 116, 137, 179–81, 189, 195; of Civil War, 327–28, 368n35; of Electoral College, 194–95; identity politics, 180–81, 261, 339; of immigration, 296; labor and, 113–14; of manufacturing, 256–59; for middle class, 200; racial politics, 115–17, 172, 175, 336; of Reconstruction era, 115; of Secession Commissioners, 111–12; of slavery, 108, 367n4; in the South, 195–96; of temperance, 198; in US, 179–80, 194–96
pollution, 147–48, 293, 330–32
population: demography of, 65–68, 66, 71–72; immigration and, 62–63, 111; of US, 71–72, 98–99, 171–72, 202–3, 326; war and, 173–74
populism, 61–62, 94, 356n1
Portugal, 126
potato famine, 17–18
power phases, 33–34, 350n5; efficiency phases and, 152; immigration and, 303; labor in, 262; in manufacturing, 152, 246–47; for railroads, 257; self-sufficiency in, 35; from war, 146–47, 176
propaganda: in the South, 111–12
property: for Densmore family, 273, 288, 304; economics of, 268–69, 305; Land Grant Act, 312; taxes for, 353n17
psychology: of American Dream, 104; of American Exceptionalism, 99, 200; biology and, 105, 224; of Densmore, E. E., 300–301, 307; of environment, 182; of family, 45–46;

psychology (*continued*)
of immigration, 24; of infant mortality, 226–27; of Long Depression, 196–97; of populism, 94; of racial politics, 175; of self-sufficiency, 104, 183–84, 197; of the South, 189; of US, 336–37; of work culture, 85–87, 155–58, 160–62, 320–25
public education, 174–75
public-private partnerships, 32
public work, 63–65
puddlers: boilers and, 192; Civil War and, 149, 154; wages for, 176; work culture of, 106, 109–10, 121–22, 156–57, 192–94, 259
Pumpkin Flood, 30

Quantrill, William, 172, 189

racial politics, 336; of Pennsylvania, 115–17; psychology of, 175; in US, 172
Rager, Susan. *See* Dunsmore, Susan
railroads, 199–202; Great Railroad Strike, 199–200, 203–6, 219–21, 223–24; history of, 199–206, 257; Long Depression for, 201–2; Maryland for, 97; Pennsylvania Railroad Company, 168–69, 199–203; power phases for, 257; titans of, 98; underground railroad, 359n14; wages and, 199, 202
Rand, James, Jr., 277
Ray, Alan, 299, 303, 309
Reconstruction era: military during, 173; politics of, 115; for the South, 173–74, 195; taxes during, 172
Red Fox (ship), 139–40, 206, 363n60
Reed, G. W., *141*
Reed, John, 82
regional dynamics, 65–68, *66*
religion, 357n7; for education, 174; in England, 16–18; family and, 165–66; Tent Presbyterian Church, 86–87; in US, 20, 61–62, 131

resources, 54, 175. *See also specific resources*
Revolutionary War, 17–18
rifles, 261, 373n30, 373n32
riots, 220–21
rivers: diseases in, 353n9; for infrastructure, 91; riverboats, 134–39, *208*, 230–31, 288
Robber Barons: in banking, 329; corruption and, 232; for culture, 202, 255–57, 333–34, 337; Golden Age and, 182; labor for, 276, 323; Pinkertons and, 38, 219–20, 222, 263–66; self-sufficiency for, 255–58
Rockefeller, John D., 190, 286
rollers, 162–63, 176, 241–46, *245*, 258, 372n8
Roosevelt, Franklin D., 222, 312, 333
Roosevelt, Theodore, 155–56, 287, 337
Rudolph, Henry, 244–46, *245*
"runaway slave" law (1850-1851), Maryland, 117
Ryland, Elizabeth, 121, 158
Ryland, John, 158
Ryland, Sylvester, 158
Ryland family, 158–60

schools, 54–56, 78
Scotland, 16–18. *See also* Europe
Scott, Thomas, 369n2
Scott, Winfield, 108
Scudder, Deborah. *See* Hart, Deborah
Secession Commissioners, 111–12
self-insurance, 137
self-sufficiency: biology and, 117–18; in coal, 69; of colonies, 4; community and, 54–58; for corporations, 202, 224, 244–48, 262; of coylers, 70; in culture, 12, 14–15, 198, 321; of Densmore family, 74–81, *77*, 197, 319; environment and, 30, 327; family and, 85–87, 328, 334; government for, 58; immigration and, 16–24; manufacturing and, 35; National

Road for, 62, 88; networks and, 81–84; of Old Robert Dunsmore, 11, 87–89; in power phases, 35; psychology of, 104, 183–84, 197; for Robber Barons, 255–58; unregulated, 200; in US, 43, 97–98; of Vandergrift family, 316; well-being and, 37, 112. *See also* wages; work culture
Shades of Death, 10–11
In the Shadow of the Mills (Kleinberg), 151
Shanabarger, Samuel, 248–49
sharecroppers, 196
shipping: clerks, 298; economics of, 33; of freight, 139–41; of oil, 142–43
Sholes, Christopher, 277
slavery: Confederacy for, 116; economics of, 35, 67, 112, 114–15; in education, 366n1; environment of, 111; family and, 315; farming and, 114; history of, 1–2, 182; importing and, 367n7; plantations, 34–35; politics of, 108, 367n4; "runaway slave" law, 117; taxes and, 180; underground railroad for, 359n14; work culture as, 98. *See also* Civil War
Smith, George W., 103
Snyder, William, 83
Sok Chul Hong, 330
the South: biology in, 98; for blacks, 179; iron for, 162; the North and, 112–13, 118, 173–74, 179–80, 331; politics in, 195–96; propaganda in, 111–12; psychology of, 189; Reconstruction era for, 173–74, 195; wages in, 199. *See also* Civil War
Spain, 18
Standard Oil, 190, 204
steamboats, 137; oil and, 124; for Pittsburgh, 170–71
steel: economics of, 167–68; iron and, 152–53, 256–59; for Pittsburgh, 185
Stewart, Andrew, 82
Stone, Charles P., 289, 296
Stone, Grace (née Grace Wheaton), 289

Stone, Grace Virginia, 289
stress, 103–4, 148, 151, 174, 181–87. *See also* biology; work culture
strikes: Great Railroad Strike, 199–200, 203–6, 219–21, 223–24; Homestead Strikes, 263–66; by unions, 263–66; wages and, 331
Stuart, Jeb, 121
Stuart, John Moody, 297
Stuyvesant, Peter, 127–29, 131–32, 329
subscriptions, 54
Sutton, Esther, 60

taxes, 362n59; for animals, 78–79; census records for, 15, 76; for coylers, 59–60; for England, 129; for family, 39; history of, 37, 94–95; immigration and, 32; in Maryland, 89; in Pennsylvania, 54; for property, 353n17; during Reconstruction era, 172; slavery and, 180; in US, 337; for wagoners, 38–39
teamsters, 80. *See also* unions
technology: of coke, 186–87; for culture, 283; education and, 299; efficiency phases for, 319; for farming, 35; of forges, 53–54; for frontier, 36; iron as, 42; for oil, 51–52; from Pittsburgh, 322
temperance, 198
Tent Presbyterian Church, 86–87
Tilden, Samuel J., 195
tobacco, 34, 38, 149, 365n47
Tomlinson, Jesse, 11
towns, 54–55
transportation, 283; animals and, 46–48, *47*, 58; economics of, 29; efficiency phases for, 33–34, 64, 94–98, *96*, 289, 297, 299; history of, 12, 14, 31–32; Jefferson for, 33; National Road for, 34; for public work, 64–65; trolley cars, 296–97; weight for, 33, 46–49, *47*
trolley cars, 296–97

tuberculosis, 274–76

Ulster, 16–18
underground railroad, 359n14
the Union. *See* Civil War
unions: corporations and, 262; history of, 355n13; immigration for, 372n1; non-union workers, 265; strikes by, 263–66; teamsters, 80; for work culture, 260–61
United States (US): Amnesty Act in, 189; biology of, 4–5, *335*, 335–36; blacksmiths in, 8–9; calories in, 187–88; class in, 221–23; culture of, 22–23; Dunsmore family in, 2; economics in, 45–46, 80–81; efficiency phases for, 4–5, 35; England and, 114; Europe compared to, 3; France compared to, 28; history of, 87–88; identity politics in, 339; immigration to, 12, 19; infant mortality in, 99; infrastructure of, 41; Jamestown Colony in, 18–19; KKK Act in, 172; longevity in, 5, *6*, *7*, 44, 188, 280, 291, 336; manufacturing in, 232–33; National Guard, 220–23; patents in, 277–79; politics in, 179–80, 194–96; population of, 71–72, 98–99, 171–72, 202–3, 326; psychology of, 336–37; racial politics in, 172; religion in, 20, 61–62, 131; resources in, 54; self-sufficiency in, 43, 97–98; stress in, 183–84; taxes in, 337; wages in, 57; war for, 61; well-being in, 311–14; work culture of, 155–56; World War II for, 311–14. *See also* census records; height
unpasteurized milk, 79
unskilled labor, 198–99, 238
urban life: culture of, 283–84; education and, 373n3; history of, 326
US. *See* United States

Vandergriff, George, 205

Vandergriff, Ida, 205, 369n63
Vandergriff, Julia, 205
Vandergriff, William, 204–5, 219–21
Vandergriff, William, Jr., 205
Vandergrift, Abraham, 133
Vandergrift, Benjamin B., *xx*, 139
Vandergrift, Benjamin F., 206
Vandergrift, Benjamin F., *xxi*, 139–40
Vandergrift, George, 42–43, 124–25, 137, 139, 186
Vandergrift, Jacob (great-grandson), 133–34, 315
Vandergrift, Jacob Jay ("J. J."), 138, 140–43, *141*, 169–70, 189–90, *208*; business acumen of, 129, 317, 329; death of, 287–88; family of, 270–71; success of, 230–31
Vandergrift, Jacob L., 124, 128, 130, 132, 316
Vandergrift, James M., *xx*, *141*, 170, 231
Vandergrift, James S., 171, 317
Vandergrift, John, *xx*, 124–25, 136–37, 170–71
Vandergrift, John C., 171
Vandergrift, Joseph, *xx*
Vandergrift, Lewis F. L., *141*, 171, 317
Vandergrift, Louis, 231
Vandergrift, Mary (née Mary Hart), *xx*, 133–34, 135, 186
Vandergrift, Paulus L., 126–28, 128–29, 132, 316, 367n26
Vandergrift, Samuel, *xx*, 136–37
Vandergrift, Sarah Ann Hoffman, 144, 229
Vandergrift, Scudder, 197
Vandergrift, Sophia, 59, 229–30
Vandergrift, William George, 369n63
Vandergrift, William Knowles, 124–25, 137, 144, 146, 186
Vandergrift family, 132–33, 137–38, 169–71, 190–94, 219–20; Birmingham for, 144, *145*, 146–47; Civil War for, 139–42, *141*; class for, 204–5, 281; Densmore family and, 139–40, 270–71, 288–90; 1880s for, 230–32; family member tables for, *xx–xxi*; Hart

family and, 315–17; height of, *341, 343, 345, 347*; history of, 5, 125–30; immigration of, 19–20; migration of, 186; in Pennsylvania, 105, 197, 287–88, 328–29; self-sufficiency of, 316; well-being of, 315–17. See also specific family members

Vandiegrist, Jacob Leendertsen. See Vandergrift, Jacob

Virginia, 32–33, 352n21

wages, 79, 349n2; biology and, 328; after Civil War, 232–33; coal and, 70; economics of, 103; efficiency phases and, 246–49; farming compared to, 60–61, 101–2; food and, 168–69, 189; immigration and, 260, 276; income and, 102–4; inflation and, 178; in iron, 243–44, 252–55, *253*; after Long Depression, 224–25; for non-union workers, 265; in Pittsburgh, 166; for public work, 63–64; for puddlers, 176; railroads and, 199, 202; for rollers, 162–63, 176, 244–46, *245*, 258, 372n8; for shipping clerks, 298; in the South, 199; strikes and, 331; in US, 57; after war, 187; work culture and, 198

wagoners, 79, 349n2, 355n13; animals for, 70; clothing for, 83–84; floods for, 30; food for, 46–47, *47*; frontier for, 95; migration and, 28, 48–49, 84; Old Robert Dunsmore, as, 57–58; in Pennsylvania, 353n28; as pioneers, 8–9, 12, 25–26; Shades of Death for, 10–11; taxes for, 38–39; West Virginia for, 36. See also transportation

war: culture after, 184–85; for Densmore family, 184; economics after, 122–23; for family, 103–4; history of, 280; infant mortality and, 311; infrastructure after, 173; iron for, 105–12; *The Legacy of the Civil War* (Warren), 118; against Native Americans, 189, 195; population and, 173–74; power phases from, 146–47, 176; resources after, 175; for US, 61; wages after, 187; work culture and, 314. See also *specific wars*

Warman, Elizabeth Densmore, 357n35

Warman, Francis, 249–50

Warman, Nehemiah, 83, 105–6, 165–66, 177–78, 267

Warman family, 105–6

War of 1812, 39–41, 50–51, 136, 341, *341–43*; bounty lands from, 60; height in, 124

Warren, Nehemiah, 249–50

Warren, Robert Penn, 118

Washington, DC: during Civil War, 119, 121; the North and, 179

Washington, George, 11, 27–28, 31–32, 99, 338

Wayne, Anthony, 23, 50

weight, for transportation, 33, 46–49, *47*. See also biology

well-being: before Civil War, 98–103; class and, 200–203, 223–25; culture and, 65; of Densmore family, 317–19; diet and, 187; in 1880, 232–36, *236–37*; family and, 85–87; of Hart family, 314–15; self-sufficiency and, 37, 112; in US, 311–14; of Vandergrift family, 315–17; worldviews and, 165–69. See also environment; height; longevity; weight

Westinghouse, George, 202

Westinghouse Manufacturing, 299, 303, 305–7

West Virginia, 324; history of, 29–31, 38, 142; labor in, 297–98; for wagoners, 36. See also frontier

Wharton, Samuel, 61

Wheaton, Grace. See Stone, Grace

Wheaton, John, *213*, 289, 301

Wheaton, Samuel, 144, 191–92, 289, 299

Wheaton, Samuel, Jr., 289

Wheaton, Sarah (née Sarah Ann Hoffman), 191
Wheaton family, 285–89. *See also specific family members*
whiskey, 37–38, 61, 370n12
WIC. *See* Dutch West India Company
widows, 184–85, 198. *See also* Civil War; war
winter, 29
women, 1–2; in demography, 355n22; longevity of, 349n2; mtDNA and, 302, 304, 309, 376n65; as widows, 184–85, 198. *See also specific topics*
work calories. *See* calories
work culture: biology and, 313, 330–31; calories and, 100–102, 192, 238, 245–47, 303; of coal, 291–94; of Densmore family, 255–59; diseases for, 291–92; environment of, 228, 244; ethics of, 298; in iron, 236–37, 250–52; of manufacturing, 276–77; plantations and, 35; psychology of, 85–87, 155–58, 160–62, 320–25; of puddlers, 106, 109–10, 121–22, 156–57, 192–94, 259; riots by, 220–21; as slavery, 98; unions for, 260–61; of US, 155–56; wages and, 198; war and, 314; working conditions, 199, 233, 241–50, *245*, 332–33
worldviews, 165–69
World War I, 345, *346–47*; labor and, 280, 305; manufacturing for, 303; medicine from, 311
World War II, 294, 296, 311–14
Würster, William, 273

Y-DNA, 302–3, 307, 376n64

Made in the USA
Columbia, SC
23 December 2021